Film and Fashion in Japan, 1923–39

Film and Fashions

Series Editor: Pamela Church-Gibson

This series explores the complex and multi-faceted relationship between cinema, fashion and design. Intended for all scholars and students with an interest in film and in fashion itself, the series not only forms an important addition to the existing literature around cinematic costume, but advances the debates by moving them forward into new, unexplored territory and extending their reach beyond the parameters of Western cinema alone.

Titles in the series include:

Shoe Reels: The History and Philosophy of Footwear in Film
Elizabeth Ezra and Catherine Wheatley (eds)
Fashion on the Red Carpet: A History of the Oscars®, Fashion and Globalisation
Elizabeth Castaldo Lundén
Documenting Fashion
Elena Caoduro and Boel Ulfsdotter (eds)
Film and Fashion in Japan, 1923–39: Consuming the 'West'
Lois J. E. Barnett

https://edinburghuniversitypress.com/series-film-and-fashions

Film and Fashion in Japan, 1923–39

Consuming the 'West'

Lois J. E. Barnett

EDINBURGH
University Press

Edinburgh University Press is one of the leading university presses in the UK. We publish academic books and journals in our selected subject areas across the humanities and social sciences, combining cutting-edge scholarship with high editorial and production values to produce academic works of lasting importance. For more information visit our website: edinburghuniversitypress.com

Edinburgh University Press Ltd
13 Infirmary Street, Edinburgh, EH1 1LT

Typeset in 12/14 Arno and Myriad by
IDSUK (Dataconnection) Ltd

A CIP record for this book is available from the British Library

ISBN 978 1 4744 9770 1 (hardback)
ISBN 978 1 4744 9771 8 (paperback)
ISBN 978 1 4744 9772 5 (webready PDF)
ISBN 978 1 4744 9773 2 (epub)

Contents

Figures

Acknowledgements

This book could not have come to be without the constant vigilance, care and guidance that I have received from so many individuals not only during the writing and research process of this book, but throughout my life. My name may be on the title page of this book, but in truth, like the films studied herein, it is a collaborative work. I so value this opportunity to label it as such before you begin to read it.

I would like to thank my supervisory committee, Dr Isolde Standish, Dr Angus Lockyer and Dr Griseldis Kirsch, for their support throughout this process. I would particularly like to thank Dr Standish for her kindness and support since my undergraduate years. I would also like to thank the Chair of the SOAS Centre for Media and Film Studies, Dr Lindiwe Dovey, for her kind encouragement.

This research would not have been possible without the funding and nurturing guidance of the Great Britain Sasakawa Foundation and the British Association for Japanese Studies. I particularly thank Mr Stephen McEnally and Mr Brendan Griggs of the GBSF for their kindness and support.

I am indebted to the kind assistance of so many institutions in Japan during my research, who I thank wholeheartedly for making me feel so welcome. Many thanks to the staff of the National Film Center, Bunka Gakuen University, the Shiseido Corporate Museum, Waseda University's Tsubouchi Memorial Theatre Museum and the National Diet Library.

Finally, I would like to thank my family, friends and colleagues – and this is quite a list. I will be forever grateful to my partner Dan Adams, my Mum and Dad and Aunty Vivienne – thank you so much for putting up with me being glued to my laptop every Christmas and filling up your house with photocopies and old magazines. Many thanks to my colleagues Kerstin Fooken, Iris Haukamp, Irene González-López, Laz Carter and Amy Matthewson – this whole process would have been so much harder without having you all to look up to. A special mention goes to Mr Keith Saunders – thank you not only for introducing me to the wonderful language which is so crucial to this work, but for always being there. Thank you so much to all of my friends who have always supported me: Felix Brender, Phaedra Skuce-Gunn, Lucie Jennings, Katō Shiori and family, Yamazaki Aya, Chrissy Brown, Nina Köntges, Disa Andersen, Freya Sharp, Natalie Booth, Kyle Whittington, Claude Lattin, Vickie Basham, Richard and Aja Spencer-Smith, Jordan Arnold, Asaba Yuiko, Geoff French and Dr Iain Reid. Many thanks to all at the Beauchamp Lodge Settlement and the Brilliant Club.

I couldn't have done this without you all cheering me on.

Note on translation

All translations are my own unless otherwise stated. Japanese names are given according to Japanese convention (surname first). Macrons are used to indicate long vowel sounds when transliterating Japanese words.

I dedicate this book to the loving memory of my uncle Prof. Kevin C. Gatter, my grandfather Geoffrey Gatter, and my dear friend Phil Ray.

Thank you for teaching me how to write, to understand, and to live.
I would not be me without you.

Introduction: Defining, theorising and approaching Japanese film, fashion and modernity

'In all societies the body is "dressed," and everywhere dress and adornment play symbolic, communicative and aesthetic roles' (Wilson 2011, 3). In Japan, following the Meiji revolution of 1868, dress was 'the most easily accessible grammar and vocabulary of modernity', directly aligned with the pursuit of what was 'desirable', rather than 'polluting', in the modern world of industry, urbanisation, and empire. 'As in many other countries, the desire to act "modern" and to be part of modernity could most simply and immediately be fulfilled by means of clothing' (Slade 2009, 85). However, not all sartorial expressions of modernity were considered 'desirable'. This was particularly the case when modern clothes appeared on film, given the important role that clothing played in constructing character. Cinema thus became entwined with other 'undesirable' modern qualities, which were criticised by conservative figures. This is succinctly illustrated in differing responses to 'Modern Boy' and 'Modern Girl' imagery which will be explored in this book.

In this book, I outline and evaluate the perceptions, approaches and discourses surrounding the use of Western fashion in Japanese films produced between 1923 and 1939. I select this time period due to two specific events which triggered significant changes in style and content in the Japanese cinema: the 1923 Great Kantō Earthquake and the 1939 Film Law. I concur with Gennifer Weisenfeld's view that 'for many Japanese, the earthquake recapitulated and accelerated the ruptures and dislocations of modernisation, which had been subjects of intense debate long before the temblor hit . . . The shock of the quake became the shock of the modern,' with fashion and the cinema both existing as arenas for exploring and expressing such 'shock', triggering a high occurrence of fashion images onscreen (Weisenfeld 2012, 10). The 1939 Film Law imposed stringent censorship and controls on the use of celluloid to support the war effort, with 'feature films censored at the level of scenario' in accordance with strict tenets prohibiting, amongst other factors, 'that which may corrupt morals or undermine public moral principles' and 'that which may hinder the development of the national culture' (Nornes 2003, 1962). Frivolous focuses on consumerist content such as fashion, particularly considering the polarised attitudes to some forms of Western-style dress which will be explored in this book, were no longer permissible, providing a logical end point to this study. In order to analyse the fashion imagery contained within these films, I build on Slade's and Wilson's suggestion that we 'read' the 'grammar and vocabulary' of sartorial choices semiotically in order to decode their role in representing the wearer's intellectual and social outlooks. In Japan, where dress formats took on new meanings as expressions of a multi-faceted modernity, clothing was a loaded cultural universal, through which one can explore the simultaneous specificity and universality of Japan's own modernity. However, this study is not limited to 'decoding' the semiotics of sartorial elements onscreen. It also considers audience responses and Japan's position within the global film industry, insights into which may be found within literary accounts, magazines and other printed ephemera, such as film posters and advertising campaigns. This allows for the reconstruction of the contemporary audience and consumer environment, within which to contextualise the semiotic readings, thereby illuminating the motivations of the conjoined film and fashion industries to feature Western attire onscreen.

Slade's association of fashion with modernity is mirrored in Leo Charney's assessment of the cinema as 'a crucible for ideas, techniques, and representational strategies already present in other places' (Charney and Schwartz 1995, 1). Japan's appropriation of Western attire, examined through the lens of cinema, connects to wider, global debates on modernity and the place of the individual within mass culture. How were new, Western-derived concepts of masculinity, femininity and social acceptability appropriated within new modern spaces – not only the cinema itself, but the urban environment replicated onscreen – as well as within wider society? How were they met and opposed by conservative principles and movements? Answering these questions requires linking the film and fashion industries and placing the local within the global, necessitating a multi-disciplinary approach. This approach includes evaluating how these concepts were illustrated onscreen via the usage of Western clothing, examining the responses of contemporary audiences, and situating both not only within the socio-political developments within Japan during the 1920s and 1930s but also with reference to narratives concerning gender performativity, national identity and modernisation. Rebecca Ann Nickerson studies the gendered material culture of Japan in the 1930s and 1940s to 'demonstrate how women functioned as objects in the quest to define Japanese cultural identity' (Nickerson 2011, ii). Similarly, I explore how costume both reflected and shaped new, gendered constructions of national and individual identity. Two qualifications are important. First, in order to understand the way in which Western fashion objects appeared onscreen as 'signifiers of modernity', I not only consider entirely Western-inspired ensembles, but also the inclusion of Western-derived accessories within otherwise conventionally Japanese dress formats (for example, hats, scarves and cosmetics). Second, both classical cinema and the early-twentieth-century fashion industry conceived of gender as a male/female binary, with little to no acknowledgement of non-binary, transgendered or non-heterosexual consumers. I therefore focus on 'male-' or 'female-focused' clothing items. This is appropriate given the post-Meiji context. Although Japan had a tradition of (male) homosexuality, the new Meiji state adopted Western-inspired gender and marital norms, including a 'sodomy ordinance, drafted by the Ministry of Justice in 1872 ... [which] punished all "sodomites" with ninety days in prison' (Faure 1998, 219). The film and fashion industries in the 1920s and 1930s subsequently generated marketable gender archetypes informed by global cinematic norms. This book will explore the relationship between these archetypes, the Western-style fashion items implicated in their imagery, and Japanese audiences. Japanese cinema's use of Western costume allowed for a two-way communication of modernity, simultaneously shaping and responding to audience attitudes to the socio-political changes that were influencing mass consumer culture. Film thus provides a way of ascertaining the place of Western fashion within Japanese society and economy, together with a consideration of Japan's place in the world, during the interwar period.

I use 'Western attire' as a catch-all term for dress formats originating from non-Asian (and specifically non-Japanese) sources. Given my focus on the 1920s and 1930s, this primarily refers to (but is not limited to) the appropriation of the cut and style of Hollywood dress aesthetics, embodied by the flapper and suited man-about-town. A 'Western-style' garment engages with the body itself by creating specific coded silhouettes in order to generate meaning. This contrasts with the historical use of fabric and pattern to differentiate socio-economic status within the uniform, square shapes of 'Japanese' garments such as kimono, *hakama* trousers and *haori* kimono-sleeved jackets. This does not mean that there was a clear-cut distinction between 'Japanese' and 'Western' outfits. Sartorial duality was evident in Japan from the Meiji era, when a Western-style appearance was promoted by the government and print media as a means of modernising the populace of Japan as a military power (Dalby 1993, 83). Nor was the idea of self-modernisation via the adoption of Western aesthetics limited to clothing. Western-style accessories, such as imported umbrellas and pocket watches available from Japanese department stores, as well as certain hairstyles such as the male cropped *zangiri-atama*, also 'signified a modern attitude' (Dalby 1993, 71). Everyday working people, of all genders, could thereby affordably partake in nationwide modernisation efforts. Many clothing ensembles from the 1880s onwards, worn at all levels of society, included both conventionally 'Japanese' and 'Western' attributes. Such outfits, for example, a kimono paired with Western accessories such as hair slides, handbags or hats, are described here as 'hybrid outfits'. 'Western attire' thus denotes not simply the wearing of Western articles of clothing, but the adornment of one's person in a manner popularly perceived to be symbolic of the wearer's Westernised modernity in terms of silhouette, accessorisation and appearance. This definition fulfils two purposes. First, it places the wearing of Western-style fashions in the 1920s and 1930s within a longer narrative of Japanese sartorial development since the Meiji Restoration of 1868. Second, by acknowledging this longer 'Japanification' of Western styles, it does not reduce fashion to a 'recent and specifically Western development' but understands the Japanese case as an example of fashion's nature as 'a process of continuous change . . . exist[ing] in all known societies' (Kawamura 2005, 106–7), thus minimising orientalist dichotomies.

To explore this process, I have used two kinds of primary materials: the films themselves and contemporary print media, which provide insight into audience reception of both the films and the fashion. The print media consist of both film- and fashion-related publications. The film-related publications had different audience demographics, for example the highbrow *Kinema junpō* was focused on a male readership, while popular fan-oriented publications such as *The Play and Movie*[1] and *Sutā* (*Star*) aimed for a mixed-gender audience, but all discussed both domestic and international film productions. The fashion-related publications range from department store promotional magazines to specific Western-style fashion periodicals such as *Fasshon* (*Fashion*) and *Sutairu* (*Style*). Most were female-focused or mixed gender in terms of their desired audience but, when possible, I have also included specifically male-focused publications, particularly *Shinseinen* (*New Youth*) magazine, which had its own men's fashion column.

The majority of films I examine belong to the 'contemporary drama' (*gendai-geki*) genre, in which characters wear contemporary clothing and exist in contemporary settings and situations. This is intended not to marginalise the significance of the equally popular *jidai-geki* (historical costume drama) films of this period, but to highlight the role of cinema as a 'sensory-reflexive horizon for the experience of modernization and modernity' (Hansen 2000, 10). Due to their contemporary settings, the films provided an immersive replication of the sensations of modern life. This was facilitated by factors such as 'continuity editing . . . [which] creates the effect of a closed diegesis, a seemingly autonomous fictional world which the viewer can access fantasmatically as a privileged and invisible guest' (Hansen 2000, 11). By featuring a recognisable modern urban landscape and relatable issues, the contemporary drama film also attempted to capture the ephemeral quality of everyday life, which characterised modernity: 'the negotiation between ephemerality and stasis emerged as a defining feature of modernity' (Hansen 2000, 11). The characteristic attempt to 'freeze fleeting distractions . . . [and] moments of "present" experience' (Charney and Schwartz 1995, 2–3) also made it an apt setting in which to showcase the transient nature of fashion itself, which similarly aims to capture the momentary and allow the subject to sensuously experience an illusionary 'present' as something pleasingly tangible:

> [Fashion] is poised ambiguously between present and past … fashion freezes the moment in an eternal gesture of the-only-right-way-to-be … clothes are objects, but they are also images … the 'now' of fashion is nostalgia in the making. (Wilson 2011, vii)

Although neither of these media may have been able to truly represent an immersive 'present', their success in providing a sensational imitation lay at the core of their success in continually attracting modern audiences and consumers. This was reflected in the rapid expansion of cinema in Japan, with 300 movie houses appearing in the thirteen years following the building of the first cinema, the Asakusa Denkikan, in Tokyo in 1903 (Standish 2006, 18). The Japanese contemporary drama film of the 1920s and 1930s thus becomes an intriguing site for analysing the interaction between fashion and film, together with other discourses surrounding modern space and experience.

To examine this interaction, I will focus on the early careers of the directors Ozu Yasujirō, Shimazu Yasujirō, Naruse Mikio and Mizoguchi Kenji. Many of their films focused on contemporary settings and issues, including work in the *shōshimin eiga* ('lower middle-class film') genre and films with prominent female roles. Many also survive into the present day. During this time period all four directors produced features for the Shōchiku film company, 'the embodiment of "Japanese Modern"'. The pre-eminence of Shōchiku was in part the result of the company's Kamata Film Studios being the only Tokyo studio left standing after the 1923 Kantō earthquake. The earthquake provides the starting point for this book due to its impact not only on the domestic film industry but on the wider popular culture and Tokyo's physical urban landscape (Wada-Marciano 2008, 128). While a focus on Shōchiku films is therefore unavoidable, I also examine other films to identify trends across the cinematic spectrum, for example the independently funded works of director Kinugasa Teinosuke.

Although the films surveyed share these generic qualities, they also exhibit specific directorial approaches in their sartorial depiction of Japan. The period was a volatile one, a decade of 'antinomy between Japanese modernity and rising nationalism . . . [pervaded by] the sense of a Japanese national subject's split between the call to modernize and the contradictory longings for the mythic cohesion of the past' (Wada-Marciano 2008, 50). Dress was easily employed onscreen as a means of articulating these concerns without noticeably subduing or interfering with a film's overall visual style, purpose and effect. With its constant presence as an ephemeral object in the everyday sphere, it was able to carry connotations of class and wealth, modernity or 'tradition' (a concept itself subject to constant change and reinvention) or indeed a combination of these qualities. The semiotics of dress and costume within the films all address the identity conflict inherent to the experience of a contemporary Japanese audience but via different narratives and styles. A Saussurean approach to semiotics is helpful here, since it takes into account the immediacy of meaning while acknowledging that a 'sign' (in this case, clothing) can never be totally meaningless, with its meaning shaped by its context, in this case the filmic narrative, the cinematic technology, and the broader socio-economic climate (Saussure 1974, 102–3). It is of course impossible to generalise successfully about audience experience, given the multiplicity of individual responses. Nevertheless, it would have been impossible for audiences not to be affected by the constant clash between modernity and nationalist conservatism which permeated the 1920s and 1930s, not only in Japan. This book addresses a gap in existing scholarship, exploring the relationship between sartorial change and its onscreen representation in Japanese films between 1923 and 1939, thereby throwing light on the way in which Western attire was appropriated and adapted within modern Japan. Although chronologically and geographically specific, the interwar Japanese case suggests the potential of this approach in other times and places, for exploring fashion and cinema as agents in the ongoing social negotiation of modernity.

The interdisciplinary approach of this book requires engaging with work on not only Japanese history and cinema, but a range of comparative and theoretical issues: fashion and the body, the cinema and modernity, and gender studies, as well as work on the intersection of these areas. The inspiration for such an approach comes from Michel Foucault (1969), who likens the treatment of discourse not to linguistics, but to the arrangement of life itself, with subjects discussed in relation to each other rather than an overarching structure. In building on this suggestion, it has been equally important to engage with work that suggests how best to construct a historical survey and demonstrates how to apply theory to the relevant primary sources – magazines and printed ephemera, alongside the films themselves, drawing upon both English- and Japanese language scholarship. The existing literature on Japanese cinema in the 1920s and 1930s provides a wealth of insight into the local and global context within which films were produced and consumed, and into particular directors, performers and productions. But this book breaks new ground in a number of respects. Most significantly, there is currently no work on the way in which Western-inspired dress in Japanese film was a semiotic mode of articulating modern experience, no work on the way in which the link between fashion and film was expressed in print media, and very little work on the role of Western fashion items in everyday Japanese life. To do this work, an interdisciplinary and multimedia-based approach is required, but this means challenging some assumptions in the existing literature, about the academic value of non-linguistic visual and material culture, as well as the relative standing of different forms of visual culture – film and fashion as against art and theatre. In the existing literature, fashion is presented as a marginal indicator, with fashionable tropes such as the Modern Girl (*moga*) bobbed haircut becoming shorthand for an array of factors related to modernity. There are studies of fashion in film in the West, but their assumptions and findings must be adapted when exported to a non-Western (and specifically Japanese) context. Another striking omission is the place of the masculine in the appropriation of Western fashion as influenced by the cinema: what was the effect of the Western-style male outfit onscreen, or the impact of the Westernised Japanese male star on his Japanese audience? Finally, to answer these questions, it is essential to evaluate the films of the period on an equal basis, correcting the bias in English language scholarship towards the more well-known directors of the 1930s.

This work questions the role of Western-style fashion within the immersive sensory-reflexive experience provided by Japan's transnational film industry and how the cinema in Japan influenced a sartorial shift towards the wearing of Western-style products and participation in Western-style spaces. This cannot be answered by the existing body of literature. The everyday wear of the kimono and other indigenous styles has been consigned to the past; what is unclear is why and how this change took place. In this book, I posit that the key decades were the 1920s and 1930s and that cinema had a central role in enacting the change. To the author of a 1922 *Shukujo gahō* (*Ladies Pictorial*) article, entitled 'The Advantages of Japanese Clothing', an overarching adoption of Western-style clothing throughout society would have appeared ludicrous. Identified only as 'Takaki, Professor of Medicine', he states that 'nothing surpasses Japanese style' and that 'a Western-clothed lifestyle is not suitable for Japanese women', listing various reasons why he believes this to be so. These include the assertions that Western clothes do not allow for sufficient freedom during exercise, that they are 'too long and inconvenient' for everyday life and Japanese-style homes and furnishings, and that they go against national identity: 'as Japanese people follow the ways of the world, and even citizens eating a Japanese diet become fewer . . . we must not forget these features and fashions of Japanese clothing' (*Shukujo gahō* 1922, 2).

This article and others like it produced during the 1920s and 1930s, known popularly as *ryūkō kiji* ('trend articles'), which 'articulated things Western' (Wohr, Sato and Suzuki 1998, 54), make clear associations between dress and geo-culturally defined spaces and practices, with clear distinctions between dress which is appropriate for domestic (Japanese) space and external (Western) space. Gaston Bachelard, writing in a European context, states that

> outside and inside form a dialectic of division, the obvious geometry of which blinds us as soon as we bring it into play in metaphorical domains. It has the sharpness of the dialectics of *yes* and *no*, which decides everything . . . it is made into a basis of images that govern all thoughts of positive and negative. (Bachelard 1958, 211)

However, Bachelard also raises the query of the physical and metaphorical role of 'doors' deeming them 'an entire cosmos of the half-open . . . schematiz[ing] two strong possibilities, which sharply classify two types of daydream' (Bachelard 1958, 222). What is yet to be explored is the respective and combined roles of clothing and the cinema as such 'doors', allowing the individual to traverse both physical and metaphorical spatial binaries, for example, 'Eastern' (specifically 'Japanese') and 'Western', male and female, modernity and tradition modernity, public and private, individual and mass experience, urban versus suburban. Bachelard describes such polarities as 'daydreams', reminding us of the role of fashion and the cinema in prompting consumerist aspiration by attempting to 'freeze' present experience. Fashion and film can be considered as agents which allow the spectator, by wearing Western-style attire, to construct their own 'doorways' and position themselves in a physical and hypothetical space which is simultaneously both and neither.

Spatial divisions are frequently articulated via clothing onscreen during the 1920s and 1930s and carry specific gendered undertones: female characters in domestic spaces conventionally wear kimono, while business-suited men return from their Western-style workplaces to change into *hakama* pants and *haori* jackets. It is in the hybrid outfit that boundaries become blurred and identities become complex. The very same issue of *Shukujo gahō* that championed the wearing of Japanese fashions featured advertisements starring kimono-clad women sporting fur stoles and cloche hats. Men and women adopting such hybrid outfits appeared onscreen in both internal and external settings but with distinctly nuanced implications. This aesthetic and ideological hybridity continues, with contemporary Japanese designers both at home and abroad expressing sentiments of 'Japaneseness' within their collections. Nowadays, though these rely mainly upon the 'Japanisation' of existing Western styles. For example, the iconic Japanese designers of the 1970s, Kenzo Takada, Yohji Yamamoto and Rei Kawakubo, sought to introduce elements of the kimono to conventionally Western designs. Kawamura has described this as a process by which 'the combination of Japanese and Western elements force the destruction of both in order to reconstruct something completely new' (Kawamura 2013, 24).

The print media I examine in this book suggests that the 'destructive combination' we see today is not entirely new, but the product of an ongoing negotiation of nationality and modernity, sartoriality and space, which was facilitated by the cinema's 'sensory-reflexive horizon'. Japan's interwar print culture sheds light on both the inclusion of Western fashion products onscreen and their implications for what it meant to be simultaneously 'modern' and 'Japanese'. Using cinema to investigate the process leading from the wearing of indigenous attire towards the widespread adoption of Western-style clothing ensembles and varying degrees of sartorial hybridity will contribute to the understanding not only of the history of Japan's dress culture but of contemporary relationships between film, fashion and identity in Japan and worldwide.

Since the key relationship between fashion and film has yet to be theorised in regard to a non-Western (specifically Japanese) context, some adaptation of Western theory is necessary. Within this general problem, there are three areas that require theoretical elaboration: the status of fashion; the relationship between the spectator and the cinematic space; and the treatment of media and primary materials. A preliminary issue is how to define 'modernity' in both a global and a Japanese context, which requires elaborating the theoretical factors specific to the temporal context.

Iwamoto Kenji focuses on the linguistic background of Japanese conceptions of modernity, exploring multiple terminologies to describe 'the modern' and explaining the links between modernity as a period of time and the theoretical issues surrounding modern Japanese films:

> What is modernism [*modanizumu*] in regards to Japanese films? I would say that films concerning modern science (or perhaps just 'science') born at the end of the nineteenth century received a baptism of the earliest origins of the modern age. Therefore, film was an excellently of-the-moment media, which could make the age's consciousness and unconsciousness begin to work together. Most of all, whether you say '*kindai-shugi*' or if you say '*modanizumu*', the subtle values within these words vary. In the case of the former term, be it thought or science, European rationalism embodied the traversing between two positive and negative polarities, and even today is becoming an era of reflecting this same negative polarity. Considering this, already in pre-war Japan, 'overcoming of the present' [*kindai no chōkoku*] was being chanted, and so the nation, its ideology and its history was faced with being burdened with this ponderous problem; the use of '*modanizumu*' was lighter and carried an image of 'frivolousness', 'brightness' and 'newness'. More than

> the thought of *kindai-shugi*, more than the image of *modanizumu*, I wonder about how these points entered the realm of Japanese film. (Iwamoto 1991, 6–70)

Iwamoto juxtaposes the two Japanese terms *kindai-shugi* and *modanizumu* as being based upon 'thought' and 'image' respectively but suggests that cinema was able to unite them from the end of the nineteenth century due to its combining science and present experience. Fashion, too, relies on image to convey meaning. As a consumable product, relying on positive associations and the constant pursuit of 'newness', it might seem to embody *modanizumu* rather than *kindai-shugi*. However, as with the cinema itself, it is impossible to truly separate the image-driven concept of fashion from the 'thought' of *kindai-shugi*. Fashion is a medium influenced by and influencing social change and issues external to the aesthetic and consumer sphere, evident not only in the emphasis on Western attire in government-enforced dress reforms since the Meiji era but the moral panic surrounding the Modern Girl.

My definition of 'modernity' therefore relates more closely to *modanizumu*, but also acknowledges its relationship with the rationality of *kindai-shugi*. I choose the term 'modernity' rather than 'modernism' in line with other English-language scholarship, in which the latter implies 'a stylistic term' and a Western context, whereas 'modernity' 'denotes a phase in societal development' (Bullock and Trombley 2000, 539–40). This echoes Iwamoto's differentiation of *modanizumu* and *kindai-shugi*. It thereby allows for a discussion of Japanese modernity which both fits within a geographically specific temporal context and refers to global conceptions of modernity, drawing on discussions of different geographies and temporalities, which are nevertheless subject to the same shaping factors pertaining to the 'modern'. This echoes the work of Harry Harootunian, who cites 'thinkers as different as Walter Benjamin and Miki Kiyoshi and Georges Bataille' in order to understand the way in which interwar Japan 'was perched to embark upon the production of commodities for mass consumption … [an] experience which established what Japanese called "modern life" in the short space of roughly two decades'. Harootunian summarises this experience as the moment when Japan was 'overwhelmed by modernity' (Harootunian 2011, x, xv). It is this approach of applying specific theoretical responses to globally shared socio-political experiences, particularly concerning new conceptions of space, cinematic and scientific technology, and consumerism, which informs my assessment of the role of dress in articulating Japanese modernity both on- and off-screen.

With respect to fashion, both Wilson and Slade emphasise fashion as a signifier, which may be 'read' visually. This echoes Bruzzi, who sees characters as 'constructed through their costumes' due to fashion functioning as a semiotic visual device, which does not rely on narrative (Bruzzi 1997, xv–xvi). What I have yet to discuss is the anthropological connotations of Wilson's assertion that 'in all societies the body is "dressed", and everywhere dress and adornment play symbolic, communicative and aesthetic roles' (Wilson 2011, 3). Gary P. Ferraro and Susan Andreatta describe 'cultural universals' as the basis of the anthropological belief that 'despite variations in specific details, all cultures have certain common features'. In 1945 George Peter Murdock published a non-exhaustive list of these universals, including 'body adornment', which have arisen as factors contributing to 'solutions to a whole series of problems facing all human societies' (Ferraro and Andreatta 2010, 38–44). Wilson's assertion that semiotic adorning of the body is a practice common to all societies, read in conjunction with Murdock's concept of 'cultural universals', allows for a discussion of how Japan's appropriation of Western attire, through cinema, initiates wider debates upon modernity and the place of the individual within mass culture. This prompts consideration of the place of new, Western-derived concepts of masculinity and femininity within the Japanese context. It also augments the relevance of gender theorists such as Butler, working on non-Japanese contexts.

A transnational perspective can also be brought to the question of the spectator's relationship with the cinematic space. Most current works on this issue come from non-Japanese perspectives. Film itself may be considered a 'grammar and vocabulary of modernity', as Slade designates fashion. Charney and Schwartz suggest that film is a means of visually reacting to the pressures and sensations of modernity, which exist in industrialising countries worldwide. They argue that cinema facilitated 'a developing mass audience', which was motivated by the desire to 'freeze fleeting distractions and evanescent sensations' via the 'talismanic innovations . . . the telegraph and telephone, railroad and automobile, photograph and cinema'. They conclude that 'modernity can be best understood as inherently cinematic' (Charney and Schwartz 1995, 1–3). This concept of film as a visual technology with the ability to psychologically and physically respond to the modern spectator's desire to grasp present experience aligns with Ben Singer's assessment of Georg Simmel's 1903 essay 'The Metropolis and Mental Life'. Simmel describes modernity as 'an intensification of nervous stimulation' given the qualities of the urban environment:

> the rapid crowding of changing images, the sharp discontinuity in the grasp of a single glance, and the unexpectedness of onrushing impression: these are the psychological conditions which the metropolis creates. (Singer 1995, 74)

Simmel delineates a psychological change in response to the 'shock of modernity', the 'radical increase in nervous stimulation and bodily peril' which arose as a result of the industrialisation of everyday urban life (Singer 1995, 74). Simmel emphasised not only the stimulation and sensation that came with modern urbanisation, but the intrinsic link between an individual's exposure to 'changing images' and their psychology. Not only the cinema's bricolage of changing images, but the urban environment itself is key to modern life as experienced by the cinematic spectator; the city itself is the cause of the 'rapid crowding' and 'changing images' described by Simmel. Innovations such as advertising, the department store, and the cinema – all of them stages for the performance of fashion – were part of everyday experience within the city, fundamentally changing the psychology of the urban inhabitant, generating a modern experience and outlook unattainable in a rural setting.

It is this dangerous new urban environment which provides the context for what Tom Gunning terms the 'cinema of attraction'. This was an 'exhibitionist cinema', based on Fernand Léger's understanding of cinema's power to 'make images seen . . . and show something', relying upon its position as 'the newest technological wonder' in order to garner the attention of modern audiences with a thirst for the new (Gunning 1986, 63–5). By creating a space in which the sensation of the present itself, alongside the dangers it poses, could be impressed upon a knowing audience within a physically safe setting, the cinema was institutionalised as a means of coping with the collective psyche of fear and bombardment forced upon the subject by the new terrors of the everyday. The cinema only replicated the shock of the present, rather than fulfilling the wish to experience the 'now', thereby perpetuating mass cinema-going, driving consumption, and sustaining modern experience, within which the 'old' and the 'new' are constantly juxtaposed. 'The new is experienced as modern because the old and archaic are still around' (Harootunian 2011, xxiv). This was mirrored within the urban Japanese landscape following the Kantō earthquake, with new 'modern-style' buildings springing forth amongst surviving older structures, and within the contrasting garments of the hybrid dress ensemble, all of which both affected and reflected the changing psyche of the interwar Japanese spectator.

This consumerist experience can be related both to the negotiation of mass and individual evoked by the cinematic space and to a consideration of how gender pertains to this dynamic. Hansen, similarly to Charney, relates the spectator's physical and emotional immersion within the cinematic experience to the modern desire to 'freeze' the present. This immersion was facilitated via cinematic techniques such as continuity editing (Hansen 2000, 11). Mary Ann Doane links this experience to consumerism in the way it incites the female spectator to self-identify with star images onscreen:

> In her desire to bring the things of the screen closer, to approximate the bodily image of the star, and to possess the space in which she dwells,

> the female spectator experiences the intensity of the image as lure and exemplifies the perception proper to the consumer. The cinematic image for the woman is both shop window and mirror, the one simply a means of access to the other. The window/mirror takes on then the aspect of a trap whereby her subjectivity becomes synonymous with her objectification. (Quoted in Petro 2002, 43)

Laura Mulvey concurs with this assessment, adding that the female screen body also holds an erotic power: 'traditionally, the woman displayed has functioned on two levels: as erotic object for the characters within the screen story, and as erotic object for the spectator within the auditorium' (Mulvey 1975, 11). Judith Mayne interprets this statement as describing the means via which the male spectator may self-identify with the screen image, with the erotic female screen body itself acting as 'lure' rather than the aspirational space surrounding it as in the case of the female spectator. 'For Mulvey, the mainstream cinema is made to the measure of male desire, and the various devices central to the classical Hollywood cinema all serve to facilitate the identification of the male spectator with his like, the male protagonist onscreen' (Mayne 1993, 18). In her 1981 reassessment of her original article, though, Mulvey adds that the female-identifying spectator possesses a fluidity in terms of which gendered characters she identifies with onscreen, and that this is particularly complicated by works centred around a female protagonist (Thornham 1999, 123). Considering the arrival of masculine-style women's fashions (particularly those associated with the 'action' and bodily freedom of the sporting world) and the popularity of androgynous Western star personae such as Marlene Dietrich (who openly endorsed Shiseido cosmetics) this raises the question of the effect of gendered dress formats on the textual self-identification of all genders. What is clear from these observations is that the dialectic between spectator and screen enabled by the cinematic space can serve to utilise the feminine, either subjectively or objectively, to inspire consumerism. However, the role of the masculine in this dialectic is in need of further questioning.

There are two points for further consideration with respect to this dialectic. What is the specific place of Western-style fashions? And is the masculine only a secondary participant? Writing in a European context, Jürgen Habermas describes mass media as 'a conduit for social forces channelled into the conjugal family's inner space by way of a public sphere that the mass media have transmogrified into a sphere of culture consumption' (Habermas 1991, 162). In the Japanese context, Western clothing was initially worn only within the male official sphere and was regulated by state edicts, both functioning as 'public' performances. This led, however, to sartorial change for all genders, dress conventionally existing as a 'private' identity-coding practice. Given the role of media (such as film) as 'mediators' between the public and private, it is impossible to ignore the importance of masculine cinematic self-identification in relation to filmic motivations for consuming Western-style commodities. The relationship between masculinity and the emergence of Western-style content in the Japanese cinema of the 1920s and 1930s, particularly in regard to the treatment of the body and costume onscreen, was reinforced by the thoroughly patriarchal leadership at its core, with all studios in the sole control of conservative male figures. For example, following a trip to Europe and Hollywood in 1929, Shōchiku head Kido Shirō was determined to recruit actresses from the Japanese countryside with 'shapely legs who could wear Western-style clothes' (*kyakusenbi joyū*) (Standish 2006, 56).

Critical discourse analysis provides a way to understand the power dynamics underpinning the primary materials that document this role of media as a 'conduit' between public and private spheres. This is based on Foucault's concept of 'orders of discourse', which Norman Fairclough describes as 'social structurings of linguistic/semiotic variation or difference . . . [L]inguistic and semiotic systems make possible (can "generate") texts which differ without limit, but the actual range of variation is socially delimited and structured, i.e., through the ways in which linguistic and semiotic systems interact with other social structures and systems' (Fairclough 2013, 358). This means reading both the relevant print media and ephemera and the films in reference to their social contexts. Fairclough and Wodak summarise the method as considering discourse as 'a form of "social practice" . . . imply[ing] a dialectical relationship between a particular discursive event and the situation(s), institution(s) and social structure(s), which frame it' (Fairclough and Wodak 1997, 258). There is therefore a link between statements on screen or the printed page and actual social developments: 'the discursive event is shaped by [these structures], but it also shapes them' (Fairclough and Wodak 1997, 258). Media can thereby 'help produce and reproduce unequal power relations between (for instance) social classes, women and men, and ethnic/cultural majorities and minorities through the ways in which [it] represent[s] things and position[s] people' (Fairclough and Wodak 1997, 258). Given Frederick's assertion that many prominent Japanese women's magazines, such as *Fujin kōron*, have 'always been written and edited primarily by men' (Frederick 2006, 27), this reminds us that any text cannot be read within a vacuum but must instead be assessed in light of the power dynamics exerted by and upon its creator(s), audience, and socio-cultural context.

Note

1. Despite being a Japanese-language magazine, this publication's title is in English.

Part I

On sartoriality and speaking: 'Expressive' women and Western attire

Chapter 1

Fashionable female imagery between media formats: Tanizaki Jun'ichirō's *Naomi* (1924) and the concept of marketable female star 'types'

This section explores expressivity and sartoriality. I focus on how cinema constructed a relationship between these two concepts, by drawing on new models of Western-inspired femininity. In its definition of 'expressivity', the *Oxford English Dictionary* notes that it is not only language that can 'effectively convey . . . thought or feeling', but that facial features can have expressive power. This raises the possibility of 'expressive images', which manipulate such visual cues for specific purposes. Onscreen, this might include furthering a film's narrative or constructing a star's persona. In print media, as well as film, expressive images might be utilised for commercial purposes, for example, using an 'expressive' female star's endorsement to promote a commodity. This is not to downplay verbal expressivity. Onscreen, female characters express emotion and intent through their action and verbalisations, which can be manipulated for narrative effect and persona construction. Vocal expressivity reached new heights with the introduction of sound: volume, accent and dialect, as well as frequency of contribution, all became new ways of creating 'expressive' stars onscreen. Actresses' voices themselves became sites of commentary, with aspects such as dialect subject to tropes of geography and class. As with 'code-switching' (Stockwell 2002, 8), accent and dialect were employed both to generate identification and to enact distance, for example by Mizoguchi Kenji, using the Kansai dialect[1] in *Osaka Elegy* (*Naniwa erejī*, 1936). 'Expressivity' in this section therefore refers to a subject's ability to convey their internal concerns and desires via any and all physical avenues. It thus connects to the question of how a character or actress 'expresses' her public personality, as well as how those with authority over her – directors, producers and print media editors – intend such expression to be perceived as part of her identity. This was connected to the general 'commodification of images' in the early twentieth century, which relied on a certain ambiguity in the images available to fans, 'who could take them as the embodiment of these stars' personalities, their sexual bodies, or both' (Fujiki 2013, 124). This commodification was heightened as the star image was transferred to other consumer goods. Film-related images of expressivity and the body were combined, with new Hollywood-derived aesthetics emerging within Japan (and their interaction with existing aesthetic ideals) acting as a cohesive element between these two factors.

The onset of modern spaces, practices, and political reforms threatened to disturb the gendered hierarchies of patriarchal society. De Beauvoir famously described how such hierarchies were enabled by the denial of public expression to women:

> Women – except in certain abstract gatherings such as conferences – do not use 'we'; men say 'women', and women adopt this word to refer to themselves; but *they do not posit themselves authentically as subjects.* (de Beauvoir 2011, 28, emphasis mine)

Thurman notes, however, that expressivity can be used to subvert such hierarchies and that '[i]nstead of rejecting "Otherness" as an imposed cultural construct, women ... should cultivate it as a source of self-knowledge and expression' (Thurman 2011, 14). In the interwar period, it was the Hollywood 'flapper', the forerunner of the Modern Girl elsewhere, who emerged in the new, modern spaces and threatened to disturb the existing social order. In 1922, self-proclaimed ex-flapper Ruth Hooper claimed that the flapper was a reaction to the end of the war: '"Yes", say we who won our freedom in the slippery paths of war, "Peace", and the outcome of it all is the flapper' (Hooper 1922). Other developments also contributed to her emergence, however: the increasing number of women entering the workplace and living independently; the introduction of electric lighting, which facilitated the notion of city 'nightlife'; the onset of female suffrage, increasing levels of female post-secondary education and university attendance (Kalagher 2014, 4). These phenomena not only allowed women to voice opinions within designated female spaces, but also to engage with stereotypically 'masculine' physical and intellectual spaces. Hooper herself describes the flapper as a female archetype, whose expressive qualities directly engaged the position of men:

> A flapper is proud of her nerve – she is not even afraid of calling it by its right name. She is shameless, selfish and honest, but at the same time she considers these three attributes virtues. Why not? She takes a man's point of view as her mother never could, and when she loses, she is not afraid to admit defeat ... (Hooper 1922)

This characterisation of the flapper in terms of her expressive qualities portrays her as the actively subversive 'Other': her expressivity empowers her to exert her autonomy.

The direct effect of modernisation on feminine self-expression was evident across the globe, not least in female artistic production. In the Chinese context, Ng notes that 'women's position of powerlessness in patriarchal society' had made it 'difficult for women to write a certain way or to express a viable subjectivity', but the May Fourth language reform movement had allowed women to gain their own 'literary space'. As a result, women writers during the 1930s were able to 'contend directly with the state of their perpetual object position of passivity as receivers of the male gaze . . . They manoeuvred to gain their textual self-determination by manipulating the gaze' (Ng 2010, 41–2). Ng suggests that female expressivity was a subversive force, with the power to destabilise patriarchal systems, but she focuses on the intellectual class and does not address aesthetically expressive images. De Beauvoir and Ng do not explain the prevalence of expressive imagery within global popular media, which were targeted at both male and female consumers: despite their superficially subversive feminine power, they did not solely appeal to women. Consumerism therefore must be considered. An expressive appearance was an innate feature of the Modern Girl, or flapper: 'numerous iconic visual elements including bobbed hair, painted lips, provocative clothing, elongated body, and open, easy smiles enabled us to locate the Modern Girl around the world in approximately the same years between World War I and World War II' (Weinbaum et al. 2008, 2). These aesthetic features suggest the importance of sartoriality in constructing expressive images. Clothing can therefore be used as a heuristic device through which we may study the context of sartorial elements – their relationship to the body, to narrative, to space, and to (perceived) 'natural' elements. The significance of fashion as artifice, and its role in creating marketable fantasies, cannot be ignored, particularly as it is used in film, which relies upon the artificial construction of images and events. 'Sartoriality' points to the dual status of fashion products, as both tangible, with physical, sensory qualities, and symbolic, carrying meaning even in print or on screen.

Hooper's article on the flapper is accompanied by an illustration of a masquerade. Male and female attendees wear largely historically derived outfits and are all depicted engaging in some kind of movement, whether that be dance or romantic activities. The image's centrepiece, a short-haired girl wearing large hoop earrings and a grass skirt, represents the author herself: 'I wore a hula-hula costume.' She stares directly at the centurion with her hands on her hips; he appears somewhat startled. Hooper recounts her experience: 'the poor male fry feared that costume as one would fear the devil and his angels, perhaps because the paper of the skirt kept dropping bit by bit, or perhaps because my arms and neck were so brown from sunburn that you could never tell just where they left off and the brown bodice began' (Hooper 1922). Hooper implies that it is the flapper's fashionable image, and its propensity to enable her emotional and bodily expressivity, that is her most disturbing element, rather than her unconventional attitudes. Hooper describes flappers as though they are members of an educational hierarchy: the 'prep school type – still a little crude', lacks 'the finish of the college flapper' (an attendee of a women-only college), who is eclipsed by 'the co-ed flapper . . . [who] has attained a certain poise and dignity that an ordinary college specimen lacks' (Hooper 1922). The defining link between all these women, alongside their education, was their appearance. With the arrival of mass-produced, off-the-peg fashions this 'educated' appearance, loaded with intellectually and bodily expressive power, became accessible to women outside the socio-economic groups with access to education. Peril notes the market opportunity: 'by giving consumer items names like "campus" or "co-ed", manufacturers hoped that nonstudents would associate the college girl's youth and freshness – or her sexuality – with such products' (Peril 2006, 116).

Through the fashion commodities associated with flappers, any woman with disposable income could engage with its aesthetics and expressivity, including its educational connotations, regardless of class. It is via the mass industries, including film and fashion, that 'higher class' ideas become accessible to a 'lower class' demographic. Film or fashion are not, like female autobiography, an individual form of self-expression. Mainstream films of the 1920s and 1930s were produced for the financial benefit of predominantly male-backed companies. While individual women could benefit from the expressive power of the flapper aesthetic, their engagement with the issue of women's position within society would remain superficial without access to the spaces in which women could express themselves as described by de Beauvoir. This allowed the flapper aesthetic to appeal to both male and female consumers, while provoking mixed male responses. Some men were threatened by the flapper's expressive power, regardless of her socio-economic position, but others found this erotically appealing. 'Women as well as men . . . dress as much for reasons of status as for sex appeal; but does not power bear a relationship to sexual allure?' (Wilson 2011, 91–2). Alongside the visual appeal of the flapper's increasingly exposed body, some perceived her autonomy as a source of excitement rather than threat. For the male reader, Hooper suggests, the attraction of the flapper was her spontaneity, which she twinned with her role as an equal partner in leisure activities: 'she will never make you a hatband or knit you a necktie, but she'll drive you from the station hot [sic] Summer nights in her own little sports car. She'll don knickers and go skiing with you; or, if it happens to be Summertime, swimming; she'll dive as well as you, if not better' (Hooper 1922). The 'shocked' or startled male party guest who looks on at the flapper in horror in the cartoon illustrating

Hooper's article may instead be considered as an intrigued voyeur, excited by the flapper's challenging gaze.

In Japan, a 1928 *Play and Movie* article, entitled 'Two Sketches: *Bonnō* from First National Pictures', featured two images of actresses, including one of Betty Compson, also wearing a hula outfit, parting the skirt to expose her legs, and staring into the camera with the same challenging smile. *Bonnō* carries a number of Buddhist-derived meanings, referring to 'any passion, attachment, working of the mind, or subsequent action that hinders the attainment of enlightenment' (Baroni 2002, 33). Perhaps the closest English translation is 'forbidden fruit'. Given the context, of a 'popular', mixed-gender-focused publication and its accompanying images of scantily clad Hollywood actresses, the term is clearly being used colloquially. But the actresses are certainly presented as sinfully attractive, their expressive power laden with potential spiritual harm for the male viewer. Compson appears beside Dorothy Mackaill, a former dancer in the Ziegfeld Follies. This was a series of elaborate theatrical revues, which were famed for their use of parody and elaborate costuming produced by celebrated designers and which frequently featured songs about the fashion industry (van der Merwe 2009, 22). Film stars who had performed in the Ziegfeld Follies were quickly associated with these realms of fashionable dress and subversive pastiche, frequently revolving around the body. Another notable Ziegfeld graduate was Louise Brooks who was spotted for the Paramount studios while performing in the 1925 Follies, and who gained immense popularity in Japan (Koszarski 2008, 49). Images of the Ziegfeld Girls appeared in Japan in both magazines focusing on theatrical content and more general interest publications. Consumers of popular culture in Japan during the 1920s and 1930s would have been aware of their Japanese derivative groups. Kobayashi Ichizō was inspired to create the Takarazuka Revue, which debuted in 1914, in part due to the success of the Ziegfeld Girls. In 1928, Shōchiku produced its own revue in response to the popularity of chorus-girl groups (Haggerty and Zimmerman 2003, 24). Mackaill's star persona is therefore imbued with the chorus girl's subtly subversive sense of beauty, fashion and dance. In the *Bonnō* photograph, she wears a tennis skirt and a polo jersey, reminiscent of the college girl advertising images and her own active past. Like Compson, a full view of her legs is provided as she adjusts her stockings; she is shown laughing, open-mouthed. The photo provides a candid, active impression: the image suggests that Mackaill is not laughing to please the camera but expressing her emotional autonomy. The sartoriality of the two images positions the women as two sides of a single coin: Compson as the 'wild', 'Other' flapper; Mackaill as the active, sporty co-ed. The Japanese commentator appreciates both: 'Not only is [Mackaill] a noble princess with a beauty that puts any flower to shame, but as she lifts her hem, we get the added extra of her shameless, charming smile'

(*The Play and Movie* 1928, 4). He finds Compson equally exciting – her hula attire especially causes him to add a further expressive dimension to his commentary on the image: 'Brazenly calling out like a street hawker, and dancing wearing this curious costume: this is Betty Compson' (*The Play and Movie* 1928, 4). In the photo, Compson's mouth is smiling but closed; she is not 'calling out'. The commentator seems to have derived an expressive, uncontrollable, almost masculine persona purely from Compson's outfit and positioning. He imbues her image with the power to satisfy his 'desire to go' to Hawaii and see the hula dancing of its 'dazzling beauties', instilling it with similar immersive qualities to the cinema itself.

The flapper's desire for expressive power not only was enabled but could be curtailed by her cinematic and sartorial consumption, allowing her to remain simultaneously a profitable and relatively 'safe' ideal, a site for power 'play' rather than a subversive force. An early 1930s advertisement provides an example of consumerism being employed as a political 'decoy' for women: 'Following a lead caption "when lovely women vote", the text concludes that their inevitable choice is Listerine toothpaste' (McDonald 2003, 51). Her consumption set the flapper archetype apart from her predecessor, the 'New Woman'. While flappers could be political, this was not necessary. They thrived on subconsciously political connotations, expressed via their sartorial choices and bodily and emotional expressivity, rather than partaking in political activities. In Japan, 'the Modern Girl icon was a rare means to take power away from the New Women who challenged political certainties and respectability . . . If the Modern Girl was to be seen, the New Woman was to be heard or at least read' (Silverberg 2008, 358). While 'a "Modern Girl look" was singled out as a key mechanism that allowed women to disrupt class boundaries and to challenge established gender relations', (Weinbaum et al. 2008, 12) this was not necessarily an effect intended by the everyday female consumer. The prevalence of Modern Girl images worldwide throughout the 1920s and 1930s suggests their popularity among a mainstream consumer demographic, rather than as the sole preserve of female activists and their allies. What the expressive images of the flapper and her sartoriality provided was the possibility of 'dressing up' in ideas without any lasting commitment. It was this element of masquerade which also allowed the Modern Girl worldwide to playfully subvert gender norms, albeit within existing patriarchal hierarchies. Butler notes that 'on the one hand, masquerade may be understood as the performance production of a sexual ontology, an appearing that makes itself convincing as a "being"; on the other hand, masquerade can be read as a denial of a feminine desire that presupposes some prior ontological femininity regularly unrepresented by the phallic economy' (Butler 1990, 64). Despite their daring fashion choices, Modern Girls performed a male-directed and attractive femininity, illustrated by the widespread popularity of Japanese and Hollywood stars in conventionally 'masculine' attire, both onscreen and in publicity photographs.

In the Japanese context, the expressivity made possible by Western-style dress formats was not simply the product of Western-style modernisation initiatives, but of the way in which Western-derived associations were mobilised in the Japanese popular imagination. Concerns surrounding female consumption of Western-inspired dress norms and exposure to Western-derived intellectual ideas had persisted since the Meiji era (1868–1912). For many women, it was the 1872 School System Law, which introduced compulsory primary education for all, and the subsequent emergence of the schoolgirl, which provided an entry point into Western fashion, fostering the popularity of hybrid outfits. Already by the middle of the decade, the press was noting that girls were adopting masculine speech patterns and life goals, seemingly undifferentiated from their male counterparts. An 1875 letter describes overhearing two girls wearing masculine *hakama* trousers and discussing their desire to 'become teachers and make their own money rather than getting married, so that they can freely go to the theatre and keep a gigolo' (Nakamura 2006, 274). By 1879 the Imperial Rescript on Education was 'remonstrating against too much Westernisation' (Nakamura 2006, 274). Girls were banned from wearing *hakama* in school and the kimono became school uniform between 1879 and 1882. Still, the schoolgirl was synonymous with *hai-kara,* a term initially derived from the English 'high collar' appearing on men's shirts, but which described anything fashionable, and which could be expressed literally, with white layered *ban-eri*[2] collar pieces added to the uniform kimono. Even in the first instance, then, modernisation was not simply a matter of adopting Western practice. Similarly, following World War I, increasing female expressivity was not purely 'Western'. Expressivity was common to women (and their images) worldwide, as they experienced the modern world and its opportunities, but took various forms depending on context. One example in interwar Japan was the new phenomenon of women seeking love marriages, which had greater resonance and cultural specificity, given the prevailing custom of arranged marriages, in line with family obligations. It is here that the role of cinema in forming and propagating expressive images becomes truly transnational. The meaning of the image, in this example those of Hollywood romances, was determined by the territory in which it was being exhibited.

Consumerism itself was not new in Japan. The 'great cities' of the Tokugawa period, between 1603 and 1868, have long been recognised 'as centres of consumption' (Francks and Hunter 2012, 5). 'Western' consumer norms were therefore grafted onto, and prompted the adaptation of, existing 'Japanese' practice. But by the early twentieth century, the 'transnational character' of

Japanese consumption was unmistakeable. The consumer was exposed to 'a whole complex of practices from salesmanship, advertising, and consumer credit to mass formal education in home management . . . designed to generate the desire and the possibility to possess branded goods that placed women and families either proudly and pleasurably in the middle class or made them anxiously seek to join it' (Gordon 2012, 15). While the practices allowed the consumer to purchase a sense of identity, their transnational crisis meant that this also produced an identity crisis, nowhere more evident than in discussions of the Modern Girl, herself a transnationally constructed consumer image. Companies produced print media to promote the consumer products associated with this image, thereby further contributing to its development. In June 1926, the in-house magazine of Shiseido Cosmetics published a round-table discussion on the Modern Girl (*Shiseido geppō* 1926, 5–6). Superficially, the discussion seems to provide information, but it is clearly intended to market the brand's products, the prices of which are printed below the body of text. The introduction emphasises the location of the discussion ('Meguro . . . behind the Fudōson temple, in one tatami room'), but the participants are not named and do not come to any real consensus about the Modern Girl's true 'identity'. This is related to her leisure activities (which include visiting both the Kabuki-za theatre and the Hollywood-style cinema), but the only constant is her use of cosmetics: 'The Modern Girl's lips are a devilish red, her face powder is purple and green, or sometimes yellow, and used plentifully. Her rouge is also vivid, she draws on her eyebrows and beauty spots and lines her eyes with ink.' She wears both kimono and Western clothing. Her consumerism is mentioned in neutral, rather innocuous terms: 'Basically, Modern Girls just like new things, don't they?' Other participants describe her as purely American. According to Shiseido, the Modern Girl both works, and does not; she is married, and she is virginal; she is scandalous, and she is progressive; the only defining feature of the Modern Girl is that she is an avid consumer of the brand. Print media used the *moga* to appeal to a diverse audience, presenting her and her associated anxieties as a malleable fabrication, easily adaptable to maximise consumer participation.

By the mid-1920s, there were links within the Japanese popular imagination between Western clothing and inner character. This was facilitated by the interconnected nature of Japan's media and consumer climate, which saw publishers, department stores, cosmetics companies and film studios constantly referencing each other's products and advertising them, with one popular media theme being the internal and external Westernisation of women. Emblematic of this phenomenon was the success of Tanizaki Jun'ichirō's novel *Chijin No Ai* (*A Fool's Love*, also referred to as *Naomi*), despite its initial serialisation in spring 1924 in the *Osaka asahi shimbun* being halted due to government censorship (Suzuki 2005, 357). The novel's titular character embodies the social concerns of the time. The protagonist, Jōji, 'discovers' her working in a cafe and attempts to shape her internally and externally into a perfect 'Western' wife, purchasing Western-style outfits and shoes and providing her with language and dancing lessons. Naomi's 'vamp'-like powers increase as her clothing becomes increasingly Western, to the extent that the narrator no longer recognises her towards the end of the novel, when she appears wearing 'a pale blue French crepe dress . . . [and] high-heeled, patent leather shoes decorated with fake diamonds' (Tanizaki 1985, 207–8). There is a correlation between the purchasing of a Westernised appearance and the creation of a new identity, with increased autonomy and sexual power. Naomi is dangerous, wreaking havoc once enlightened (or perhaps tainted) by her Westernisation, but her power is also attractive, presenting the reader with a multi-faceted and problematic view of the Westernised female.

This allowed Tanizaki's narrative to enter the independent commercial sphere; publication of the novel was taken up from November 1924 to July 1925 by *Josei* (*Female*), 'a high-brow literary magazine targeting female readers' (Suzuki 2005, 357). *Josei* differed from other women's (and literary) magazines of its time in that it was initially founded by the company Nakayama Taiyōdō as a promotional material to raise the profile of the Club (Kurabu) cosmetics company, which had a reputation as the most 'Western' Japanese cosmetics brand available at that time (Ishii 2005). This reputation was maintained by the firm's widespread advertising not only in targeted publications (such as *Fujin gahō*, which catered specifically to its female target market) but in national newspapers, including the *Asahi shimbun* and *Yomiuri shimbun* – the firm's 'Western' aesthetic being clearly displayed using large pictorial accompaniments, a stark contrast to conventional text-only Japanese newspaper advertising. Club cosmetics' endorsement of *Josei* magazine by the time of *Naomi*'s publication was evident only through its (relatively minimal) employment of advertisements for the firm's goods within the publication (Tipton 2009, 194). The novel proved to be a successful investment – it became a best-seller for the publishing house Kaizōsha, with over fifty printings in the first two months of publication (Suzuki 2005, 357). According to the *Yomiuri shimbun*, *Naomi*'s Western-styled heroine also led to a movement coined as 'Naomi-ism' (*Naomizumu*) arising amongst young urban women which encouraged the assumption of a Westernised aesthetic and persona, including fashion and cosmetics – a clear benefit to Club (*Yomiuri shimbun* 1925, 4).

The *Yomiuri shimbun* links the trend's aesthetic components to daring behaviour:

> 'Naomi-ism', the new word coined in honour of the novel's female heroine Naomi, who possesses a fierce and perverse sexuality, seems to be all that is on the red painted lips of those following this secret fashion trend . . .

> Even the daughters of certain venerable masters of modern literature have experienced *Naomi*'s electric shock, and can be heard nagging their fathers – 'hey, buy me a copy!' The old masters can only smile bitterly with embarrassment. (*Yomiuri shimbun* 1925, 4)

This commentator refers to the position of the *Naomi*-inspired trend amongst existing adherents to the Modern Girl aesthetic (they refer to the same 'female students' which held a key role in forming the consumer image worldwide, alongside their 'red-painted lips', a constant in the image's iconography) alongside the text's ability to 'corrupt' the daughters of the intellectual class, resulting in embarrassment for the male elite. Considering that Club's advertising was relatively scarce in *Josei*, and that this commentator refers to 'Naomi-ism' as a 'secret fashion trend', it is possible that the publication of the novel constitutes an early form of covert marketing.

Terence A. Shimp and J. Craig Andrews describe covert marketing as 'messages that appear *not* to be marketing communications but that actually are' – he uses the example of internet 'viral' advertising campaigns in order to illustrate this: 'unsuspecting recipients of such messages presume that the favorable word of mouth is from an actual consumer who really likes the brand, when in fact the "buzzer" has been hired to deliver a disguised sales message' (Shimp 2008, 622). At this time, the Westernised Modern Girl image was still the aim of only a distinct minority in practice – Barbara Sato notes, 'According to one of the first surveys to record the changing fashions and lifestyles after the earthquake, out of over one thousand men and women observed in the summer of 1925 on the Ginza . . . ninety-nine per cent of the women wore traditional Japanese dress . . . the small number found consisted primarily of the *modan gāru*' (Sato 1993, 364). It would make sense to target this autonomous group with an ostensibly 'neutral' literary product laden with fashion imagery, and to then allow the group itself to generate the 'buzz' required for the desire to purchase the *moga* consumer image, meaning that desire for its related goods could transit throughout society in a seemingly organic manner. If we consider early-adopters of the *moga* consumer aesthetic as members of a fashion 'subculture', and that 'there are instances when the marketing happens from within the subculture, but more often, subcultural dress and aesthetics are selectively borrowed from outside without regard for the subcultural ideology and style guidelines, and redesigned and branded in a way to become a commodity for the mainstream to consume' (Winge 2013, 107), then the covert marketing of a Western-style aesthetic functions on two levels, satisfying two consumer groups. The subtle sponsorship of *Naomi* satisfies counter-cultural notions of 'authenticity' – via Tanizaki's narrative, its associated fashion artifacts become predominantly associated with Naomi's subversive behaviour rather than mainstream commercial interests, as is described in the *Yomiuri shimbun* gossip column. Yet the text's presentation as a highbrow literary work within a periodical targeted at 'well-educated, middle and upper middle class women' (Ishii 2005) justifies its merit amongst mainstream, aspirational consumers – it becomes a 'gateway' for further discussion of the *moga* as a purchasable consumer image and her aesthetics, embodied by a series of further articles appearing in *Josei*, such as 'The *Modan Gāru* and the Origin by Mutation' in December 1925 (Sato 1993, 368). It is not until June 1926 that Club's most prominent rival in the Western-style cosmetics market – Shiseido – publishes its round-table on the Modern Girl in *Shiseido geppō* (*Shiseido Monthly*). *Josei*, financed by Club, appears to be more invested in propagating the *moga* image as a purchasable, named archetype directly alongside *Naomi*'s success. Even Tanizaki himself was fully aware of the pulling power of Naomi's visual appearance – when updating *Josei*'s readers of the novel's plot since the cessation of its publication in the *Osaka asahi shimbun*, a process achieved in only a few concise sentences, he places the most emphasis on Naomi's journey from 'fifteen-year-old café waitress' to 'luxuriously *hai-kara* ['high-collar'] grown woman' (Tanizaki 1985, 83).

It is difficult to conclusively determine whether or not the subversive 'Naomi-ism' trend was specifically orchestrated by the Club cosmetics company, or if it truly was a grass-roots consumer reaction to the text's content, or if it even existed in the form described in the *Yomiuri shimbun*. The term 'Naomi-ism' does not seem to appear in women's magazines and is only used by external commentators. However, it is apparent that the text's depiction of a Westernised aesthetic aligned with female expressivity allowed its literary content to transcend social and media boundaries, disrupting the conventionally 'male' literary sphere and entering the realms of a feminine consumer sphere. There are clear motivations for Nakayama Taiyōdō to feature *Naomi* in *Josei* as a text with specifically relevant marketing potential, and its position within an intertextual multimedia network with interests in marketing the *moga* consumer image is clearly demonstrated: the editorial decision to feature *Naomi* in *Josei* was made by Osanai Kaoru, who set up the Shōchiku Acting School in 1920 (Tsubouchi 2000, 102) and trained the popular Western-style actresses that the studio's official history credits with the company's exponential popular success during the early 1920s (Nagayama 1996, 562). The very characteristics which led to the novel's restriction by state-influenced media were the very aspects which generated financial gain for the fashion, cosmetics and commercial publishing industries – an expressive female character emblematised (and enabled) by her Western-style appearance and alignment with cinematic stars.

Tanizaki's cinematic references when describing Naomi emphasise this association by invoking star images, combining the individual reader experience and the mass cinematic experience. In the text's original published form, as a serialised feature in the *Osaka asahi shimbun*, this experience is enhanced by its position on the page, reproduced alongside the paper's reviews of imported cinema, a section entitled 'Screen'. The printed page and the cinema provide different immersive experiences for the reader and the viewer, with different implications for the individual's relationship to their consumer practices and desires. Reading 'is best done alone, in a quiet place, and to the exclusion of other activities . . . Reading is "anti-social"; it isolates the reader from live interactions' (Meyrowitz 1986, 124). Reading is also never fully immersive. The reader has to choose what to read and make an effort to do so, rather than passively 'receiving' images. In a cinema, by contrast, the viewer has to go to a designated space, where they undergo the same immersive experience as many others. As discussed in the Introduction, it is this act of participation, rather than their content and style, which allows films to provide the sensory reflexive horizon described by Hansen (Hansen 2000, 10). They could thereby cater to the everyday subject's desire to 'freeze' the ephemeral 'moments of "present" experience' (Charney and Schwartz 1995, 2–3). This sense of immediacy was noted by the novelist Satō Haruo. 'My favourite among the symbols of modernity is the motion pictures. When I reflect on them, I feel duty bound to live in the present' (quoted in Harootunian 2011, 23).

We also need to acknowledge that this kind of 'classical spectatorship is fundamentally gendered, that is, masculinized, which makes textually dominant routes of identification problematic for the female viewer' (Hansen 1994, 5). Nonetheless, the cinema was able to foster a specific relationship between 'femininity and consumerism and the spectator', creating a desire on the part of the female spectator for the star onscreen (Petro 2002, 43). The screen allows the female spectator to envision herself, first, appropriating the star's lifestyle via sensory immersion in her image, then materialising it via modern 'feminine' spaces such as the department store, thereby coding her own identity. This is a reaction which is unique to the cinema as an audio-visual medium; due to the singular visual quality of the printed page, print media is unable to provide the all-encompassing and immersive 'sensory reflexive horizon' as described by Hansen, due to both its lack of spatial involvement (unlike the cinema, which exists as a space itself, simultaneously providing both individual and mass experience) and its singular, one-way avenue of consumerist dialogue from page to a single reader. Shimp and Andrews note that 'magazine advertising is not intrusive; readers control their exposure to a magazine ad' (Shimp and Andrews 2008, 367) – the page directs the peruser to purchase; however, she does not 'see herself' within those pages, since only the 'window' described by Doane persists and not the 'mirror' supplied by the cinema. Due to the perusal of magazines as an individual activity within an undefined space (and the position of the magazine as a physical commodity in itself as an item to be bought and consumed, rather than as a leisure activity itself), print media lacks the immersive, sensory and mass involvement which generates the immediate and direct self-identification of the viewer with its subject which is produced by the cinema and which motivates the female subject to desire 'purchasing' the image of the star and her surroundings. The action of the cinema urging spectators to consume is visceral in its origins – its immersive nature eliminates the individual's choice to receive marketing messages and replaces it with involuntary exposure.

Tanizaki's references to Hollywood star images provide a 'bridge' between the printed page and the cinematic and private and public spheres, manifested in the book's position as a portable physical object. The text's simulation of the cinematic quality is further strengthened by Tanizaki's referencing not only of cinematic imagery but of its technology and techniques – he describes how Jōji utilises photographs of Naomi in order to document her 'progress', a literary interpretation of the Hollywood montage sequence. His descriptions of Naomi's actions, dress and persona with direct reference to named stars act essentially as marketing brand names, which are immediately evocative of both the consumerist allure of the cinematic space and specific marketable feminine archetypes. This is reinforced by his inclusion of actual marketing brand names, providing examples of both Japanese and Western brands: 'her cigarette is Dimitrino slims, her newspaper, the *Miyako*. She also reads magazines like *Classic* and *Vogue*' (Tanizaki 1985, 234). Isolde Standish describes how 'the *modan gaaru* ... crossed the boundaries of the public and private, becoming a symbolic figure of the city, which is both modern and degenerate' (Standish 2006, 60). I argue that the ability of cinematic star images to transit between media (and consequently the mass and individual spheres) allowed this specific *moga* image itself to form and proliferate, culminating in a specific set of associations between fashionable appearance and internal character which motivated consumer processes on both public and private levels.

The concept of a recognisable fashion archetype – in this case the Modern Girl – moving between media and through different spaces prompts a discussion of the relationship between fashion archetypes, the urban space and the cinema. Fashion and cinema act simultaneously as capitalist trap and lure, with urban space as their necessary centre. The 'unnatural ... social arrangements' of the city gave rise to a formalised fashion system (Wilson 2011, 9) and were also easily captured in film. The cinema itself relies upon unnaturally constructed depictions of human society in order to generate the narratives of beauty and success that attract audiences. Not only is the city itself frequently employed as the stage for these narratives, but they are mirrored in the audience's physical surroundings: even in a rural setting, the cinema carries connotations of technology and modernity, as well as the rapid succession of changing images which pertain to the city. Wilson describes fashion as homogenising 'national and regional difference' into a 'distilled moment of glassy sophistication'. The same was true on the Japanese screen, embodied by the actress wearing hybrid dress. Film and fashion images could transition seamlessly between the page and the screen, the promotional display and the living clothed form. The city was the space within which this media mobility was achieved. But the sense of freedom, suggested by fashion and perpetuated by the cinema, were restricted by the capitalist economics, which both birthed them and allowed them to thrive. 'Fashion *speaks* capitalism ... [W]e live as far as clothes are concerned a triple ambiguity: the ambiguity of capitalism itself with its great wealth and great squalor, its capacity to create and its dreadful wastefulness; the ambiguity of our identity, of the relation of self to body and self to the world; and the ambiguity of art, its purpose and meaning' (Wilson 2011, 14–15). These ambiguities are never resolved but are instead perpetuated by the transnational and transmedial nature of the Japanese cinema, which therefore feeds a desire to create and consume expressive, fashionable images and engage in behaviours, sartorial and social, which are compliant with them.

Richard Dyer's concept of the constructed 'star persona', in which stars play characters on- and off-screen within predetermined archetypes, is key to understanding the role of cinema in providing marketable behaviours and aesthetics across multimedia texts (Dyer 1998, 99, 109). Deborah Shamoon notes that the stars which Tanizaki cites when describing Naomi predominantly fit with the 'vamp' archetype, and Tanizaki expresses her consumption of their star images as a process of adopting their mannerisms, which alters (and Westernises) her overall physical appearance in the eyes of the text's narrator:

> Apparently, she studied the actresses' movements when we went to the movies because she was very good at imitating them. In an instant she could capture the mood and idiosyncrasies of an actress. [Mary] Pickford laughs like this, she'd say; Pina Menicheli [sic] moves her eyes like this; Geraldine Farrar does her hair up this way. Loosening her hair, she'd push it into this shape and that. 'Very good — better than any actor. Your face looks so Western.' (Tanizaki 1985, 36)

Tanizaki presents the aesthetic and behavioural emulation of these star images as a transformative action – despite Naomi's race and nationality being fixed, this action allows even her actual face to appear Western. The exception to Tanizaki's use of 'vamp' film stars is Mary Pickford, who was selected as a *Kinema junpō* cover star in November 1916 based purely on her facial appearance (Fujiki 2013, 91). Nicknamed 'America's Sweetheart' in the US press, Pickford was best known for her 'Little Girl' roles and held appeal as an accessible, non-threatening sex symbol (Whitfield 2007, 300). Considering her frequent promotional visits to Japan throughout the 1920s and 1930s, arranged by the Kamata Shōchiku Studio, she had a significant Japanese following and was featured in print media aimed at cinema audiences and young women (Fujiki 2013, 189). Rather than only referencing subversive, active and sexually loaded star personae, the inclusion of Pickford provides an approachable aesthetic which was less challenging of existing Japanese expectations of women, but which nevertheless still held the marketing power of a Western-derived Hollywood bodily image. This was an existing technique in the Japanese cinema, even prior to the 1923 earthquake – Murata Minoru's *Souls on the Road* (*Rojō no reikon*, 1921), produced by Osanai Kaoru as the first full-length feature created by the Shōchiku Kinema Research Studio, featured actress Sawamura Haruko (a graduate of the Shōchiku acting school) fully appropriating Pickford's visual aesthetics by wearing her hair in pigtails, with cutesy Western sailor dresses, and exhibiting a playful, girlish expressive persona.

This concept of *moga* actresses with 'harder' or 'softer' (but still Westernised) aesthetics endures throughout the Japanese film industry of the 1920s and 1930s. A film in which this is clearly illustrated via the usage of Western clothing is Shimazu Yasujirō's *Our Neighbour, Miss Yae* (*Tonari no Yae-chan*, 1934), produced by the same Kamata Shōchiku Studio which arranged Mary Pickford's Japanese tours (Fujiki 2013, 189). Starring actress Aizome Yumeko's own publicity shots reference Pickford's appearance following her role wearing solely Western attire in Ozu Yasujirō's *Dragnet Girl* (*Hijōsen no onna*, 1933) the previous year, entailing that a Western-style appearance was becoming an established aspect of her own public persona. Shimazu was known to directly reference Hollywood cinema as source materials for his works (Wada-Marciano 2008, 36) and engaged in the industry-wide practice of creating Japanese 'equivalents' of Hollywood stars in order to generate revenue not only from films themselves but from related merchandise, such as cosmetics and fashion lines promoted by actresses such as Natsukawa Shizue, the 'Japanese Clara Bow', who alongside Irie Takako featured in fashion catalogues for the Mitsukoshi department store (*Osaka Mitsukoshi*, 1932). Aizome's character Yae wears her hair in loose pigtails with minimal cosmetics and a loose, high-necked cotton dress with a bow at the neckline – a clear visual reference onscreen to Pickford's demure persona. Yae's attire, combined with the casting of Aizome Yumeko and her Westernised star persona, acts as a means of 'Japanising' Hollywood images in a way which is accessible and palatable to a variety of Japanese audiences – both the consumerist youth market and conservative figures via her fashionable but 'respectable modern persona' (Fujiki 2013, 279).

While *Naomi*'s Westernised titular character is portrayed as a wholly negative force, Shimazu's film provides a wholesome, yet still Hollywood-derived alternative which could appeal to women wishing to participate in Western-style fashion trends without negative connotations. The juxtaposition of this respectable image with Yae's older divorcee sister (Okada Yoshiko), a woman who adopts a hybridised *moga* appearance, wearing a brightly coloured kimono with pin-curled hair and cosmetics, presents the audience with a generational divide symbolised via Western attire. Yae's sister's dialogue encapsulates the concerns raised by the press and which feature in *Naomi* – she states, 'I could live by myself and work in a cafe,' which her mother confirms 'would never be acceptable' – her dress format is fully coherent with the audience's presumed expectation of her inner character. This also corresponds with Okada's star persona, which entailed 'a foreigner discourse, aligning her physical body with the sexual Otherness of Western cinema . . . [carrying] the transgressive sexual terms that often mark mixed identity . . . a sexually autonomous figure' (Wada-Marciano 2008, 96). Yae's characterisation is entirely different – she is portrayed as energetic and sporty but morally innocent; her sister remarks that she 'can't be pure like Yaeko' and ultimately Yae's virtue leads her to succeed romantically where her sister cannot. In this sense the trope that the hybridised *moga* must always be punished for her poor morals may also be applied to Shimazu's work; however, the film offers an attractive, younger alternative role-model for viewers seeking a Western-style heroine. The film manipulates Hollywood dichotomies (the inoffensive Pickford-type versus the subversive Clara Bow-inspired figure) in order to make the hybridised *moga* appear not only dangerous but dated – Yae's Westernised dress does not dictate a morally bankrupt character, but instead girlish charm. Her ultimate 'victory' at the film's climax, in which she joins the male lead's family when her own family relocate to Korea, enforces her position as an aspirational character; she embodies the promotion of a total external Westernisation for young women as a virtuous aspect preferable to the older and hybridised *moga*, so long as they retain distinctly 'Japanese' moral characteristics.

The concept of marketable fashion 'types' is something which appears within global fashion marketing contexts – Wilson describes how consumers were categorised by 'personality type' and encouraged to make their purchases accordingly by Bullock's department store in Los Angeles in the 1920s (Wilson 2011, 124). In the Japanese context, the word '*taipu*' was adapted from the English 'type' in order to import this concept. An August 1936 *Nihon eiga* (*Japanese Film*) magazine article promoting PCL's *Older Brother, Younger Sister* (*Ani imōto*, 1936) describes actress Takehisa Chieko as follows: 'As a man, ha ha! What can I say? Takehisa Chieko is the type who is perfectly suited to her "older sister" role' (*Nihon eiga* 1936, 10). The article's author then describes her role in the film: 'This "older sister" until now has known nothing but hardship. She couldn't know when she would have her next meal. Until the day she returned home . . .' (*Nihon eiga* 1936, 10). She is pictured wearing bold cosmetics, pearl earrings, white gloves and a hat with a black-and-white, peplum-waisted pencil dress and carrying a square, white handbag, held at the very centre of the image. This is a clearly an affluent image – the photo's caption implies that the film's character manages to gain money despite her impoverished background, and the article's comments imply that Takehisa's looks factor into this characterisation. *Nihon eiga* was a companion publication to *Shufu no tomo* and was aimed at a predominantly female market – it included not only advertisements for *Shufu no tomo* itself, but also fashion 'style guides' within its issues. The commentary on this image, accompanied by its fashion content and situation within a magazine of this nature, implies that the female reader's desire to conform to this attractive and resilient 'type' may be achieved via an approximation of her sartorial style. The practice of arranging actresses by 'type' also affected the variety of goods which they advertised – while *moga* archetype Irie Takako and the hybridised Natsukawa Shizue promoted Western style fashions in the 1932 *Osaka Mitsukoshi* catalogues, ranging from Dietrich-style trench coats to Clara Bow cloches, in the January 1931 edition of their fan magazine *Kamata*, the Shōchiku studios employed images of more 'accessible' stars such as Tanaka Kinuyo and Takao Mitsuko (both of whom held modern yet respectable personae, as demonstrated by Aizome) in order to promote match holders, an altogether more utilitarian product. Stella Bruzzi describes fashion in the cinematic context as 'clothing as a discourse not wholly dependent on the structures of narrative and character for signification', allowing for characters to be 'constructed through their costumes', particularly in terms of gender and sexuality (Bruzzi 1997, xv–xvi). Fan-focused publications and related promotional materials allowed women to construct their own everyday 'characters', by utilising these materials themselves and film archetypes onscreen as a guide. Essentially, these 'types' allowed women to simultaneously express themselves (by projecting a proscribed identity) and abstract themselves into codified objects. This is coherent with de Beauvoir's discussion of artifice in the European context, in which she states that the 'dressed' woman 'is the character she represents – but is not. It is this identification with something unreal, fixed, perfect . . . that gratifies her; she strives to identify herself with this figure and thus to seem to herself to be stabilised, justified in her splendour' (de Beauvoir 2011, 509). Wilson further elaborates that dressing to 'type' involves 'becoming something other than and more stable than one's fluctuating and moody self. But the problem is that – except on celluloid – the attempt to achieve an absolute, petrified state can never succeed' (Wilson 2011, 125–6). Film becomes a site which enables the audience as consumer to view the 'types' sold by fashion and related industries in both an immersive and perfected form; it acts as a stabilising agent which allows the viewer to categorise both others and themselves, acting as a means of comprehending both the criticisms and praise levelled at various sartorial archetypes expressed in print media.

Deborah Shamoon notes that 'while images of modern girls appeared sporadically in the early 1920s, it was not until the late 1920s and early 1930s that the modern girl look became widespread both in media and women's fashion' (Shamoon 2012, 1068). The moral panic surrounding the *moga* (or 'Modern Girl') which had been proliferated by print media intensified by the mid-1930s, with films such as Mizoguchi Kenji's *Osaka Elegy* (*Naniwa erejī*, 1936) directly referencing the role of newspapers and magazines in forming a negative image of Western-attired women. Conservative male figures such as Fujita Tsuguharu, an artist who painted in the Western-inspired *yōga* style, described a distinct relationship between dress, the cinematic and vocal expression: 'when dressed in Japanese costume, [women] must behave according to Japanese customs of modesty and quiet, and it is wrong for them to imitate American movie actresses' (Brown and Minichello 2003, 21.) Fujita's commentary presents the Japanese female appropriating the American cinematic body via her attire as being inherently un-Japanese, with Fujita defining Japanese identity expressed through costume in terms of moral and vocal characteristics. Considering the presentation of the Americanised cinematic female as being the antithesis of the kimono-clad Japanese woman, it is to be assumed that her characteristics would also be the opposite of 'modesty and quiet' – immodest and vocal. A number of journalists expressed similar opinions during the late 1920s, with Kiyosawa Kiyoshi describing 'modern girls [as] Westernised young women . . . girls who secretly socialise with young hoodlums, have sexual relationships with foreigners and have day jobs . . . they embody resistance against male-dominant morality and society' (Wada-Marciano 2008, 87). While Fujita's comments were most prominently aimed at young Japanese devotees of American stars such as Clara Bow, whose appropriation of her bodily image similarly 'tended to highlight contradictions between her fans' consumption habits and their national identity' (Fujiki 2013, 270) it is an observation which may be easily applied to the portrayal of Westernised Japanese women within the cinematic sphere. In the late 1920s, Japanese female-focused print media frequently defined female beauty in comparative terms, with publications such as *Shufu no tomo* determining the allure of the Western star's cinematic body as rooted in her 'genuine beauty of facial expression . . . [being] natural and reflecting her culture' following an interview with the wife of an entrepreneur working in Hollywood (Fujiki 2013, 134). While opinion concerning the Westernisation of young cinema-going Japanese women was mixed in content, there were incentives for filmmakers to provide outwardly Westernised female Japanese stars onscreen who exhibited not only the physical but also emotional qualities pertaining to their Hollywood counterparts; a Westernised appearance implicitly denoted an outwardly expressive character.

Notes

1. The Kansai dialect is a dialect of Japanese predominantly spoken in Osaka, Kyoto, Kobe and other regions of Western Japan.
2. *Ban-eri* were decorative collar pieces added to the neck of a kimono made of a fabric of the wearer's choice, reflecting different tastes and trends, popularised in the late Meiji/early Taisho period.

Chapter 2

Sartoriality and expressivity pre- and post-sound: The vernacular voice, the Western-attired woman and the city

In a 1929 essay for *Fujin kōron,* Shōchiku's chief producer Kido Shirō encouraged 'new' Japanese women to approximate the physical body of the Euro-American woman via increased exercise (Fujiki 2013, 134). Though this is the opinion of only one substantial figure in Shōchiku's operation, it is impossible to ignore the increasing appearance of Westernised female characters in the films produced by directors such as Mizoguchi Kenji for the studio's Dai-Ichi Eiga division, founded by Kido in response to Nikkatsu's 1933 expansion (Shoemaker 1979, 10). Mizoguchi's 1936 diptych *Osaka Elegy* and *Sisters of the Gion* (*Gion no kyōdai,* 1936) were initially intended to be part of a trilogy, with the plot of the final film focusing on a Japanese man's relationship with a Western woman, also to be set within the Kansai area (McDonald 1984, 49). This indicates an increasing involvement of Westernised femininity throughout the sequence of the films despite their separate narratives. This also illustrates a desire not only to explore the place of Westernised versus conventionally Japanese women in the modern spaces of this region, but also their position in a comparative context with an actual Western female occupying these same spaces, transcending mere emulation via dress and aesthetics and solidifying this concept of inner character being directly aligned with a woman's physical and national identity by allowing the Western female to directly replace the Westernised Japanese woman's position in a modernising society. Wilson states that 'fashion . . . substitutes for the real body an abstract, ideal body . . . the body as an idea rather than an organism' (Wilson 2011, 58). Considering the marketing of the Westernised female body as a desirable vessel for a more active and expressive female beauty by the film and print media industries, it is apparent that the usage of Western clothing to denote the modern outspoken woman and her relationship with a changing world, its technology and its past is a constant semiotic signifier throughout these films which would have been comprehensible to both men and women with experience of the modern consumerist city and the global film economy. This chapter explores the role of Western fashion objects in constructing the identities of female characters onscreen, particularly in reference to the onset and use of sound and new concepts of 'expressive' modern female stars, the representation of the city space and the response to Western-style fashion objects as expressed in contemporary print media. I aim to address several core queries: were Western clothing and accessories purely used onscreen to denote outspoken and expressive 'modern' women, who adopted them as an outward signifier of an internally 'modern' outlook inspired by Hollywood actresses, or did they carry more subtle nuances? How are Western-inspired fashion objects utilised onscreen to encourage the viewer to consume? I will respond to these questions via film case studies, discussed in correspondence with contemporary print media aimed at both male and female audiences.

Mizoguchi's diptych raises not only the query of 'type' enacted by sartorial contrast, but also the role of sound and technology in constructing expressive images of women. Jane Nicholas notes that 'the elision of differences between representations of machines and modern women's bodies was a significant aspect of feminine modernity . . . interlocking discourses of speed, progress, efficiency, youth, and beauty further brought together modern women's bodies, cars, and movies with the theme of desire and want for both bodies and goods' (Nicholas 2015, 193). This theme also appears in the iconography of the Japanese cinema: a promotional image of the actress Sakai Yoneko (Figure 2.1) which in the May 1924 issue of *The Play and Movie* depicts her operating a film camera while wearing kimono. Despite her demure costuming, Sakai was known for her 'vamp' roles, appearing in films such as Murata Minoru's *Night Tales of Honmoku* (*Honmoku yawa*, 1924) and Mizoguchi's *Queen of Modern Times* (*Gendai no joō*, 1924), a fact which illustrates that Mizoguchi was no stranger to modernised, expressive female stars by the time he created his 1936 diptych. Her operation of the film camera enacts a symbiosis: while dressed in 'traditional' attire, her active use of film technology and her challenging gaze immediately mark her persona as 'modern', while her established 'vamp' persona marks the camera as equipment facilitating the 'feminine modernity' and its consumptive connotations described by Nicholas. Changing technologies facilitate new means to generate meaning, with the addition of sound enhancing the 'immersive' nature of the cinematic experience by more closely replicating reality. Rather than relying on the *benshi* human narrator to explain and punctuate the moving image in a wholly artificial process of generating meaning, the audience is instead involved within a diegetic use of sound, much as they would experience in everyday life. A comparison which can be used to succinctly analyse the role of sartoriality pre- and post-sound is the respective relationships between

Figure 2.1 Photograph of actress Sakai Yoneko, *The Play and Movie*, May 1924. Courtesy of Kokusai Jōhōsha.

female expressivity and the usage of Western fashion (two key themes which denote the 'modern' woman as a commercial image) as they appear in Shimizu Hiroshi's silent film *Undying Pearl* (*Fue no shiratama*, 1929) and Gosho Heinosuke's *The Neighbour's Wife and Mine* (*Madamu to nyōbo*, 1931). *Kinema junpō* critic Tamura Yukihiko described *The Neighbour's Wife and Mine* as 'not only the first talkie produced by the [Shōchiku] Kamata studios, but the first all-talkie production made by the Japanese film industry – through this film, we will begin to see talkies made in Japan, too!' (Tamura 1931, 77). This quality of technological advancement, and its alignment with a modernising Japanese cinema, is advertised as the film's key selling point. Advertisements appearing in the *Yomiuri shimbun* promote the film as 'Japan's first all-talkie production' and its screenings were prefaced with 'the premiere of the first ever Japanese-made "sound-news" films', increasing the immersive cinematic experience by providing real-life Japanese news scenes complete with diegetic sound and demonstrating practical uses of the technology beyond its entertaining novelty (*Yomiuri shimbun* 1931, 2). Like Mizoguchi's diptych, these two films rely upon a 'traditional/Japanese' versus 'modern/Western' female dichotomy, enacted primarily through dress and iconography; however, due to their respective usage of sound (or lack thereof) their expressivity is depicted through varied means.

Undying Pearl utilises the motif of two sisters in order to enact a dichotomy, made clear solely through the usage of clothing from the onset of the film, which opens with Toshie (the more 'traditional' sister, played by Yagumo Emiko) dreaming of her sister Reiko (Oikawa Michiko) leaving with Shozo (Takada Minoru), her love interest. The couple are both wearing Western clothing, and their image is superimposed over Toshie's kimono-clad appearance. This sequence repeats several times, ensuring that the audience is aware of the predominance of the couple's Westernised image, and when Toshie wakes from her dream, we see she is wearing a garment with a layered collar, suggesting a kimono, even as she sleeps. The first view the audience sees of Reiko outside of this dream sequence is her stockinged legs and the hem of a striped dress as she climbs the stairs; she then undresses off-screen and puts on a pair of striped Western pyjamas. This cements the association between Reiko's Western-style attire and a Westernised interior persona: rather than restricting her wear of Western clothing to the public sphere, she wears Western garments even while sleeping. This action subverts the male practice of wearing Western dress in the workplace – 'Western clothes (called *yōfuku*) were worn in public, where modern men did their work. Returning home, many slipped off the external symbols of civilisation and modernity and slipped on the relaxing kimono' (Molony 2010, 86). Oikawa's Westernised form embodies the *moga*'s threat to the Japanese home space, which is reinforced by the usage of an inter-title, the preserve of the silent film, which cements the relationship between Reiko's Western-style attire and promiscuity: 'This is the story of two sisters – Toshie and Reiko – and a man. Narita Shozo was one of Reiko's many boyfriends. But for older sister Toshie, Shozo was the one and only man she had ever dreamed of loving.' This inter-title, while interrupting the immersive effect of a 'closed diegesis' by reminding the audience that they are witnessing a constructed narrative, nevertheless elevates the viewer to the status of 'a privileged and invisible guest' as described by Hansen in regard to the immersive classical Hollywood cinema by providing them with additional information external to the action onscreen (Hansen 2000, 11). The viewer of the silent cinema, when provided with informative inter-titles such as this, is not simply a voyeur watching events unfold blow-by-blow as in the sound cinema, instead, they watch from an elevated position of 'knowing', included within the narrative. It is in this way that despite the sound film more closely replicating reality due to its usage of diegetic sound that both media manage to immerse the viewer within the cinematic experience. In Shimizu's film, these inter-titles allow the audience not only an insight into events, but into the character's interior perceptions and opinions, which are not always overtly expressed within the narrative. These 'interior thoughts' frequently concern Westernised spaces; when Toshie enters a dancehall, populated entirely by revellers in Western or hybridised attire, in order to 'save' her disgraced sister, the audience is informed that 'for a woman like Toshie, coming to a place like this was like jumping into a lion's cage, but she did it for her sister's happiness'. This ensures that the audience is aware that a 'virtuous' woman such as Toshie would never be found for her own enjoyment in such an establishment. Another states, 'Fine food at a European restaurant. And a stroll around the lively streets of Ginza. Even these things tormented Toshie.' This usage of inter-titles distances Toshie's 'traditional' persona from a whole plethora of *moga*-related activities and spaces, and simultaneously associates them with her sister's subversive persona, creating both a moral and spatial distance between the pair. These non-dialogue-based inter-titles ('expository inter-titles') are a vital part of what Kristin Thompson describes as a 'judicious combination of expository intertitles, dialogue titles and exemplary character action [which] create[s] a fairly knowledgeable and communicative narrator' (Bordwell, Staiger and Thompson 2003, 27). 'Expository inter-titles' can act as either a reliable informant (dispensing new information) or as a means of eliminating ambiguity, reassuring the viewer that their assumptions are correct – while, for example, it is likely that an audience would already associate a wholly Westernised appearance with promiscuity prior to the interjection of the inter-title, the inter-title's confirmation of this being the case in terms of Reiko's characterisation elevates the viewer not only to a position of 'knowing' privilege, but also moral privilege. However, it must be noted once again that while the character played by Oikawa represents a Westernised threat in the film's narrative, it is apparent that the film itself (an adaptation of a story by Kikuchi Kan) was marketed as a star vehicle for Oikawa herself, and that the illicit allure of the *moga* image was intended to become part of her established star persona – this becomes clear in her later collaborations with Shimizu, including *Japanese Girls at the Harbour* (*Minato no nihon musume*, 1933) in which her character Sunako shoots her love rival and becomes a sex worker. An article marketing the film in the *Asahi shimbun* credits 'new star Oikawa Michiko' before any of her co-stars and is accompanied by a large image of Oikawa standing tall before a seated Takada Minoru (Figure 2.2), dominantly grasping his necktie; the couple are reflected in the mirror of her dressing table, the preserve of the cosmetically inclined *moga* (*Asahi shimbun* 1929, 5). While Oikawa's star persona and onscreen appearance in *Undying Pearl* appears to hold immoral connotations of female dominance and consumerism, it also appears to have been an attractive draw for audiences, once again highlighting the Westernised *moga*'s conflicted, yet lucrative consumer image.

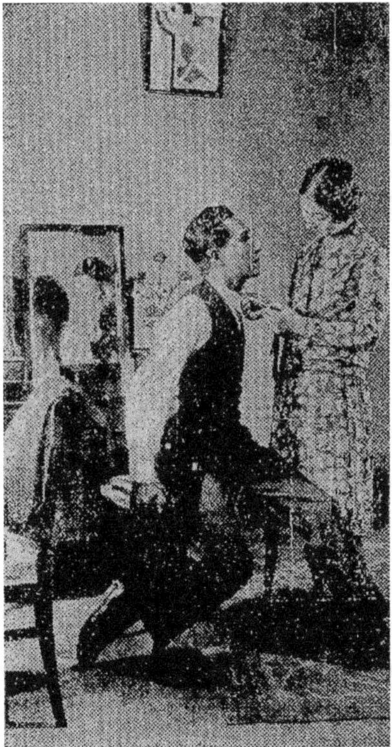

Figure 2.2 Promotional image for *Undying Pearl* (1929) featuring Oikawa Michiko and Takada Minoru. *Asahi shimbun*, 13 October 1929.

I discussed the role of speech and the act of speaking in female expressivity in Chapter 1; while the sound film more immediately achieves this connection and carries the additional connotations of accent and the emotional qualities of the voice, the silent film may still utilise the motif of Western attire alongside the frequency with which a female character is credited with dialogue in order to create an image of vocal expressivity. Aside from Reiko's sartorial appearance, her alliance with Western consumerism is made clear by the word choice used in her dialogue: she announces to her sister, 'I'm in the mood for European food;' she insists that Shozo buys both herself and her sister cosmetics; she laments that the bus she travelled on during her honeymoon 'was not a Hudson', an American brand of motorcar. Her dialogue imbues her with active, spontaneous connotations: she announces, 'I suddenly want to go to Hakone. Can we go right away?' In contrast, Toshie rarely speaks for herself at all, with most of her opinions either conveyed via letter or the omniscient narrator informing the audience. She is almost wholly passive, only taking action when she believes it to be in the best interests of others, embodying the concept of *giri* (familial obligation) – she agrees to her mother's wish for Reiko to marry Shozo, despite her own desire for romantic love. While the dialogue and imagery of the film portray the two sisters as polar opposites, it is this desire for romantic love which most strongly illuminates Toshie's conflicted persona. While she wears kimono and tries to behave in a way which only benefits others, she works as a typist, not only a thoroughly modern occupation, facilitated by new technology, but one which had become expressly feminine. While a 1905 job advertisement appearing in the *Asahi shimbun* requesting the attention of 'a person compliant with the use of a typewriter' to work at the Yokosuka naval munitions factory makes no reference to the desired applicant's gender (*Asahi shimbun* 1905, 1), by 1929 the role gains more glamorous connotations, with the same newspaper in December of that year introducing the MGM actress Fay Webb to Japanese audiences as 'a famous typist', providing the aspirational story of her humble origins working in New Jersey (*Asahi shimbun* 1929, 2). Despite Toshie's supposed dislike of the *moga*'s material trappings, in one sequence she wishes to appropriate them for herself, imagining herself surrounded by pearls and holding a large, feathered hat which belongs to Reiko; in another she envisions herself in hybridised attire, with permed hair and dressed in a brightly striped kimono, riding in a car with her boss, who has proposed to her. The inter-titled dialogue exploits this conflicted identity, highlighting it to the audience – after her boss' proposal, Toshie visits him at his home and meets his young nieces, who are dressed in typical *moga*-style short dresses, stockings and high heels. The most prominent of the women has a Louise Brooks-style bobbed haircut: she is played by Date Satoko, who would later appear as the jazz singer next door in *The Neighbour's Wife and Mine*. She tells her uncle, 'It's said that all typists are just no-good *moga*', and he replies, 'You don't know anything about working women. There are some decent typists too.' Toshie appears to be visibly offended by these words while the young women laugh amongst themselves; when their uncle describes Toshie as his receptionist his niece retorts, 'A female secretary? Uncle, you're very stylish!' At first, Toshie silently listens as these vociferous *moga* archetypes criticise her for the very characteristics associated with their own subculture; finally she gains her own expressivity and states, 'I do some secretarial work, but really, I am a typist. I don't know what you mean by "decent" but I am proud of my work and have nothing to be ashamed of.' The scene relies on comic irony; rather than the *moga* being a lower-class woman who supports herself through work in order to fund a lavish consumerist lifestyle beyond her means, she is a middle-class snob who undeservedly takes the moral high ground in the face of a 'virtuous' woman who works to support herself out of necessity. The film's script even manages to imply a relationship between expressivity and sound despite its silent medium; following Toshie's outburst, the camera now focuses on her boss's three children, one of whom asks, 'What is a typist?' The film cuts back to the *moga* nieces, who are still idly chattering and giggling, before the eldest of the children – a young girl in Pickford-style pigtails – responds, 'They make more noise than a piano!' while waggling her fingers in mime. The nieces burst into riotous laughter, appearing hypocritical – the choice of a Western instrument – the piano – as an analogy, aims the criticism as much at the nieces as Toshie. Despite the film's silent quality, its references to sound and speech manage to efficiently depict 'expressive' women, with their attire carrying specific coded connotations. A woman who wears conventionally 'Japanese' attire and aims to be selfless in her actions, but who is nevertheless subject to the allure of Western-style consumerism and Hollywood-style romantic love, Toshie exists as a summary of the various conflicting discourses surrounding a Westernised appearance experienced by the contemporary female spectator.

Initially titled *Tonari no zatsuon*, or *The Noise Next Door*, Gosho's *The Neighbour's Wife and Mine* similarly depicts the dichotomy of a *moga* versus a conflicted hybridised yet expressive persona, executed primarily via the use of sound. Clothing is intrinsic in depicting this dynamic, and both principal actresses – Tanaka Kinuyo, the protagonist's wife, and Date Satoko, his jazz-singer neighbour – swing between both 'Japanese' and 'Western' sartorial poles. When the audience is first introduced to the jazz singer, she appears largely conventional, wearing a *yukata*[1]; she scolds the protagonist after he mistakenly stumbles into the female section of the local bathhouse. The male protagonist and his artist companion (styled to resemble comedy duo Stan Laurel and Oliver Hardy, providing a link to the Hollywood cinema also via depictions of the masculine) do not react in any negative way towards her appearance, instead remarking on her beauty. Here, clothed in a 'conventionally Japanese' manner, she is considered no threat. Contrastingly, Tanaka's portrayal of the protagonist's wife is largely negative, despite her wearing kimono and an old-fashioned Japanese hairstyle throughout the film – rather than withholding her emotions in the interests of the welfare of her husband and consequently their family's income (he is a scriptwriter who is trying to finish a manuscript within a tight deadline), she constantly nags and shrieks in a thick Kansai accent, ruining his artistic flow. Gosho later recalled the following concerning the casting of Tanaka:

> When we cast Tanaka Kinuyo, who speaks with a Kansai accent, we broke the rule stipulating that all dialogue had to be delivered in standard Japanese, the way radio announcers speak. Contrary to expectations, her delivery imparted lifelike nuances to the dialogue and offered a valuable suggestion for solving the problems faced by the talkies that followed. (Iwamoto 1992, 322)

Tanaka's dialect embodies a new realism enabled by the 'all-talkie' sound film by speaking in a dialect which is not affected – the convention of utilising a 'standardised' accent and dialect immediately suggests the sphere of a constructed media narrative. Rather than the audience's sensory immersion being interrupted by dialogue, as in the case of the use of inter-titles in the silent film context, the act of speaking furthers the sense of immersion by involving sound, another of the audience's senses. Gosho's choice of the Kansai-accented Tanaka appears to have been successful according to a review in *Kinema junpō*: 'none of the cast have conventional stage experience – but rather than being a hindrance, this really makes the delivery of the lines more natural. The tone of delivery is just as in everyday speech, and further creators of Japanese talkies must take notice of this' (Tamura 1931, 77). This wholly immersive usage of sound adds a sense of hyper-realism to the film, particularly its replication of everyday Japanese life – the home is fitted with *shoji* paper doors, a shared quality with the audience. The irritation or voyeurism of overheard sound makes the audience privy to what is usually unseen – this embodies an exciting sensation, new to the Japanese experience as this was the first talkie, enacting a distinct contrast to the 'informant' nature of the omniscient narrator present in the silent film's inter-titles. The review bears this out, expressing delight at the immersive quality of the film's soundtrack and comparing it positively to American sound pictures:

> Until now, when watching an American or European talkie film, what they most made me feel was that the sounds I heard building up were beautiful sounds. But if you make a complete sound production, then you must also include annoying or unwanted sounds – if a 'complete' sound film does

> not do this, then you cannot call it a 'complete sound film'. . . although this film is completely original, the sounds are by no means not beautiful. The first American-made talkies were just filmed live performances, structured like a film – sound was not a priority. (Tamura 1931, 77)

While Tanaka's character only wears kimono in her active scenes, following an argument within which her husband criticises a nagging change to her speech ('Now all you say is "why", and "but"!') we see an old photograph of her on his desk in which she is smiling and wearing a beret. He turns this photograph over, implying the completion of a process whereby her appearance and speech have changed together simultaneously – when she wore Western clothing, she was pleasant to speak to, now in kimono she is a tiresome nag. When the writer is interrupted by the jazz band, and goes next door to investigate, Date Satoko's costume and performance depicts a reversal of this change: while she was initially relatively quiet and innocuous while wearing kimono at the onset of the film, she now appears singing and dancing the Charleston wearing a short dress, which is sleeveless and cinched at the waist with a leather belt – a noticeable change in silhouette from her kimono earlier and highlighting her bodily form. Her dress has a bib front and is made from a boldly striped fabric; the 'bib' softens the otherwise overtly sexualised look – her ensemble simultaneously references the Pickford and Bow Hollywood archetypes. Date's performance is initially provocative – the protagonist recoils when she lights his cigarette, implying that she is 'dangerous' and that he is literally 'playing with fire', but he comes to enjoy her song 'Age of Speed' ('Supeedo no Jidai'), the performance of which within the new diegetic sound technology (she is accompanied by a full jazz band, including conductor) aligns Date's body with the 'feminine modernity' embodied by technology as described by Nicholas. It is this song which leads the protagonist to complete his script – rather than representing the dismantling of the Japanese family, Date's Westernised jazz persona (and its related expressivity) indirectly benefit it. In its coverage of the film's production, the *Yomiuri shimbun* newspaper overtly linked Date's vocal performance within this new technology to both her expressive star persona and its ability to sell external products related to the film, describing with surprise how her performance was picked up by Western record label Polydor, creating a product of hybrid Western–Japanese identity: 'It has been decided that Date Satoko, of the Kamata Studio that made *The Neighbour's Wife and Mine,* will record the brazen theme song "Age of Speed", and, upon seeing just how unexpectedly great her performance really is, Polydor Records have enthusiastically decided to release a run of the recordings' (*Yomiuri shimbun* 1931, 10). In contrast to her initially conventional appearance in *The Neighbour's Wife and Mine,* it appears that subsequent to the film's success this alignment of the female body (and its commodified appearance) with modern technologies also applied to Tanaka – a promotional postcard distributed by *Housewife's Friend* in 1932 features Tanaka as the face of Modern (Modan) brand shampoo: she wears full Western dress, including high-heeled shoes, and appears beside other technological symbols of modernity, a motorcar and a motorcycle. It is apparent that, regardless of characterisation, by merely appearing within the first Japanese talkie film itself, both of its principal actresses gained distinctly 'modern' public identities, reflected in their subsequent film roles. Similar to her characterisation in *The Neighbour's Wife and Mine*, Tanaka continued to perform a mixture of conventional and 'modern' roles – in the immediate years that followed the film's release she played a subversive Western-style gangster girl (*Dragnet Girl* [*Hijōsen no onna*], 1933) while also appearing in a number of *jidai-geki* period drama films. While Date already held a recognised *moga* allure in her roles with Shimizu for Shōchiku, as seen in *Undying Pearl* and *This Mother Is Sinful* (*Kono haha ni tsumi ariya*, 1931 – released only a few months before Gosho's film), *The Neighbour's Wife and Mine* solidified this image – Date continued to play similar roles following the film's release, including in Shimizu's two-part *Seven Seas* (*Nanatsu no umi* 1931–2), in which her costuming references Clara Bow's aesthetic to an even greater extent than in Gosho's film.

The contrast between the modern girl and housewife archetypes is most obviously executed via dialogue, exploiting the sound element further – when the protagonist returns home, he is confronted by Tanaka shouting, 'Did you just go around to play with that modern girl? That's the Madam next door!' Tanaka spits out the words *modan gāru* and *madamu* in disgust, the Western-derived terms providing emotion in a way impossible in the silent cinema. His reply confounds the importance of sartoriality in constructing identities onscreen – 'She's just wearing Western clothes.' She retorts, 'Madams these days are dangerous . . . I would say that it was definitely something erotic [*ero*]!' The reversal of the 'modern' versus 'traditional' roles of the two women is made complete when Tanaka then stabs the protagonist with her long Japanese hairpin – despite her branding the Madam as 'dangerous', it is she who causes him harm using a Japanese fashion accessory. The choice of the title *Madamu* to describe Date's character imbues her with simultaneously alluring, Western, expressive and subversive connotations. Articles from the *Yomiuri shimbun* and *Asahi shimbun* illustrate that in the 1880s and 1890s, '*madamu*' was used purely as a salutation for a French woman, but by 1907 the term had already gained pace as one of aesthetic hybridity as a brand name for cosmetics and hair products purported to be used by the actress Sadayakko, who had herself worked in France; since this time, '*madamu*' already held connotations of a Western-derived consumer image. At this early stage, Madamu cosmetics were being marketed as 'Western disguise cosmetics', ostensibly promoting their use as a means of pursuing a cosmetically Caucasian appearance onstage; however, the advertisement's publication within a mainstream national newspaper aims it at a general consumer audience rather than the theatrical sphere (*Asahi shimbun* 1907, 5). By 1911, the association between the brand-name Madamu and a Western cosmetic appearance now overtly targeted the everyday consumer, yet their relationship with the theatre remains – a 1911 advertisement for the brand advertises it as 'a gift from the actress Kawakami Sadayakko' (*Asahi shimbun* 1911, 7). The term gains greater prominence and more scandalous undertones following the release of Frank Lloyd's *Madame X* (1920) in Japan in 1922, the plot of which revolves around a woman who is thrown out of her home when she is accused of adultery, shoots a blackmailer dead and is convicted of his murder. Posters for the film appear on the walls of the jazz singer's home as she dances in *The Neighbour's Wife and Mine*, aligning this filmic archetype with the movements of her Westernised body. Japanese advertising for *Madame X* emphasises the immorality featured in the plot (it is subtitled *Whispers of Darkness*) and also hints at the same voyeurism created by *The Neighbour's Wife and Mine*'s usage of sound: another subtitle reads, 'Nothing left unnoticed!!!' (*Asahi shimbun* 1922, 2). The word '*madamu*', by the time that *The Neighbour's Wife and Mine* is released, appears to have become synonymous with not only a Westernised appearance, but also a modern, illicitly attractive appearance: in *Kinema junpō*'s synopsis of the film, designed to entice readers to view the film at the cinema, '*madamu*' is repeated several times, and her alluring character is placed at the centre of its narrative:

> From next door, loud jazz can be heard. Filled with rage, Shinsaku (the playwright, a play on 'New Work') goes around to talk to next door, but when he least expects it, he is lost for words when he is seduced by the beautiful 'modern madam' [*modan madamu*] of the title. While she does so, she sings the song 'Speed Up!', making Shinsaku do his work ... his script is a success – his wife now has a smile on her face and there is not a cloud in the sky. And so, the Madam next door sings 'My Blue Sky'. (*Kinema junpō* 1931, 79)

That the argumentative dialogue sequence between Tanaka and the male protagonist utilises multiple 'buzzwords' of the time as seen in print media, and would have been the first time Japanese audiences would have physically heard this vocabulary onscreen, instantly makes the 'talkie' film both a current and fashionable product of its time and relatable to real-life Japanese audiences who would use these words themselves in conversation, further enhancing the effect of the 'sensory-reflexive horizon' described by Miriam Hansen. This makes an initially Western format (the talkie) into a localised format, albeit with hybridised language loanwords such as *modan gāru*, *ero* and *madamu* – this hybridity is reflected in the outfits seen onscreen; the entire film is hybridised in its aesthetics and even plot. The relationship between the film, the use of Western-style loanwords and the purchasable Modern Girl consumer image is symbiotic; in the same way that the film utilised print-media derived 'buzzwords' in order to localise the immersive talkie format and realistically depict the moral panic surrounding the Modern Girl onscreen, Club cosmetics appropriated the specific modern-style vocabulary of the film – namely the title of the film's theme song 'Age of Speed' – in order to market its cosmetics products. Just as Club utilised Tanizaki's *Naomi* in order to promote its products in 1925, in August 1931, a month after *The Neighbour's Wife and Mine* was released in cinemas, it commissioned a half-page informative cosmetics article in the *Yomiuri shimbun* entitled 'Cosmetics *A La Mode* for 1931'. Ostensibly a general article on the latest cosmetics, the fact that the article mentions only Club products and a large pictorial advertisement for the company makes its financial agenda clear; a large section of the article is entitled 'You Can Do It in Just One or Two Minutes: Fresh Elegance With Speed Make-up', and the products advertised are introduced with the following words: 'If you're in a hurry to go out, but you still want that "Female Student Look", here are four kinds of quick cosmetic products, filled with the spirit of the "Age of Speed"' (*Yomiuri shimbun* 1931, 3). Yet again we see cosmetics aligned with the image of the 'fresh' female student seen in the promotion of the flapper consumer image propagated worldwide. The film did not merely appropriate Western-derived language in order to describe connotations applied to Western-attired women; it shaped and encouraged its use in a commercial context.

Another issue raised by the argument between the protagonist and his wife is female-focused jealousy, centred around Date's Western-style clothing. Tanaka sits at her sewing machine noisily pedalling, then asks the protagonist to buy her some Western clothing, which he refuses to do until he has completed his assignment. At the onset of the film, Tanaka makes her feelings towards adult Western clothing clear, regarding it as an unnecessary expense and the preserve of her husband – it is apparent that she does not sew Western clothing for him herself, as she states that 'a tailor came today, and we owe him two a month'. While her children wear solely Western attire, this would have been neither unusual nor expensive, with women's magazines such as *Shufu no tomo* providing easy-to-follow patterns for housewives to make their own practical children's clothing at home. A supplement supplied with copies of the magazine in June 1932, entitled 'The Complete Guide to Making Children's Summer Clothing' presents a multitude of styles for both girls and boys and features exclusively Western garments; while the booklet is ostensibly promoting only the creation of Western clothing for children, with the accompanying instructive illustrations featuring a woman wearing similar Japanese housewives' attire to Tanaka, the booklet also features a small selection of adult designs described as 'fashionable Western clothes for female students' – the designs are superficially not aimed at the publication's target market (*Shufu no tomo* 1932, 158). While the other outfits in the booklet state the ages which they are aimed at, from the infant to the adolescent, these are the only outfits which do not specify the age for which they are designed, and rather than simple patterned cotton poplin as suggested for other garments, the annotated illustrations suggest the usage of luxurious (and expensive) fabrics such as spun crepe, spun silk and lace. A skirt and shawl set within this category is supplied with recommendations on which hats would best accompany it, directly referencing Tokyo department stores by name: 'Any of this summer's latest styles will do, but we recommend one from Ginza's Matsuya or Matsuzakaya department stores, or products made by the Chiyoda Hat Making Company Ltd' (*Shufu no tomo* 1932, 46). The booklet provides examples with a variety of difficulty levels, and a basic guide to the equipment recommended for home Western tailoring, with particular emphasis on the modern electric iron and sewing machine (although the author insists that these are not necessary, but 'will make sewing Western clothing at home more convenient'; furthermore they add that the sewing machine can 'also be utilised to achieve a fine finish when tailoring Japanese clothing' (*Shufu no tomo* 1932, 51, 157). The booklet at first glance presents home tailoring as foremost a practice conducted in service of the family in compliance with existing housewife norms, including the production of Japanese-style garments; however, the booklet also provides the reader with the same basic skills required to tailor fashionable clothing for herself, albeit concealed amongst more conventional, 'selfless' images and rhetoric. While women had been exposed to Western-style home sewing en masse following the foundation of several high-profile sewing schools (notably the Women's Academy for Cultural Sewing [Bunka Saihō Jogakuin] in 1923) and radio sewing lessons broadcast by NHK in 1926, the emphasis of these classes (unless aimed at women seeking vocational skills in the textiles industry) was clearly on the household, rather than the sartorial desires of the woman herself (Gordon 2012, 121–4). While articles produced by women's magazines during the 1920s do provide allusions to self-made Western clothing and accessories, these predominantly involve some form of frugality in service of the home space – a 1924 *Fujin kurabu* (*Women's Club*) article by Okumura Hanako of the Okumura Sewing School describes how 'a beautiful springtime handbag' can be easily fashioned from leftover fabric scraps (Okumura 1924, 7), and *Shufu no tomo* carried an article entitled, 'How to Convert Disused Kimono into Western Style Clothing for Women' in 1925 (Sato 2003, 147). Considering the appeal of the female student as a component of the *moga* consumer image – and the conflicted connotations of this image itself – the insertion of these fashionable outfits for adult women within a guide for making children's clothing provides a subtle reference to the desire to market these garments (and their related consumer fantasies, embodied by the cinema and the department store, which according to this guide could purportedly be recreated at home utilising the same basic skills involved in fashioning a child's simple smock) even to relatively conservative feminine archetypes such as the Japanese housewife. The ensembles appear as an almost guilty pleasure, a distraction from the housewife's homely duties (hence their concealment amongst more 'selfless' designs), and it is this factor which is referenced as Tanaka sits at her sewing machine. She appears to be frustrated as she cannot make her own Western clothing herself as she would with kimono – she throws a piece of kimono fabric aside in anger, another bodily expressive act. While Date's Western-clothed appearance initially appears to threaten the home space – only to indirectly benefit it – it is in fact Tanaka's desire to appropriate it which causes domestic disharmony by not only generating a sense of inadequacy concerning her performance in her marital role, but also introducing the prospect of additional expenses. Like Toshie in *Undying Pearl,* Tanaka wishes to wear Western clothing in order to assume the attractive power of the jazz singer's body in a process akin to the female spectator's desire to assume the star's bodily power by purchasing an emulation of her sartorial appearance. However, a key difference between Toshie and Tanaka's character is that Tanaka openly, vocally, expresses her desire to do so – and she is rewarded, rather than punished for this. However, her sartorial Westernisation is not without compromise: at the end of the film, she finally appears wearing a hybridised style – a vibrantly striped kimono, permed hair, earrings and a scarf worn as a shawl; her hair is up, but not cut, and she carries an elaborate handbag. The hybrid style is presented as a compromise for women who are either economically unable to fully Westernise, or hesitant to adopt its aesthetics on moral grounds. Tanaka's character is now open to modern ideas and is more affectionate – she wants to fly in an aeroplane to Osaka (another alignment of the feminine with technology as described by Nicholas) and says that they will die together. Now wearing Western clothing once more, her temperament has reverted to that of when she was younger and wearing berets. Rather than holding a conflicted female persona as embodied by Toshie in *Undying Pearl,* her hybrid attire represents the completion of a process which harmonises 'desirable' expressivity (i.e. one which is inoffensive to men) with a partially Western-derived fashionable appearance. These two films both portray female characters who do not necessarily embody a polarised dichotomy, but instead the space in-between its two polarities. Via the different uses of form and style innate to either sound or silent film respectively, these films provide examples of how women can be simultaneously 'modern' and 'expressive' via their sartorial consumer choices, a quality which is scarce within polarising and confusing print media.

The novelty of the 'all-talkie' film, and the use of accent in order to generate the heightened sense of immersion, which was praised by Gosho's critics, experiences significant longevity, despite the simultaneous ongoing production of *benshi*-supported Japanese silents enduring until the mid-1930s. Five years after the release of *The Neighbour's Wife and Mine,* Tanaka Kinuyo recounts her experiences of appearing in the first all-talkie production:

> The acting methods of the silent era now had to completely change – I was worried about how strange my accent would seem onscreen, and even though I remembered my lines I would bungle them; the job became more difficult for more and more film actors. And so, in this era, the likes of Suzuki Denmei, Takada Minoru and Okada Tokihiko had to leave, and new stars marched in one after the other. (Tanaka 1936, 20–1)

Tanaka's account describes the effect of changing technology on the Japanese star and narrative conventions, as well as her own fears concerning her native Kansai accent, which were proved to be unfounded, as noted above. Tanaka's observations denote a correlation between the talkie cinema's new immersive synchronised environment, which generated an arguably more 'realistic' sensory-immersive experience facilitated through factors such as Tanaka's Kansai accent, and new, less polarised, depictions of women. Rather than purely embodying 'moral' characteristics (such as the *giri*, 'obligation', exhibited by the 'self-sacrificing young maidens' described by Tanaka) or a one-dimensional innocuous 'cheerful' expressivity, Tanaka's experiences denote a new, more emotionally complex expressive characterisation arising as a result of the new realism encouraged and enabled by the synchronised sound cinema.

Critic Hatoyama Suruga concurs with Tanaka's perspective that the onset of sound heralded a new standard for recruiting acting talent but has a different take on its desirability and significance (Hatoyama 1936, 26–7). He suggested that it was possible to replicate 'reality' even without sound. In Japan, 'it is polite not to speak while eating', so it was accurate for actors 'not to speak while eating their meals onscreen'. It was therefore possible to understand the continuing success of some pre-talkie stars even in the sound era. On the other hand, while he acknowledged that on first hearing, an accent might be charming, 'by the second or third listen [its] heaviness becomes irritating'. While he recognises that 'audiences follow novelty', he suggests that the success of the talkie depends on its relationship with star persona rather than its replication of reality. Hatoyama makes this point with reference to a male star, Ōkōchi Denjirō, whose first words in *Tange Sazen: Part 1* (*Tange Sazen dai-ippen,* 1933), revealing his natural voice, provided a kind of voyeuristic insight: 'Isn't it ironic that it took the grand appearance of the talkie to expose the heavy accent of this star, who has been gaining resonance nationwide?' (Hatoyama 1936, 26). He notes that this also applies to actresses:

> Even if they have great faces, since the talkie, an actor's only requirement is a voice … And so, sometimes when they are recruiting actors, and a quite shamelessly cheeky girl is there, she will say something like, 'hey, I've got confidence!' in a regional dialect, embarrassing the judge; however, the Japanese public will adore her all the more for it. (Hatoyama 1936, 26)

Hatoyama suggests a new standard for actresses alongside the new, well-rounded archetypal roles described by Tanaka. The silent cinema had focused purely on aesthetic beauty and non-verbal expressivity, but the onset of sound provides a new ideal, making vocal expressivity equally important to an actress's aesthetics. Hatoyama also hints at a positive association between a regional dialect and a gently subversive 'pluckiness', which draws the expressive Japanese actress even more closely to the Hollywood-derived image of the flapper, particularly the heavily Bronx-accented Clara Bow. However, rather than the talkie allowing a Japanese actress to approximate the behaviour of the flapper, Hatoyama suggests that the success of regionally accented actresses with audiences was due specifically to their local appeal:

> From the onset of the talkie, we have enjoyed becoming able to hear the mispronunciations and strong accents of both the great swordplay stars and beautiful actresses. Through accent, an unexpected familiarity between the star and audiences from the same region grows. (Hatoyama 1936, 26)

In my discussion of the function of sound in *The Neighbour's Wife and Mine*, I demonstrated the role of using Japanese loanwords, common in contemporary print media, in order to localise the talkie film's overtly Hollywood-inspired sound technology, and how this related to the promotion of Western-style fashion goods as desirable objects to a Japanese consumer base. Hatoyama and Tanaka's observations denote that as the Japanese adoption of synchronised sound technology matured during the mid-1930s, not only did the criteria for successful actresses and varied female roles develop alongside it, but the medium experienced a shift towards representing specific, localised archetypes via accent. Hatoyama's observation that 'through accent, an unexpected familiarity between the star and audiences from the same region grows' adds new depth to my application of Doane's description of the consumer relationship between the female viewer/consumer and the onscreen star image as 'shop window/mirror' in the 1930s Japanese context; Hatoyama's observations describe how for localised audiences the star image was drawn ever closer to the viewer's own experiences, generating an even greater proximity between the quasi-attainable star image and the viewer's own identity. Yet Hatoyama's irritation at hearing the repetition of localised accents in talkie films elucidates the potential of the accented actress to cause the very opposite reaction in the viewer who does not share the geographical experience that she portrays – the accent serves to enact distance between the viewer, which can be exploited in order to depict stereotypes for comic or emotive effect. Mizoguchi's diptych *Osaka Elegy* (*Naniwa erejī*, 1936) and *Sisters of the Gion* (*Gion no Kyōdai*, 1936) – released in the same year that both Tanaka and Hatoyama's observations were published – combines the Kansai accent of its star Yamada Isuzu with a Western-style Modern Girl sartoriality, yet her manifestation (and personification of the city) is made specific to either Kyoto or Osaka respectively.

Aaron Gerow describes how following the cinematic reforms of the Pure Film movement of the 1910s, in which 'each and every shot must bear a meaning or intention founded in the choice and judgement of the filmmaker', that 'the word may have been divorced from the image, but the image was to be coded like the word . . . the image was to be freed of signs of speech and writing only at the price of the image internalising a code as "linguistic" as writing and speech' (Gerow 2010, 22). This suggests two separate forms of communication – the visual and the aural – holding specific but distinct meanings; however, despite this effort to separate the meanings of the audio and the visual, due to the simultaneous involvement of both inherent to the 'talkie' film's technology itself, these two semiotic systems are united in combining existing linguistic forms (including not only the meanings of words themselves, but also intonation and dialect, both of which it has been established are key to the reception of the 'talkie') with existing visual forms. It has been established that 'in all societies the body is 'dressed', and everywhere dress and adornment play symbolic, communicative and aesthetic roles' (Wilson 2011, 3) and that body adornment is a cultural universal as described by George Peter Murdock (Ferraro and Andreatta 2010, 40.) This presents audio-visual technology as not only putting an age-old semiotic system into visual motion within a mass-media context, acting as another means of articulating the immediacy of modernity, but also vocalising it, uniting the sounds and meaning of language with the coded nature of dress and fashion. This suggests that the enduring public interest in immersive audio-visual technology may be explored as a means of uniting two universal semiotic systems – fashion and the spoken word – in order to create a hybrid means of expressing meaning which is relevant to the modern, film-literate and sensory-immersed audience. This coincides with Judith Butler's interpretation of Foucault's statement that 'the soul . . . is produced permanently around, on, within the body' in terms of gender performativity, stating that 'the soul is a surface signification that contests the inner/outer distinction itself, a figure of interior psychic space inscribed *on* the body as a social signification that perpetually renounces itself as such' (Butler 1990, 184). To consider a philosophical interpretation of the purpose and origin of the voice from an Aristotelian-Thomistic perspective, which dictates that 'voice is a sound that is a striking of the air breathed in through the windpipe . . . which striking caused by the soul' (Crowley 1996, 108) – or, more simply, that the voice is an exterior expression of, and caused by, the interior self – then by this logic it may be established that gender construction may be facilitated by clothing as such a signification of interiority '*on* the body' and hence hold the ability to exert a direct influence upon the voice as an expression of such. Mizoguchi's diptych places a direct emphasis on this relationship between speaking and the speaker's wearing of Western, Japanese or hybrid dress, practically and humanly illustrating the relevance of technological development to the engagement of the modern spectator with existing social practices within the ever-changing city environment.

Osaka and Kyoto represent the dichotomy between 'modernising' Japan and 'traditional' Japan. The positioning of Western attire within each further complicates the relationship onscreen. In print media Osaka was synonymous with the *moga*, 'a locale which offers nearly as many possibilities as the *moga* does to examine the price of Japan's modernization' (Kirihara 1992, 36). *Osaka Elegy*'s focus on a young working woman (particularly one working in a technological capacity, as a telephone operator) who presents herself as a Westernised *moga* was not an unexpected means of exploring the issues of the ultra-modern Osaka onscreen, due to the prevalence of women like her featured throughout the popular image of the city itself. Osaka's relationship with the *moga* becomes part of what Mori Toshie describes as 'both the dark and light side of social change' inherent to modernisation (Mori 2007, 40); in the same way that the *moga* simultaneously embodied the alluring aspects of women's independence while being 'a particular icon of *modanizumu*[2] . . . mentioned derogatorily and perceived as being sexually and morally decadent', the city's architecture itself becomes a double-edged critique of modernity. Mori describes the film's closing sequence filmed on Ebisu Bridge, a 'symbol of urban modernisation' built in 1925, as hinting at 'the dark and light sides of the modernisation process of the previous decade, as if to suggest that the hope and expectations of modernity were only an illusion, just like the shimmering image on the river' (Mori 2007, 43–4). The rhetoric surrounding Osaka in contemporary print media reinforces this association between the city, the scandalous *moga* and daring Western-inspired body aesthetics with a zealous sensationalism that is not applied to other Japanese cities, with the trends sported by Osaka Modern Girls carrying particularly 'extreme' connotations. A 1928 *Asahi shimbun* article 'The Osaka-Made Modern Girl Look' describes 'the huge, shocking tattoo trend' sported by Osaka Modern Girls, particularly those working as waitresses in cafes (*Asahi shimbun* 1928, 7). While the article's content concentrates on the tattoos on the bodies of these independent working women who were already subject to a nationwide moral panic, describing their motivation to adopt the aesthetic as 'a new low in the whole-body Westernisation of appearance inspired by the smiling flapper' (again aligning a Westernised appearance with expressivity), the article's subtitle states that 'even university students are indulging in this disgraceful behaviour' (*Asahi shimbun* 1928, 7). The article takes the marketable and aspirational image of the female student – a positive proponent of commercial Westernisation – and frames Osaka itself, with its subversive Modern Girl adherents, as a polluting agent, permanently damaging the 'fresh' and youthful connotation of the female student's body by marring it with tattoos of Western-inspired motifs. The cinema is not exempt from these criticisms – the author particularly reviles tattoos which allude to the 'names and associations' of 'students' favourite actresses' (*Asahi shimbun* 1928, 7). This concept of Osaka as a corrupting city is coherent with Tomoda Jun'ichirō's review of *Osaka Elegy* published in *Kinema junpō*, describing Yamada's performance as follows:

> It takes a breadth of maturity and enthusiasm to perform this role: a young woman who, for three hundred yen, walks the path between the lifestyle of a telephone exchange worker and that of a concubine, leading to her downfall. She is the opposite of a hero, but we are moved to sympathise with her; women and women's circumstances are meticulously portrayed ... The woman is played by Yamada Isuzu, and the points in her acting which express the transformation of [the character's] lot in life are admirable. (Tomoda Jun'ichirō 1936, 106)

Rather than the condemnation of the tattooed *moga* appearing in the *Asahi shimbun*, Tomoda instead sympathises with Yamada's portrayal, as though she were a helpless victim of the city's ruthless culture of Westernisation. The print article read by Ayako at the onset of the film cements this association between commercialism, women and Osaka's position during the financial decline of the mid-1930s; reading 'Woman ruined, all for money,' the headline ensures that the audience is fully aware that women, money and commercialism entwine wholly negatively in the film.

Yamada Isuzu's character Ayako's pursuit of fashion is a factor innate to the film's portrayal of Osaka as a centre of commercialisation and individualistic consumption; while it is impossible to truly ascertain contemporary audience attitudes to Osaka residents, Mizoguchi made his own observations clear in *Kinema junpō*:

> People from Osaka do not care what others think. They are too busy pursuing self-interest, too shameless to value self-restraint... *Ninjō* ['humane feelings'] to them means little or nothing – nothing when weighed in the balance against business interests. (Quoted in McDonald 1984, 40)

Tomoda's assessment of the Osaka depicted onscreen concurs with this:

> Mizoguchi depicts the varied humanity which dwells in this city – the rich who seek to satisfy their lust, those who have become mean in their old age, the doctors who act as though they are judges, families which behave like parasitic insects, the young man who cannot even be passionate in love and all who are burdened with lives of selfishness – he openly admits this poisonous outlook, and portrays a process of poisoning of human life. He transmits the harshness of the city and its everyday texture of fearfulness with no regrets. (Tomoda Jun'ichirō 1936, 106)

Considering this connotation of the city of Osaka as a centre of consumption, commercialism and 'self-interest', it is apt that these factors are expressed via the clothing featured in *Osaka Elegy*. The association between Osaka and subversive dress has existed since the Edo period, when its wealthy merchant class employed extravagant dress as a means of crossing class boundaries, ultimately resulting in the Shogunate imposing restrictions upon the clothing permitted to be worn by merchants (Slade 2009, 36–7). Even excluding the negatively received relationship between Osaka and the Western-attired *moga*, Osaka holds an innate association with the purchase of Western clothing; a 1936 *Yomiuri shimbun* article promotes Osaka over Tokyo as the best city to purchase both tailored and off-the-peg Japanese-made Western-style garments, generating a more neutral relationship between the Kansai dialect and Western attire (*Yomiuri shimbun* 1936, 9). Mizoguchi's own words however relate the sound of the dialect back to the same themes of Osaka as a corruptive city noted by Tomoda; he imbues it with bodily connotations, stating that the *Kansai* dialect used in *Osaka Elegy* played a vital role in aurally 'describ[ing] the stink of the human body ... paint[ing] human beings who are implacable, selfish, stingy, sensual [and] cruel' (quoted in Le Fanu 2005,74). Osaka appears to be almost the 'natural habitat' of the *moga*, and the combination of the Kansai accent and Western attire is wholly expected. When we are introduced to Ayako in her brightly patterned kimono and with shingled Western-style hair, particularly following her perusal of the aforementioned print article, we expect her to be a subversive character personifying the commercialist city from the onset; despite her sartorial appearance being initially 'hybrid' in construction, we immediately identify her with the *moga* subculture, and we are not surprised by her appearance in the city of Osaka. Her dress format becoming fully Western in style at the film's ambiguous climax, including a cloche hat pulled down over her eyes, signifies the completion of the city's corruptive process of Westernisation as described by Tomoda.

Sisters of the Gion's construction of Kyoto as a location is more conflicted in nature; however this concept of the personification of the popular image of the city is also present. Kyoto is presented as embodying the duality of Japan's modernisation; rather than the single figure seen in *Osaka Elegy*, the two sisters each embody 'modernity' and 'traditionalism' respectively. Considering the depressed economic climate of the mid-1930s, which is discussed in the narratives of both films, it is important to note that specifically in Kyoto, the two industries which continued to flourish despite these difficulties were the city's historic textile and kimono-making industries and the emergent film industry, which made Kyoto its new centre for creating the hugely popular *jidai-geki* (period drama) films, while *gendai-geki* set in contemporary settings continued to be produced in Tokyo (Brumann 2012, 48). Considering the film's focus specifically upon Kyoto and a narrative which revolves around the sisters' relationship with a kimono merchant, the film itself actively engages with both of these industries. From the moment they appear onscreen, the two sisters embody not only the city's position between the 'traditional' and the 'modern' from a cultural perspective, but also one which is economic, echoing the conflicted identity of the Modern Girl commercial image itself.[3] At the onset of the film, the younger sister, Omocha (Yamada Isuzu), is introduced in a Western silk negligée with a cropped hairstyle, in contrast to her sister Umekichi's kimono and elaborate wig – despite both being involved in the same 'traditional' occupation as geishas, Omocha's attire immediately relays new attitudes to the body as an economic resource in a changing, modern society. This illustrates an association between Western clothing and a new relationship with the physical body which had been present within Japanese society since the Meiji era (Downer 2003, 52), with the tubular, uniform shape of the kimono being contrasted with the structured shape of Western attire highlighting the bodily form itself. Omocha's negligée reveals her bare arms and décolletage and clings to her form, demonstrating this contrast when viewed in-frame alongside her more conventional sister. The expensive appearance of the silk negligée, a specialised item available only from expensive department stores, imbues this newly physical sexuality with an aggressively consumerist tone, posing a threat to her sister's modest traditionalism. This image of a physical sexuality particularly pertaining to the Western-clothed star onscreen appears in a Kawaishi cartoon published in *Nihon eiga* depicting a woman in a low-cut Western dress with defined cleavage, a hat, permed hair and stiletto heels. Behind her is a Greek goddess statue – their bodily forms are directly compared. A man with a Chaplin moustache is measuring her hips with a tape; another man photographs her from behind. The cartoon is accompanied by the following caption: 'The salesclerk's honour: taking the measurements of a big star at a Western clothes store. "I better photograph this moment inch by inch!"' (*Nihon eiga* 1936, 34). The sartorial juxtaposition of the sisters presents a friction between the modern and conventional pervading even the most ingrained of Kyoto's cultural industries – its geisha houses – imposing the position of film and technology itself alongside Kyoto's textile industry onto the bodies of women themselves. As in *Osaka Elegy*, Yamada's Kansai accent plays a role in the construction of a more well-rounded female character as described by Tanaka Kinuyo, aurally enacting an even greater expressive contrast with her Tokyo-born standard-accented opposite, Yoko Umemura. Dialect is crucial to representing this duality of the city, an observation noted by *Kinema junpō* critic Mizumachi Seiji:

> In Mizoguchi's previous work 'Osaka Elegy' he used Osaka vocabulary, and this time we have Kyoto vocabulary. Of course, it must be remembered that this is a unique phenomenon in Japanese film throughout this year, but, in the case of Mizoguchi, it is easy to observe how he is indebted to provincialism . . . Through the use of dialect, he becomes able to represent the present character of the region. (Mizumachi 1936, 128)

Mizumachi combines a number of responses to the talkie format; he acknowledges Hatoyama's assertion that the talkie's usage of regional accent exists as a popular gimmick for audiences, yet he also acknowledges its role in reconstructing reality. He also approves of the multi-faceted portrayal facilitated by the use of accent, as noted by Tanaka in her description of new female talkie roles. However, the most striking element of his review is his personal identification with the portrayal of the city onscreen, facilitated by dialect, in the familiar manner described by Hatoyama:

> But I can gladly say that, having lived in Kyoto, I know more about the daily lives of women of [Omocha's] ilk than the typical audience member, and it takes just one of these unscrupulous women, when seen through the eyes of the typical audience member, to evoke empathy with the old-fashioned manners of the older sister – therefore, the appearance of the younger sister's realism is bound to be thought of as repulsive. (Mizumachi 1936, 128)

Mizumachi's comments depict him relating the 'realism' of Yamada's portrayal, facilitated by her accent, to his own life experiences, and he uses this 'interior knowledge' of who he perceives as the real-life women of Kyoto in order to elevate his own position above that of the everyday viewer and to enact empathy with Umemura's conventional geisha figure. This is a practical example of how a geographically specific archetype, enabled by localised dialect and dress, allows the local audience member to generate a personalised identification (or distance) with the star image onscreen, adding a further dimension to Hansen's assessment of the classical silent cinema's immersive ability to provide a 'fantasmatic' audience experience 'as a privileged and invisible guest' (Hansen 2000, 11).

The same fashionable connotations applied to Osaka also relate to Yamada Isuzu's own star image and public persona. In related publicity materials, Yamada adopts a hybridised sartorial image similar to her characters in Mizoguchi's films; while she is not as overtly 'Western' in appearance as her Modern Girl star contemporaries such as Okada Yoshiko, she appears more subtly and stylishly 'modern' when she is contrasted with more conventionally 'Japanese' stars. A feature in the August 1936 edition of *Nihon eiga* – published after the release of *Osaka Elegy* in May and prior to *Sisters of the Gion* in October – showcases her alongside another Nikkatsu actress, Hanai Ranko, a *jidai-geki* actress known for *Kageboshi: The Noble Thief of Edo* (*Edo kaizoku-den: Kagebōshi*, 1925) and later *The Stylish Retainer* (*Oshare hatamoto*, 1935). Both actresses wear kimono but are accessorised and presented wholly differently. Hanai sits modestly on the side of a bridge in a Japanese walled garden, her hair is in a conventional Japanese up-do, and she wears minimal makeup. Her kimono is as conventional as her hairstyling – it is decorated with a simple pattern of chrysanthemum flowers. Yamada is presented standing before a clean modernist brick wall topped by a globular streetlamp, smiling directly to camera with her hair in a simple bun lying on the nape of her neck, only slightly visible from the camera's angle – the same style worn in *Osaka Elegy*. Her makeup is also worthy of attention, particularly her brows, which are drawn in an elongated arch reminiscent of images of Clara Bow and other Hollywood stars, particularly those from the silent era. Subtle comparisons are drawn between Yamada and Bow during *Osaka Elegy* at the onset of the film – the newspaper article consulted by Ayako mirrors scenes from Bow's appearance in *It* (1927), in which print media is used as a narrative device intersected with close-up shots of Bow's face – and the headline on the opposite page refers to 'Western Fashions for Springtime', clearly aligning the protagonist with the Modern Girl's thirst for fashion, as also portrayed by Bow's role. Using the look of Joan Crawford as an example, David M. Lugowski discusses the role of cosmetics as a means of conveying emotion within silent film, and its evolution within the 1930s: 'Crawford calibrates slight muscle movements around her mouth and eyes . . . to convey a succession of emotions . . . her makeup was designed to highlight her larger-than-life features . . . she literally embodies the 'we had faces' philosophy that was such a part of Gloria Swanson's own silent-era fame . . . and that was part of Swanson's influence upon Crawford' (Lugowski 2011, 136). Yamada's use of cosmetics therefore not only visually aligns her with Bow and her Hollywood contemporaries, but also with their ability to convey their emotional expressivity onscreen. Yamada's hybridised appearance is not criticised by *Nihon eiga* magazine, which specialised in popular commentary specifically on Japanese films – 'she has become someone who we can call a great actress within the Japanese film world' (*Nihon eiga* 1936, 9). Yamada and

Hanai are presented as equally attractive and talented actresses, each fulfilling wholly different roles in regard to their sartoriality. Yamada's subtle hybridity is presented as a fashionable asset, making her star persona an incentive for casting her in subversive Modern Girl roles. While Yamada's Kansai accent allows the female consumer with a direct connection to the Kansai area to experience a personal process of self-identification with (or distancing from) her star image, alongside relating her to Osaka's established *moga* imagery (proffering her as a localised version of stars such as Bow, as alluded to in *Osaka Elegy*) her hybrid appearance ensures that her image 'type' remains adaptable to a number of contexts and audiences rather than purely representing the Osaka *moga* aesthetic.

It is easy to define the relationship between speech, sartoriality and the modern city space in Mizoguchi's diptych in purely dichotomous terms, as a means of exploring both modernising cities' amalgamation of the past with the present as a combative process. However, my analysis reveals a complex semiotic system combining both speech and sartoriality which utilises two specific locations in order to explore nationwide and global issues. The film's manipulation of audio-visual technology via accent facilitates a sensory-immersive cinematic experience which allows this uniquely modern semiotic system to examine the modernising Japanese city and film industry itself, acting as an intermediary between the audience and both national and international media and consumerist trends. The film's concentration on both sartorially and internally Westernised female characters transcends mere gimmick; while it is clear that their involvement was at least partially an economically motivated reaction to increased interest in Hollywood star personae and new female 'talkie' archetypes as professed in related print media, the interaction between the Kansai accent and a sartorially Westernised appearance is also indicative of the emergence of dress as an indicator not only of filmic character 'types' in terms of age, class and socio-economic standing, but of identifiable and specifically Japanese geographical archetypes.

Notes

1. A *yukata* is a casual, unlined cotton kimono, worn in informal settings such as festivals and to local bathhouses.
2. The Japanese interpretation of Western 'modernism', which entailed 'the lightness and frivolity of the new' accompanying sweeping social change (Iwamoto 1991, 6–7).
3. The use of the term 'sister' here does not necessarily denote a biological relationship: it is never made explicit in the film that the two women are biological siblings; instead it is possible that they are deemed 'sisters' via the geisha house seniority system.

Chapter 3

Fashion commodities onscreen: The modern housewife in Naruse Mikio's *No Blood Relation* (*Nasanu Naka*, 1932) and masculine female attire in Ozu Yasujirō's *Dragnet Girl* (*Hijōsen no onna*, 1933)

The relationship between Western-inspired fashion commodities onscreen and purchasable character 'types' was recognised and propagated by related industries. The idea of characterising oneself through one's media consumption and fashion item purchases transcended the cinematic space into the spectator's everyday life, with the cinematic connotations sometimes diluted by the advertising company in order to normalise the delights of the screen for everyday consumption by ordinary folk rather than being purely the domain of the stars of the screen. I have already outlined the concept of character 'type' expressed via fashion imagery and identified some examples of more subtle collaborations between the film and fashion industries in Chapters 1 and 2. One such subtle example is the Osaka Mitsukoshi department store's employment of the Nikkatsu actresses Irie Takako and Natsukawa Shizue as models in their fashion catalogue – there is no reference made to their position as film stars by name or to the studio that employed them. This allowed for a versatility in the reception of the advertising imagery – while cinema fans could experience a greater attraction to the commodities displayed via their connection with the stars they recognised, the fashion items displayed could also function as desirable items in their own right, devoid of cinematic connotations. Considering the criticisms levelled at the cinema, particularly concerning its consumerist elements, this illustrates the inescapably pervasive nature of cinematic iconography throughout popular culture – particularly fashion. This aspect was noted by Marxist literary critic Hirabayashi Hatsunosuke: 'from the outfit of the cafe waitress to the uniform of the boy scout, there is nothing that has not been influenced by film' (Harootunian 2011, 22). However, overt advertising for fashion commodities was also featured onscreen across the studio system. This included the usage of locations within the narrative related to the corporate sponsor – in Fushimizu Osamu's *Tokyo Rhapsody* (*Tokyo rapusodei*, 1936) produced for Tōhō, the male and female leads meet in the Shiseidō Parlour, an elaborate Ginza-based Western-style restaurant owned by the cosmetics firm. Advertisements could also appear narratively within the cinematic frame. In Gosho Heinosuke's *Izu Dancer* (*Izu no odorikko*, 1933), produced for Shōchiku, Tanaka Kinuyo's character is told she must become a geisha in order to settle her family's debts to a backdrop of Club cold cream advertisements. Shōchiku and Club had a well-established advertising relationship, as noted by Daisuke Miyao in *The Oxford Handbook of Japanese Cinema*: 'the Club cosmetics company was the most prolific advertiser, both in cinema pamphlets and through the ubiquitous 'Club toothpaste' illuminated sign in Shōchiku films of the period' (Miyao 2013, 119). The neon sign described by Miyao is a piece of stock footage, often inserted into the film's narrative with little attention paid to their role within the film's diegesis: in Ozu Yasujirō's *Dragnet Girl* (*Hijōsen no Onna*, 1933) the film's gangster protagonists attempt to escape the police while enrobed in its flashing light, while in Ozu's *An Inn in Tokyo* (*Tokyo no Yado*, 1936) the protagonist merely takes a cursory glance up at it while making his way around the city. In comparison to Club's minimal advertising in its companion magazine *Josei*, these segments are hardly subtle. The inserted advertising certainly did not go unnoticed by critics: in his review of *The Neighbour's Wife and Mine*, Tamura had only one substantial criticism:

> The single unpleasant thing is Club toothpaste advertising blatantly displayed throughout; I don't know how much advertising revenue this makes, but I really wish they would stop such things from now on. (Tamura 1931, 77)

Club's products ranged from cold creams to soaps and face powders – it is of interest that the commodity chosen to feature in these films (which were predominantly aimed at female audiences – Wada-Marciano describes them as 'Shōchiku woman's films' [Wada-Marciano 2008, 88]) was toothpaste, rather than any other cosmetic item. Writing from a global perspective, Thomas Schatz notes that 'cosmetics [became] synonymous with Hollywood . . . no more potent endorsements were possible than those of the women who manifestly possessed the most "radiant" and "scintillant" eyes, teeth, complexions and hair' (Schatz 2004, 184). This observation is also concurrent with Japanese print media, written even from overtly male perspectives – an article by critic Hosokawa Haruhiko published in *The Play and Movie* in November 1928 entitled 'The Goodness of Clara Bow' relates her appeal specifically to how 'she completely shows us her white teeth when she smiles' (Hosokawa 1928, 10). Idealised white teeth were linked to Hollywood archetypes and their innate expressivity, while bolder cosmetics such as lipstick were still the preserve of the subversive Modern Girl, and even the sex worker in some films. The camera lingers on Okada Yoshiko's character, who works illicitly in nightclubs in order to support her brother, as she applies her lipstick in Ozu's *Woman of Tokyo* (*Tokyo no onna*, 1933). Cosmetic products such as shampoos and toothpastes, which subtly improved on 'natural' physical features, were an accessible means of gaining an expressive Hollywood appearance. This makes multi-purpose personalities such as Tanaka Kinuyo, who could deftly switch between both 'traditional', 'pure' roles as seen in *Woman of Tokyo* (in which she wears kimono throughout) and subversive gangster girl roles as in *Dragnet Girl* (in which she wears only Western attire), so useful; while she could market neutral household items, such as the match cases sold by Shōchiku, she could also market 'socially acceptable' cosmetic products, appearing 'modern' without *moga* connotations. The 1932 Modern Shampoo postcard distributed by *Shufu no tomo* states that Tanaka herself uses the shampoo despite her hair being concealed beneath a beret: 'A famous user of *Modern* shampoo is Shōchiku's Tanaka Kinuyo' (*Shufu no tomo* 1932). It is implied that the films themselves in which Tanaka appears will advertise the effectiveness of the shampoo, rather than the simple postcard image alone. While the overt usage of cosmetics appears to be frowned upon in onscreen narratives, it is quite apparent that their advertisement onscreen – at least for more accessible goods – was not. However, it must also be recognised that such blatant advertising techniques were not necessarily appealing to all audiences.

A film which utilises overt fashion advertising within its form and narrative is Naruse Mikio's *No Blood Relation* (*Nasanu Naka*, 1932), produced for Shōchiku. The film's opening titles contain a Mitsukoshi *mon* crest, an instantly recognisable brand image – the film itself is essentially presented as another Mitsukoshi 'product' alongside its fashion and lifestyle items. This was not the first time that Mitsukoshi had worked in conjunction with Shōchiku, particularly within a fashion context: in 1927, it held what it described as 'Japan's first fashion show', rendering it using the *katakana*[1] *fasshon shō* in the company's magazine and directly referencing the Western spectacle (Mitsukoshi 2015). The show itself, while featuring kimono as its focus, was displayed in both a new Western-style space (the Mitsukoshi Hall, an exhibition and performance space newly built that year on the sixth floor of the Tokyo Nihonbashi store) and exhibited the styles upon the bodies of Shōchiku film actresses, who embodied the cinematic – Mizutani Yaeko, Azuma Hideko and Kobayashi Nobuko (Okada 2011, 8). Naruse's 1932 film was not Mitsukoshi's first foray into featuring its premises on film – Mitsukoshi's Ginza store was featured as a filming location in Kaeriyama Norimasa's independently produced film *The Glory of Life* (*Sei no kagayaki*) in 1919 (Bernardi 1997, 373).

While the 1927 fashion show fused star bodies to new Westernised Japanese spaces, and this was promoted and commented upon by related print media, it lacked the immersive cinematic experience which drives the consumer to attempt to fulfil their desire to obtain the star's appearance via their attire; this is a factor inhibited by the show's lack of Western-inspired goods, removing any relationship to a fashionably expressive Hollywood-inspired aesthetic. Mitsukoshi's earlier appearance in Kaeriyama's film similarly exploits only one aspect of the audience/consumer dynamic – while audiences were exposed to the brand within the cinematic space, unlike the 1927 fashion show its featuring was a subliminal nod to the brand, rather than an event publicised by print media. Naruse's film, in its acknowledgement of Mitsukoshi's involvement, becomes a site in which the commercially focused spatial relationships between the cinema and the department store – both public spaces – and the private but transferrable sphere of print media collide, with both the star's body and the commodities she uses acting as interchangeable agents seamlessly transitioning between media types and spatial spheres. The film's existence allows its fashion images to circulate freely, with Mitsukoshi and Shōchiku acting as productive origins, with new meanings independently radiating from them as they progress from the screen into external spaces; by visiting Mitsukoshi's stores or perusing their catalogues, or by consuming the stars' images in related print media, the connections between the fashion items and these various spheres strengthen and allow for the construction of new consumer meanings and desires. Lash and Urry describe how 'If production happens at one time and at one place, circulation allows that production to vary as commodities are cast adrift and acquire mobility to flow through changing spaces at shifting times' (Lash and Urry 1994, 1). Mitsukoshi's multimedia relationship with Shōchiku, which reaches its peak in the creation of *No Blood Relation*, allows these commodities to be 'cast adrift' across the widest selection of media possible at that time, while at the same time ensuring that they remain anchored to the brands as named producers. This enacts a cycle which mirrors that of the satisfaction-seeking consumer/spectator described by Doane; the spectator views a brand-oriented film in the cinema, then purchases a featured fashion commodity in the brand's department store, then views the same stars in a magazine stocked there, perhaps for a different film or wearing a different outfit. The spectator is then simultaneously inspired to both return to the cinema and to the dress rack; the providers of these spaces aim to satisfy this desire by producing more film and fashion objects, buoyed by print media and its relationship to their respective spaces. The overt branding which features in *No Blood Relation* ensures that the cycle repeats within Shōchiku and Mitsukoshi rather than their competitors. Whereas *Naomi* allowed its readers the opportunity to reminisce about the immersive cinematic experience and to fantasise about appropriating the star's image themselves within their own homes via its content and the book's physical tangibility, *No Blood Relation* offered a complete immersive experience, which via the purchasing of actual fashion items from the film extended the screen to the multimedia, everyday world around the spectator. The spectator/consumer could move and live within a world which directly replicated that which they saw onscreen via their consumption choices.

As with store catalogues, the film features images of various fashion items in close-up, which function both as solitary fashion objects and within the film's narrative. The items are even referred to frequently in the film's script, and these references provide the items onscreen with further connotations: when a woman's clutch handbag is stolen by thieves at the film's onset not only is the item concerned visually focused upon in one of these series of close-ups (the factor of its theft in itself implying the item's desirability and association with affluence, as something 'worth' stealing) but it is referred to by onlookers as a '*handobaggu*', the English word 'handbag' rendered in *katakana*. The repeated usage of this terminology marks the item as a Western accessory, made conveniently accessible to the Japanese consumer via the department store; rather than the accessories worn by Hollywood stars in imported films, which female spectators were inspired to consume by the screen but which were ultimately unobtainable due to their geographical and economical situations, exact copies of the items onscreen were available to consumers not only across Tokyo but in Osaka and Sapporo, where a store was opened shortly before the release of Naruse's film (Mitsukoshi 2015). In the same way that reading a copy of *Naomi* could allow the reader to reminisce about the cinematic experience within the private sphere through the text's portable nature, purchasing the exact items which appeared onscreen allowed the female spectator/consumer to authentically purchase the star's bodily image and in the case of accessories carry it with her, impressing the immersive cinematic image directly onto her own appearance. This linguistic marking of Western accessories is compliant with the goals of Mitsukoshi's first executive director, Hibi Ōsuke, who in the *Tokyo nichinichi shimbun* in December 1904 announced that the brand's predecessor, Mitsui Gofukuten, 'had changed its name to Mitsukoshi and that it would henceforth increase the variety of goods it stocked and sold, and become like an American department store . . . Mitsukoshi will deal with a variety of products just like the American department store' (Tamari 2006, 101). Hibi specifically uses the *katakana* term '*depātomento sutoa*', and the titling of the article these remarks appear in as 'The Department Store Declaration' designates the importance of this adapted term and others like it – language allowed the American concept of the department store to be transformed; the Mitsui Gofukuten, essentially a simple drapery, transitioned into a hybridised space, stocking Japanese-made Western-inspired items such as the '*handobaggu*' which appears in Naruse's film. This intention was made clear in the Declaration itself, which describes how internationally derived patterns would be presented to Japanese clientele via both print media (a monthly journal entitled *Jiko* [*Vogue*]) and didactic exhibitions, which appeared within the stores themselves (Tamari 2006, 101). Tamari Tomoko notes that these exhibitions 'aimed at introducing new lifestyles, which were based on a new aesthetic sensibility, [and] were further designed to educate Japanese people on how to be good citizens' (Tamari 2006, 101). Just as Tanaka Kinuyo presented an image which was both modern and respectable in order to market 'acceptable' Western-style commodities, Mitsukoshi's 'Japanisation' of conventionally Western goods and spaces allowed for new narratives to be constructed surrounding these items, drawing their appeal away from the niche *moga* market and towards the everyday consumer.

The focus on these fashion items onscreen entails an early form of product placement, whereby 'the good feelings associated with the scene are transferred to the brand' (McCarty and Lowrey 2012, 24). As in Mizoguchi's diptych, Naruse's film relies upon a dichotomy enacted by sartoriality. Okada Yoshiko portrays Tamae, a Japanese actress who has achieved success in Hollywood and has returned to reclaim her daughter from her estranged husband; she wears an exaggerated Western style – her hair is always permed, her dresses always fitted and her calves always on display. The only exception to this is when she dons kimono to meet with her former mother-in-law; however, the example she wears is brightly patterned in accordance with *moga* convention. Her opposite is her ex-husband's new wife Masako (Tsukuba Yukiko), who wears only kimono and is portrayed as an ideal mother, beloved by her stepdaughter, who rejects her birth mother despite her worldly wealth. Masako takes a job as a shop girl at Mitsukoshi in order to support her husband's debts; rather than the Hollywood portrayal of shop girls as subversive figures, enabled by their financial independence (as embodied by Clara Bow's character in *It*) she instead utilises her extra income in order to benefit her family, embodying the Meiji-era ideal of *ryōsai kenbō* ('good wife and wise mother') within a modern context and demonstrating an ability to be involved in consumerism (including the sale of Western fashions) without compromising her morality. This is not an isolated depiction of a moral working woman in a Western-style space; in Ozu's *Dragnet Girl* (another Shōchiku film) Tanaka Kinuyo's gangster delinquent views another girl working in a branch of the British record store His Master's Voice (HMV) as an aspirational figure, stating, 'I'm not a dependent girl. I can be like Kazuko. I can be as good as her;' the righteous typist Toshie in Shimizu's *Undying Pearl* provides an earlier example.

This dichotomous characterisation creates a problematic element when considering Mitsukoshi's aims of presenting desirable (and purchasable) lifestyles alongside nurturing good citizenship – while Masako's character is a positive role model, it is not only her appearance which is examined onscreen. Prolonged shots are also featured of Okada Yoshiko's gloved hands, adorned with diamante details, or of her cloche hat and fur-trimmed overcoat. McCarty and Lowrey's description of the psychological processes involved in successful product placement dictate that the 'unconditioned stimulus' evoke 'good feelings' within the audience; that items worn by Okada's character are also featured as promoted objects dictates that her character, too, was intended to inspire positive consumerist desires.

An answer to this quandary may be found in the relationship between Okada's star persona and her characterisation within the film: I have already discussed Wada-Marciano's assessment of Okada's 'foreigner discourse ... [which] aligned her physical body with the sexual Otherness of Western cinema' (Wada-Marciano 2008, 96). While Wada-Marciano's assessment of Okada is primarily grounded in her later appearances in *Woman of Tokyo* (1933), *Our Neighbour, Miss Yae* (1934), and *An Inn in Tokyo* (1936), within which she plays a sex worker, a divorcee and a homeless single mother respectively, her association with marginalised female archetypes (particularly those with connotations of Westernised 'Otherness') had already been established by the time of her appearance in *No Blood Relation* in 1932. The March 1927 issue of *The Play and Movie* includes a colour image of Okada advertising Murata Minoru's film adaptation of *La Traviata* for Nikkatsu (Figure 3.1), in which she took the starring role of Marguerite (rendered in Japanese as *Tsubakihime*, the 'Camellia Princess'), a courtesan who dies of tuberculosis after a fraught love affair (*The Play and Movie* 1927, 15). This was a well-known theatrical role in Japan, one with specifically Western connotations – Joseph L. Anderson notes that 'throughout the history of *shinpa*, the most popular story from abroad continued to be that of the ill-fated and sacrificed heroine of *Tsubakihime*' (Anderson 2011, 561). The image presents Okada as not only Westernised, as per her role (she sports the same previously discussed elongated Clara Bow eyebrows and dark lipstick as Yamada Isuzu), but wild and uncontrollable – she gazes upwards in despair, with long, unbrushed, dark hair tumbling to her waist. The private life of Okada would come to embody these qualities in the media publicising the film. Murata had intended the two leads to be played by Okada and Takeuchi Ryōichi, and began shooting with them, but 'before shooting was finished, the two eloped and disappeared', causing a huge scandal and creating 'a huge amount of publicity'. Murata had 'to begin shooting all over again with different stars', but the final product fell short.

Figure 3.1 Promotional image for *La Traviata*, featuring Okada Yoshiko, *The Play and Movie*, March 1924. Courtesy of Kokusai Jōhōsha.

'The star had become that important. The role of Marguerite was intended for Yoshiko Okada. It was not transferrable' (Komatsu 2005, 374–5).

Despite featuring an actress who embodies scandalous recklessness in her publicised private life, who plays a character who sartorially references the Hollywood cinema and who immorally rejects her familial responsibilities, *No Blood Relation*'s narrative maintains a moral stance (in compliance with Mitsukoshi's aims) by essentially exiling Okada's character – the film ends with her returning to America by ship. While conservative circles could view this as a fitting punishment, a denouncement of Okada's national identity, other viewers could interpret this ending as an exciting form of immersive escapism, with the concept of 'running away to Hollywood' embodying a cathartic excitement realistically unthinkable for the everyday Japanese woman. Articles such as 'The Voice of a Female Extra' by Misono Teruko, which describes the experiences of a very ordinary Japanese girl (she clearly states that 'I was not a "modern girl" and I was raised in downtown Tokyo' [Misono 1927, 12]) as an extra in the Japanese film industry appeared in magazines such as *The Play and Movie* as early as April 1927; there was a clear fascination with the prospect of assuming even a minor role onscreen, and the idea of a major career in Hollywood must have held an even greater allure for the everyday female spectator. Okada is characterised in terms of a subversive, but lucrative 'Bad Girl' discourse, with such 'Bad Girls' having 'big, devouring appetites – for sex, for adventure, for freedom, for handbags' (Miller and Bardsley 2005, 6). Okada's 'exile' thus becomes a culmination of subversive, 'Bad Girl' attractions; the clothing that she wears becomes associated with geographical and expressive freedom and unabashed consumerism. The Mitsukoshi store becomes a safe space within which to sartorially indulge such fantasies. Rather than being forced to choose between the 'virtuous' kimono-clad type and the 'subversive' Western Bad Girl persona, the marketing of fashion objects which carry connotations of both 'types' within the same space encourages the consumer to 'mix and match', providing a multitude of options to appeal to different consumer groups.

I have isolated the role of 'type' in marketing Western fashions both on- and off-screen – these 'types' have relied upon representations of either over 'Western' or 'Japanese' femininity. An outlier is the concept of a sartorially masculine, yet still markedly female persona – in the Hollywood context, prominent examples include Marlene Dietrich and Greta Garbo. Yoshimoto Mitsuhiro describes the prominence of these personalities within the pre-war film landscape, and their intrinsic relationships with American-inspired consumerism, which made the use of the cinema as a propaganda machine difficult as international tensions gained momentum during the 1930s: 'when Charlie Chaplin, Greta Garbo, Marlene Dietrich, and Gary Cooper were at least as popular as Japan's biggest movie stars, when the Japanese were so enamoured with the American scenery, commodity culture and way of life, how could the Japanese film industry have made propaganda films that showed devilish images of Americans in any convincing way?' (Yoshimoto 2000, 84). In the Hollywood press, much attention is paid to Garbo and Dietrich's costuming, both on- and off-screen, and this is used in order to construct their sexualities. Journalist Rilla Page Palmborg describes Garbo's off-duty wardrobe, comprised of 'men's low shoes . . . men's tailored shirts . . . men's silk ties . . . men's pajamas' and hats 'in mannish style'. She suggests how her fashion choices informed her physical movements, quoting two male friends: 'Garbo strides along like a man and fairly races across the ground . . . she plays tennis like a man too' (Horak 2014, 280). Horak notes that Palmborg also alludes to Garbo being homosexual, as a possible reason for her off-screen masculinity: 'Garbo's off-screen masculinity was one of the key 'mysteries' that journalists hoped to solve. Clearly sexual inversion was an explanation that could not be stated in print' (Horak 2014, 280).

The 'mystery' of the masculine female star was also applied to Dietrich's persona – *The Travel Bulletin* in 1935 attributes her popularity in Japan to this very factor: 'unquestionably Marlene Dietrich is the most popular movie star in Japan. This comes probably from the fact that she has a certain unknown quantity in her art that appeals to the Japanese public, that mysterious appeal whose power is in inverse ratio to what is understood of it' (*The Travel Bulletin* 1935, 49). This factor was also noted by Japanese critics themselves; literary critic Kobayashi Hideo describes experiencing an 'inexplicable attraction' when viewing *Morocco* (1930), the first subtitled sound film exhibited in Japan, in which Dietrich appears wearing a top hat and tails. His writings concerning the film describe 'the workings of a double anxiety of identifying with a Western, orientalist gaze' (Lippit 2012, 4). Seiji M. Lippit attributes Kobayashi's reaction to *Morocco* as being based upon the narrative's geographical location: 'the desert landscape of Morocco – with all its familiar cultural and natural markers of orientalism – becomes a site of exoticism' (Lippit 2012, 4). Edward Said's concept of 'Orientalism' relies upon the hierarchical 'Othering' of the perceived person or country; he describes Raymond Schwab's 'notion that "Oriental" identifies an amateur or professional enthusiasm for everything Asiatic, which was wonderfully synonymous with the exotic, the mysterious, the profound and the seminal' (Said 2014, 51). These are all terms which could be applied to the masculine-attired personae of Garbo and Dietrich – both actresses already held a geographically 'exotic' appeal in the Hollywood context due to their European nationalities; their attire further exoticises their bodies. The confusion of being 'doubly Othered' (one who by their very female definition is 'Other', but who is dressed in a parody of the 'Absolute' male, generating an appearance of a hybrid gender) enacts a distance between the spectator and the star; she gives the impression of not only being transnational, but moving across gender boundaries. The star's air of sexual 'mystery', which can seemingly be resolved only by accusations of homosexuality, entirely removes the male spectator from the dynamic. Rather than the female existing as an accessory to the male, as suggested by de Beauvoir (2011, 27), the male is rendered wholly irrelevant. These observations make the setting of *Morocco*, which allowed Kobayashi to vicariously experience a Western orientalist perspective despite his own non-Western origins, a fitting location. Marjorie Garber notes the following: 'Why cross-dressing in Morocco? Because the one was already, in European as in North American eyes, the figure for the other. Araby was the site of transvestism as escape and rupture' (Garber 2006, 646). This adds a further dimension of 'Otherness' to Dietrich's cross-dressed form – she is an 'Other', portraying an 'Other' gender, within an 'Other' space; her body becomes a site of disorientation, regardless of the spectator's geographical situation. Returning to de Beauvoir's assessment of woman as intrinsically 'Other', alongside the flapper's power to exploit this dynamic via her expressivity, the power of masculine attire to trigger an attractive hierarchical confusion exists as a paradoxical factor. If the aim of the cinematic female, according to Laura Mulvey, 'traditionally ... has functioned on two levels: as erotic object for the characters within the screen story, and as erotic object for the spectator within the auditorium' (Mulvey 1975, 11), then why clothe your female star in a manner which renders her inaccessible to her male viewer? Judith Mayne interprets this statement as describing the means via which the male spectator may self-identify with the screen image, with the erotic female screen body itself acting as 'lure' rather than the aspirational space surrounding it as in the case of the female spectator: 'for Mulvey, the mainstream cinema is made to the measure of male desire, and the various devices central to the classical Hollywood cinema all serve to facilitate the identification of the male spectator with his like, the male protagonist onscreen' (Mayne 1993, 18). While Dietrich wears male attire, she is still aesthetically feminine; her hair is long, blonde and permed – she wears cosmetics. In the same way that the flapper, despite her expressive power, remained attractive to a heterosexual male populace as her power could be subdued via her preoccupation with consumerism, Dietrich and Garbo similarly remained within male-dominated constructions of heterosexual beauty. While their masculine attire superficially allotted them the power to exist as agents free from the constraints of the gender dynamic, their visual alliances to Hollywood feminine conventions ensured they remained anchored within it. As the 'types' featured in Naruse and Mizoguchi's films allowed their female characters to be appealing to different spectator demographics (and to inspire the consumption of different fashion products as a result), Dietrich and Garbo, when in 'masculine' mode, were able to inspire self-identification in both male and female spectators. In her 1981 reassessment of her 1975 article 'Visual Pleasure and Narrative Cinema', Mulvey adds that the female-identifying spectator possesses a fluidity in terms of which gendered characters she identifies with onscreen, and that this is particularly complicated by works centred around a female protagonist: 'she may find herself secretly, unconsciously almost, enjoying the freedom of action and control over the diegetic world that identification with a hero provides' (Thornham 1999, 123). Masculine female star personae simultaneously embody aspirations for male- and female-identifying spectators; the heterosexual male spectator values her as aspirational object, while the female spectator desires her potential for activity and manipulation of gender boundaries.

Dietrich's top-hat-and-tails persona is scarce in Japanese print media; when Dietrich or Garbo appear, they are usually depicted in the same feminine modes as their contemporaries. A 1936 advertisement for *Desire* (1936) in *Stage and Screen* refers to *Morocco* but shows Dietrich adorned in lavish furs, jewels and cosmetics as opposed to her trademark suits. Garbo and Dietrich's masculine personae rely not only on their sartoriality, but how their physicality, physiognomy and persona are depicted onscreen; both actresses had deeper, European-accented voices and long-limbed frames, all offset with androgynous facial aspects – Garbo's pronounced jawline, Dietrich's high cheekbones. These structural factors are what make their use of masculine attire both particularly striking and alarming; although Clara Bow was also photographed in 1927 wearing a masculine outfit of white tailored shirt, braces and necktie, when adorning the compact height of her body (5 feet 3 inches) and combined with her girlish face and persona, the look gives the impression of fancy dress rather than a threatening androgynous hybridity. Horak describes how Garbo was described as 'a tall, lanky, mannishly attired woman' in the Hollywood press (Horak 2014, 280), and Martha Gever notes how 'Von Sternberg's precise orchestration of various cinematic elements – framing, lighting, costume – present isolated parts of Dietrich's body (e.g., legs, face) or her entire body as perfect objects. On screen she becomes a phallic substitute, a "phallic woman", who wards off the association between a female body and the "fact" of her castration' (Gever 2003, 30). These actresses' masculinity is not linked purely to their attire, but to their overall presentation, including cinematic technique. In *The Aesthetics of Shadow*, Daisuke Miyao notes that the role of lighting in constructing Dietrich's onscreen persona was also noted in Japan by cinematographer Ogura Kinji, who claimed that '[Sternberg] prepared lighting perfectly in such a film as *Dishonored* (1931), considering the shape of Dietrich's face' (Miyao 2013, 207). Direct visual references to Dietrich's masculine persona in the construction of Japanese actresses in the 1930s appear to rely more heavily upon the usage of such lighting and softer, more feminine cues, such as heavy jewellery, relaxed poses and a permed hairstyle, than on sartorial appropriation.

A rare example of a direct appropriation of Dietrich's masculine sartoriality is a photograph of Shōchiku actress Chihaya Akiko appearing in *Kinema junpō* in May 1932 (Figure 3.2). Chihaya wears a top hat and tails; her bare hands clutch a large pair of men's white gloves, effecting a gendered contrast in size, a cigarette dangles from her lips and even her facial expression replicates Dietrich's studied nonchalance. Superficially, the image appears to have no bearing on her characterisation in film roles, existing purely as a novelty – rather than portraying Western-style, masculinely attired heroines, it appears that Chihaya was exclusively cast in *jidai-geki* period dramas. However, considering the actress's personal life, the image carries new undertones; Miyao notes in *The Aesthetics of Shadow* that Chihaya was involved in an affair with the director Kinugasa Teinosuke following the limited release of his independently produced experimental film *A Page of Madness* (*Kurutta ippēji*) in 1926 (Miyao 2013, 121), a film which Jasper Sharp notes 'was critically well regarded, but its experimental approach meant that it could only be screened in a limited number of theaters' (Sharp 2011, 136). This led to Kinugasa taking the print of a subsequent film – *Crossroads* (*Jūjiro*, 1928), a '*jidai-geki* without sword-fights' that featured Chihaya as its female lead – overseas to Europe with the intention of reaching a more artistically inclined audience. The film gained distribution rights in Berlin – a city which not only came to be synonymous with Dietrich but with the vibrant Weimar nightlife from which she originated. Katie Sutton notes the usage of masculine attire, embodied by Dietrich's beloved tuxedo, influencing fashions in Berlin itself – 'dark, cleanly tailored replicas of the male tuxedo . . . reached the height of popularity in 1925/26 . . . related garments such as women's tailored suits remained popular well beyond the mid-1920s and managed to achieve a more permanent place on the female fashion scene during the Nazi era' (Sutton 2013, 43). Chihaya's association with Kinugasa's experimental, avant-garde film style, particularly considering its transnationality, becomes imprinted upon her body via her clothing; just as Dietrich was exoticised by her orientalised setting in *Morocco*, Chihaya exoticises the Berlin tuxedo for Japanese audiences, a symbol of her position as a nascent transnational star. Particularly considering Kinugasa's initial origins as an actor known for portraying female roles onscreen as an *oyama* for Nikkatsu in the 1910s (Sharp 2011, 136), her masculine attire enacts a fascinating role reversal; her subversive background and associations allow her to appropriate Dietrich's image in a manner altogether more convincing than Japanese actresses with more conventional career paths.

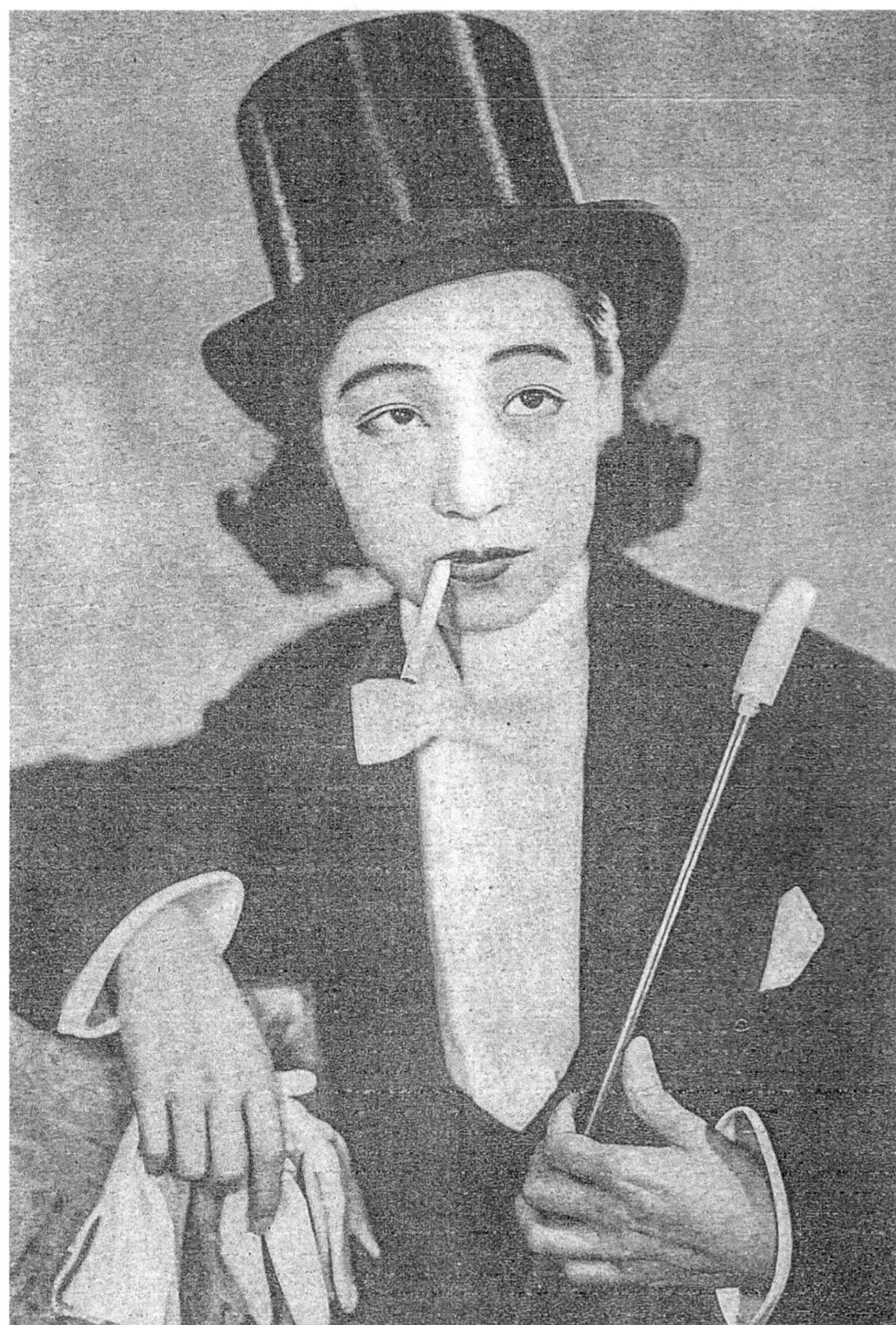

Figure 3.2 Photograph of actress Chihaya Akiko, *Kinema junpō*, May 1932.

While the conventionally 'feminine' aspects of Dietrich's star persona appear to be widespread within 1930s Japanese print media, emulations of her look exhibited by local stars are not totally devoid of subversive connotations, particularly in reference to the star's perceived sexuality. An image of actress Saijō Eriko published in *Nihon eiga* in June 1936 (Figure 3.3) is shot with the exact same overhead lighting employed by Sternberg; she sports the same softly curled hairstyle and elaborate jewellery and idly toys with a cigarette. Like Chihaya, Saijō provides a perfect replica of Dietrich's world-weary glare. However, unlike Chihaya, Saijō had already been overtly linked to female cross-dressing in the entertainment press. Prior to her film career, Saijō was a performer in the Shōchiku Revue, which, like its rival predecessor the Takarazuka Revue, featured women in cross-dressed male roles, an aspect which in itself provided her with a degree of gender flexibility in her star persona. However, much more notable was her affair with a masculinely attired woman, Masuda Yasumare, which culminated in a joint suicide attempt. The scandal was made public by Saijō herself in an autobiographical column in *Woman's Review* in February 1935 – a year before the Dietrich-referencing promotional photograph was taken. Jennifer Robertson notes that Saijō herself performed in the Shōchiku Revue solely in female roles, and in stark contrast to the sartorially masculine Masuda, her overt femininity allowed her a degree of impunity in the press – 'the media focused mostly on Masuda, whose masculine appearance was perceived as a marker not only of aggression but also deviance. Saijō, on the other hand, was treated more leniently for the likely reason that her feminine appearance did not make her appear different enough to be perceived as a heretic' (Robertson 1998, 193). The article even attributed Saijō's initial attraction to Masuda to her masculine attire, which referenced the cinematic sphere in itself; 'the cross-dressed fan's physical beauty – especially her straight, white teeth, her round [Harold] "Lloyd" spectacles, and her "Eton Crop" (a short hairstyle) – impressed the actress, and the visits became a daily affair' (Robertson 1998, 193). Rather than the still noticeably female appearance of Dietrich and Chihaya, photographs of Masuda show a convincingly cross-dressed figure (Figure 3.4) – Saijō herself concurs with this: 'for those who didn't know who they were [Saijō and Masuda, walking together], they probably looked just like heterosexual lovers' (Robertson 1998, 195).

Rather than existing as a playfully subversive visual device, Masuda's 'authentic' portrayal of sartorial masculinity is portrayed in Saijō's article as a means of enacting trickery, allowing for the perversion of Saijō's conventional femininity – Masuda's image is one of pure threat, with no benefit to the male observer. Yet, curiously, the title of another *Fujin kōron* article (written by male journalist Nakano Eitarō, who found both women collapsed in the Tokyo hotel

Figure 3.3 Photograph of actress Saijō Eriko, *Nihon eiga*, June 1936.

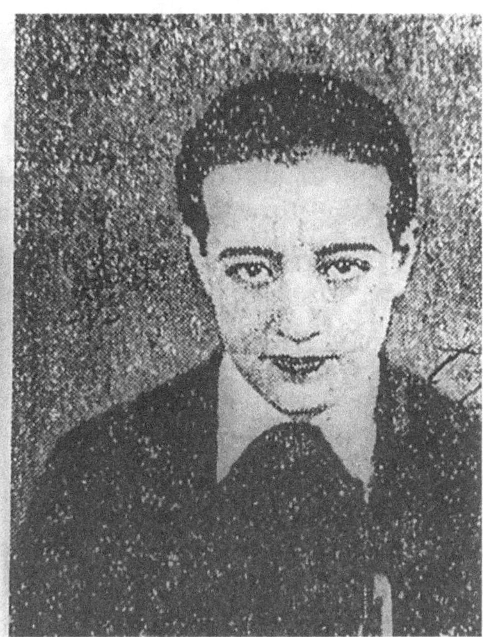

Figure 3.4 Photographs of Saijō Eriko's lover, Masuda Yasumare, *Fujin kōron*, 1935.

and called for medical help) refers to her as a '*dansō no reijin*' – a 'male-dressed beautiful woman', implying that despite her masculine persona she still holds a conventionally attractive feminine beauty, providing subtle echoes of the subversive attractions to masculinely represented stars such as Dietrich. This becomes somewhat of an epithet for Masuda; the *Asahi shimbun* also describe her as a '*dansō no reijin*' (or the single noun '*dansōreijin*') throughout the headlines of their coverage and refer to her only by her feminine birth name 'Fumiko', ensuring that her identity remains conventionally 'female' to the reader throughout. However, it is the legacy of Saijō's lesbian affair which leads to her entering the film sphere; Robertson notes that following the scandal Saijō 'left Shōchiku to pursue a career in film and disappeared from that revue's fanzines, where before she had been featured regularly' (Robertson 1998, 196). Saijō was featured as a dancer in Watanabe Kunio's *Symphony of the Backstreets* (*Uramachi no kōkyōgaku*) on 15 May 1935 – around the same time that her confessional article was published in *Woman's Review*. The film itself appears to predominantly be a vehicle for the Teichiku Record Company, produced by Nikkatsu – it was an American-style musical, with its title song 'Love is the Same as Luggage' (*Koi wa nimotsu to onaji yo*), which was available for consumers to purchase themselves, being performed by Alice Fumiko Kawabata, a Japanese-American jazz singer. E. Taylor Atkins notes that Kawabata arrived in Japan in 1932 at the age of sixteen, determined 'to teach her audiences what to appreciate, to show them that jazz was not necessarily vulgar' (Atkins 2001, 81). By featuring Saijō in an overtly Western-style but still consciously 'Japanese' musical, alongside a star who carried the same connotations, Nikkatsu began to set the stage for Saijō assuming an identity similar to Dietrich's – a woman with a controversial sexual identity, with connections to the musical stage, but who carried connotations of a Japanese, rather than purely Western identity. Considering Frederick's assertion that many magazine articles of the 1920s and 1930s were written by men under female pseudonyms, it is entirely possible, considering the temporal proximity of the date of the article's publication and her first feature film's release date, that Nikkatsu either orchestrated, or actively encouraged Saijō's public 'confession'. This is a motivation made plausible by the article – Robertson suggests that despite its story being told from Saijō's perspective, its elements were 'likely edited by Saijō or someone else in a way that exonerated the actress from any complicity in a double suicide attempt . . . a strategy designed to minimize the incident's damage to her acting and modelling career' (Robertson 1998, 54). By seizing ownership of the event's narrative, Nikkatsu ensured that it could be manipulated not only to ensure that Saijō could still be effectively used as a star without significant moral condemnation, but that it could also be exploited for its potential benefits. Saijō's attempted lesbian double suicide imbues her with qualities of titillating escapism rather than pure scandal; Robertson notes that 'historically in Japan, suicide or attempted suicide was recognised and to a certain extent valorised as an empowering act that illuminated the purity and sincerity of one's position and intentions' (Robertson 1998, 196). In this way, Saijō's actions could be presented to her female audience as the ultimate means of conveying her expressivity; this most ultimate expression of her desires is achieved without the patriarchal constraints of a male love interest. Robertson concurs with these connotations pertaining to Saijō's suicide attempt, stating that it 'suggests an apparently ironic correspondence between the resolve to commit suicide and the resolve to challenge on some level a family-state system in which women were rendered docile and subservient' (Robertson 1998, 196). By directly aligning her physical and sartorial appearance with Dietrich's feminine guise in her promotional image (Figure 3.3) for her first film with a major role, *Roses of Remembrance* (*Tsuioku no bara*, 1936), released a year after the scandal, Nikkatsu effectively repurposed the negative connotations of Saijō's romantic history in order to attract audiences seeking an expressive star unrestricted by the constraints of the patriarchal *ie* family system. This is in contrast with the characterisation of her male-attired lover in the *Asahi shimbun*. Prior to the suicide attempt, the paper detailed on 28 January 1935 how the 'male dressed beauty' was accused of the theft of 10,000 yen by her own mother and sister (facilitated by her dress mode – 'as she was dressed as a man, she could put the money in her pockets' [*Asahi shimbun* 1935, 11]), reinforcing her position as a threat to the family unit; another article produced on 28 March 1935 is entitled 'Male-Dressed Beauty Goes Off the Rails Again', detailing how Masuda 'was suddenly discharged from hospital during evening visiting hours on 27th [March 1935] along with forty other women' (*Asahi shimbun* 1935, 11), implying that she is a risk to public safety as she is no longer institutionalised. By aligning her appearance with Dietrich's feminine guise rather than her masculine tuxedo, the studio ensured that despite these connotations, Saijō still remained superficially approachable to both male and female audiences alike, who may have been alienated by the same full adoption of masculine attire exhibited by Chihaya. Her contrast with her entirely convincingly masculine lover enacts a paradox by ensuring that she is inherently feminine in comparison; while via her suicide attempt she is portrayed as an active, expressive agent, this contrast ensures that she remains an innocent entity, corrupted by Masuda's masculine trickery rather than assuming its form herself.

This analysis of the transit and manipulation of Marlene Dietrich's sartorial iconography across the bodies of Japanese star personae suggests that by association with the Hollywood star's specific connotations and public history, the performance of 'masculinity' or associations with alternative sexualities were not achieved solely via the usage of conventionally masculine attire. Instead, it is apparent that it is an overall star-derived 'look' which creates this effect – Saijō's heavy jewellery and permed hair alone would not distinguish her as holding any specific identity; however, when viewed in composite with the photograph's composition and lighting, the viewer associates Saijō with Dietrich. The fact that images of overtly masculine-attired female stars are scarce within Japan's interwar film industry would superficially suggest that masculine attire for women was a purely eccentric pursuit, limited to only the most avant-garde of stars. However, more subtle visual references to aesthetic masculinity (and the subversive expressivity which made it illicitly attractive) could be acceptably achieved via the usage of isolated 'male' fashion items within an otherwise 'feminine' ensemble. The adaptable Tanaka Kinuyo also appeared with a masculinised sartorial persona in Ozu Yasujirō's silent film *Dragnet Girl* in 1933, in which she plays a typist dating a small-time gangster. Her sartoriality embodies a swinging between two gender stereotypes: the two outfits we see her wearing most commonly in the film are a long, pale-coloured satin ballgown and a cloche hat with a trench coat and she wears high-heeled shoes and stockings with both ensembles. When we first see Tanaka in her ballgown she is visiting her boyfriend at a boxing gym – he remarks, 'You think this joint's a dancehall?' when he sees her, simultaneously implying a feminine superficiality and her alignment with stereotypical Modern Girl spaces. The relationship between the gown itself and Tanaka's body carries contradictory connotations; in the boxing gym, we see her from a front-facing angle, and while the dress is close-fitting to her body, it is high-necked with a long hemline – the pale-toned (most likely white) fabric adds further connotations of chastity and a soft femininity. However when we see her in a more private setting in the presence of just her boyfriend, we view her from behind, revealing that the dress exposes her back; the dress also interacts with the now freer way in which she moves and behaves – the straps of the dress slide downwards to expose her shoulders (a particularly erotic body part in the Japanese context) as she sits on her boyfriend's lap, smoking a cigarette. It is clear that Tanaka's character is one of duality regardless of her attire – duality itself being one of the themes of the film, in which the gangster couple debate whether or not to pursue a non-criminal life; however, it is only when she dons the trench coat that she engages in overtly criminal, dangerous or masculine behaviours. The trench coat is worn by Tanaka – always softened by her high heels and a cloche hat – when she extorts money from her boss, when she intends to shoot her love rival, and when she attempts to flee the police.

In the Hollywood cinema, the motifs of which are frequently referenced in Ozu's films, the trench coat is linked to the masculine gangster icons, such as Edward G. Robinson in *Little Caesar* (1931). While the origin of the coat itself was specifically masculine, designed as a garment to protect the World War I officer during trench warfare, it was the screen that transformed it from utilitarian men's garment to female fashion item. Patricia D. Stokes concurs with this, attributing its popularity amongst American women to Garbo: 'by 1930, [women] were wearing what Garbo was – berets, trench coats, turtlenecks became classics' (Stokes 2005, 65). Tanaka in her trench coat embodies a merging of masculine, feminine, subversive and Hollywood elements; the film itself, despite being part of the macho gangster genre, focuses upon Tanaka as its 'masculine' gangster star, replete with his costume, appealing to the section of the female-identifying audience wishing to imagine herself as an active male character onscreen as described by Mulvey. Tanaka is even punished for her passive, emotional femininity: when she suggests to her boyfriend that they should 'go straight', he throws her out, throwing her high-heeled shoes at the door as she leaves – she is assaulted by the aspects of her sartoriality which mark her as feminine. When Tanaka appropriates this male role, we yet again see a Japanese actress mimicking the subverted sexuality of androgynous stars such as Dietrich, not only via her semi-masculinised aesthetics but via her actions. In *Morocco*, we see Dietrich in full male attire kiss another woman in full view of the camera; in *Dragnet Girl* the homosexual undertones are less apparent, but still evident, when rather than killing her kimono-clad love rival, it is implied that Tanaka kisses her off camera: 'I hate to say this, but I like you,' she remarks. The camera focuses on the legs of the two women, one in *zori* sandals and kimono (her legs themselves entirely concealed), the other in stockings and heels peeking beneath her masculine trench coat, enacting not only a contrast of femininities between conventionally 'Japanese' versus 'Western', but also feminine versus masculine. At first glance, Tanaka even appears to be wearing a crisp white shirt and tie beneath her trench coat, also referencing Dietrich; however, when she returns home to her boyfriend, and announces, 'I can tell why you fell for her, I've taken to her too,' she removes her trench coat to reveal that the 'necktie' is in fact a very feminine bow at her neck, a feature of a fitted dress. She also allows her hair to fall to her shoulders, assuming an entirely feminine appearance in the presence of her boyfriend. It is at this moment that she is thrown out, after she professes a desire to become a virtuous working woman like her love rival – it appears that not only does her boyfriend view her as an inconvenience to his criminal career, but also his romantic and gender-based visions; her quasi-homosexual attraction to his love interest threatens to replace his male role. That this duality takes place upon the body of Tanaka Kinuyo normalises partially masculine aesthetics, while adding an 'edgier' facet to her versatile persona: if a simultaneously 'modern' yet innocuous star such as Tanaka could wear aspects of a male style, then surely the everyday woman could, too.

The usage of 'token' masculine items as part of a feminine ensemble appeared not only in films themselves, but also in fashion magazines, particularly in the late 1930s. In *Fasshon* (*Fashion*), *Sutairu* (*Style*) and *Yōsō silhouette* (*Western Clothing Silhouette*), a publication which offered advice on Western men's and women's tailoring to women sewing clothes at home, articles appear which feature masculine items and tailoring interspersed amongst dresses, skirts and kimono. Hollywood actresses occasionally appear in trousers, but they are described in little detail. Japanese actresses seemingly appear only in trousers when they are engaged in a sport which necessitates their wear, such as skiing. *Sutairu* acknowledges this phenomenon; in a June 1939 feature on early summer fashions, an un-named Caucasian model (who appears to be Warner Brothers actress Ann Sheridan) is depicted wearing a military-styled utilitarian trouser suit alongside Hollywood stars Bonita Granville, Ginger Rogers and Bette Davis. The commentator remarks, 'When it is summer every year, here at *Sutairu* we are repeatedly introduced to this struggle: why is the slacks pantsuit so unfashionable in Japan?' (*Sutairu* 1939, 13–14). Masculine dress elements are predominantly limited to the upper body; a popular combination in the late 1930s was a sharp tuxedo jacket (often in a conventionally male fabric, such as a bold pinstripe) paired with a crisp tailored dress shirt, similar to that sported by Dietrich – however the effect is softened by a long, A-line skirt in a matching fabric. *Sutairu* showcases such suits on multiple actresses in the late 1930s, ranging from Kazami Akiko (then a new star, who held a soft, girlish star persona [Natsumura 1939, 8–9]; Figures 3.5, 3.6 and 3.7) to Yuri Akemi (Figure 3.8), a musical film star with similar Western-style connotations

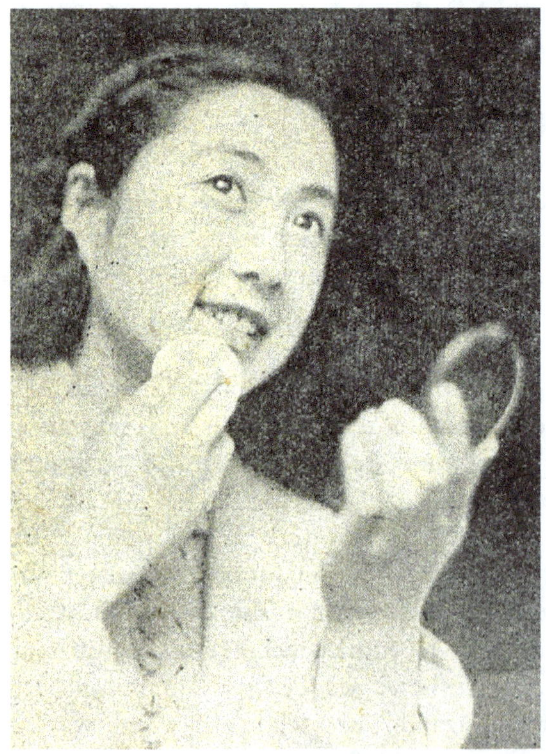

Figures 3.5–3.7 Actress Kazami Akiko wearing a tailored skirt suit, *Sutairu* (*Style*), July 1939.

Figure 3.8 Actress Yuri Akemi wearing a tailored skirt suit, *Sutairu* (*Style*), May 1939.

to Alice Fumiko Kawabata (*Sutairu* 1939, 42). The quasi-masculine style of the suit itself appears to both complicate and diversify the bodily image of the expressive female star; in a *Sutairu* interview conducted by Natsumura Senkichi, Kazami is quoted as stating 'I look like such a baby!' when viewing a photograph of herself wearing such a suit, and Natsumura infantilises the actress's expressive features – she 'smiles sweetly, with a spirited, girlish face', has 'innocent eyes' and a 'childlike smile' (Natsumura 1939, 8). The interview also contains commentary on the actress's weight gain, a factor which Kazami does not deny: Natsumura asks, 'You've put on a little weight, haven't you?' to which Kazami replies, 'More than a little. Actually, I've put on a lot' (Natsumura 1939, 8). However, rather than being criticised for this, Natsumura instead praises her sense of humour – 'As she is so amusing, Miss Kazami and I both laughed heartily together' (Natsumura 1939, 8–9). Her look is described as having a 'fresh coquetry' and little attention is paid to her bodily form. Kazami is photographed using a cosmetic compact, once the feminine preserve of the Westernised *moga*. Her aesthetic representation can be interpreted in order to simultaneously appeal to a number of desirable traits – her quasi-masculine outfit and use of cosmetics marks her as modern and fashionable, while her body shape itself is obscured, allowing for emphasis on the face and an innocent, youthful and asexualised, yet still modern and expressive star persona.

A photograph of Nikkatsu actresses Higure Satoko and Ōuchi Tokuko (Figure 3.9) wearing these suits is supplied with the following caption: 'Beautiful smiles; vociferous laughter; intimate and friendly. They are modest, but appealing at the same time' (*Sutairu* 1939, 30). While they are praised for their facial and aural expressivity in line with Western actresses, the concealment of their physical forms within the quasi-masculine style ensures that they remain modest and approachable, in contrast to masculinely attired Hollywood actresses. This 'modest but appealing' factor allowed the suit to also be marketed towards everyday women. *Fasshon* features contributions from readers in a recurring feature entitled 'Fashion Answers' – in 1935, a reader who identifies herself only as 'Namiko', rendered in *katakana* as though it were a foreign name, describes her desire to sew herself one of these suits, and the way in which its form relates to her own body shape:

> I think I would like to make myself a suit for the springtime. Please advise me on which style to choose. I am five feet five inches tall with no curves. I will look like a man, and I believe I may look strange in a blouse, but I would still like to make myself one. (*Fasshon* 1935, 7)

The editor's response makes no comment on the author's body type or its gendered connotations, instead simply providing seasonal advice – they suggest the use of a wool-based fabric, that blouses are practical in the transitional

Figure 3.9 Photograph of Nikkatsu actresses Higure Satoko and Ōuchi Tokuko wearing masculine-style tailored suiting, *Sutairu* (*Style*), June 1939.

stage between spring and summer and to create a skirt with pleats in the front and back in order to keep up with contemporary trends. The male-inspired suit appears to no longer be the preserve of the cinematic and has made the transition to the desires of the everyday female consumer regardless of her body shape or sexual identity.

Rather than fearing a 'masculine' appearance, the visual cues of Western-inspired male sartoriality have become adapted to the extent that Dietrich's construction of a threatening yet alluring hybridised approach to masculine femininity has become neutralised – a 1935 *Fasshon* article which was purportedly written by Dietrich herself makes no reference to her clothing at all, instead offering only makeup and skin-care tips (*Fasshon* 1935, 10). This is not to say that the masculine features of these ensembles were being ignored – a photograph featured in *Yōsō silhouette* in 1939 (Figure 3.10) depicts a Japanese model with a trilby hat pulled over her eyes (similarly to Yamada Isuzu at the climax of *Osaka Elegy*) and wearing a tailored masculine-styled skirt suit; she accessorises this with a feminine patent leather handbag and a pair of white ladies' gloves. It is captioned thus: 'This classic tailored suit has the exact same basic lines as a men's suit, but if the body concealed within it is female, it must be tailored with full knowledge of that inner femininity' (*Yōsō silhouette*, 1939, 1). By 1939, the appeal of masculine-based attire for Japanese women, despite (or perhaps buoyed by) its connotations of expressivity and flexible sexuality, had been acknowledged; however, it had been manipulated in correspondence with existing Western-derived ideals of feminine sartoriality to the extent that it had become a new hybrid style devoid of subversive connotations, with feminine accessories always present.

Komatsu Hiroshi states, 'The stars advertised by film companies and the adaptations of novels written by popular authors helped the cinema become more and more popular. Most of the films produced were dependent on their stars. That was the result of the acceptance of the American star system by Japanese cinema' (Komatsu 2005, 374). It is this system focused around the advertisement of the star image, featuring film itself alongside related books, magazines and fashion or cosmetic items, which allowed a Western-derived fashionable appearance to transit from the screen to the collective consumer consciousness of its female-identifying Japanese audience. While the cinematic experience itself provided the initial immersive 'sensory-reflexive horizon' which by its very nature encouraged the female spectator to consume with the aim of appropriating the star's bodily form (and as a result her lifestyle and innate power), this multimedia sales environment based around the star image extended the immersive experience of the screen to the everyday living world of the spectator. This enacted a pervasive linkage between public and private spaces, from the cinema to the department store, to the home space,

Figure 3.10 An uncredited Japanese model wearing a trilby hat and skirt suit, *Yōsō silhouette*, 1939.

with coded consumer imagery constantly changing and fluctuating within the tangible objects of newspapers, books and magazines in the same manner as the immaterial flickering momentary image onscreen. In the same way that audiences wished to grasp the momentary immediacy of modernity by consuming more and more cinematic experiences (that is, by attending more screenings at the cinema), female spectators engaged in consumption in order to physically own the momentary and embody it themselves – '[Fashion] is poised ambiguously between present and past . . . fashion freezes the moment in an eternal gesture of the-only-right-way-to-be . . . clothes are objects, but they are also images . . .' (Wilson 2011, vii). Between 1923 and the state-controlled 1939 Film Law we see this relationship between the screen and fashion industries become both more obvious and more sophisticated, with star images and fashion brands merging onscreen, in-store and in print. This affected film form and style, altering factors ranging from casting, to narrative, to a film's soundtrack and shot focuses. The concept of the expressive female image became a transnational marketing tool with the Hollywood cinema as its locus, which became subject to adaptation within the Japanese context. While connotations of female autonomy and the ability to subvert patriarchal systems (albeit tempered by its intrinsic link with consumerism, controlling its true power) acted as motivations for both male and female audiences to experience attractions to the image of the expressive cinematic female, its link to a Western-style fashionable appearance is augmented in the Japanese context, treading a fine line between threat and respectability. Studios producing *gendai-geki* dramas utilised sound and silent cinema in order to portray expressive women and their relationship with Western attire in a manner which both fulfilled moral standpoints and the public thirst for Hollywood-style aesthetics and personae, frequently portraying female characters wearing more 'modest' interpretations of Hollywood styles and engaging in 'acceptable' expressive behaviours which do not threaten patriarchal structures. Characters outside of these parameters are subject to either condemnation (Okada Yoshiko in *No Blood Relation*; Yamada Isuzu in Mizoguchi's diptych) or reformation (Tanaka Kinuyo in *The Neighbour's Wife and Mine*). There is no single Western-style appearance that is promoted by these films; while some advocate a hybridised appearance (Tanaka Kinuyo's appearance at the end of *The Neighbour's Wife and Mine*) other productions use it in order to portray subversion (Okada Yoshiko in *Our Neighbour, Miss Yae*, Yamada Isuzu in *Osaka Elegy*). A means of stabilising these conflicting images and maximising their appeal comes in the form of 'types' based upon Hollywood personae, which allowed the consumer/audience to construct their own star-inspired sartorial persona via their consumption habits (a factor subject to variation, ensuring a diverse market for multiple varieties of fashion item) and the studios and fashion companies to select stars to promote their goods, depending on the Japanese star's own adherence to these 'types'. This alignment of Japanese stars as 'equivalent' to their Hollywood counterparts not only allowed for an expansion of their marketing appeal, even as star archetypes emerged which threatened the gender binary such as Dietrich and Garbo, but also allowed studios to protect their investments. The rebranding of disgraced lesbian revue girl Saijō Eriko as a 'Japanese Marlene Dietrich' not only legitimised her story but could attract new audiences, while Okada Yoshiko's pseudo-foreign 'bad girl' discourse helped to market her films and fashionable appearance, even when she was removed from productions as 'punishment' for her romantic adventures. The films analysed here – despite many featuring dichotomies of extremes imposed upon the bodies of their female characters via their clothing – present a spectrum of Western-inspired expressive and sartorial identities, rather than the two conflicting polarities apparent in print media. The key to making these fashion trends and their related expressivity digestible to Japanese audiences lay in the ability of the film and fashion industries to dilute their connotations, a task achieved partially via the aforementioned types, but also through the usage of accessorising, the mixing of coded fashion objects upon the body of the Japanese actress. That even the innately subversive adoption of masculine-style fashion items could be presented as an acceptable outfit choice when paired with otherwise 'feminine' fashion objects is testament to the versatility of this hybridity, whether that be a pairing of 'Japanese' and 'Western' fashion objects or 'feminine' and 'masculine' aesthetics. This raises the query of the role of hybridity in the context of fashion ensembles worn by men, and the role of Westernised and gendered aesthetics across the bodies of multiple gender identities. This dynamic can be observed in the popularity of sportswear for men and women arising in the 1920s and 1930s.

Note

1. *Katakana* is a phonetic alphabet in Japanese used primarily for 'loanwords', which originate from languages other than Japanese. In this example, the English wording 'fashion show' has been transliterated to *fasshon shō* using this alphabet, signifying its foreign origin in both wording and concept.

Part II

Sportswear and hybridity: The national body and gender

Chapter 4

Sportswear and hybridity: The middle-class housewife as hybridised consumer archetype

In Part I, I established that Western-style clothing and cosmetics allowed for a Hollywood-derived concept of an expressive, assertive female image to become a marketable ideal for the emergent female consumer, and that it was the combined efforts of the film- and fashion-related industries which presented this ideal in a sensory-immersive context to the consumer-as-audience-member. The purchasing of the goods depicted onscreen and in cinema-related print media allowed women to 'purchase' the connotations of the fashion item's relevant female star personalities, allowing the female consumer to engage in new identity coding practices and to align her aesthetic appearance with developing Hollywood-inspired approaches to gender, sexuality and the socio-economic position of women in society. New Hollywood-derived attitudes to the female physical form were also implicated in the process of the construction of saleable identities, with the transnational 'flapper' image equally entailing a physical (and increasingly bodily exposed) expressivity alongside her non-physical assertive emotional qualities. Yet Western-style fashion goods – and the pursuit of a new 'Western-style' Japanese body encased within – were not the reserve of the female consumer who self-identified with the 'flapper', and this image of female physicality and expressivity did not solely target the Modern Girl demographic.

Here I examine the role of the onscreen sporting world and its related consumer fashion objects in aligning state narratives (which focused on personal physical development and Western-inspired eugenics for the benefit of the nation) with the consumerist leisure activities of the middle-class family unit and the individuals to whom this image was marketed as an ideal. This involved not only the female consumer (typified onscreen and in print media by the housewife archetype) but the aspirant middle-class man and by proxy their children – the next generation of Japanese citizens. This concept was hardly unique to Japan, with the most obvious comparison being seen concurrently in

Germany. The Third Reich similarly utilised imagery and rhetoric focused on the female body to target women as catalysts to increase the size and physical health of the German family unit: 'Women were encouraged to devote their time and energy into producing the next generation of German citizens and were rewarded for their efforts' (Silva 2018, 8). Propagandist Günther Kaufmann's work was 'directed towards young women specifically', using female-focused beauty practices and norms to instil the Reich's familial values; he wrote that 'taking pleasure in human beauty must emanate from feminine vanity and must be accompanied by a rigorous culture of physical hygiene and a certain elegance' (Silva 2018, 8). Crucial to this process were depictions of physicality and athletic health: 'They encouraged the athleticism and healthfulness of their members and encouraged the conformity of the young girls and women to fit the German ideal' (Silva 2018, 8). Women living under the Third Reich, who had experienced new freedoms during the Weimar Republic, including voting rights, the ability to stand for political office and greatly increased financial freedom and presence in the workplace, were now expected to return to prior ideals summarised by the phrase '*Kinder, Küche, Kirche*' – 'Children, Kitchen, Church'. While the roles of women had not experienced such strikingly rapid change in the Japanese context, women were still faced with the dichotomy of the imagery and opportunities of the rapidly modernising world around them versus a similarly retrospective state-focused tenet: 'good wife and wise mother' (*ryōsai kenbo*), a Meiji-era concept rooted in patriarchal Confucian family and household structures. One means of harmonising these factors, to harness the bodies of women as vehicles for the health and prosperity of the national family unit – in both contexts – was via sporting imagery and the promotion of a beautiful, hygienic and fit body across media.

Roland Barthes' analysis of electoral photography suggests how images can be used to convey a sense of 'kinship' between the state and everyday family life: 'photography . . . establishes a personal link between [the candidate] and the voters; the candidate . . . suggests a physical climate, a set of daily choices expressed in a morphology, a way of dressing, a posture'. As with the flapper in the previous section, here too a 'type' is employed not only to prompt a purchase, but political engagement, allowing the individual to view himself in the politicised image: 'a photograph is a mirror . . .; it offers to the voter his own likeness, but clarified, exalted, superbly elevated into a type . . . the voter is at once expressed and heroized, he is invited to elect himself . . .' (Barthes 1991, 91–2). Barthes' concept of the politically loaded photographic 'type' can be combined with Hansen's idea of the cinema as 'sensory-reflexive horizon' (Hansen 2000, 10), as well as Doane's observation that the cinematic space functions as 'both shop window and mirror, the one simply a means of access to the other' for the female spectator-as-consumer (quoted in Petro 2002, 43).

Images of the sporting body, too, can thus become both commercialised and politicised by encouraging the immersion of the spectator in the image.

John Hoberman has posited that 'political ideology [was] an animating force in the pre-1989 sports political universe' (Edelman and Wilson 2017, 29). In the Japanese context, Sandra Collins has demonstrated how Japan's performance in the 1932 Los Angeles Olympics, and the media coverage thereof, proved a turning point for Japanese self-perception: 'Only 32 years after Natsume Sōseki lamented upon his reflection in a British shop window in London as "small, ugly and yellow", a Japanese Olympic athlete described his body as "tall, powerful and seemingly white" prior to and during the 1932 Olympic Games' (Collins 2007, 37). The idea of Japan as an outward-facing 'new sports nation', with the concept of the cultivation of the body at its core, was transmitted from the national to the individual sphere via archetypes in commercial and state-endorsed media. The cinema was a key mechanism for this transmission, alongside other media such as print, exhibitions and beauty contests. The relationship between star bodies and sport in the Japanese cinema –showcased in clothing, activity and motifs – thus presents ample opportunities to observe the effort to immerse the Japanese subject simultaneously in cinematic, commercial and political narratives. Images of the hybridised star body suggested a favourable eugenic melding of Japanese and Western characteristics – but ensured that this process was always rooted within the concept of a specifically Japanese national identity.

Barthes suggests how the idea of a 'nation' is itself the product of 'myth-making', in an analysis of a photograph of a black soldier saluting (presumably to the French tricolour): 'I see very well what it signifies to me: that France is a great Empire, that all her sons, without any colour discrimination, faithfully serve under her flag, and that there is no better answer to the detractors of an alleged colonialism than the zeal shown by this Negro in serving his so-called oppressors' (Barthes 1991, 115). Standish combines this analysis with Claude Lévi-Strauss's assertion that the core function of myth is to 'ensure the permanency of the group', applying it directly to Japanese national narratives generated via the cinema during the colonial occupation of eastern Asia (Standish 2013, 13–14). Such myth-making practices helped to form a collective Japanese 'national identity' from the Meiji era onwards, as many historians have emphasised. Vlastos summarises the consensus:

> In Japan as throughout the industrialised world, the rise of the nation-state in the late nineteenth century produced an outpouring of new national symbols and rites such as flags, anthems, and holidays, as well as new (e.g., public health) or reorganised (e.g., armed forces) state institutions that created and imposed their own discourses of social control. The idea of 'the nation', after all, stands as the mega invented tradition of the modern era. (Vlastos 1998, 8)

The characteristic of such myth-making is the repurposing of history, with 'traditional' events and practices invested with new significance by the myth-making authority. Shintō[1] was perhaps foremost among these. The new Meiji government built on the work of Edo-period *kokugaku* ('National Learning') scholars, who insisted that Shintō was an all-encompassing, uniquely Japanese phenomenon, to present Shintō as 'the cultural will or energy of the Japanese people' (Kuroda 1981, 2–3, 19). The state could thereby present the Meiji settlement cosmetically 'as a return to ancient ways, whereas in fact it was heralding some of the greatest changes Japan has ever faced' (Picken 2004, 87). Sports were also subject to revisionism, with existing practices repurposed into 'national' sports via a manipulation of their 'history', making myths out of actual bodies. Vlastos cites the Japanese sport of sumo wrestling in order to depict how the bodily aspects of myth-making around sport intensify its power as a national sign, citing Dipesh Chakrabarty: 'ideas acquire materiality through the history of bodily practices, they work not simply because they persuade through their logic ... the past is embodied through a long process of the training of the senses' (Vlastos 1998, 7). Given the spectator's sensory immersion in the cinema, the appearance of the Japanese sporting body onscreen intensifies this process.

Sport was hybrid, however. Even for 'traditional' Japanese sports, myth-making was required to incorporate non-Japanese influences and remove any 'foreign' connotations. Inoue Shun has described how Kōdōkan judo was the product of the transformation of 'a Tokugawa-era martial art, into a "national sport" [*kokugi*] and body culture' (Vlastos 1998, 163–4), within an unfavourable climate for 'Japanese' martial arts. Its founder, Kanō Jigorō, succeeded by combining the best moves of the 'traditional' martial art with the latest understanding of human physiology, thereby creating the foundation of 'a new, "scientific" martial art ... which is best suited to today's world'. This approach could be justified as part of national heritage, while also being future- and outward-facing. Kanō was instrumental in securing Tokyo's hosting of the 1940 Olympics, encouraged women to practise the sport, and even sent one of his star pupils to the United States to demonstrate it internationally. Finally, Inoue notes that in the 1930s and 1940s the process of imbuing 'historically Japanese' sports with progressive connotations was mirrored in the application of historical narratives also to Western sports. Since '"imported sports" were ... based on Western individualism and liberalism ... they should be "Japanized" through *budō*, which embodied Japanese spiritual values ... *Budō*, originally a modern hybrid typical of late Meiji culture, was redefined as "timeless" and utilised to infuse Western-type sports with "pure" Japanese spirit' (Vlastos 1998, 172). Both conventionally 'Western' and 'Japanese' sports featured in the popular culture landscape of the 1920s and 1930s, each with their own mythical significations. Given the focus of this book on Western attire, this section only addresses images of Western sports onscreen and in print media – but does so with an awareness of the hybridity in these mythical sporting images of Japanese men and women. The role of conventionally 'Japanese' sports images (e.g., representations onscreen of sumo or kendo practices) within a cinematic context is in need of further research. This chapter specifically focuses on depictions of women interacting with a Western-inspired sporting world onscreen.

Japan's emergent 'new middle class' presented a more accessible alternative than the Modern Girl. Garon has shown how their aspirational status relied on 'Westernised' education and was outwardly expressed, whether male or female, via a consumerist lifestyle. 'In middle class homes, women assumed the privileged status of housewife, who managed the household, read the new housewives' magazines and partook of inter-war consumer culture' (Garon 2009, 309). Tipton has described how this 'affluent lifestyle . . . became the ideal for most Japanese during the 1920s' and was propagated in the mass media via the rhetoric of a 'cultured life' (*bunka seikatsu*), a concept which became entwined with the words '*modan*' and '*modanizumu*' towards the end of the decade (Tipton 2008, 107). Harootunian notes that this 'new culturally lived experience' was 'targeted [at] the city salaryman and his family', primarily via the department store, which alongside 'popular discourse . . . and advertisements . . . kept the spectacle of endless consumption constantly before the population' (Harootunian 2011, 16). This spectacle, already visible to the female audience described in the previous chapter, was also targeted at the middle-class male and his family, prompting new questions about the cinema's role in generating desire for Western fashion among these various target audiences.

In fact, the consumable markers of a 'cultured life' in large part reached the market via the female image, albeit with different moral connotations to the Modern Girl. In the wake of World War I, 'officials in charge of "social education" became convinced that "improvements" (usually Westernisation) in food, clothing and shelter would strengthen Japan and raise living standards' and founded a 'daily life improvement campaign' by way of response. This campaign was influenced by figures such as Hani Motoko, who had founded *Fujin no tomo* in 1903. This was a publication 'aimed at middle class women who were taking on the role of household manager', within which the 'new consumer goods were presented not as luxuries, but as higher-quality, simpler, and sometimes less expensive replacements for traditional, wasteful expenditures' (Minichello 1998, 323). This approach, aligning Western-style lifestyle goods with state-condoned cultural advancement and frugality, continued to use female-focused media consumption, but with a focus on the household rather than the individual consumer.

The advertising materials of the cosmetics company Shiseido illustrate how a fashionable, Western-style appearance could be marketed to the middle-class Japanese housewife and, by extension, her family. The company opened a Western-style art gallery in 1919 and developed an American-inspired 'chain store' system in 1923, following which it experienced exponential growth, with over 2,000 contracted retail stores offering Shiseido services and experiences, such as skincare consultations (Shiseido 2023). As early as 1922 the brand was associating itself with the 'Western knowledge' being marketed towards the middle classes. To do so, it drew on a scientific concept of 'healthiness', for example in pamphlets entitled with the German word '*Kosmetik*', which advertised consultations with a 'skin specialist', before the opening of a new Tokyo store (Shiseido 1922, 1). It alternated this image of wholesome middle-class healthiness with that of the Modern Girl, as described by the in-house *Shiseido geppō* (*Shiseido Monthly*) in 1926:

> The Modern Girl is a young woman who holds modern [*kindai-teki*] beliefs. Particularly, I think it means a woman who chooses Western clothing over the kimono. You can see her intelligence shine out; her individuality is made clear … In other words, she is a woman who shatters notions of a conventional appearance and recognises herself through her clothing and cosmetics, and who beautifies herself as much as possible. (*Shiseido geppō* 1926, 5)

This image contrasts with a 1924 photo feature in the middle-class women's magazine *Fujin kurabu* (*Women's Club*). Spanning two pages, the left-hand section of the article detailed 'Japanese hairstyles suitable for young ladies during *Hanami* [viewing the cherry-blossom]', illustrated with three conventional Japanese coiffure styles, taken from behind (*Fujin kurabu* 1924, 12). The right-hand section offered a Western-style alternative, 'Two Fashionable Hairstyles', with front and rear views of a smiling model wearing a simple chignon, alongside a young girl with short, curled hair. The accompanying text noted how the 'incredibly fashionable [*hai-kara*]' styles had been achieved at the company's 'Milan' salon 'by gently using curling tongs. The chignon respected 'your unique beauty' and so would 'make you very happy', but the presentation of Western hairstyles alongside conventional Japanese styles as suitable for children and 'demure young ladies' at a 'traditional' seasonal event served to make Western hairstyling as a wholesome pursuit suitable for the whole family (*Fujin kurabu* 1924, 11). The article also highlighted new technology, consistent with the idea that the middle class were meant to value the convenience provided by Western-style technological advancements rather than their associated luxuries. The chignon had been endorsed as good for the nation since the Meiji era. As early as 1885, a woodblock print by Ginkō Adachi had depicted a woman having her hair arranged by a maid while surrounded by photographs of various

Western-inspired hairstyles, emphasising the benefits of such styles for the nation. Shiseido's efforts to market both to the individualistic Modern Girl and the middle-class family provides a concise illustration of the ability of the same Western-style fashion products to appeal to supposedly contrasting female consumer archetypes, dependent on the particular media context.

Shiseido's advertising material consistently promoted Modern Girl and middle-class imagery side by side. In 1927, the company released *The Pocket Book for Women* (*Go-fujin techō*), which provided 'educational' information about Western lifestyles, explained novel Western domestic technologies, and was laced throughout with details about beauty and fashion. The book offered a portrait of the 'cultured life', combining an individualist emphasis on fashion and beauty with middle-class family concerns about advancement and convenience. The Shiseido advertisements featured iconography inspired by Modern Girl cinematic icons such as Louise Brooks, whose short geometric bob supports an article exploring the fashionable haircuts of Parisian women:

> Here we show a trend that it would not be an exaggeration to say that Parisian women, or in fact all French women, adhere to – the cropped haircut. Young women of the countryside, maids, salesgirls, housewives and their husbands all have short hair. If you were to go out and get this short haircut for yourself [in Japan] it would be outstanding, as it is unthinkably fantastical and stylish. But on the contrary, [in France] it has come to be seen as normal. (Shiseido 1927, 105)

The appeal to the individualist consumerism of the Modern Girl is clear, given the emphasis on 'unthinkably ... stylish', the 'salesgirl' archetype, and the Hollywood-inspired illustrations. But there are echoes of the earlier *Fujin kurabu* article, given the wide spread of the fashion in France. The reference to France also strengthens its connotations of European-influenced middle-class life. A similar effect is evident in a two-page spread entitled, 'Images of Household Electrical Appliances', with one side dedicated to standing lamps and the other to various hairstyling tools:

> In your quiet room, the electric standing lamp emits a dreamlike light, gently waking you and bringing you back to reality. Lamp 'A' and Lamp 'B' are both suitable for a husband and young lady's room – 'A' is an extravagant French-made example and 'B' is an understated German design. Articles 'C' and 'D' are both Pelouze Hair Irons, without which it would not be possible to create Western hairstyles ... 'E' and 'F' are convenient electric hairdryers, which can dry your washed hair in just forty-five minutes, and 'G' is the electric clothes iron that we all know. (Shiseido 1927, 33–4)

The text notes that the goods are manufactured in the West, but transfers them to a domestic setting, allowing the reader to envision them within her own middle-class Japanese surroundings.

In Part I, I established that the immersive cinematic experience induced the female spectator to consume Western-style fashion goods in an effort to approximate the onscreen star's bodily appearance and her surroundings. The Shiseido handbook interweaves the ostensibly Modern Girl desire to approximate the appearance and lifestyle of onscreen stars with the middle-class desire for efficiency in service of the family and state, which would manifest in a 'cultured life'. Shiseido's aim was to align its own Japanese-made beauty products, services and spaces with these Western-style goods and their associated lifestyles. The company's cosmetics and consumer experiences were presented as an accessible yet 'authentic' means of attaining the lifestyle seen onscreen. Shiseido's mixed approach to advertising – with Western-style goods as the common denominator – shows how the Modern Girl and middle-class housewife existed primarily as consumer images, rather than mutually exclusive consumer identities. Shiseido could market its cosmetics, products and services with both Modern Girl and practical housewife imagery, allowing both to be seen as aspirational, in their in-house media and specifically middle-class women's magazines. In other words, it was possible for consumer images to be neither 'Modern Girl' nor 'middle-class' exclusively, but an effective and appealing combination of the two. Consumers could choose to craft their own individuality via their consumption habits.

This was underlined by Kon Wajirō's famous survey of 1,180 men and women in the Ginza at various times of day during the early summer of 1925 (Figure 4.1). Kon's headline finding was that only 1 per cent of the women wore wholly Western-style clothing, with the remaining 99 per cent retaining the kimono (Sato 2003, 49), despite the fact that Modern Girl iconography could be found in every corner of the interwar Japanese advertising landscape, particularly its cinema. This impression, of a stark and uneven contrast, was underlined by the summary pictogram which Kon used to illustrate his findings. This depicted a woman divided into two halves, one clad in kimono and wearing *geta* sandals, the other in a cloche hat, sheath dress, and high heels. A closer examination of Kon's survey, however, presents a less polarised image of female dress: 'the pages and pages of drawings and analyses of the specific parts [of outfits worn by the survey subjects] work against a simple dichotomy between East and West' (Silverberg 1992, 39). The survey itself breaks down the broad categories, differentiating, for example, between different types of high-heeled shoe, necktie, or cosmetics, suggesting a more varied aesthetic. For example, in the summary pictogram, he located cosmetics on the 'Western' half of the image, but elsewhere he notes that of the fifty-nine women he surveyed between the times of 15:45 and 16:00 on the ninth day of the survey, a majority (62 per cent) were found to be wearing some form of facial cosmetics, 48 per cent wore 'light makeup' (*usugeshō*), 14 per cent wore 'heavy' (*nō*) makeup,

Figure 4.1 Index image summarising the findings of Kon Wajirō's survey of the dress styles of 1,180 men and women in the Ginza, 1925. Courtesy of Kogakuin University Library.

and one solitary participant wore lipstick (*beni*), with only 38 per cent going bare-faced.[2] Kon also provides detailed pictograms of individual observations, each annotated with date, time of day, and side of street. Admittedly, in the detailed pictogram of overall female style (conducted at the same time, albeit with a slightly smaller sample size of fifty-two participants), he notes that 90 per cent wore a form of kimono (divided into six sub-categories) with only 10 per cent wearing 'Western clothing' (categorised simply as *yōfuku*[3]).

Still, his detailed findings suggest a middle ground between 'Japanese' and 'Western' clothing styles. Most women were wearing both 'Western' cosmetics and 'Japanese' kimono (Kon 2011, 126–7).

Kon himself appears to acknowledge the existence of hybridised dress: he situates the apron, a staple of both the housewife and the cafe waitress, in its own category, between the kimono and *yōfuku*. He notes the wearing of Western-style accessories, for example a scarf (*sukāfu*) within the various kimono-based ensembles. Similarly, all except four people wearing Western-style shoes were wearing Japanese clothing. All except one woman carrying a handbag, marked as a Western item in the summary pictogram, were wearing kimono (Kon 2011, 126–7). Kon's survey was not an exhaustive depiction of dress styles worn within Tokyo at the time, as even he admitted, but it does suggest how Western-style cosmetics and accessories were being incorporated into Japanese clothing styles, not only onscreen or in relevant print advertising (Kawazoe 2004, 31). It is also worth noting that the survey itself originally appeared in the middle-class women's magazine *Fujin kōron*, aimed squarely at the female Japanese middle-class consumer. Fashion goods marked as 'Western' were not inherently elements of a Modern Girl aesthetic but were purchased and worn in conjunction with Japanese dress aesthetics. Just as the Shiseido *Pocket Book for Women* allowed the reader to use Western household objects as objects of desire through which to transform her home into a centre of 'cultured life', so the wearing of the Western-style accessories, cosmetics, and hairstyles associated with the Modern Girl aesthetic allowed the wearer to 'bring the things of the screen closer', but not too close. The consumer could choose which aspects of the Modern Girl, and so of *modanizumu*, to adopt, while still fulfilling the valued role of the educated, technologically informed, middle-class housewife.

Female characters appearing in Japanese films reflect this hybridised image. Naruse's *No Blood Relation* (1932), produced for the Shōchiku studios and supported by the Mitsukoshi department store, stars Okada Yoshiko, who epitomised the Modern Girl both on- and off-screen. The camera lingers on her Western outfits and accessories in a series of prolonged shots, which seemingly perform no narrative or diegetic function. An approachable alternative, however, is offered by her rival. Masako, her estranged child's stepmother, performed by Tsukuba Yukiko, embodies the selfless middle-class mother to the extent that she throws herself in the path of a motorcar to save her stepdaughter. When her husband's company experiences financial difficulties, in order to support her family, Masako starts working in the Mitsukoshi department store in its Western clothing department. She is shown sorting through folded dresses and accessories and assisting customers in a scene reminiscent of Clara Bow's shop-girl role in *It* (1927). That film had sparked an '*Itto*' boom, with the print media using the term as a neologism for *are* ('that'), indicating a subject distant from the speaker. The association with Bow remained ubiquitous. A photo feature in the February 1928 issue of *The Play and Movie* depicted a heavily made-up Bow in a form-fitting, short-sleeved dress, with permed hair, high-heeled shoes and a small dog – itself a marker of middle-class status (Skabelund 2011, 160). The feature was captioned with the words, 'it . . . It . . . IT' (sic) in *hiragana, katakana* and roman script. The term also took on a life of its own, however. An article by film critic Ishii Bunsaku in the same magazine in September 1928 told 'The Story of "It"':

> The word 'It' [*are*] has come to mean 'the shape of beauty in 1928.' However, it is not the case that this beauty is found only in exterior appearance. Standing out against the beauties of *ukiyō-e* woodblock prints, nowadays there is no use in a beautiful form if there is no soul. Such round-faced beauties do not have the modern flavour. It is said that beautiful women now have what is known as a 'moving beauty' [*ugoku utsukushisa*] – a charm has come along which is based on more than pure doll-like beauty and includes sex appeal. 'It' may not be a representative word for 'beauty', but I think instead it is a word which describes the sex appeal found in the wit and cheerfulness it is certainly necessary to have in modern life. 'It' does not represent beauty, but it has come to represent 'a thing that is impossible to place, but which makes people either like or dislike you'. (Ishii 1928, 9)

Ishii went on to identify Elinor Glyn as the inventor of 'it', in a 1907 novel, debunking the assumption that the term should be necessarily associated with Clara Bow, her flapper image, or the 1927 film. Rather, 'it' referred to an innate non-physical quality, meaning that it could also be found in a housewifely character such as Masako. This suggestion is underlined by the film's treatment of Okada Yoshiko's character, Tamae. Her Western-style appearance was much closer to that of Bow – at one point she wears an outfit strikingly similar to Bow's 1928 photograph in *The Play and Movie* – but she is portrayed as a scheming woman, who abandons her daughter and is essentially 'exiled' to the United States, hardly embodying the charm of 'it' as described by Ishii. The camera focuses on Tamae, in Western dress, but also on Masako. She wears kimono throughout, but also a chignon and a kiss-lock purse, supplied by Mitsukoshi. The film does not use Masako's body to market the firm's Western dresses, coats and hats, but still highlights her role as a housewife with a 'cultured lifestyle', as defined by her accessories and her domestic surroundings.

Masako's family home is a huge, Western-style, detached house in vast grounds, furnished entirely with elaborate Western furniture. Her stepdaughter also benefits from the 'cultured lifestyle' sold by Mitsukoshi: she first appears onscreen playing in a lush garden with a European-style China doll and a Western-style toy kitchen set; her hair is in a short bowl-cut, and she wears a simple, sailor-collared Western dress. Masako's surroundings closely resemble the model of Western-style home and family living described in publications such as Shiseido's *Pocket Book for Women*. Mitsukoshi was using the domestic setting, together with the archetype of the housewife to market not only home- and family- targeted items, but also Western-style accessories for the middle-class housewife herself. This was consistent with Mitsukoshi's educational exhibitions in their stores. In these, the female spectator was able both to acquire 'knowledge' of Western-style homewares and lifestyles and to learn how to consume effectively so as to transform her family surroundings into the ideal that appeared onscreen and in print. These in-store exhibitions resembled the cinema itself:

> Department stores also sought to provide scaled-down versions of spectacular spaces, catalogues of the world of goods … The practical sensibilities needed in order to know what to buy, how to consume it, how to wear it, how to put it in an ensemble, a suitable context with other goods, were complex. In short, this required the effort to learn a new type of 'good taste'. To learn and naturalise a new set of sensibilities with which to organise experience, along with the skill of how to juggle this in relation to existing ones, which still operated. To this end, department stores provided learning spaces and pedagogies through a variety of activities, along with suitable narratives, on what it meant to be modern in the Japanese sense. (Tamari 2006, 103)

The cinema intensified this education in consumption, extending the female spectator's desire to 'own' not only the actress's bodily presentation, but her onscreen family environment. The film shows scenes of the immaculately dressed child gleefully playing with her ornate toys, sneaking out of her bedroom to join Masako in her own elaborate Western-style bedroom, ensconced in soft lighting and surrounded by elegant furnishings. This was family bliss as a lavish, purchasable environment. The film provided an immersive example of how a spectator could use commodities to transform her real-life situation, presenting it not only as a desirable middle-class environment, but as moral instruction. Masako embodies this 'blending' of the lure of the star and the respectability of the middle-class housewife, as depicted in exhibition spaces and print media. She was an 'acceptable "it" girl', living a virtuous existence in Westernised, consumerist spaces and enjoying the use of selected, Western-style goods, without the stigma of the wholly Westernised Modern Girl archetype.

The choice of Tsukuba Yukiko to play the role of Masako reinforced this blending of archetypes. Scouted as a sixteen-year-old performing in Fukuzawa Momosuke's Imperial Theatre by Shōchiku's Kido Shirō, images from Tsukuba's earlier career from 1924 depict her in a Bow-like manner, wearing short hair, Western clothing, and cosmetics (*Kinema junpō* 1980, 456–7). A June 1928 *Play and Movie* article, however, suggests a more complex star persona. It begins by portraying Tsukuba as a beautiful, but accessible figure. Having long wanted to appear on the stage of the Kabuki-za theatre, she finally achieved her goal:

> After the curtain fell, her alluring figure appeared in the corridor of the Kabuki-za with the appearance of someone who had just taken a bath, wearing a *yukata* and with her hair tied in an effortless bundle. And so, with a friendly charm, she sweetly wound her way through the crowd – many of her fans were truly taken aback by both the beauty of her face and body and her elegant manner. (*The Play and Movie* 1928, 10)

Despite her beauty, the article emphasises her difference from the distant, almost disembodied image of the successful star. 'Her face was clear. Yet, her crooked lips distorted its uniformity.' This image of a desirable but imperfect, approachable star is consistent with Tsukuba's role as hybridised housewife in *No Blood Relation* – a star, but one with 'everyday' qualities, so as not to threaten gender and societal norms, her 'imperfect' facial features drawing her closer to the female spectator-as-consumer who can identify with her onscreen. However, the author also notes her preference for certain kinds of onscreen roles, admiring the 'vamp' figures aligned with the Modern Girl archetype, typecast in 'concubine roles', and playing characters with an 'evil woman's face'. He suggests that she was not suited to these, since she could not pull off the necessary 'style of makeup' and was, besides, too innately 'sweet'. But he suggests that this risqué element to Tsukuba's star persona was mimicked in real life, detailing her failed attempt to found her own production company with fellow Shōchiku star Moroguchi Tsuzuya, with whom it was alleged she was having an affair. On screen and in person, Tsukuba was neither entirely the wholesome girl-next-door, not the vampish, dangerous Modern Girl. *No Blood Relation* thus featured two actresses who had pushed against the boundaries of social norms and the film industry. While Okada's role as exiled actress was consistent with her star persona, following her abandonment of her role in Murata Minoru's adaptation of *La Traviata*, Tsukuba's role as hybridised housewife made no reference to her public transgressions.

Her casting in *No Blood Relation* was not Tsukuba's first foray into marketing a blended aesthetic. In October 1927 Tsukuba appeared as a model in *Shufu no tomo*, advertising an exhibition organised by the publication to 'represent this autumn's new trends' (*Shufu no tomo* 1927, 15). The exhibition focused on *meisen* silk kimono from the Isesaki region, suitable 'for sunny days or frosty days', on the surface a conventionally Japanese outfit choice (*Shufu no tomo* 1927).

Figure 4.2 Image of actress Tsukuba Yukiko advertising an exhibition of autumn fashions, *Shufu no tomo*, October 1927.

However, Francks notes that *meisen* silk was developed in the 1890s as a cheaper alternative to conventional silk. 'By the 1910s, power looms . . . and a new method of dyeing . . . made possible the production of highly coloured and patterned, but relatively cheap, clothing fabric'. The *meisen* kimono thus 'provided the vehicle by means of which to introduce the techniques of the fashion system to the marketing of Japanese-style clothing . . . [bringing] the concept of the mass-market fashion item to a wide market of inter-war consumers'. The vibrant, bright designs of *meisen* kimono were often influenced by Western fashion trends, such as art deco, and as a result 'the *meisen* label could be attached to anything from cheap-and-cheerful mass market silk kimono to the high fashion outfit of the "modern girl"' (Francks 2012, 168–9). Like the blended East-meets-West persona of Tsukuba herself, and the hybrid approach of Mitsukoshi and Shiseido's advertising, *meisen* kimono managed to blend Western and Japanese dress aesthetics, appealing to both the thrifty housewife demographic via their low prices and the fashion-oriented woman who wanted to incorporate a Western aesthetic into her dress ensemble.

This was evident in the 1927 advertisement in which Tsukuba appears (Figure 4.2). All seven designs on the opposite page use bold colour, with a distinct art deco influence: a particularly striking example features a mottled pale pink and green background studded with playing card suits. The image of Tsukuba accompanying the advertisement reinforces the idea of a bright, eye-catching Japanese garment, placed firmly within a Westernised space, with the model acting almost as an intermediary, revealing a blend of these attributes. Just as in *No Blood Relation*, five years later, Tsukuba is pictured in a lavish Western-style living room, gazing into a large birdcage inhabited by two green parrots. The cage itself rests on an art deco wicker table, together with an open book, suggesting an educated middle-class housewife. The image is in vibrant full colour, and the emphasis is clearly on Tsukuba's kimono, which has a bold, bright, triangular pattern. Accentuating the Western theme, her hair is in a chignon, her face is powdered, and she wears a pink-toned lipstick and multiple gold rings on her fingers. She leans on a wooden chair, upholstered in another vibrant blue and green deco-style fabric and accented with a sumptuous red velvet cushion. Despite its humble price point, the *meisen* kimono was being marketed as suitable for wear within the educated middle-class home. Tsukuba's hybridised star persona allowed her to represent a glamorous but socially acceptable consumer archetype.

This usage of a 'blended' female consumer archetype to market Western-style goods – enabled not by bodily adornment alone, but by a *partially* adorned body within Westernised surroundings – echoes the thinking of Kobayashi Ichizō, who was involved in multiple business ventures focused upon the female consumer, including consumer exhibitions, the all-female Takarazuka Revue theatrical troupe, founded in 1913, and a beauty salon and college in Tokyo's Nihon Theatre in 1937 (Robertson 1999, 387).

> Every woman could be a well-coiffed and costumed star, so long as she shone on the home stage ... The problem with the Modern Girl is that she would *go* shopping – an occasion for flanerie – instead of *do* the shopping – an occasion for linking the household's economy to the capitalist private sector and the state ... Inside the Takarazuka auditorium ... the 'masses', and female aficionadas especially, were recast as consumers, and the commodities on sale ... became part of the machinery of modern Japanese citizenship. (Robertson 1999, 387–8, emphasis as in original)

Robertson places attitudes and marketing practices such as Kobayashi's within the context of female citizenship, particularly in reference to the state-promoted trope 'good wife and wise mother' (*ryōsai kenbo*) (Robertson 1999, 384). This concept of performing 'on the home stage' via clothing, cosmetics and accessories spatially transports the act of shopping from the self-centred domain of the Modern Girl to this state-approved sphere of monogamous marriage, which according to Kobayashi and his peers 'constituted the only legitimate context for female consumer citizenship' (Robertson 1999, 388). In contrast to the superficial consumerism of the Modern Girl, an onscreen reminder that 'females acting on their own behalf outside of the household, or outside of the context of marriage, were regarded by the state as socially disruptive and anomalous' (Robertson 1999, 388), Kobayashi actively encouraged household-based performance as a female duty rather than a self-indulgent extravagance.

An overt example of this on the screen appears in Gosho Heinosuke's *The Groom Talks in His Sleep* (*Hanamuko no negoto*, 1933), a comedy which follows the middle-class life of an infatuated newlywed couple. Yukiko (Kawasaki Hiroko) and Yasuo (Hasegawa Kazuo) are deeply in love, to the extent that their displays of affection arouse the jealousy of Yasuo's co-worker Tamura (Kobayashi Tokuji), whose own wife Chikako (Shinobu Setsuko) is a shrewish nag who even scolds him for peeling too many onions. One such display centres on Yukiko presenting her new hairstyle to her husband – again, a neat chignon, but this time the style's consumerist associations are heightened by the addition of a thoroughly Western accessory, an ornate, rhinestone hair slide. Until this point, Yukiko has only worn a kimono and conventional Shimada coiffure, accented with Japanese hairpins, but now she weas a housewife's apron and a new Western hairstyle. It is clear that Yukiko is enjoying her latest beauty treatment, and that this enjoyment is partially female-focused. Before Yasuo returns home, she asks her maid Kiyoya – herself a marker of middle-class life (Sakai 2008, 31) – 'What do you think of my new hairdo?' 'It looks perfect.' The ensuing scene when Yasuo returns home entails all the markers of the housewife as consumer: he brings her a gift – a magazine, wrapped in paper – and exclaims that her new hairstyle is 'so beautiful'. The contrast with her former 'Japanese' self is made clear as she shows off her new chignon, next to a photograph of her in her Shimada coiffure. Yukiko assumes the role of the female star within her home as she poses for photographs. The connotations of the scene, and the association of the feminine with consumerism, are cemented when Yasuo almost drinks a bottle of Club cosmetics facial milk. The product is mentioned by name. 'Ah, so *that's* what keeps you looking so beautiful,' Yasuo remarks, as the camera focuses upon Yukiko's complexion. The product placement is again clear. However, in contrast to the examples in the previous chapter, which took place in the city, illuminated by neon lighting – the natural habitat of the Modern Girl – this time the branded product appears within the home, alongside other housewife staples such as the magazine and a Western chignon hairstyle, as a commercial product conducive to marital bliss.

Like Tsukuba Yukiko, Kawasaki Hiroko was an actress with a blended star persona, appearing as early as 1929 in Shimizu Hiroshi's Shōchiku short, *Stick Girl*, as one of the 'stick girls' of the title. This was an unequivocally Modern Girl role, stick girls being 'female gigolos who like walking sticks attached themselves to men', cited by Tanizaki Jun'ichirō as one of the things that most disappointed him about the post-earthquake Westernisation of Tokyo (Slade 2009, 112). The film is no longer extant, but stills and short reviews published in *Eiga jōhō* suggest that it addressed topical issues concerning gender and sexuality among young men and women in Tokyo and served largely as a vehicle to market Shōchiku's latest crop of both male and female stars. Kawasaki herself does not appear in the stills, but her female co-stars and fellow 'stick girls', Tamaki Yasuko and Tatsuta Shizue, both appear in full Western dress with bobbed hair, exhibiting all of the key markers of the Modern Girl aesthetic. Tamaki is pictured sitting on a bench wearing a short skirt and high heels, with her lower leg fully exposed, with a dark-coloured lipstick and a cloche hat. Tatsuta also wears a cloche hat and cosmetics and draws her fur-trimmed coat close to her body while riding in a motorcar. Both of the women are romantically engaged, rather than housewifely partners: Tatsuta leans in cheek-to-cheek with her male co-star Yūki Ichirō in the motorcar; Tamaki is seated on a bench with her arm around the smartly dressed Nishikiori Takeshi, as Yūki looks on jealously. The review accompanying the stills notes: 'New women have appeared on the Ginza streets who say that for just an hour – for a price – we can take a stroll together, as I look so lonely alone. We call them "Stick Girls". This is perfectly captured by . . . this 'Modern Nonsense' film (*Eiga jōhō* 1929, 28).

Yet the following year Kawasaki took a role much closer to her housewifely persona in *The Groom Talks in His Sleep*, that of the virtuous Yasue in Ozu's *Walk Cheerfully* (*Hogaraka ni ayume*, 1930). Yasue is a kimono-clad maiden with a Western chignon, replete with diamante hair slide, who refuses expensive jewellery offered to her by her boss. Like Masako, she is a virtuous working woman, a stark contrast to her Modern Girl opposite, gangster moll Chieko (Date Satoko) who conspicuously applies face powder from a compact at her desk. Yasue assists her widowed mother with her household duties, including the care of her younger sister. Her virtue is such that Chieko's gangster boyfriend Kenji (Takada Minoru) chooses to leave her and his life of crime behind, becoming a window cleaner in order to win Yasue's love. This effort to 'go straight' is impeded by Chieko convincing the police to arrest Kenji, but Yasue promises to wait for his return, further cementing their union. The transformation from individualistic delinquent to productive family member is achieved at the film's climax. Yasue is arranging flowers, wearing a housewife's apron, boiling a kettle, and admiring bottles of Western cider and beer in the room that was formerly the gangsters' hangout. Kenji returns from prison and embraces Yasue and her sister, in a pastiche of the image of a husband or father returning home. Even though Yasue is not yet married, she already embodies a 'good wife and wise mother': her relationship with Kenji has already produced a productive household unit.

From these examples it is clear that the East-meets-West hybridity of the middle-class housewife aesthetic offered an approachable alternative to the Westernised aesthetic of the Modern Girl. While borrowing some elements of her aesthetics, it presented an opportunity to combine cinematic spectacle and everyday experience, informing both the silver screen and the family home. Middle-class 'household performance', facilitated by the purchase of onscreen goods and beauty practices, can be seen as a restrictive female ideal for audience members, but it offered flexibility in regard to the star personae of some actresses, and diversified the appeal of Western-style fashion products such as cosmetics, accessories, and hairstyling apparatus. Actresses and commodities could transition seamlessly and marketably between the archetypes of the single woman and the middle-class family, reaching not only female consumers, but their husbands and children.

Utilising the image of the 'good wife and wise mother' to market to the family via the middle-class female can be seen to be both a commercial and state interest. Robertson suggests that consumption was a distinctly female endeavour, nurtured by the state as a duty both to the family home and the military state, which 'exploited a perceived link between consumer citizenship and eugenic citizenship, the latter of which was also expressed in terms of "pure blood" [*junketsu*] and the concomitant necessity of "mental hygiene"'.

She also suggests that the concept of familial 'hygiene' was transferred to the actual female body, the betterment of which became a subject of consumer exhibition (and corporate sponsorship).

> [S]pecial attention was paid ... to the improvement of female bodies, which were evaluated and measured according to a physical aesthetic of 'healthy body beauty' [*kenkōbi*]. Numerous healthy body beauty contests were staged in the 1930s, including the Miss Nippon contests of 1931 and 1934 ... jointly sponsored by the *Asahi shimbun* and Takashimaya department store. (Robertson 1999, 389)

At first sight, using a sponsored beauty contest as means to encourage women to nurture their bodies (and by proxy those of the whole nation) may appear incongruous alongside the ideal of the middle-class housewife. It was, after all, the Modern Girl archetype who was known for displaying her bodily form, alongside her consumerist tendencies, and using fitted Western clothing to do this. The association between Western clothing and bodily form, and the contrast with middle-class family life, became a feature of Shiseido's vision of the Modern Girl, as discussed in 1926:

> a woman must decide to wear Western clothing for herself. Western clothing fits closely to the natural body. Women wearing the latest Western clothing seem almost foreign; you can see the elegance of their natural body. (*Shiseido geppō* 1926, 6)

The Miss Nippon beauty contests also coincided with prominent film events, which firmly situated the beauty contest alongside the European cinematic image of an actress's unclothed bodily form. The Japanese release of the Louise Brooks film *Prix De Beauté* (*Miss Europe*, 1930) was extensively advertised in double-page spreads in film magazines such as *Kinema junpō*, featuring close-up scenes of Brooks undressing as she puts on her bathing suit, provided by the French fashion house Maison Alexandre. The Nikkatsu film *Miss Nippon*, released in April 1931, also emphasised the Modern Girl image, rather than eugenic family-oriented ideals.

Miss Nippon starred Japan's own Modern Girl archetype, the actress Irie Takako, who also modelled Western clothing for department stores, including Mitsukoshi. A still from the film in *Eiga jōhō* (*The Movie Pictorial*) depicts a typical Modern Girl, wearing only Western attire, including a striped headscarf, with bobbed hair peeking beneath, a matching scarf, and bold cosmetics, standing behind a sofa upon which two men in Western-style suits are seated, gazing up at her. The accompanying caption notes: 'Itō Takako (Irie Takako) is a woman representing modern Japan, but she is in love with the wholly un-modern poor company worker Yūkichi (Izome Shirō)' (*Eiga jōhō* 1930, 21). The film's plot depicts the Modern Girl as a consumerist working woman, disrupting the productive heterosexual unions advocated by the state with her romantic drive and multiple relationships:

> Irie Takako is . . . 'Miss Nippon', the young, pretty, smartly dressed director of a company in the Marunouchi building, who with wealth, beauty and youth at her command goes after life and gets mostly what she wants, except the biggest prize she seeks, the young serious-minded and hard-working draftsman employed in her office . . . (*The Japan Times* 1931, 3)

Irie's character is intended to serve as a 'type' within the complex network of romantic relationships, to be contrasted with other female archetypes. While the film did not contain a beauty contest, the Westernised Modern Girl's body is crucial to its desired appeal. The cover of the sheet music for the title song features an illustration of a curvaceous female nude, with bobbed hair, stockings and black high heels, in clear reference to Irie's screen image. The similarity between Irie's onscreen role and her public persona, and between her character's name (Itō Takako) and her own, echoes Louise Brooks' role in *Miss Europe* two years earlier, in which she is referred to as 'Lulu', a nickname which had stuck since her appearance in *Pandora's Box* (1929). *Miss Europe* and *Miss Nippon* focused not only on the actresses' bodies and personae within the film, but on these same qualities off-screen. Given this association of the Miss Nippon brand with the Modern Girl image, as well as the emphasis of the beauty contest on the public exhibition of the female body, it is difficult to see how it could be aligned with the ideal of healthy, educated, middle-class wives advocated by the Japanese state.

Nonetheless, these contests were able to combine the lure of the cinematic (and its related consumerism) with a socially acceptable, 'selfless' image of the Japanese female, whose physical fitness and 'hygienic' qualities benefited not only her family – as with the housewife emulating the cinematic performer in her own home – but a wider Japanese future. The state was directly involved in the creation of these contexts, which were a way of presenting the 'results' of eugenics initiatives since the mid-1920s, to be judged by middle-aged male judges, ranging from a physician and a girls' school principal to visual artists (Robertson 2001, 15). The rhetoric of 'healthy body beauty' was not a new phenomenon in the 1930s. The term *kenkōbi* was in use as early as 1924. An advertisement in *Fujin sekai* included 'tips to lose weight, gain weight, improve muscle tone or complexion for those who wish to become beautiful' (*Asahi shimbun* 1924, 1). The Miss Nippon contest thus reflected the culturally and institutionally hybrid character of New Japan to an even greater extent than the hybridised female Japanese star. The 'standard' by which the women were judged relied not only on 'purity of spirit and blood', but also a 'body that met the classical Greek standards of shape and proportion'. A British man, Glenn Shaw, was appointed to provide an 'objective perspective' due to his own lack of Japanese national heritage (Robertson 2001, 15–16). This concept of a 'Western' bodily appearance might appear to be the realm of Kido Shirō's 'actresses with beautiful shapely legs' (*kyakusenbi joyū*), but the entry requirements excluded 'girls whose professions depend on their figures', including actresses (Robertson 2001, 1). The ideal marketed here and sponsored by corporate entities such as the Takashimaya department store was a woman who seamlessly melded the ordinary and the extra-ordinary: a woman who was Japanese, but with a Western bodily appearance. The Westernised Japanese body was not just the individualist, barren project of the consumerist Modern Girl. Consumption was presented here as a way of performing a woman's public procreative duty: the hybridised female body itself became the desirable product.

These ideals were not wholly at odds with the aims of Japan's cinematic studios. On 18 February 1931, the same year as the initial Miss Nippon contest, Shōchiku held a beauty contest of its own. This appeared on the front page of *The Japan Times*, headlined 'exotic beauties passé in Japanese films this year; healthy types preferred'. The contrast was expressed in terms of Hollywood archetypes: 'girls ape Clara Bow and Janet Gaynor, but lay off Greta Garbo', with an accompanying photograph of the entrants in swimsuits noting that 'girls not of the "erotic" but of the healthy type were chosen'. Like the *Miss Nippon* contest, the selection process was pseudo-scientific, including measuring the entrants' bodies, observing their performance in swimsuits, and testing them on 'oral intelligence', supposedly to assess their 'healthiness' inside and out. The reward for the winners was 'minor roles in their debut in the movies'. Alongside the obligatory university doctors and physicians, the judges included a 'leading woman novelist . . . three sportsmen. . . . [and] Kamata studio officials and actors' (*The Japan Times* 1931, 1), blending genders and the official and popular spheres. The Shōchiku contest presented the cinema as a vehicle for Japanese versions of 'healthy' Hollywood stars, facilitating rather than hindering state ideals. Rather than 'ideal' bodies selected as didactic archetypes by state representatives, the public was encouraged to emulate the participants' figures at a quasi-'peer' level, by aspirational rather than authoritative figures. The fit, hybridised female body was a desirable 'product' promoted by the state, but Shōchiku's beauty contest advertised the same product via the cinema and star system, just as it marketed consumer goods for Club and Mitsukoshi. As in the cinema, so in the contest: the female spectator could imagine her own body receiving the approval of both men and women, emulating the romantic and familial relationships presented onscreen. For the male spectator, the clear alignment of the fit bodies of 'ordinary' Japanese women with successful Hollywood figures transferred the allure of the female screen star to the everyday female Japanese citizen, providing that she complied with the eugenic standards promoted by the contest.

Not every beauty contest was based on the new Western-inspired, but still 'Japanese', healthy beauty ideals, nor did audiences always welcome the prospect of Western-style Japanese actresses being selected purely based upon their merit as 'healthy body beauties'. *Eiga jōhō* published an anonymous article on the Shōchiku contest (accompanied by Figures 4.3 and 4.4), concluding that 'the result was very disappointing'. 'Before, actresses with beautiful shapely legs were recruited at Kamata, but from this point on these so-called "film actresses" simply lack sophistication' (*Eiga jōhō* 1931, 13). It is also clear that, despite the promotion of the beauty contest as an element of the state's eugenic project, contests were still held which served purely as consumerist spectacles, in line with the Modern-Girl connotations initially applied to such events, and that the Modern-Girl-esque female image remained popular with some audiences.

An advertisement for the Universal Studios film *The Good Fairy* (1935) was accompanied by a 'competition announcement':

> The original story of 'The Good Fairy' has a heroine (Margaret Sullivan) who is a female worker in an unusual cinema building. We at Universal, who sponsor this original story, wish the very best for all female cinema workers in this country and everywhere, and so we have decided to hold a contest, subject to the regulations listed to the left, to find the quintessential 'Miss Movie-House Beauty'. (*Kinema junpō* 1935, 22)

Rather than celebrating the 'healthy body' of the Japanese woman, the contest instead celebrated not only the working woman's body but her role in the space of the cinema, aligning the everyday Japanese female subject's body with that of the specifically Western screen star. She is lauded for her independence rather than her duty to family and procreation. Her emulation of the star is not conducted at home, but in public. Like the Miss Nippon and Shōchiku pageants, Universal employed a range of judges, both male and female. All were Japanese, from various backgrounds, but all had links to Western-style popular arts and media, suggesting a similar hybridity as the other contests, but for a distinctly different aim. They included artist and illustrator Iwata Sentarō, known for his portraits of beautiful women; author and jazz critic Shioiri Kamesuke; the film critic Tanaka Saburo; and the writer Okada Saburo, who wrote the story that would later become Mizoguchi's *Osaka Elegy*. The only judge directly related to a film studio or an American organisation was Itō Tatsuo, in charge of United Artists' Japanese operations. The only female judges were the dancer Takada Seiko, who had studied ballet in New York

Figures 4.3–4.4 Contestants at the Shōchiku Studios beauty contest, *Eiga jōhō*, March 1931. Courtesy of Kokusai Jōhōsha.

(Akoh 2002), and the Shōchiku actress Okada Yoshiko. The contest took place only a year following Okada's appearance in *Our Neighbour, Miss Yae* (1934), as the miserable divorcee sister of the protagonist, a striking contrast to the glamorised working woman celebrated by the contest. The judges were listed 'in no particular order' (*Kinema junpō* 1935, 22). Crucially, 'health'-oriented figures – the doctors, physicians and sportsmen who anchored the committees in the other contests – were absent. The Universal contest hinged on personal status and gain. The contestant's beauty was measured in terms of her ability to resemble the star in a 'real' setting. Applicants were to submit a 'recent photograph with a good likeness, rather than one which is just flattering'. The contest would compare these photos to the 'real-life product' [*genpin*] and the winners would be rewarded with either with a cash prize (fifty yen for First Prize, twenty yen for two Second Prizes) or 'a year's subscription to a women's magazine of your choice' (for the five Runner-Up winners). The Universal contest was neither a state-mandated, health-oriented spectacle, like the Miss Nippon contest, nor a way of using state rhetoric to film products in order to make them more 'Japanese', like the Shōchiku event. On the one hand, it suggested co-operation between the American and Japanese film industries, in celebrating the consumerism of the single working woman, who was to be rewarded as a beautiful 'product', carved in the screen star's image. Hollywood and Japanese cinemas were equal partners in the transnational landscape. While primarily a commercial attraction to garner audiences, the contest also performed a diplomatic role, implying Universal's desire to be seen to be in support of not only Japan's domestic film industry, but its imperial project, despite rising anti-Japanese sentiments in the United States. The contest is described as aimed at women 'from anywhere in the country [Japan], including Suzhou, Kantoshu and Shanghai', acknowledging these Japanese-occupied territories in China as part of Japan itself (*Kinema junpō* 1935, 22).

The various beauty contests in Japan held fluid connotations, but at their core they were tied intimately to consumer images and their allusions to the female star body as archetype. The beauty contest allowed the agency hosting it to impress their agenda upon the female image via a process of hybridisation. The Modern Girl, be she Hollywood- or Japan- based, was melded with the ordinary Japanese woman, generating profit while propagating ideology ideals, with 'healthy body beauty' being just one of these possible marketable attributes.

Notes

1. Shintō describes a set of beliefs and practices indigenous to Japan. The word '*Shintō*' literally means 'the way of the *kami*', a Japanese word for divine power and specifically gods and deities, distinct from Buddhism, which was introduced to Japan in the sixth century CE.

2. Kon's characterisation of cosmetics as 'Western' is curious given the history of cosmetics in Japan. Cho Kyo documents the use of powder to whiten the complexion in *The Tale of Genji* in the eleventh century and suggests this was Chinese-inspired (Kyo 2012, 24). The Japan Cosmetics Industry Association adds that during the Edo period (1600–1868) the repertoire of female cosmetics expanded to include lip rouge, nail varnish and eyebrow pencil, with companies such as Bien Senjoko marketing these via tie-ins with *ukiyo-e* prints, indicating that neither these products themselves nor their advertising were inherently Western influenced (Japan Cosmetics Industry, 2017). Kon doesn't say why he thinks using cosmetics is 'Western' practice. Given the contemporary prevalence of brands such as Club and Shiseido, which used Western-style advertisements, it may be he is mainly referring to the use of mass-marketed, clearly Western-influenced products such as these.
3. *Yōfuku* is a generic Japanese term simply meaning 'Western clothing', with no specific details or origin, as opposed to *wafuku*, the generic term simply for 'Japanese clothing'.

Chapter 5

Women and the sporting body

The Shōchiku beauty contest, with its reliance on male sports personalities and both male and female films stars as judges, raises the question of how fashion and sport intersected to promote a fit, hybridised female aesthetic onscreen. The sporting world, together with images promoting bodily health and fitness, were a key junction for the Modern Girl and middle-class housewife archetypes. As explored in Part I of this book, the image of the Modern Girl included her incarnation as a nubile female student. The addition of sportswear to star dress ensembles allowed the female form to be presented at its most physically expressive, in exaggerated physical motion, and, in the case of the swimsuit and other revealing costumes such as the tennis skirt, bodily exposed. Superficially, this aligned the female sporting body with the Modern Girl. However, as with the hybridised housewife aesthetic and the fit, 'Western-style' body advocated by the state, 'Modern-Girl-esque' factors gained new connotations when transferred to different contexts. The significations of the sporting female body and its sartorial markers were fluid.

Sportswear was 'occasion wear', a genre made possible by the industrial revolution, which weakened 'the seasonal imperatives of the agricultural calendar' and imposed 'a new and more rigid demarcation between "work" and "leisure"'. 'There was a move from display to identity . . . individuals participated in a process of self-docketing and self-announcement, as dress became the vehicle for the display of the unique individual personality' (Wilson 2011, 155). In both Japanese and Hollywood cinema, sportswear could be aligned with the Modern Girl, but also with affluent middle-class leisure and the sports activities possible in a university environment, both implying sufficient wealth for leisure or higher education. By choosing sports-related fashion items, the female Japanese subject could appear not only as middle-class and educated, but also eugenically 'fit'. Many of the Miss Nippon pageant winners 'were active sportswomen . . . most[ly] from middle class households'. Gōto Keiko, the 1934 winner, was an avid tennis player, presented in print media 'modelling Western-style sportswear as well as a kimono' (Robertson 2001, 24). What was being consumed was the *image* of a prosperous, educated middle-class lifestyle, rather than actual physical commodities. Tipton notes, 'Many members of the new middle class struggled financially during the 1920s . . . They were often no more than "*poor people dressed in Western clothes*," the lifestyle portrayed for them by the mass media and advertisements remaining as elusive for them as for most Japanese' (Tipton 2008, 107, my emphasis). The gap between the lifestyle of the star and that of a majority of the audience would have heightened the attraction of the affluent lifestyle portrayed onscreen. As Marshall McLuhan noted, 'the movie . . . offers as product the most magical of consumer commodities, namely dreams . . . [it] has excelled as a medium that offers poor people roles of riches and power . . . in the 1920s . . . the world lined up to buy canned dreams' (quoted in Jenkins 2014, 59). In Britain, for example, sport and the cinema were the key leisure activities of the working classes during the 1920s and 1930s, but access was 'sharply divided'. 'Not all people could participate as equal consumers . . . cinema became the major form of leisure for the working class in general . . .' (Horne, Tomlinson and Whannel 1999, 244).

Cinema was thus an affordable alternative to sporting activities, which were out of reach for the majority of the audience. It provided an affordable window into the sporting activities imported from Hollywood and the affluent middle-class 'cultured life' advocated by the state and mass media. Weisenfeld shows how sport was blended with other consumerist spheres. A February 1934 advertisement for the Morinaga confectionery company featured:

> the simple double image of a happy young woman in a smart ski outfit with her cap jauntily cocked to one side placed next to the name of the milk chocolate product . . . The image reinforces the copy that proclaims Morinaga chocolate as a perfect treat to share with a friend when one hits the slopes to engage in winter sports . . . Combining disparate spheres of consumption, in this case food and sports, was an effective tactic of doubling pleasurable expectations. (Weisenfeld 2009, 16–17)

Weisenfeld suggests this advertisement was effective due to the economically challenging context: 'chocolate . . . offer[ed] much needed healthy calories for the still comparatively undernourished Japanese population . . . for contemporary audiences, eating chocolate and skiing were both healthy activities'. The visual composition of the advert 'tripl[ed] the leisure connotations by alluding to entertainment in moving pictures' (Weisenfeld 2009, 17). Sporting images – particularly the sportswear-clad figure – became a signifier for an affluent middle-class lifestyle, with the cinema both delivering and further 'glamorising' this image.

Sportswear's ability to span media formats and commodity iconography meant it could convey the 'educational' aspect of Western sports to the Japanese populace. The Japanese government was keen to impress the value of sports and leisure time: a 1923 Osaka City Government survey of 'Leisure Lifestyles' concluded that sport would 'unleash creative energy' and 'promote a more "civilised" populace' (Leheny 2000, 175). The changing government attitude towards Western-style sports was made evident in print media:

> In September 1911, the Tokyo Asahi Shimbun ran a series of articles entitled 'Yakyū sono Gaidoku' (Baseball and Its Evil Effects) ... Baseball, it was argued, had four principal vices: (1) it consumed time that could be better put to use for studies; (2) it resulted in severe fatigue among the players and prevented them from studying and pursuing other activities; (3) its games were frequently followed by parties and dinners where the players (even the students) would drink alcohol; and (4) its play, such as pitching and hitting, relied on 'unnatural' motions or activities. (Leheny 2000, 176)

Yet by the mid-1920s the Ministry of Education, alongside the Ministry of Home Affairs, was sponsoring youth baseball and sporting contests for school-age students, stressing instead that baseball illustrated the virtue of 'teams that fought together for a common goal, and a spirit of self-purity that derived specifically from its being an amateur sport' (Leheny 2000, 176). An article published in *The Japan Times* in 1930 noted that 'the present most popular and most effective sports are almost all what may be called "Western" ... Track meets, tennis tournaments, baseball series, rowing races and such like are very common events in the life of Young Japan' (Clement 1930, 3). The article compared these to male-focused, 'aristocratic' Japanese sports, such as 'fencing and archery', noting that the Western sports appealed to women, encouraging them to socialise and compete with their male peers. It also notes how Western sport could be easily adapted to the Japanese context via substitution and language: 'the real national game of Japan is baseball. In the street of a large city or a small town or in country districts, one may see boys (and even girls) with bat (stick) and ball calling out "*wan sutoraiki*," "*tsu bāru*", "*outo*"[1] ... special mention should be made of what athletics has done for the Japanese girl student, who is now strong, healthy and vigorous ... a Japanese girl, Miss Hitomi, holds three world records' (Clement 1930, 3).

Women were being targeted as consumers by the film, fashion and print media industries, bolstered by government initiatives intended to strengthen the modern Japanese family unit. Harootunian notes, however, that the increasing number of working women, unconstrained by the household unit, meant that the idea of 'cultural living' resulted in 'the establishment of a "feminine culture"'. Sport, alongside education, was a formerly 'male preserve' that allowed some women to escape the 'seclusion and isolation women had experienced as virtual prisoners of the household' (Harootunian 2011, 17). 'Leisure-related policies . . . were contradictory and meandering', united by 'a preoccupation with the meaning of leisure: what kind of recreation would be good for the Japanese, and whether leisure ought to be modern (i.e., Western) or traditional' (Leheny 2000, 176). The cinema did not provide an answer, but it did provide a stage on which 'Western' sports could be represented within a Japanese and/or traditional context. Just as in Part I the promotional materials for Shiseido equipped the housewife with the knowledge of the Western-style household goods she needed in order to appear 'educated', so the cinema allowed all sexes and classes to engage with sport, regardless of their economic means – an engagement which could be furthered via the viewing and purchasing of sports-related fashion objects.

Sportswear thus functioned as a signifier of consumption, rather than as a 'uniform' for an activity, foreshadowing the post-industrial, occasion-based fashion system: 'images of desire are constantly in circulation; increasingly it has been the image as well as the artefact that the individual has purchased . . . fashion is a magical system, and what we see as we leaf through glossy magazines is "the look"'(Wilson 2011, 157). Sportswear on screen or on a star's body became another site where the two 'magical' systems of film and fashion entwined. The featuring of sportswear onscreen successfully reproduced an iconographic aspect of the 'canned' American way of life, but domestic productions using Japanese stars took this process a step further, placing these Western-style sporting goods and practices in an idealised version of the everyday lives of the Japanese subject. The Modern Girl and Modern Boy were both depicted onscreen wearing sporting 'looks', albeit with diverse audience effects, given the conflict between the sporting world's association with state-mandated 'healthiness' and the Modern Girl and Boy's connotations of frivolousness:

> In images of Modern Boys and Modern Girls, there is a lightness sparkling on the edges of old customs. On the one hand, that lightness is related to 'frivolousness', which has become a derogatory term . . . There were also Modern Girls and Boys . . . who participated in sports . . . in the display of the 'bathing-suit beauties', the healthiness of exercise becomes entwined with eroticism. (Iwamoto 1991, 50)

For the female consumer, though, the fashion objects of the sporting world were markers of middle-class success, enabled by her new-found disposable income, showcasing the new bodily ideal of fitness and mobility, with its attractiveness bolstered by the allure of the screen star. The viewing of the sportswear- or swimsuit-clad form would have inspired mixed feelings among the audience, given the depressed socio-economic climate of the period. Similarly, in Soviet society at the same time, the ideal of a 'sporting life' contributed to a widespread 'rising body image fetish of the 1920s and 1930s', with '[c]lothing . . . simultaneously empowering an individual or group with a sense of identity and dividing people according to status' (Grant 2013, 19). Sportswear could be divisive, both as a status symbol in unstable economic times and due to its role in displaying the body for visual assessment, transferring the logic of the beauty contest to the everyday sphere of the spectator.

The arrival of standard sizing, together with sporting lifestyles and sportswear, allowed for the direct comparison of body types in terms of shape and fitness level. In the Western context, 'as the mass market developed, so did the sizing of garments. This was equally contradictory, for it aimed to individualise garments, yet sorted individuals into groups, and as such could also be seen as part of the increasing uniformity of mass society' (Wilson 2011, 124). Sizing was innate to the mass-marketed, Western clothing experience. Like the beauty contest, it provided a point of comparison for the specificities of the body. The disparity between ready-to-wear and pre-existing sizing norms was even more pronounced in Japan. While its shape and sizing can vary slightly, the kimono is largely a uniform garment, which can be adapted to a variety of different body shapes and sizes without measuring or physically altering the garment to suit the specific contours of the wearer's body. Even in a department store, the kimono shopping experience remained the same. The emphasis was on whether a fabric's pattern and design were suitable for the season or occasion, rather than whether or not it flattered the wearer's body by allowing it to conform to conceptions of an 'ideal' silhouette. In the Takashimaya department store during the 1920s, which originated as a simple kimono drapers (*gofukuten*), despite the addition of display windows, Western-style chairs, and advertising posters, customers continued to follow the fabric-driven consumption practices necessitated by the kimono as a garment. The buyer would 'select designs for fabrics . . . and bolts of cloth were brought for them to inspect' (Sapin 2004, 319–20). Western clothing, however, allowed the viewer and the wearer to 'see the elegance of their natural body' via its fitted silhouette (*Shiseido geppō* 1926, 6). The swimsuit provided the most explicit contrast, and a new way to eroticise the female form. An 1887 woodblock print showcases the difference: two women turn away from each other, the swimsuit-wearing woman reclining on a rock while the kimono-clad figure stands. The latter has the stance and silhouette of conventional prints of beautiful women (*bijinga*), while the Westernised figure draws the eye to her physical form, heightened by the fitted clothing. Prior to Western intervention, Japanese women swam stripped to the waist; the Western bathing suit both clothed and sexualised women's bodies (Downer 2003, 52). The erotic connotations of swimwear persisted into the early twentieth century, as is evident in the beauty contests of the 1930s. Given its new connotations with middle-class affluence, health and fitness, sportswear now provided a way to market Western-style occasion-wear to all genders with varied social positioning.

The categorisation of women's bodies into standardised measurements and body shapes allowed for a culture of comparison, of the Japanese body with the Western body and of the female consumer-as-audience-member with images in film and print media. The former context was clearly illustrated in a 1934 article in on an upcoming beauty contest. The centrepiece is two images, one a close-up of 'Miss France', the other a photo of Gōto Keiko – Miss Nippon – posing in her tennis outfit and a beret with her racquet under her arm. The caption reads: 'Just one month to go until the Miss Europe beauty contest – high hopes for Miss Nippon'. The article focuses on the two women's ability to wear Western clothing, particularly the swimsuit: 'Miss France is a girl with a cheerful appearance, her body is beautifully balanced, and she has blue eyes and blonde hair . . . but coincidentally our own Miss Nippon, who was elected by our *Weekly Asahi* readers, is attracting her own popularity in Paris' (*Asahi shimbun* 1934, 5). The choice to feature a photograph of Gōto in her tennis outfit, rather than one of her modelling kimono, appears to be a source of pride for the author. Sporting competition is transferred to competitive comparison of female bodies, with Gōto representing the physical aptitude of Japanese women on the global stage.

It was largely a male audience who were being encouraged to compare the virtues of the female form. A two-page photo spread, 'On Ōiso's Silver Sands', presents a bevy of bathing beauties from the Shinkō studios, all posing for the camera or engaged in sporting activities (Figure 5.3). Yamaji Fumiko, Miss Kobe 1930, kicks a football around the beach (Figures 5.2 and 5.4). Kuji Yukiko, the star of the sports-themed *Youth Olympics* (1938), stands on a swing, swinging athletically (Figure 5.1). Kuji is lauded both for her strength and physical attributes. 'Swing swing! Small, but strong – the wondrousness of Kuji Yukiko's shapely legs and body' (*Eiga jōhō* 1938, 32). The largest image is a line-up of six actresses, all in the same pose, wearing swimsuits with the same core silhouette, with a tied belt around the waist, highlighting and enhancing the actresses' curvaceous figures. Yamaji stands at the far left of the line-up and is the only one with a swimsuit monogrammed with her initials, in Western order, 'F.Y.'. Yamaji's background as a pageant winner further aligns the image with the beauty contest, while the addition of the monogram underlines the relationship between sportswear and a fit and healthy bodily form.

An article in March 1935 suggested how the monogram as a middle-class fashion trend could be used to align oneself with the sporting world. Monogramming was suitable for both men and women and used on many

Figures 5.1–5.4 Images from a two-page photo spread featuring actresses from the Shinkō studios. Kuji Yukiko swings athletically on a swing while Yamaji Fumiko, in a monogrammed swimsuit, plays with a football on the beach. *Eiga jōhō*, October 1938. Courtesy of Kokusai Jōhōsha.

fashion items: 'The most popular is the handkerchief, but among men white shirts, walking stick handles, cigarette cases, cufflinks, dressing robes etc. are now initialled. For women, initials appear on handbags, gloves, the top pockets of blouses, brooches, hair and dress clips, and, on dresses, anywhere that can be embroidered'. The article adds, 'for a large gentleman's handkerchief, the most important thing is that the initials are boldly embroidered; for ladies, it is best to stay with small examples, for a sporting style' (*Fasshon* 1935, 13). Handkerchiefs are not sportswear, but the association with sport is clear. This was enabled by the monogram's sporting and campus origins. In Europe and Hollywood, it had been popularised by French designer Jean Patou, who founded the first specialised sports couture boutique 'Le Coin Des Sports' in 1925 and created sportswear for prominent tennis stars such as Suzanne Lenglen (Tilbury 2016). Patou's designs featured in French films; he provided the pageant costumes for Louise Brooks in *Miss Europe* (Parrill 2006, 321). His designs suggested the wearer's appreciation of the sporting world, rather than actual participation: 'the women who would see Patou's fashions and advertisements in magazines had no need to chase a ball, dance or play golf… women's primary driver in adopting the new look was to appear "modern"' (Tilbury 2016). This idea of a fashionable rather than functional sporting aesthetic also led Patou to monogram his garments, essentially becoming the first couturier to use a logo, ensuring that those viewing the garment were aware not only of the wearer's affluence, but of their involvement in the sporting and cinematic world invoked by Patou's garments (Shaeffer 2001, 18). The monogram on Yamaji's swimsuit performs a similar role, heightening both her sporting aesthetic, and her incorporation of Western cultural elements into her Japanese star persona.

The 1935 *Fasshon* article compares the practice of monogramming to the Japanese use of a family crest (*mon*) on kimono, identifying the former as the more 'modern' alternative, as a statement of one's 'personality', and suggesting how the Western monogram can be adapted to the Japanese context:

> In Japan, there are people using the family's crest, but the effectiveness of this depends on the crest itself … Ladies, you can use initials almost anywhere … We have provided samples of initial combinations, fonts etc for your reference. However, since this is a foreign practice, the monograms are in three-character groups. Three letters are easy to assemble and will look better, so try making your monogram into three letters. So, you don't have a Christian name? We understand, it's not easy. Try adding one of your boyfriend or girlfriend's initials. (*Fasshon* 1935, 13)

A *mon* denoted the individual's membership of the family unit, but a monogram signalled one's individuality, independence, and romantic affiliations, innate to the plotlines of Hollywood cinema and aligned with the Western-inspired sporting world. Yamaji's monogram only has two characters, removing any overt connotation with a romantic relationship. But, given her persona as a pageant winner and progressive woman – she was known in the 1930s as one of the few women to own her own motorcar and driving licence – the monogram underlines her embodiment as a fit, strong Japanese woman, enjoying the liberties and attractions of the modern world and its sporting accoutrements. This was in line with her other promotional activities. In 1937, Yamaji was featured in a 'stars of today swimming event' hosted in Yokohama, where she and her peers were described as 'mermaids' (*Yomiuri shinbun* 1937, 7). In the *Eiga jōhō* photo spread Yamaji is positioned as an exemplar to whom the other actresses can be compared. The uniform poses allow, and the accompanying text encourages, the reader to compare their bodies: 'All lined up in a row – feet and breasts upon breasts. Whose body is the most attractive? Whose feet are the longest? Who has the most perfectly round breasts? You, male fans, decide the score!!' (*Eiga jōhō* 1938, 32). Despite the allusions to the sporting world and the 'healthy body beauty' rhetoric of the government-supported beauty contest, the images and captions segment the star's body into fetishised, comparable parts.

The 'erotic' and the 'healthy' are constantly combined in presenting the actress's body for the male gaze. In a 1938 image, Ōkawa Momoyo lies on her front at the beach in Enoshima, with an open-backed swimsuit displaying the breadth of her shoulders and the curve of her buttocks. The headline and caption emphasise her 'healthy body beauty' (*Eiga jōhō* 1938, 12). In 1932, a *Kinema junpō* summer photo spread features kimono-clad, Shimada-coiffured actresses, as well as Western-style bathing beauties, but the text only comments on the bodies of the latter. Nikkatsu actress Fushimi Nobuko wears a bathing suit on a sailing boat: 'white sails, white skin; cutely erotic'. Shinkō Eiga's Suzuki Sumiko, 28 years old, with an established reputation as a 'vamp actress', reclines in a swimsuit with her legs extended: 'the beauty of long legs stretched out beneath the bright sunlight – why, oh why, can the new girls starting out on the erotic path never match the pulsing attraction of the screen veterans that they so desperately seek?' The most blatant example is an image of Tōkatsu star Isuzu Keiko, standing on a stairway wearing a swimming hat and swimsuit: 'radiant with beauty, health and youth' (*Kinema junpō* 1932, 28–9). The swimsuit's association with the star body (particularly the Hollywood star body) had existed since its first appearance in Japanese cinema, in Shōchiku's *Amateur Club* (*Amachua Kurabu*, 1920), worn by Hayama Michiko (Tsuneo 1955, 15). Here, too, the swimsuit was a way of directly comparing Hayama's body with the Hollywood star image, via a distinctly sexual gaze. In the opening scene, Hayama appeared in the same style of suit and the exact same pose as an image of Annette Kellerman which had appeared across Japanese print media, producing a '"repetition" of bathing beauties' (LaMarre 2009, 275). Kellerman was an Australian swimming star and international film actress. The relationship between the swimsuit and her body was intrinsic to her star image; she had been one of the first women to wear a one-piece bathing suit in public, rather than full-length pantaloons, and she had designed her own line of swimsuits in 1912 (Schmidt 2008, 97). Kellerman was the first major star to appear nude, in *A Daughter of the Gods* (1916) (Robertson 1993, 9–10). She was also an early female health and fitness advocate, penning a number of mail-order health and beauty manuals during the 1910s, including 'The Body Beautiful' in 1912, which 'promised that . . . every woman could achieve a level of physical beauty that was essential to the wearing of a body-hugging one-piece bathing suit with confidence' (Schmidt 2008, 17). Kellerman was thus an apt template for Hayama's character, Chizuko, in *Amateur Club*, who embodied connotations of both fitness and romance: 'even though Chizuko is a woman of action (exotically tomboyish and even warlike), she can also be a girlfriend' (LaMarre 2009, 275). Hayama's role, as a Japanese facsimile of Kellerman, becomes an invitation to the viewer – particularly the male viewer – to compare the two star bodies. The swimsuit performed a triple role in making female bodies available for the male viewer's comparison, in terms of physical fitness (in line with government initiatives), their proximity to existing film star bodies (originating from the Hollywood and Japanese studio systems) and their eroticism (combining both fitness and filmic models).

However, the female consumer was also meant to engage in bodily comparison, which promised both emancipation and restriction. The print media encouraged the female reader to compare her own body to bodies on screen and of the women around her, represented by other readers. *Fujin gahō*'s 'Style Book' was a seasonal publication advertising Western patterns for purchase by Japanese consumers. The 1934 version contained detailed diagrams comparing different Japanese female body types, both nude and dressed, both to each other and to the Western model depicted in the pattern book's advertisements (Figure 5.5). The diagrams and the text, penned by Kawakita Renshichirō, an architect known for designing cinemas and shops, presented the diagrams as scientific exercises:

> [The model's] height is usually around seven to seven-and-a-half times the height of their head, but usually Japanese women are only six to six-and-three-quarters times the height of their head … Furthermore, there are many variations in body shape. And so, here at 'Style Book' we have undertaken rigorous research into the body types of Japanese women. The *Fujin gahō* offices have surveyed and measured around five hundred women, and from the results of this survey we have discovered that there are over twenty different Japanese female body types. We scaled these body types down to a tenth of their size, and by printing them on thin paper, we have managed to perfectly re-design the 'Style Book' designs to fit. (Kawakita 1934, 30)

Kawakita goes on to spell out these differences and show how the designs can be adapted – the look 'fixed' – even for the type whose 'breasts appear to

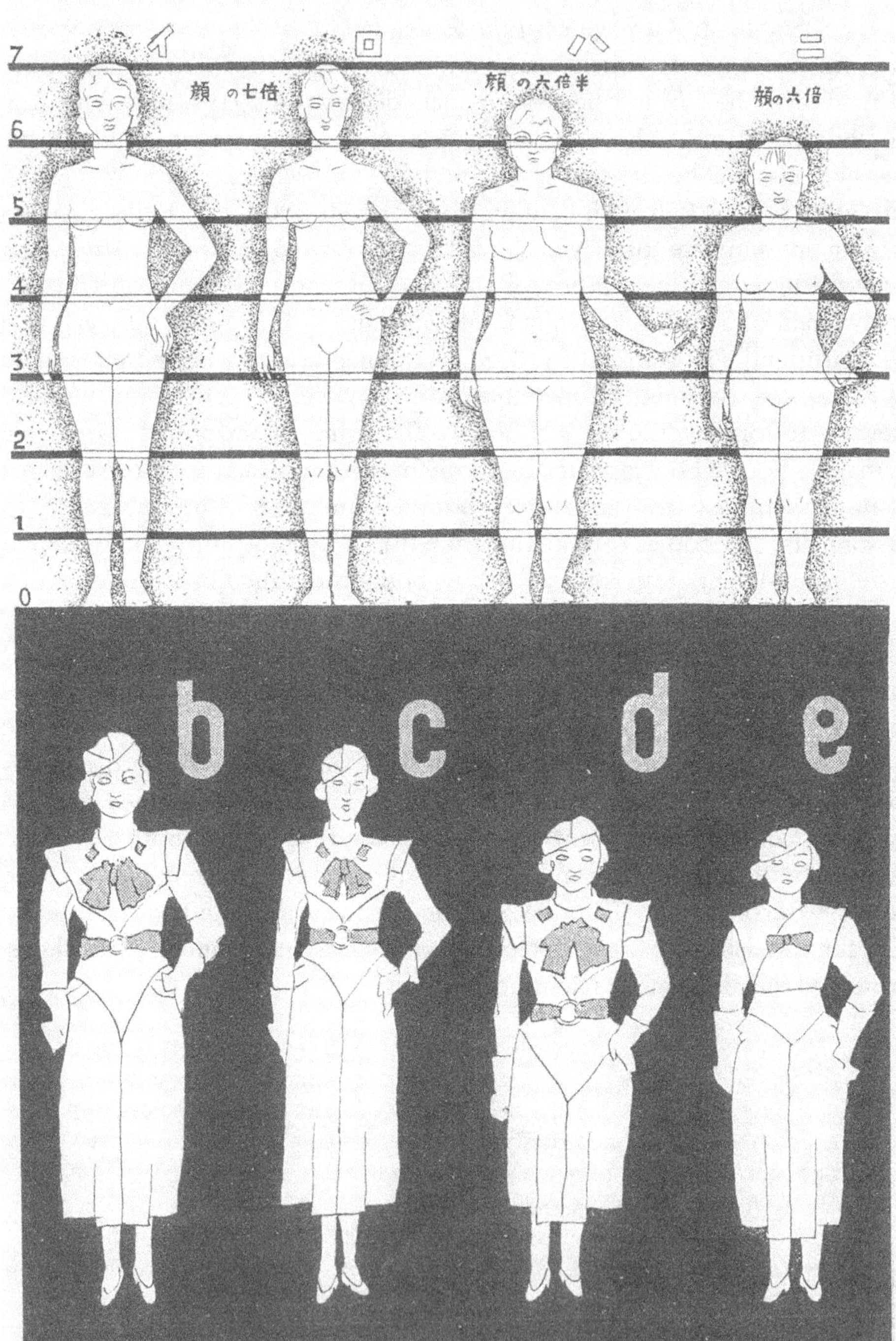

Figure 5.5 Diagram of different Japanese female body types and how homemade Western clothing may be adapted to flatter them, *Fujin gahō* 'Style Book', 1934.

vulgarly stand out much more' than the others (Kawakita 1934, 30–1). The reader is encouraged to identify herself among these 'types' and to adapt the designs in order to fit the advertised silhouette. The article notes, too, that it is possible, in one instance 'to incorporate some "Japanese style"', in the form of a kimono-style cross-over detail on the collar and bust of the dress, with a discreet bow rather than the flamboyant neckerchief detail apparent in the original Western design. The ideal aesthetic was not a wholesale emulation of Hollywood-style aesthetics. Rather, the article suggests that combining Japanese and Hollywood aesthetics was a superior alternative for a Japanese woman whose body did not exactly match Western ideals. What is clear, though, is the body was being viewed as something to be 'fixed'. The consumer was required to identify her physical shortcomings and address them – sartorially or physically – in order to achieve the look.

The female subject was being asked to approximate a physical form presented in the print and film media. This culture of comparison with respect to Western-attired, particularly sportswear-clad, bodies allowed the fashion industry to market products as necessities, claiming they would allow the consumer to approximate the cinematic female 'standard'. An advertisement for 'Eva' brand hair removal cream appeared in March 1936, alongside swimsuit photos of Japanese and Hollywood stars. The illustration showed a Caucasian woman, running along a beach with her arms raised, exposing her hairless armpits and legs. A large arrow pointed towards her body: 'first, remove that armpit hair!' (*Kinema junpō* 1936, 186). The accompanying text linked the removal of hair to the wearing of swimsuits, using scientific terminology to present itself as catering to the desire for a 'cultured life'. Removing armpit hair with Eva cream, it proposed, would 'prevent acidic corruption and fermentation . . . give you a look of the palest beauty . . . make your vivacious curves stand out naturally' and so allow you to 'enjoy the joys of summer' (*Kinema junpō* 1936, 186). Treatments promising paleness were nothing new: 'dermal consciousness is ancient in Japan, and traditional beauty standards from centuries ago emphasized pale, translucent skin' (Miller 2006, 35). Here, though, the product is presented as a means of appropriating a Hollywood-inspired conception of bodily beauty. It promises to showcase the user's 'curves' and is positioned alongside images of star bodies. This was not simple emulation, based on race (Miller 2006, 4 and 23), but adaptation, with the star body acting as the catalyst for the proliferation of the hybridised female image. This combined indigenous ideals with global influences, generating a new, augmented, but still 'Japanese' form, just as the Miss Nippon contests promoted a robust, 'Western-style' body with a 'proven' Japanese heritage. What is clear is that there was a 'correct' way for the female Japanese body to be shaped and showcased, in line with the image of the Western-style sporting star. The Japanese female consumer's body had to fit within idealised notions of the Western clothing form.

This was most apparent from the mid-1930s. Women were simply told which bodily preparation methods were necessary for particular styles of clothing. An August 1935 article, 'Quick Beauty and Weight Loss Methods', stresses the need to lose weight before wearing a swimsuit, illustrating this with images of a Western model exercising in shorts and a polo shirt (*Fasshon* 1935, 20). A month later, 'Let's Streamline Our Bodies' discussed body weight and 'correct' posture, insisting that the female consumer fits into both her Western clothing and her modernised surroundings, with images of a Caucasian woman in a swimsuit and a text combining beauty and health:

> This is the streamlined age. Streamline, streamline! A car, a building, kimono or Western clothing, everything now has a streamlined shape, but are our bodies being left behind? Must our bodies have a tire hanging from their waists, a hunched back and no distinction between the chest and the stomach? *Non, Madame.* We absolutely must streamline our bodies – to harmonise with modernity, for beauty, and for our health. (*Fasshon* 1935, 16)

The imperative tone resembles 'fat shaming', which emerged in the West as part of 'a 19th-century anxiety about body size' and culminated in the marketing of a variety of weight-loss 'cures' as early as 1887. In the American context, 'fat both signifie[d] the "moral corruption" of particular individuals and reinforce[d] hierarchies of race, sexuality, gender and class'. Early media depictions suggested that fat bodies 'ineffectively manag[ed] the modern world' (Farrell 2011, 19–20, 27). In 1930s Japan, too, the import of Hollywood-derived conceptions of morally loaded bodies meant that self-maintenance of the middle-class female body became a matter of moral duty. The use of 'we' suggested that such work would serve both herself and others, with the out-of-shape female Japanese body encumbering both herself and the nation. Given the contemporary socio-economic climate, this made for some confusion around the female physique and the sporting world; skiing was being used to market high-calorie foods such as confectionery to an impoverished populace at the same time as the swimsuit was used to motivate the female consumer to 'streamline' her body and so assert her position within the Japanese class structure. Weight gain in itself is not the factor to be feared: the appreciation of 'healthy' curved bodies and the demonisation of excess fat were both innate to the experience of Western clothing, with its emphasis on silhouette as opposed to size. 'Fashion required the redistribution of fat into desirable locations, rather than [its] elimination' (Farrell 2011, 36–7). The culture of comparison in print media and the cinema portrayed sport and sportswear as a way of 'sculpting' one's body and identity into a desirable, Western-inspired, but still 'Japanese' form. Exercise produced the fit and healthy body of the Hollywood-style screen star, while sporting goods and fashions indicated that a consumer had the affluence to enjoy and the education to understand the concept of Western-style leisure.

Fasshon also produced articles that acknowledged the potential for anxiety, not simply instructing the female consumer on 'correct' bodily form, but empathising with her and acknowledging the effects of such comparison on the female consumer's body image. In 1935, *Fasshon* produced a series of articles on the 'correct' way of wearing Western clothing, each focusing on different aspects of Western-inspired outfits. One of these, subtitled 'About the Waist' was written by an author calling themselves 'Futaba Hikari', purportedly a woman, but potentially a man using a female pseudonym to produce a sense of identification and trust between reader and author (Frederick 2006, 27). Futaba discusses the Japanese waistline, comparing the reader's body to the Western-inspired ideal and highlighting a widespread dissatisfaction with Japanese body image:

> In terms of body composition, the Japanese person's waistline is much lower than the Westerner's. As you probably already know, a Japanese person has a long torso. On a Western person, the waistlines of bodices and skirts are cut to fit on the natural waistline. So when we wear them, inevitably they are always too short . . . So is this body, with its long torso and long legs, flawed? Many people are self-deprecating, saying that our bodies are clearly misshapen. From an objective viewpoint, [the Western] body, with its longer legs and shorter torso, is more dynamic, so it must be more beautiful. But I do not think this has to be the case. *I think Japanese people are too self-deprecating about this.* (Futaba, May 1935, 6–7, original emphasis)

The article is a counterpoint to *Fasshon*'s more didactic articles. Elsewhere, *Fasshon* used the shame of comparison to elevate the fit body as an object not just of aspiration, but of necessity. Futaba, by contrast, brings the ideal body ideal within reach, suggesting adaptation, via consumer purchases of 'flattering' garments and accessories, rather than wholesale transformation. The article still portrays the consumer's body as flawed and still provides sartorial solutions to the perceived 'faults', describing the use of belts and peplums as 'camouflage' (Futaba, May 1935, 7). The aspiration remained the same, but the intensity and moral implications of the observations were reduced. By suggesting that Japanese were 'too self-deprecating', Futaba suggested the reader was closer to the ideal than she may have believed.

Piga describes the 'utopia' generated by advertising as a 'hypothetical social reality', reliant upon 'scenes imagined that impact upon implied meanings in the active consumer' (Piga 2012, 185). This utopia can be divided into two categories, depending on the position of the consumer within the narrative: 'inclusive . . . if the consumer is perceived and represented (in the scene and in reality) as halfway to social ascent, and . . . exclusive . . . if the consumer, who has already consolidated his status, is intelligent, hypercritical, and thus overvalued (but also flattered and courted) by advertising' (Piga 2012, 185). In both, the alienation of the consumer is key: 'the symbolic universe . . . is illusory in terms of the way it travels along a wave of alienation; alienation from the real and unsatisfying reality, from which one would like to escape; it follows that the escape can produce more images, impressions and appearances than behaviours really suitable to integration into the group to which one wishes to belong' (Piga 2012, 185–6). The examples from *Fasshon* discussed here employ the 'inclusive' utopia model, with the consumer presented as a work in progress. The difference between the standard didactic approach and Futaba's sympathetic approach is the degree of alienation. The didactic examples depend on strenuous physical exertion, with the exemplar being the idealised Western body and the reader not considered even halfway there. Futaba plays on the dissatisfaction this generates, empowering the reader, via the price of body-camouflaging fashion goods, and making the goal of attaining such a body feasible.

In Part I, I established that the cinema motivated consumption by prompting dissatisfaction in one's ability to grasp the constantly evolving moment onscreen. Futaba's approachable method of suggesting the pursuit of an idealised Western-style body reproduced this in a print media context. The sympathetic examination of the sporting body drew it closer to the average consumer, using direct emotional engagement in the text to imitate the sensory immersion of the screen, so allowing the reader to envision her own body more easily alongside that of the star. However, the comparison and dissatisfaction continued, prompting continued consumption of consumer goods in the desire to approximate the star body. In the cinema and print media of the 1930s, the sporting world and its body images were marketed on both aspirational and approachable levels, but both centred on a culture of comparison. Their connotations of eugenic respectability, middle-class affluence, and cinematic attraction allowed elements of the sporting world to become signifiers. Sporting connotations were applied to numerous products, regardless of their actual sporting application. Like the monogram on Yamaji Fumiko's swimsuit, sporting iconography could immediately imbue any object with the elevated status of affluent leisure, transferring its desirability from the screen to the everyday.

Another of Futaba's instructional articles, on how to wear skirts, not only commented on which skirts were suitable for various sporting activities, such as hiking, golf and tennis, but also introduced a 'semi-sports skirt, for wearing in the office or everyday use' (Futaba March 1935, 7). Futaba describes the skirt's practical functions and praises its novelty, placing it within the realm of the middle-class housewife and her thirst for convenience. 'This year's trendy skirt is less flared. From the photographs I have seen it has a pleat at the front and a bias cut. Such an innovation!' (Futaba March 1935, 7). Futaba notes that she has only seen these outfits in photographs, most likely in the same 'foreign magazines' she would draw on in discussing the Japanese waistline. In its original American context, 'semi-sport' garments 'met the needs of a contemporary American (sub)urban lifestyle rather than the requirements of actual sporting play ... [semi-sportswear] engaged desirable, nationalised, discourses of dynamism, vitality, functionalism and adaptability so enabled by their athletic invocations' (Goodrum 2013, 35). These 'desirable' connotations echo the ideals presented in the Japanese print media, including the 'dynamism' praised by Futaba as a desirable attribute of the Western body. The 'semi-sports' skirt allowed these connotations to move from the sporting arena to the middle-class housewife's home and the working woman's office. Sporting iconography also allowed them to be transferred to smaller, more affordable commodities. An advertisement on the back cover of film fan magazine *Sutā* (*Star*) promoted Smile (Sumairu) brand eye drops, an item with seemingly no link to the sporting world. Alongside a stylised illustration of an ethnically indeterminate woman's face, with a short perm and a bow-collared blouse, the advertisement listed the locations and occasions for which the product was suitable. 'For reading, for sports, for strolling, for the household, for meeting up at the cinema, for the factory ... [Smile] increases the beauty of the eyes and your health' (*Sutā* 1933). The list combines middle-class leisure activities with the 'household', and the 'factory' – the spaces of the housewife and the working woman respectively – rather than the cafe, the space of the Modern Girl. A medical product is presented as a beauty product, suggesting that caring for the physical body, through beauty rituals and health-focused care, was a positive activity for all women, regardless of their social status, and a ritual linked to a Japanese 'cultured life', rather than an emulation of Western style. Advertisements such as these, like Futaba's advice column, market the sporting world as accessible to *all* women via the purchasing of cheaper beauty products, as 'entry-level' purchases of the image of the middle-class sporting life – a stark contrast to the didactic advertisements targeting anxiety concerning one's body and social position. This multi-level approach to marketing the sporting world might be characterised as 'democratising' luxury, allowing the less affluent consumer to buy into the brand's aesthetic, with the potential to consume higher-priced goods at a later date (Jackson and Shaw 2008, 126).

Onscreen, too, the anxiety surrounding the affluent sporting body was clear. In the 26-minute fragment that survives of Mizoguchi Kenji's *Tokyo*

March (*Tokyō no Kōshinkyoku,* 1929), Natsukawa Shizue stars as Michiyo, a female factory worker, who becomes a geisha in order to support her uncle's family. She begins the film with permed hair and bold cosmetics, but also a brightly patterned *meisen* kimono, separating her from the Modern Girl archetype, but marking her enjoyment of the disposable income that working life brings. However, following a familial discussion of her fate, she wears a muted kimono and a geisha wig, becoming a 'traditional', albeit not entirely respected, archetype. When one of her clients wants to marry her, he is warned by his father (also one of Michiyo's clients) that it would not be acceptable for the heir of a prestigious company to be married to a geisha. Michiyo is aware of her role as a desirable 'product' from the film's outset. Her ability to benefit from her body is made clear in a dream sequence, where her mother appears and directs her to 'never fall in love and never depend on men, but learn to seduce them'.

The film places Michiyo squarely within the lower echelons of modern Tokyo society, with a sequence literally shot from her lower level. A calendar shows that it is Sunday, a day reserved for leisure in the Hollywood context, and an elevated shot shows a large tennis court, with a young woman with short, bobbed hair enthusiastically engaged in a game with a young man. The camera lingers, the low neck of her outfit revealing her cleavage and her skirt displaying her lower legs in motion. An inter-title then clearly aligns the sporting world with affluent, privileged youth, augmenting the camera's elevated position: 'Sunday . . . Fortunate young people devote their time to their favourite sports, just above the slums.' One of the young men, also in a tennis outfit, hits the ball over the side of the court into the housing below, where Michiyo is sitting on the ground. The sequence is filmed from behind the young men's heads, clearly aligning the audience with the privileged young men. Michiyo is wearing a kimono and *geta,* with her hair in a simple low bun. The camera angle now changes to her viewpoint as she retrieves their ball. She tries to throw it up to the men, but she misses and has to throw it again and again. An inter-title then introduces 'Yoshiki, the son of the rich businessman Fujimoto', linking his affluent status to his elevated sporting image. Yoshiki's companion remarks that Michiyo is 'really pretty', and takes a photograph of her. When the young men return to their female partners, he offers Yoshiki the photograph 'as a souvenir'. At this point one of the women grabs the camera and both of them dash athletically underneath the tennis net, with Yoshiki's male companion in hot pursuit. The scene operates on multiple levels. It exhibits the bodily athleticism of the female players, using the court and their clothing. The sporting world is depicted as a symbol of affluent success, with Natsukawa gazing up at the tennis players, but the female players are clearly threatened by her, despite her impoverished status. The two female archetypes are clearly contrasted: the wealthier women with their modern appearance, healthy bodies and social access versus the economically disadvantaged but conventional female, whose form is concealed within her kimono. The jealous behaviour of the female players suggests they are not entirely aspirational figures. It is the 'ordinary' figure of Natsukawa who is more desirable in the eyes of the wealthy young men. Given that the 1920s were a time of financial struggle for a significant proportion of Japan's working population, Natsukawa's approachable character, despite her humble circumstances, would have presented an attractive alternative to the healthy, sporting body for contemporary audiences.

Natsukawa was a popular Nikkatsu actress, known for her 'respectably modern persona' (Fujiki 2013, 279). But the favourable comparison of an 'everyday' Japanese archetype with affluent Westernised stereotypes, engaged in leisure activities, was a way of 'normalising' the star and increasing the female spectator's self-identification with the image onscreen. Nayar describes how 'celebrity culture is rooted in the everyday through [a] process where the celebrities are placed as simultaneously distant and familiar' (Nayar 2009, 2). Mass media 'constructs the star as somebody above the average human ... the celebrity [is] somebody who has transcended the usual problems of everyday life and other humans to become successful' (Nayar 2009, 126). This explains the 'jealous' reaction of the spectator-as-consumer to onscreen images of affluent and beautiful Modern Girls and Boys, as described by Iwamoto, together with an anxious desire to acquire a body resembling that of the star in order to also 'transcend everyday life'. But *Tokyo March* reverses this dynamic. It features characters who possess a 'successful' body, but also have noticeable flaws, and are even usurped by their 'ordinary' counterpart. The distant star is humanised in a process akin to that of the gossip column, wherein 'gossip about the unhappy lives of the stars helps us contend with our own ordinariness' (Nayar 2009, 126).

This mechanism of comparison is apparent throughout the film. Irie Takako also features as Fujimoto's legitimate daughter Sayuri. (Michiyo is in fact his illegitimate daughter by a geisha, making her Yoshiki's half-sister.) In *The Oxford Handbook of Japanese Cinema*, Daisuke Miyao describes how 'another thread of the narrative revolves around Irie's "ultra-modern girl", who takes pleasure in conquering all of the society men with her beauty and intelligence' (Miyao 2013, 129). A synopsis sums up how these two archetypes combine as a key attraction of the plot, accompanied by a photograph of Irie with a male co-star, wearing a fitted Western dress and in full seduction mode: 'It stars daring Modern Girls. It stars geisha' (*Yomiuri shimbun* 1929, 10). Both the ultra-modern Irie and the modest Natsukawa are portrayed as attractive, diversifying the film's star personae attractions. However, it is Natsukawa's unthreatening Japanese 'prettiness' that wins the heart of the affluent male protagonist over her sporty Modern Girl counterparts, providing an antidote to the 'healthy body beauty' images centred on the affluent sporting world, which were becoming ubiquitous in Japanese print and screen media. While dissatisfaction with their body may have driven the consumer to purchase goods associated with the star's fit body in order to more closely approximate her form, the public fallibility of stars ensured that they remained feasibly within reach. Images of the sporting world were instrumental in constructing the paradoxical female star who was simultaneously accessible and inaccessible, perfect yet fallible.

An example is the featuring of sporting misadventures in celebrity gossip columns. In May 1939, Shōchiku Ōfuna actress Takamine Hideko was filming *Love Troops* (*Aijō Butai*, 1939), which required her to learn to ski. But:

> This did not go well . . . unfortunately she twisted her ankle. [She] remarked, 'my skiing was terrible,' and truly it seems that she has neither become skilled at skiing nor grown to like it. Perhaps the next time she goes skiing they are going to send her with a walking stick – an ounce of prevention is worth a pound of cure! (*Sutairu* 1939, 37)

Skiing was particularly fashionable from the mid-1930s onwards. Austrian ski pioneer Hannes Schneider had visited Nozawa in 1930. 'The dapper St. Anton skimeister – in skis, tweed sport coat and tie – stood on the hill before hundreds of Japanese skiers to demonstrate the Arlberg technique . . . [This] marked the beginning of modern skiing in Japan', with skiing-based 'looks' appearing throughout the media. Skiing already existed in Japan, but 'the 1930s ski boom in Japan launched by Schneider's visit was so large and passionate that it led . . . to the designation of Sapporo, Japan, as the host for the 1940 Winter Games' (Sanders 2011, 30–1). Skiing was intrinsically linked to Europe in the popular imagination, encouraged by films such as those of the German director Arnold Fanck, who focused on 'films about skiing, glacier trekking and mountain climbing' before he embarked on the German–Japanese co-production *A New Earth* (*Die Tochter Des Samurai; Atarashiki Tsuchi*, 1937) (Bock 2009, 116). Skiing required expensive equipment, held exotic connotations of European travel, and was soon cemented as a prestigious middle-class leisure activity. The sport was also made slightly more accessible to the Japanese masses with the rise of domestic tourism and of '"rustic" hobbies such as skiing and mountain climbing' (Young 2013, 136–7).

Given this new accessibility, the sporting world was again applied as a motif to other fashion-related goods and practices. Japan forfeited the 1940 Olympic Games in July 1938, but in February 1939, *Sutairu* published a double-page spread discussing 'Skiing Makeup', with various female commentators providing columns advising on 'how to deal with the sunlight', 'keeping the hair natural' and guidance 'for those who always wear kimono' (*Sutairu* 1939, 66–7). The idea of skiing-specific makeup was not new. *Fasshon* had broached it in February 1935 in an article entitled, 'The Boxing Fan and the Skier: Their Makeup Secrets' (*Fasshon* 1935, 30). Both articles present skiing as a special event, emphasising the need to prepare one's body and to adapt 'Japanese' practices for the purpose. In the 1939 *Sutairu* article on skiing makeup, Hanami Kimiko noted how kimono and a related garment, the *monpe* trouser, might be perceived as old-fashioned or anachronistic in comparison to Western-style ski gear, but still attempts to present it as a potential alternative:

> In the Snow Country, girls wear *monpe* when they are skiing, and when worn with a coarse cotton striped, red scarf and suchlike, this look has a very picturesque mood. For women who usually wear only kimono, a flattering *monpe* style in something like a coarse checked wool might lead to responses like, 'Who are you supposed to be? "The Lion Dancer's" older sister?'[2] But I make this recommendation in all seriousness. While *monpe* are not yet 'national uniform' [*kokuminfuku*], perhaps they could be even more chic than baggy-bottomed ski clothing? (*Sutairu* 1939, 66–7)

Monpe had a controversial position in the late 1930s Japanese sartorial landscape, as Gordon notes. Positive responses included a 1930 article by army paymaster Kimura Matsukichi, who argued that they 'had much potential as work dress for women [as] they were "very easily sewn", inexpensive, mobile, and [for unexplained reasons] they "protected women's chastity"'. But 'the men who oversaw the army-connected National Defence Women's Association (Kokubō Fujin Kai) were distressed to find women in Osaka attending firefighting drills wearing *monpe*, and they advised against the practice'. By 1940 the *Yomiuri shimbun*'s 'Women's Page' had to respond to complaints that they 'were . . . cold in winter and clumsy for work. The problem, the column countered, was that women did not wear them properly' (Gordon 2012, 147). The 1939 *Sutairu* article acknowledges both sides of the argument. It emphasises the indigenous, rustic connotations of *monpe*, suggesting they could be part of an outfit that could rival Western-style ski gear, but evaluates them according to a Western aesthetic standard, via the use of the loanword *shikku* [chic], and acknowledges that in a skiing context, with its connotations of affluence and *modanizumu*, *monpei* would appear outdated and out of place.

The author thus champions Japanese-style aesthetics, but continues to refer to the sporting aesthetics of the Hollywood screen icon, prompting comparison and anxiety, describing her own dishevelled appearance after skiing:

> As for makeup, I was reminiscing about Claudette Colbert's skiing look, dressed stylishly in her chic ski clothing when leaving the hotel. When

> it came to doing my own makeup, this felt impossible to keep up with. However, once you've fallen over and your ears are full of snow your makeup simply slides off. It won't last more than an hour – after skiing … you will have sweated so much that you will have no face powder left, and the only parts of your makeup left will be your eyebrows and lipstick. Your cheeks will be blushing like apples, so only the tiniest amount of blush is sufficient. (*Sutairu* 1939, 66–7)

The author's experience of skiing, and its effects on her physical appearance, resembles the previously discussed gossip column on Takamine Hideko. Given the elevated social status of skiing, the acknowledgement of a star's bewilderment becomes an endearing entity, allowing the spectator-as-consumer to identify with the star and her surroundings. The star, too, must undergo a variety of rituals (including, potentially, embarrassment) to obtain the sporting image disseminated onscreen. The star's body, too, is no longer the perfect product envisioned on film. The media reporting on her 'private' life reveals her body as a 'work in progress', sustained via a fashion and beauty regime. Like the gossip columns, rather than increasing the distance between the star and the spectator-as-consumer, and thus potential consumer alienation, this presented the star look and body as attainable, that is, if one was willing to put in the effort and purchase the relevant products. The emphasis on leisure and on care for one's self and body, however normalised by the fact that stars also performed and even failed at such tasks, veiled the fact that these beautifying practices were a form of labour. Simone de Beauvoir underlines the significance of this labour:

> Dressing has a twofold significance: it is meant to show the woman's social standing (her standard of living, her wealth, the social class she belongs to), but at the same time it concretizes feminine narcissism; it is her uniform and her attire; the woman who suffers from not *doing* anything thinks she is expressing her being through her dress. Beauty treatments and dressing are kinds of work that allow her to appropriate her person as she appropriates her home through housework; she thus believes that she is choosing and recreating her own self. And social customs encourage her to alienate herself in her image. (de Beauvoir 2011, 649–50, emphasis as text)

This alienation was exacerbated by the gap between the star as active participants in public space and the female consumer as inferior aspirant within her home.

This was clear in the print media. *Fasshon* magazine published an article in May 1935 written by the infamous Hollywood publicist Scoop Conlon and translated by a purportedly female Japanese translator, with the pseudonym 'Kinema-ko' ('Miss Cinema'). It tells the story of 'a naturally plump young woman' (a proxy for the female consumer) approaching Hollywood stars, including Bing Crosby and W. C. Fields, for autographs, as they eat dinner with Conlon at a studio canteen, providing a connotation of 'authenticity'. The meal is described in almost fetishistic detail: 'a delicious, syrupy clam chowder, a huge plate of celery and olives and sliced bread . . . [and] beef steak [with] plump asparagus' (*Fasshon* 1935, 20). Restaurant dining is presented as an enjoyable, desirable leisure activity. Much of Conlon's piece describes the new tourist activity in which travellers seek out Hollywood restaurants and canteens to watch the stars eat their meals. But the overweight young woman who approaches the stars for autographs is portrayed negatively, to the point that the stars are actually put off their food, particularly when she reiterates the diet advice she has read in magazines: 'Mr Bing, could you sign this please? I already have your autograph, but I don't mind having it again. Hey, what are you eating? If you eat like that at noon, you'll get fat. A film star has to watch their figure' (*Fasshon* 1935, 20). The article then discusses various actors and actresses who refuse to eat in public (including 'Norma Shearer, Joan Crawford, Mae West', and of course 'Garbo'), contrasting them with those who delight in doing so ('mostly men', but also 'Marlene Dietrich, Myrna Loy, Jeanette MacDonald', and others). The article presents the reader with a quandary: food is not only an enjoyable consumer good, but the subject of an enjoyable leisure activity. However, over-indulging (and disobeying magazine-mandated diet advice) could result in the reader assuming the body of the subject of the stars' disgust, rather than the desirable female star body. The didactic (and conflicted) message is clear: public dining is primarily a male pursuit and the only female stars who do it all having outgoing, sexualised, and sometimes controversial star personae (particularly Dietrich). The female consumer is encouraged to appreciate fine dining, but only within the parameters deemed acceptable by film-related print media. Magazine articles such as these present diet and exercise as a way of transcending everyday life. Labour was required of the star, to achieve the appearance needed to access the star world, and of the female spectator-as-consumer, to benefit herself and her household.

The image of the fit female body as one supporting state and family was further complicated when the sporting image was combined with the more controversial aspects of the Modern Girl image, particularly her eroticised body and command of public space. The 'healthy' connotations of revealing female sporting garments – particularly the swimsuit – did not dampen their erotic associations, but almost appears to have justified the erotic allure of the images and their uninhibited publication. In real life, the swimsuit was not seen as a functional sporting garment. Its eroticism was not always welcomed in the everyday public sphere. An English-language overview of press opinion and police matters, published in 1938, includes the following:

> Summer Sports and Police: The government is eagerly urging the people to take proper exercise. Mass exercise is becoming very popular. Sports

> also are becoming popular. But what is worrying the police is the fact that in sports and exercise the people are wearing scanty clothing. Bare legs, bare arms, and even bare breasts are seen among groups of people engaged in sports and exercise. (*The Japan Times* 1938, 1)

Government initiatives were encouraging the sporting activities associated with the swimsuit, the print media was exposing female bodies and encouraging the male spectator to compare their athletic and erotic 'fitness', but the wearing of such garments in a public setting was controversial. This was an English-language publication and it is not clear whether 'anti-swimsuit' legislation was in place or enforced in Japan at this time, but the suggestion that the swimsuit met a mixed reception rings true (Schmidt 2008, 68). Six years prior to this, there is a single reference to police interest in public swimwear in the *Asahi shimbun*. 'A Peek at Seaside Trends' provides the following advice for swimsuit selection:

> Beachwear becomes more and more widespread every year, but this year swimsuits have been influenced by a worldwide trend for nudity. The curve of the back, the flank below the arms and the abdomen are all being highlighted with cut-outs, and even out in the street people are bravely exposing their bodies … it is apparent that the police have decided to issue a ban on wearing such things. So when shopping, please take ten minutes to carefully judge what you want to wear. Swimsuits, when worn with other clothing, seem to go unnoticed by the police – so wearing them with cotton beach pyjamas or capes has become a trend. (*Asahi shimbun* 1932, 10)

While there is little evidence of actual state regulation, these articles do highlight the ability of sportswear to make female bodies visible in public spaces. It was when images of the near-nude female form transcended the screen and print and entered the public sphere that their connection to the Modern Girl and the potential for panic became clear.

Male panic was also portrayed onscreen, when the sporting world allowed female transgression into masculine spaces such as boxing gyms and golf courses. In 1930, Modern Girl archetype Clara Bow was pictured swinging from a pair of gymnasium hoops, in ballet pumps and a knee-length dress, winking coquettishly. The English caption was in line with official fitness and health initiatives, aimed most likely at the female consumer: 'Exercise for health! That's the motto of Clara Bow, Paramount Star.' The Japanese caption, though, was more troubling: 'Our Clara is working out her body, making any manly guy lacking confidence look on in amazement' (*Kinema junpō* 1930, 7). The commentator appears simultaneously impressed and threatened; how can she still be sexually attractive while performing masculine exercise? Bow's sporting image was directly referenced in Ozu's *Walk Cheerfully*, released the same year. A poster of her wearing boxing gloves, shorts, and a vest appears immediately after Date Satoko's gangster moll applies her face powder. The poster hangs in the room where the male gangster characters practise boxing. The sequence of Date, Bow, and finally the men finishing a boxing session in this room align Date's body with Bow's, as a sexualised, masculinised female appropriating male space. This theme, of a masculinised and therefore threatening, but also attractive, sporting female is again referenced when Date plays golf with her male love interest, wearing a short-skirted golf outfit. She taunts and emasculates him, remarking golf is 'so easy', and leaving him to struggle. Yet rather than being rewarded for her sporting prowess, she is ultimately usurped by her conventional, kimono-clad rival. Throughout the film, she is depicted as a dangerous, malevolent character, constantly conniving and scheming for her own gain.

Overall, the images of the world of sport that depicted and were marketed towards women, including clothing, health and fitness, and physical exercise, present a confused picture. LaMarre notes:

> such photos [of women playing sports] constituted a new way of looking at women ... the cine-photographs present women who appear somehow full of power or potential, but powerful in the way that a fetish is powerful, as a restless and dynamic figure that demands constant attention ... This is the paradox of the new 'woman of motion'... in the circulation of such photographs of starlets, one can see the emergence of a subjective technology for the production of 'women in motion' which increases their range of action and circulation (imparting a sense of agency) while subjecting them to social (masculine) affection that circumscribes their movements. (LaMarre 2009, 270)

The female consumer must take part in the national sporting effort for the benefit of her family and the nation, via a plethora of consumer goods and marketed practices. The intended result is a 'fit body', which was emblematic of the middle-class lifestyle and simultaneously marketed as erotically attractive, but she must not assume the Modern Girl-derived screen sporting image *too* closely – and certainly not in a way which displaces or unnerves her male peers. The female consumer is trapped in a cycle of consumption and restriction, allowed access to the emblems, ideas, and education of physical activity suggested by the sporting world, while her own body remains restricted. Like the archetype of the hybridised housewife and the position of Western-style sport itself, in the Japanese educational and recreational landscape, the integration of sportswear and the 'sporting body' into the lives of Japanese women was subject to negotiation between existing sensibilities and imagery and new film- and media-derived rhetoric and imagery, generating a hybridised consumer response.

Notes

1. These are the American English terms 'one strike', 'two ball' and 'out', transposed directly into Japanese using the *katakana* phonetic alphabet.
2. Most likely a reference to the popular story *The Lion Dancer* (*Kakubē jishi*) by Osaragi Jirō, which was published in *Boys' Club* (*Shonen kurabu*) in 1927, but also had a large adult following, and was the subject of multiple film adaptations until the onset of the Pacific War (International Institute for Children's Literature Osaka, 2017).

Chapter 6

Men and the sporting body

At first glance, the new eugenically motivated promotion of consumption practices arising in the early 1930s was steered in the direction of the female consumer, with any effect on male household or state members being engineered via female consumption. However, the impact of sportswear on the film- and fashion-related industries – and new attitudes to 'desirable bodies' – is not restricted to the female consumer sphere. I argue that the fashionable, healthy and hybridised image of the sporting body both depicted and affected all genders. The male-identifying consumer is directly targeted in a two-fold approach – first, via the image of the fit cinematic female as object of desire for the male spectator, and second via the same image of a 'desirable middle-class lifestyle' aimed at the middle-class housewife, within which sport and health play significant roles.

Returning to the concept of the beauty contest as a companion piece to the commercial exhibitions aimed at the middle-class female demographic (for example those held by Mitsukoshi), for the male spectator the Miss Nippon pageants served similarly as a showcase of 'desirable items' displayed in a quasi-educational, categorised setting. 'Experts' (judges) defined the component parts of the 'perfect' female body, just as middle-class female-focused print media explored the virtues of modern home equipment. This transformation of the female body into a marketable product constitutes a process of direct objectification, with this exhibition-like setting within the department store satisfying the viewer's Freudian scopophilia, which Mulvey summarises as 'exist[ing] as the erotic basis for pleasure in looking at another person as object' (Mulvey 1975, 7). Mulvey notes this process of the objectified female star body being presented as a 'perfect product' in the Hollywood and European cinemas. She cites this specifically in the presentation of Dietrich's body in the work of Josef von Sternberg, in which her 'body, stylised and fragmented by close-ups, is the content of the film and the direct recipient of the spectator's look' (Mulvey 1975, 11). Mulvey describes how this fragmentation process onscreen simplifies the narrative role of the female character:

> Conventional close-ups of legs (Dietrich, for instance) or a face (Garbo) integrate into the narrative a different mode of eroticism. One part of a fragmented body destroys the Renaissance space, the illusion of depth demanded by the narrative, it gives flatness, the quality of a cut-out or icon rather than verisimilitude to the screen. (Mulvey 1975, 9)

This 'flatness' described by Mulvey is reminiscent of the print media image, the lack of 'verisimilitude' supplied by the film image generating a single, eroticised purpose in its abstraction. The close-ups of Okada Yoshiko's adorned body and made-up face in *No Blood Relation* take on a dual purpose, as not only a marketing device for Mitsukoshi's products, but as an eroticised product herself, simplified as an accessory to the narrative rather than its agent. The first Miss Nippon contest of 1931 too utilised a degree of segmentation of the female body, which was judged using an amateur photo contest – entries entailed 'a full face, a profile and a full body photograph taken on the same day', which were then meticulously scrutinised according to the strict Western-inspired criteria set by the all-male judges, before the winner and runners-up were exhibited at the Takashimaya department store in person – prior to this, all of the entries were available for viewing on the store walls, extending the event's exhibition-like quality (Robertson 2001, 13). Rather than the fragmented film image becoming one-dimensional via the close-up, this process instead utilised these true one-dimensional images in order to replicate the cinematic 'sensory reflexive horizon', with both a direct immersive element (the male participant directly walking through a corridor of these displayed, fragmented images; the eventual showcase of the living participants themselves) and an impossible desire to freeze the momentary, as described by Charney and Schwarz. The experience of the beauty contest cemented male conceptions of the physical components of a desirable and healthy female body and tethered it in the collective consciousness to cinematic images, legitimising and promoting the position of fragmented, partially clothed female bodies onscreen. The sporting female body onscreen and the reproduction of such star images in print media – particularly those which depict the body clothed in the swimsuit – becomes a means of flawlessly replicating throughout the nation this 'perfect product' both at its most exposed and in motion – in sports-themed clothing and related scenes and poses, the body is shown not only to *appear* physically superior due to its proportions and musculature, but is *proven* to be functional and strong when it is engaged in action. While the swimsuit-clad female body exists as an eroticised image, this is not its sole connotation; such eroticism becomes entwined with the rhetoric of speed, strength and exertion innate to the emergent Japanese sporting world.

Mulvey defines the relationship between the male audience member and the female star image as follows:

> The determining male gaze projects its phantasy on to the female form which is styled accordingly. In their traditional exhibitionist role women are simultaneously looked at and displayed, with their appearance coded for strong visual and erotic impact so that they can be said to connote to-be-looked-at-ness. (Mulvey 1975, 10)

In its role in allowing the female form to be exhibited, sportswear becomes a key part of this 'coded appearance', with the enactment of this subject/object dynamic inviting the male spectator to engage in his 'phantasy' by aligning his own ego with the film's hero:

> As the spectator identifies with the main male protagonist, he projects his look on to that of his like, his screen surrogate, so that the power of the male protagonist as he controls events coincides with the active power of the erotic look, both giving a satisfying sense of omnipotence. A male movie star's glamorous characteristics are thus not those of the erotic object of the gaze, but those of the more perfect, more complete, more powerful ideal ego conceived in the original moment of recognition in front of the mirror. (Mulvey 1975, 10–11)

By identifying himself with the male star onscreen, the male spectator gains power over, and even ownership of, the exhibited female star: 'by means of identification with him, through participation in his power, the spectator can indirectly possess her too' (Mulvey 1975, 11). It is via this self-identification process centred around a desire to 'own' the cinematic sporting female body that a fit and healthy body ideal for men (and its related consumer goods) could be successfully marketed via male sporting star bodies onscreen, particularly when exhibited alongside the female sporting star body.

An example of a star whose persona was central to this dynamic is Suzuki Denmei, one of the judges of the 1931 Shōchiku beauty contest – a championship-level swimmer from Meiji University who gains his first film role in Murata Minoru's *Souls on the Road* (*Rojō no reikion*) for Shōchiku in 1921, alongside Osanai Kaoru. This first role has no solid link to the sporting world in the actual film itself – he plays an aspiring violinist from Hokkaido, who travels to Tokyo against the wishes of his father (Osanai), who believes he will be unable to support his young family. However, the way in which Suzuki's body is adorned and displayed clearly positions him as possessing the male equivalent of the 'healthy body beauty' advocated for women, particularly in terms of its alignment with Hollywood-derived ideals. Suzuki wears Western hats and tailoring throughout, with his hair worn in a cropped, but natural-appearing, louche, ruffled style more in common with that worn by Charlie Chaplin than the slicked-back style worn by the likes of Rudolph Valentino, suggesting a youthful, active vitality – his hair always appears thick, healthy and with a significant curl, even in sequences in which he is meant to be playing a starving artist. He is also shot in a style more closely associated with the presentation of the cinematic female body as described by Mulvey, particularly in regard to the use of close-ups to showcase both his strikingly Western-like physiognomy and his significant height – in scenes where Suzuki is presented in full-length, he appears to dominate most of the frame. Suzuki is presented as a Japanese analogue of the Hollywood star – he is even credited under the pseudonym *Zeya Tōgo* – a pun on the English phrase, 'to go there'. His body is presented with the same sense of 'to-be-looked-at-ness' that Mulvey attributes to the female star's presentation, complicating the spectator's gendered relationship to the male star onscreen; via this conventionally 'female' objectivity, Suzuki's Western-like physical form, too, could invite the spectator's self-identification or objectifying desire. The phenomenon of the female spectator, who according to Doane wished to purchase the star's surroundings in order to 'become' her, becomes melded with the heterosexual male viewer's projection of his own ego onto the character of the male screen hero, generating a hybridised response – the male viewer wishes to possess not only the power over the narrative of the conventional cinematic hero, but Suzuki's glamorised body. For the female spectator, the 'to-be-looked-at-ness' of Suzuki's body commands eroticism, presenting his body, rather than that of the female star, as sexual object.

This is a phenomenon which Hansen observes in the female fan culture surrounding Valentino arising simultaneously in the United States between 1921 and 1926, which was centred around a male star whose body similarly manipulated gendered conceptions of the camera's 'gaze'. Hansen describes how Valentino's breakthrough picture *The Four Horsemen of the Apocalypse* (1921) 'presented him with backlighting and soft-style cinematography, textual devices usually reserved for a female star' (Hansen 1994, 259). In Japanese print media, too, Valentino is described in feminine, objectified terms – an advertisement for *The Son of the Sheik* appearing in *Film Age* (*Eiga jidai*) in 1926 markets the film with this image of Valentino at the centre of its attractions: 'Burning Lips! Magnetic Eyes! Resistless Lover! A Greater Valentino! Romance! Beauty! Action! Glowing Climax!' (*Film Age* 1926, 35, punctuation as text) Hansen posits that such modes of presentation do not constitute a pure reversal of male/female gaze dynamics, but instead complicate them, highlighting the existing male/female subject/object dichotomy:

> the figure of the male as erotic object undeniably sets into play fetishistic and voyeuristic mechanisms, accompanied – most strikingly in the case of Valentino – by a feminization of the actor's persona. These mechanisms, however, cannot be naturalized as easily as they are in the representation

> of a female body. They are foregrounded as aspects of a theatricality that encompasses both performer and viewer, and which may mean something different depending on the viewer's gender and sexual orientation. The reversal thus constitutes a *textual* difference which has to be considered case by case ... [it] thus calls into question the very idea of polarity rather than simply reversing its terms. (Hansen 1994, 252)

Taking this concept of the 'case by case' approach to examples of male stars textually presented using cinematic techniques canonically applied to female stars, Suzuki's first appearance in *Souls on the Road* enacts the same concept of a complicated reversal exhibited in Hansen's exploration of Valentino. While there are marked similarities between their overall star personae – the aforementioned 'feminine' manner in which his body is presented onscreen, his fashionably dressed appearance on- and off-screen and a reflection of Valentino's 'ethnic otherness', embodied in his quasi-Western Hollywood-style physicality and physiognomy (Hansen 1994, 259) – an outlier is Suzuki's appeal to multiple genders. Valentino's persona appears to be polarised in terms of his reception with different gender demographics: in her analysis of *The Sheik* (1921), Hansen states that 'with the film's overwhelming success at the box office, reviewers began to note its special draw with female audiences', but adds that the reviewers 'asserted a growing rejection of the star on the part of "real" men' (Hansen 1994, 259). Suzuki's star persona does not appear to experience such polarity, instead appealing to multiple genders – as noted by Peter B. High, by 1930 (alongside his frequent female co-star Tanaka Kinuyo) 'both stars were regularly featured in ads for health drinks, cosmetics, fashion wear, and a host of other products in the mass-circulation magazines ... theirs were the faces known in virtually every household in the nation' (High 2003, 14). A photograph of Tanaka and Suzuki together in *Eiga jōhō* published in 1930 (Figure 6.1) presents them as the ultimate fashionable couple, with Tanaka in a vibrant polka-dot dress with matching scarf and cloche hat and Suzuki in a sharp suit and fedora (*Eiga jōhō* 1930, 9).

An explanation of Suzuki's mass appeal can be found in the diversity of how his persona is presented onscreen: Angela Schlater describes a polarity between the archetypes of leading men in the 1920s being represented by Valentino and Douglas Fairbanks respectively:

> Rudolph Valentino embodied an 'exotic masculinity' for women to gaze upon at the movies. He symbolized a dangerous otherness that appealed to many women, but the distance of the screen made him a safe idol ... Valentino's masculinity is in direct opposition to that of Douglas Fairbanks, still a popular star in the 1920s. Fairbanks represented a normative masculinity, albeit one that negotiated social and sexual dilemmas of the time. (Schlater 2008, 98)

Figure 6.1 Photograph of Suzuki Denmei and Tanaka Kinuyo, *Eiga jōhō*, April 1930. Courtesy of Kokusai Jōhōsha.

Suzuki's persona 'blends' these archetypes, both in terms of his personal history as an athlete and his onscreen presentation: Schlater notes that Fairbanks' persona was similarly imbued with the same attributes of healthiness and athleticism, and that his treatment onscreen similarly highlighted his physicality and emphasised his height:

> An early 'health nut,' Fairbanks was very active, vital, and virile-looking. He stood roughly 5 feet 9 inches and weighed approximately 150 pounds, not a large person, but larger than the average leading man of the time. Aside from his well-developed physique, he always kept himself tan, feeling this enhanced his physical attractiveness. His dramatic and physical acting style was perfect for the silent screen. One of his most famous attributes was his upward jump. He performed the stunt with the aid of a trampoline or a springboard and often used a fence to emphasize how high he seemed to be jumping. This made him seem taller and as though he was in flight … Fairbanks often manipulated sets to make himself appear larger and stronger than in real life. (Schlater 2008, 53)

Like Suzuki, alongside his acting prowess, Fairbanks' activities were rooted firmly in the sporting world; alongside his acting career, since he was twelve years old he had taken gymnastics and fencing lessons, and in the early 1920s both his own film career and the promotional materials produced by United Artists – the production company he founded in 1919 in co-operation with his wife Mary Pickford, D. W. Griffith and Charlie Chaplin – were deeply entwined with Olympic and sporting activities (Wilson 2006, 106). Rusty Wilson notes that Fairbanks publicly befriended and supported the careers of many Olympic athletes, built extensive training facilities such as gyms and running tracks at his own residence and the United Artists studios, and 'was an official spokesman for the junior Olympics during the 1920s and 1930s' (Wilson 2006, 107–8).

Suzuki's persona becomes aligned with that of Fairbanks during a number of visits by the star to Japan in the early 1930s. One of these visits was publicised in *Eiga jōhō* using a photograph of Suzuki shaking hands with Fairbanks while wearing the exact same thick belted camel-hair coat and slicked back hair (Figure 6.2) – they are also in the company of Hayakawa Sessue, a Japanese actor who had achieved mass stardom in Hollywood, aligning Suzuki with two international cinematic heavyweights (*Eiga jōhō* 1930, 8). Both *Eiga jōhō* and *The Japan Times* describe their activities together, taking place from 1930 to 1932, as primarily social in nature (*sukiyaki* and *tempura* dinners, nights out at Ginza cafes), portraying the relationship as an organic friendship rather than an orchestrated studio visit; the two actors are presented as naturally apt counterparts (*Eiga jōhō* 1930, 8; *The Japan Times* 22 January 1932, 1; *The Japan*

Figure 6.2 Douglas Fairbanks visits Japan in 1930, pictured shaking hands with Suzuki Denmei, accompanied by Hayakawa Sessue. *Eiga jōhō*, April 1930. Courtesy of Kokusai Jōhōsha.

Times 23 January 1932, *The Japan Times* 15 June 1932, 3) Standish summarises Suzuki's persona onscreen as follows: 'he was one of the first star personas to bridge the gap between the weak romantic hero of the *shinpa*[1]-derived melodramas and the action hero of the period genres (*jida-igeki/chanbara*[2]). In cinematic terms, his athletic body is the site of action represented through metaphors of speed and movement and, through the inclusion of the romantic element, a sexual imperative' (Standish 2006, 39–40). I concur but add that Suzuki also effected a hybridised bridge between the passive 'Valentino' and active 'Fairbanks' archetypes apparent in the Hollywood cinema. This 'bridge' is achieved via thematic similarities to these personalities onscreen (in terms of shooting style and sartoriality) and his sporting persona, which in a similar manner to the hybridised housewife aesthetic employed by female stars in order to endear them to both male and female audiences, allowed studios to diversify the appeal of his body to audiences too. While Suzuki's Valentino-style quasi-objectified presentation onscreen evoked an eroticised image for female audiences, this image was tempered by his proven physical dexterity and strength which portrayed him as an acceptable model of Japanese athleticism in the mould of Fairbanks, appealing to both men and women. The treatment of Suzuki's body onscreen as a fragmented subject of the audience's gaze presents it – as in the context of the beauty contest – as a desirable product, with the role of sport masculinising it; the heterosexual male spectator does not merely identify with the agency and control of the hero's ego, but desires to obtain his body in order to achieve such agency in his own everyday sphere – including by proxy the ownership of the female star and her body.

While the athleticism and fitness of Suzuki's body is highlighted in the film, it is notable that the connotations of the sporting world are not hugely apparent in the materials promoting *Souls on the Road* – the effect of sport upon Suzuki's public persona becomes more blatantly apparent when he joins Nikkatsu in 1924. Suzuki continued to participate in swimming competitions alongside his university studies, rising to prominence as a member of the Japanese national swimming team, competing in the 1923 Far Eastern Championship Games, a multi-sport contest between Japan, China and the Philippines. These would prove to a be a landmark games for Japanese competitive swimming – this was the first time that the event had been hosted in Osaka, and throughout the swimming events the *Yomiuri shimbun* documented a string of victories for Suzuki's team, expressing them in terms of national superiority over the other competing nations: '200 yard relay: with Japan's victory, a new record continues' (*Yomiuri shimbun* 23 May 1923, 5); 'Japan's superior victory becomes more and more certain – total score: 20' (*Yomiuri shimbun* 24 May 1923, 5); 'Victory for Japan with sixty-eight points. The Philippines has only eight, and China has zero' (*Yomiuri shimbun* 25 May 1923, 5). This positions Suzuki not only as a cinematic hero, but as a *national* hero, with the athleticism of his body, alongside its Western-style appearance, fitting neatly into the eugenic rhetoric of the 1920s which would inform the Miss Nippon contest eight years later. Suzuki's persona's affiliations with the sporting world intensify following his university graduation in 1924, coinciding with the Olympics held in Paris that year, at a time Wilson describes in his survey of Fairbanks' sporting activities as 'the first time any actor showed a genuine interest in the modern Olympic games', indicating a period when new relationships began to form between the sporting and cinematic worlds (Wilson 2006, 107). This is when Suzuki joins the Nikkatsu studios – his photograph, in which he wears a suit and tie and has slicked-back hair in the style of Valentino, was printed in the *Asahi shimbun* on 3 March 1924 with the caption, 'Suzuki Denmei: the Meiji graduate swimmer who has become a Nikkatsu actor!' (*Asahi shimbun* 1924, 4). From the phrasing of this caption, despite his background already including experience as a cinematic actor, the focus is more on his role as a sports star, rather than his new ventures into Nikkatsu productions. The image of the suave, suited and perfectly coiffed Suzuki is intrinsic to Suzuki's star persona from the onset of his film career, as seen in a similar image (Figure 6.3) of a suited Suzuki enjoying a cigarette published in *Asahi Graph* in May 1924 (*Asahi Graph* 1924, 7). A photograph of Suzuki in *Eiga jōhō* in 1933 (Figure 6.4) continues to feature Suzuki in a

Figure 6.3 Photograph of actor Suzuki Denmei, *Asahi Graph* 1924. Courtesy of the *Asahi shimbun*.

Figure 6.4 Photograph of actor Suzuki Denmei, *Eiga jōhō*, October 1933. Courtesy of Kokusai Jōhōsha.

sharp suit with Valentino-esque slicked back hair, seven years after Valentino's death in 1926 (*Eiga jōhō* 1933, 8).

Suzuki's move to Nikkatsu sparks a string of youth- and sports-related roles during 1924; titles of films he starred in included *Days of Our Youth* (*Warera no wakaki hi*), *As for Youth* (*Seishun wo toshite*), and *Song of Youth* (*Seishun no uta*, also directed by Minoru). According to Hansen, in regard to general Hollywood casting practices the consistently themed casting of Suzuki cements these connotations with his body both on- and off-screen:

> the casting of a star binds the viewer all the more firmly into the fictional world of the film by drawing on more sustained structures of identification, mobilizing long-term psychic investments in particular ego ideals and primary object substitutes. At the same time the reincarnation of the star with each new film reconfirms, inflects, and keeps alive his or her publicity existence. (Hansen 1994, 246)

The 'reincarnation' of Suzuki's existing sport and film star personae into a new hybrid star category becomes solidified in his second film for Nikkatsu, *The Man Who Becomes the Sea* (*Umi ni naru otoko*, 1924). The film is no longer extant; however *Kinema junpō* provides the following plot summary:

> Young people were gathered at a coastal villa belonging to the wealthy merchant-class Urata family. Within that group, the expert swimmer Wakuyama became a popular man, but Miki, who loves Reiko, was not happy about this. When Reiko was drowning, Wakuyama rescued her. The evening before the great swimming competition, Reiko coughs up blood at the seaside, and Miki rushes her to the capital, believing she has tuberculosis. When Wakayama was holding Reiko, Wada's juvenile delinquent accomplices ambushed him and knocked him unconscious. With the great competition tomorrow, so that he may represent his Alma Mater, he leaves his sickbed, makes a splendid performance and wins a splendorous crown. After this, he knocks down Wada, who was approaching Reiko, and between two young people an eternal joy is formed. (*Kinema junpō* 1924, 21)

Kinema junpō critic Suzuki Jūzaburō responded to the film as follows:

> If it is only laborious to carry the plot, then I can't really blame the director and the cutting department for the film's more slapdash points. It is a film that you must watch without thinking of such troublesomeness. In other words, this film is simply more pleasurable than that. The atmosphere of the seaside, the studentish mood – factors such as these, along with romance and a theatrical flavour, ensure that the audience is drawn in and kept interested until the very end. For Suzuki Denmei's character Wakuyama Yutaka, dry land is not only the only bad thing for a swimmer – there's also

> Wada (Takagi Eiji) and Miki (Wakaba Kaoru). Sawamura Haruko's (Reiko) only attraction is her body in a swimsuit, but I was most grateful for the up -and-coming Ogi Ikuko, as seen in [the play] *The Peacock's Master* (*Kujaku no kimi*). Perhaps it would be incredibly rude to say so, but this film is probably director Kondō's greatest work for Nikkatsu. It is beautifully shot and the mixed tonality of the film makes it extremely pleasing to watch. (Suzuki 1924, 21)

From this review and synopsis, several clear themes pertaining to Suzuki's star persona can be isolated. Most overtly, his role as a competitive swimmer representing his university mirrors his own life events, clearly presenting the film as a star vehicle and solidifying his dual sporting- and screen- star persona as suggested by Hansen and placing the film's fictional narrative and Suzuki's onscreen character within real-life events as relayed in print media. Suzuki's sporting prowess is presented in a competitive setting not only within the context of an organised sporting contest, but on an interpersonal level, with the female body (in her swimsuit) acting as prized object, as per Suzuki Jūzaburō's evaluation of Sawamura's performance. It is via his physical strength that he is not only able to overcome his rivals as he physically overthrows them in a fistfight, but also succeeds on the institutional level in support of his university, both a socio-economic signifier of middle-class knowledge and a motif concurrent with themes simultaneously appearing in the Hollywood cinema. In Part I, I discussed the Hollywood-derived consumer stereotype of the female student as flapper, which imbued related products with connotations of youthfulness. Considering the critic's observation that one of the film's key virtues is its 'studentish mood', this positive reception of Suzuki's role presents his star persona as a male equivalent to this image, with his physical prowess holding both the connotations of a carefree middle-class and educated lifestyle while also acting as a means of neutralising the sexualised, flapper-esque connotations of the exposed female sporting body. In this context, rather than the flapper-esque female image acting as a symbol of the disruptive and non-productive single woman, who exists as an impediment to the productive heterosexual marital union, via her objectification as sporting 'prize' for both the narrative hero and her voyeuristic male audience (a factor signified by the exposure of her swimsuit-clad body) the film's climax, in which 'between two young people an eternal joy is formed' instead becomes an ideal and complete heterosexual union in line with the state's eugenic aims.

The university-based sporting narrative, replete with real-life sporting stars in the title male role, becomes a popular theme within the mid-1920s Japanese cinema. Suzuki's success with Nikkatsu in such sports-based films provoked the recruitment of an array of sporting stars by the studio, with

Suzuki's success existing as the benchmark: on 18 June 1925 the *Asahi shimbun* ran the story 'Entering Nikkatsu: The Popular Man Asaoka (Nobuo)', subtitled with the phrase, '[Suzuki] Denmei's rival steps up – a brilliant sports star,' accompanied by a list of various other (predominantly male) sports stars which the studio hoped to recruit (*Asahi shimbun* 1925, 2). Suzuki's sporting body transcends his own star persona as a national swimming hero as seen in *The Man Who Becomes the Sea*, becoming emblematic of the 'sports actor' as a genre, with the emphasis now upon the strength, physicality and dexterity of his body across sporting activities rather than his own personal sporting history. In *Wagering His Youth* Suzuki appears playing baseball, with a photograph appearing in the *Asahi Graph* in 1924 depicting him in his baseball uniform, standing in a powerful stance with his long legs apart; the magazine also featured photographs of him boxing between shoots, exposing his muscular arms (Figure 6.5) – both articles refer to him as 'a great sportsman' rather than purely an actor or a swimmer (*Asahi Graph* 1 October 1924, 18; *Asahi Graph* 5 May 1924, 6). The emergence of the male 'sports actor' as an archetype denotes a desire amongst audiences to feature male sporting bodies onscreen, with his related onscreen sporting world emblematising what *Nihon eiga* referred to in 1936 as the 'Three S'es' of

Figure 6.5 Suzuki Denmei practising boxing between filming takes, *Asahi Graph*, May 1924. Courtesy of the *Asahi shimbun*.

popular Japanese cinema – 'Sports, Speed, and Sex' (*Nihon eiga* 1936, 75). Suzuki's fit, hybridised body was portrayed as the key means for the male spectator to access this world for himself.

The prevalence of Suzuki within such films depicts the 'Sports Film Star' as a Nikkatsu archetype; however, Suzuki's association with sport continued when he returned to Shōchiku, signifying the success of the cinematic sporting star archetype across studio productions. Upon his return to Shōchiku, Suzuki's position as Japanese allegory for the virile Hollywood male star body intensifies: on 3 March 1926 he appears (playing both rugby and tennis) opposite Hanabusa Yuriko in *Undōka* – an ambiguously titled production, which could be received as either *The Activist*, playing upon the popularity at this time of the proletariat film, or *The Athlete*, an interpretation more fitting to Suzuki's persona and the film's storyline, which centres around a female tennis player (Hanabusa). A promotional image from the magazine *Eiga jōhō* depicts the film's stars: Hanabusa, smiling widely and clad in kimono, gazes up at the tall Suzuki, who is inspecting a tennis racquet. Hanabusa's aesthetic references the hybridised housewife's iconography: she is in full kimono but has a fluffy cropped hairstyle and Clara Bow's pencilled, drawn-down brows, while Suzuki wears a striped tennis jersey (*Eiga jōhō* 1926, 32). The film received a positive review in *Kinema junpō*; however, the anonymous critic had a mixed view of the film's appropriation of Western sporting and student themes:

> I am pleased that the story is more cheerful than anything, and that it touches upon the lifestyles of today's youth, however it also contains problematic aspects that can be described as 'smelling of butter',[3] and I think that already the lifestyles of today's youth smell of butter quite enough, so it would be more beneficial to stop this type of comparison [with Western lifestyles]. The adaptation is kind and attentive, with much attention to detail; however, I caught a glimpse of a number of imitations of foreign films – this film is all about the body, the whole way through from beginning to end. And so, in regard to this film's success, it must be said that this is the adaptation's greatest power. The director also depicts the lives of youth as being pain-free and without hardship. Speaking of greed, the tennis scenes, the main focal point of the film's 'fresh butter', are deceiving, as they use a body double, which left me wanting more. However, throughout the whole film a great feeling of hope for the future is displayed. Mr Suzuki Denmei perhaps over-acts his role at some points, but this will probably be seen as his most successful role to date. Hanabusa Yuriko's role is one which does not require acting – overall there is the feeling that she is too distanced from her role as a female tennis player, but from start to finish all that you can say is that her performance is passable … With today's sports trend, there is plenty here to call in audiences. (*Kinema junpō* 1926, 52)

While the reviewer's own response to the film's adoption of Hollywood-inspired themes is negative (illustrating that the concept of the Hollywood-inspired male sports star was not universal in its appeal, much like the adoption of Western-style sports and sports clothing themselves), it highlights the key themes surrounding the body which successfully drew in audiences, positioning it within the overall 'sports trend' of the 1920s, with the bodies of the film's stars existing as its 'greatest power'. As in *The Man Who Becomes the Sea*, the female lead herself is reduced to her body alone, objectified as prize for the film's hero and, by proxy, the male audience. Even the commentator himself is allured by the film's bodily focus – his annoyance at the film's usage of a stunt double in its sporting scenes suggests a desire for the viewing of the 'authentic' star body, rather than a facsimile.

This is concurrent with Su Holmes and Sean Redmond's assessment of the film fan's need to '"search" for the "authentic" person that lies behind the manufactured mask of fame ... the bare flesh confirms them [the stars] as idealised beings or as beings who are as materially fallible as we are' (Holmes and Redmond 2012, 4). The reviewer's criticism that the film is too Americanised gains new gravity in reference to both Suzuki's Hollywood-style hybridised star persona and the similarity of the film's promotional image to a Hollywood production marketed simultaneously in Japan. In the same March 1926 issue of *Eiga jōhō*, a promotional image for *Sporting Life* (1925) depicts the film's stars, Burt Lytell and Marian Nixon, both wearing tennis attire (with Nixon holding her racquet under her arm, in a similar position to Hanabusa) and locked in an embrace, their faces within kissing distance (*Eiga jōhō* 1926, 28). Suzuki and Hanabusa are pictured together in the same proximity; however, his focus on the tennis racquet dulls the photograph's romantic effect. Considering the fact that 'before the war, no films shown in Japan had kissing scenes ... the Japanese government censored international films, cutting all kisses, and no Japanese film included one', and that the usual poster used to market *Sporting Life* featured the two leads kissing, here Suzuki and Hanabusa, within the youthful sporting motif and facilitated by their sporting bodies, become the closest Japanese alternative to the classic Hollywood romantic coupling (Smulyan 2007, 84). Here the reader of cinema-focused print media is directly invited to compare Suzuki's celebrated sporting body with his Hollywood like.

This raises the issue of a culture of comparison amongst male bodies not dissimilar to the comparison of female star bodies which I have previously discussed which endures into the 1930s, in which readers are invited to admire segmented features of male bodies. In 1926 – the same year that Suzuki appeared in *The Athlete* – Osachi Higashi quotes an unnamed Shōchiku official as stating the following during their actor recruitment drive: 'Men are remembered for their arms, women, for their faces,' and a fragmented approach to male bodily beauty endures throughout the period surveyed (Osachi 1926, 100). The term '*bidan*', or 'beautiful man', becomes applied to both Hollywood and Japanese stars: in 1929 *Eiga jōhō* uses this term to describe both Ramon Novarro in *Lovers* (1927) and Takada Minoru in *Moving Spring* (*Kangeki no haru*, 1929) (*Eiga jōhō* 1929, 24; *Eiga jōhō* 1929, 26). A related term, '*danseibi*' ('male beauty') is applied to German star Hans Albers in 1934 in *Monte Carlo Madness* (*Bomben auf Monte Carlo*, 1931) – specifically a 'rustic male beauty', suggesting that the quality of 'male beauty' itself was subject to multiple interpretations and a greater flexibility than the commercial female ideal – indeed, Novarro, Takada and Albers all have very different star personae and aesthetics (*Eiga jōhō* 1934, 18). The most blatantly segmented form of male bodily admiration, referenced by the Shōchiku agent, is '*nikutaibi*' ('bodily beauty') – overt images of muscular male star bodies. These images are the closest in their presentation to the eroticised female swimsuit images – an image of Errol Flynn appearing in *Eiga jōhō* in 1938, in which he wears only swimming trunks, is captioned 'a strong chest and strong arms!' a virtually identical caption to the images of Yamaji Fumiko and her companions appearing in the same issue (*Eiga jōhō* 1938, 35). The male star body is even further segmented in a 1932 *Eiga jōhō* photo spread featuring Hollywood star George O'Brien in a variety of poses across three images; the central image is a close-up of his flexed back muscles, another focuses on his arms and chest, and the smallest image features his entire body in a boxing pose – he wears only boxing shorts throughout. The headline of the spread reads, 'Fall in love with male beauty – George O'Brien', and his body is presented as both a site of admiration and intimidation in the accompanying caption: 'When he visited Japan last year, a newspaper journalist stated that this photograph was taken right after George had had a hot bath. Knowing this, I'm wrapping a towel completely around my waist when I get out, as I cannot compete with this bodily beauty. But there is nothing as fine as this, is there?' (*Eiga jōhō* 1932, 39) This body-focused anxiety expressed by the author is similar to those expressed in articles aimed at the female consumer advocating diet and exercise – these kinds of instructional fashion articles, which also gave advice on the condition of the male body in regards to its clothing, were also apparent in male-focused print media; however, they are usually provided only from the perspective of the Hollywood star rather than from an author representing the Japanese male himself. Examples include a 1935 *Fasshon* article, 'Edmund Lowe's Style Lecture', which focuses upon the star's athletic body (Lowe himself having athletic origins similar to Fairbanks) and its relationship with clothing, including sports attire: 'Amongst the familiar faces of American films, keeping up his reputation for being tall and slender, the stylish Edmund Lowe bestows on us his supreme knowledge of male grooming and style' (*Fasshon* 1935, 20). Lowe himself highlights this relationship, and is quoted as stating, 'How do I think you should have a brand-new suit made? Well, you should fit it tightly to the stomach. It seems there's a trend for suits to fit slimmer and slimmer. However, if we're talking sports coats, wear them looser. Please' (*Fasshon* 1935, 20).

It is perhaps a sensation of intimidation which explains the lack of unclothed Japanese male *nikutaibi* images – much as gossip columns made actress bodies and lifestyles appear to be more obtainable for female audiences, the quasi-Hollywood-style, but still Japanese, bodies of stars such as Suzuki provided a more approachable alternative. Suzuki's position as Japanese allegory for the Hollywood star with significant popularity endures into the 1930s, as noted in an article in *Nihon eiga* in 1936 which acknowledges his attempt to infiltrate Hollywood, while still noting his prime position as a Japanese sports star and successes as a swimmer and competitive motorbike racer: 'his fans say, is he Kamata's Suzuki Denmei, or is it the case that instead, Kamata belongs to him?' (*Nihon eiga* 1936, 75). Suzuki's star persona was adapted during the late 1920s and early 1930s as militaristic tensions intensified – Miyao summarises how 'Suzuki Denmei, "the most Americanised star" of Shōchiku, began to play stoic Japanese men who punish flippant youngsters wearing Americanised clothes in such star vehicles as *Kare to denen* (*He and the Countryside,* Ushihara Kiyohiko, 1928). Like the hybridised housewife aesthetic, different facets of his persona could be either interpreted as 'Japanese' or 'Western' depending on the audience member's desired orientation. In *Marching On* (*Shingun,* 1930) Suzuki appears in predominantly Western clothing, and is filmed in the same close-up, soft focus, quasi-feminised mode as his earliest appearance in *Souls on the Road*; he showcases his athleticism as a means of procuring the desire of his female co-star, Tanaka Kinuyo, including a scene where he dramatically rescues her on a horse in a sequence similar to a Hollywood Western. Yet the film's war theme (despite its narrative and stylistic similarity to the 1927 Hollywood film *Wings,* starring Clara Bow – whose attire is emulated by Tanaka in the film, positioning her as a Hollywood-style love interest) ensures that Suzuki's daring physical exploits and athleticism, surrounded by military paraphernalia and aircraft, are cemented as actions in service of the state, rather than his own romantic desires. Suzuki's star persona was flexible in its connotations, but the consistent representation of his body as fit and of comparable standard to his Hollywood peers positions his sporting body as a desirable object for the male consumer – like the female consumer, he too could 'purchase the star's surroundings' – including his healthy female love interest – via acquisition of Suzuki's fit and hybridised form, facilitated via the purchase of consumer goods.

The image of the fit female form accompanied by her healthy sporting male opposite encouraged the middle-class man to consume Western-style fashion and sporting goods himself in order to transform himself into his very own everyday cinematic hero, in order to procure the everyday 'fit leading lady' for himself, and as a result further the eugenic intentions of the state. These images and the spaces in which they were exhibited equipped him with the theoretical knowledge necessary to identify a eugenically compatible, fit and strong wife in service of the state. This generated an illusory image of autonomous romantic 'love marriages', as seen in the Hollywood cinema; in practice, as noted by Mark McLelland, 'despite the range of discussions about romantic love as the ideal basis of marriage and family that took place in a variety of Japanese print media across the early twentieth century, there was little alteration in the way marriages were arranged . . . Resistance to what was still seen in some quarters as a foreign sentiment strengthened as Japan descended further into militarism in the 1930s' (McLelland 2012, 58). This association between the cinema, sports-related Western fashion and hygiene products and the desire to acquire the sporting female body as object via one's own physical prowess endures throughout the period surveyed.

In 1933, Smile eyedrops employ George Raft, wearing boxing gloves with a towel around his neck, in order to market their product to the male consumer. He is quoted as stating the following:

> my departed friend Valentino had a saying: 'The most interesting things in life are women and boxing.' During my training, I have been watching my muscular beauty [*nikutaibi*] go from strength to strength, but once I was up against a guy with which I couldn't compete; his upper cuts were so straight. But then I noticed that he had the most ridiculously charming eyes – using *Smile* eye-drops was the reason! Now my motto is: 'Women, boxing and *Smile* are what it's all about.' (*Sutā* 1933, 17)

This example aligns the product not only with the two Hollywood archetypes of both Raft and Valentino, but even implies that it may even more successfully allow access to the star's world of sports and women than the Hollywood star's own body allows; the sense of threat in Raft's quotation echoes that of the commentator observing George O'Brien, transposing this anxiety to the Hollywood star's own context. As seen in female-focused product advertisements featuring sporting motifs, and the addition of non-functional sporting motifs such as monograms to fashion items, the products themselves rarely have actual sporting applications, instead utilising the sporting motif as a shorthand for both the sexually attractive male form and his affluent cultured lifestyle; an advertisement appearing in *Sutairu* magazine in March 1939 for Men's Jockey Club Brilliantine Cosmetique pomade reads as follows:

> A gleaming cropped haircut is a most prestigious thing. A straggly dandruff-head is most crude. Horse Racing Stick Pomade: an elegant

> sense of style with the latest fragrance – invigorates the mood, feels great after washing the hair. (*Sutairu* 1939, 66)

This statement is accompanied by an image of a tall woman in riding culottes and boots – supposedly the kind of woman who would not find an unhygienic man – in other words, one who did not use this sporting male grooming product – appealing. In a reflection of nationalist sentiments building at the end of the 1930s, despite this usage of Western-style sporting iconography, the product's tagline is 'domestically made', ensuring that it remains proudly representative of Japanese rather than foreign spirits and as an item beneficial to the local economy. This highlights the position of sports, and sportswear itself, as not being marketed as a specifically Hollywood-style, Western pursuit; as seen in my discussion of female hybrid outfits, male outfits, too, could employ both Japanese and Western elements within a sporting context.

Our Neighbour, Miss Yae (1934) provides an example of this phenomenon in its opening scenes; two young brothers are depicted playing baseball together, and the camera itself is actively involved using a dolly shot. While the younger brother, Seiji (Isono Akio), wears an American-style baseball uniform, his older brother Keitaro (Obinata Den) wears a dark-coloured kimono with *geta* clogs, a conventionally 'Japanese' ensemble. However, his outfit is worn in an unorthodox way; the kimono is layered with a white Western-style t-shirt and is worn off the shoulder in a relaxed manner, facilitating a full degree of movement as required for sporting activity, and his hair is cut in a floppy style reminiscent of Clark Gable, a personality featured heavily in film fan magazines such as *Eiga no tomo* since the early 1930s (Silverberg 2009, 122). Suzuki Denmei had already worn a similar *haori* kimono jacket and t-shirt ensemble in *Marching On* in 1930 – it is possible that he too was an influence for this look in this sporting application considering his physically active star persona. In this sense Keitaro's outfit is hybridised, however its hybridity matches more closely to that utilised in the middle-class housewife's aesthetic than that of the hybridised *moga* in its connotations – rather than existing as a dangerous entity, Keitaro is instructing his younger brother on how to play baseball effectively, with his wholly aesthetically Westernised younger brother being less adept to the point of causing physical harm not only to property (a glass window) but potentially to his female neighbour Yae by missing his brother's throw. The hybridised, but more sartorially 'Japanese' young man is depicted as superior in terms of physicality and skill, despite being engaged in an American sport for which a Westernised uniform would seemingly be more appropriate. By presenting a strong male character in hybridised 'Japanese' dress who performs more effectively at a Western cultural practice than his Americanised counterpart, the film presents neither a conservative nor fully accepting attitude to Westernised youth. It is implied that a combination of Western attributes with conventional Japanese attributes could allow Japan to be more successful than Western powers at even their own cultural practices – including, perhaps, becoming a global imperial power. The wearing of Japanese attire does not neutralise the emphasis on the strength of the male sporting body, as noted by the camera's focus on Keitaro's shoulders, which are revealed by his kimono during the sporting activity. Keitaro is later featured appearing equally comfortable in a Westernised student's uniform, his form visibly sprawled over Yae's *tatami* room (a fully 'Japanese' physical space) accentuating his long limbs, essentially a reversal of his earlier appearance in kimono performing a conventionally 'Western' cultural activity – despite his attire or activity, his body is fully acknowledged as a modern, internationalised but still Japanese body. Just as the middle-class housewife was encouraged to cultivate a 'cultured life' via her educated and healthful approach to the consumption of Western-style goods and leisure practices, which was beneficial both to her own personal life and that of the Japanese state, it is apparent that this same lifestyle image, emblematised by the motifs of the sporting world, was marketed identically towards men, with the additional pull of the cinematic female existing as the ultimate desirable object.

As noted in Part I, hybridised dress ensembles were readily employed as semiotic shorthand onscreen for proscribed female 'types', dependent on the configuration of the items employed in the ensemble. The examples I discussed in Part I were predominantly employed to denote Modern Girl characters, with the look's constituent items commonly consisting of a boldly patterned kimono, noticeable Hollywood-inspired cosmetics and a short hairstyle. In Part I, I acknowledged narrative settings in which this Modern Girl hybridised aesthetic was contrasted with a more neutralised presentation of an aesthetically hybridised woman. I maintain that the hybridised aesthetic was subject to substantial variation in its connotations, and that Western-style fashion items and accessories were not solely marketed towards consumers identifying with the Modern Girl archetype and her related behaviours. What this chapter adds is that the hybridised ensemble, when applied to the bodies of female stars both onscreen and in related print media, presented opportunities for companies to market their Western-style commodities to a variety of markets simultaneously, and that the individual goods themselves – rather than solely the concept of a hybridised ensemble itself – experience a degree of fluidity in their connotations. Shiseido's cosmetics and hairstyling parlours could either provide a Modern Girl with the materials to express her individuality or introduce a thrifty middle-class housewife to the latest neat and hygienic hairstyles for her family. Likewise, the mass-produced *meisen* kimono, an ostensibly 'Japanese' garment, augmented by its deco-inspired prints and bold use of colour, appeared onscreen worn by both Modern Girl characters (Yamada Isuzu in *Osaka Elegy*; Okada Yoshiko's characters in *No Blood Relation* and *Our Neighbour, Miss Yae*) and middle-class housewife archetypes (Tanaka Kinuyo in *The Neighbour's Wife and Mine*), with Tsukuba Yukiko, an actress with a history of both Modern Girl and middle-class roles, appearing in print advertisements for *meisen* kimono featuring lavish Western-style home settings. The position of actresses such as Tsukuba, who were cast in both Modern Girl and middle-class housewife type roles does not appear to be unusual, with the hybridised aesthetic of these versatile stars both on- and off-screen existing as a means for them to transit easily between the two archetypes. Just as the commodities advertised onscreen and in print media could be implicated in a variety of consumer images, so too could a variety of female star personae, and this extended to the consumption of the female consumer. As illustrated in Kon's 1925 survey and the success of companies such as Shiseido and Club cosmetics, which relied heavily upon a Western-style aesthetic in their advertising practices (which also frequently involved the cinema, via product placement or print media channels), rather than solely dressing themselves within 'Japanese' or 'Western' stylistic conventions; instead these two aesthetics existed as poles on a spectrum along which the consumer could choose her own position, augmenting her look with whichever 'Western-style' products she desired.

I add that female consumption – and particularly the consumption of Western-style fashion products – was not an activity which was explicitly criticised by state authority; instead, it was harnessed as an act of good citizenship in line with eugenics initiatives, so long as the purchases made served such purpose. While the Modern Girl image was criticised for encouraging women to spend time and money on their own appearance, the eugenic middle-class housewife aesthetic encouraged women to immerse their families within the ideal of a 'cultured life', with Western-style fashion practices embodying values of 'modern' education, hygiene and leisure. With athletic female bodies appearing onscreen and in state-endorsed public spectacles such as beauty contests, the female spectator is not only immersed in a new consumer culture advocating the selective curation of a collection of Western-style fashion goods, but becomes exposed to a plethora of goods intended to allow her to sculpt her own body to closer approximate that of the screen star. It is via the state-endorsed ideal of the 'cultured life' that a hybridisation of not only external aesthetics, but of the new ideal Japanese body encased within, could be promoted – it is here that the intersection between Japan's nascent outward-facing sporting world, Western-style fashion products, Japan's transcultural cinema system and all constituent members of the model Japanese middle-class family (husband, wife and children) becomes clear.

In Part I, I explained the immersive process in which the female star image provoked the female spectator to consume Western-style fashion products; in this chapter I reassert the position of the female star image as not only inciting the female spectator to consume these products herself, but for the healthiness of her own family, and by extension, that of the state. The female star image becomes the consumer 'lure' described by Doane not only for the female spectator herself but by proxy her male counterpart and their children. The practice of consumption itself remains the domain of the female but has a direct effect on other members of her household regardless of gender; other family members become part of her emulation of the star's surroundings, facets adorned via her consumerism in pursuit of the 'cultured life' aesthetic goal. The position of the sporting world as a motif in this dynamic is similar to the position of the versatile and adaptable hybridised aesthetic itself in the case of the female Japanese star; the iconography and vocabulary of the sporting world could be applied to a plethora of commodities (regardless of their actual physical sporting applications) in order to evoke connotations of this fashionable, cultured sporting lifestyle and personal environment. In a contemporary context, Paul Blakey describes the UK sportswear market in the 2000s as 'a major crossover market serving sport as fashion as well as sport as function' (Blakey 2011, 39). The 1923–39 Japanese sportswear market also served this dual purpose, with both functional sportswear items sold alongside other lifestyle goods marketed using sporting iconography or vocabulary. Like the sports-inspired monogram, the connotations of healthiness, leisure, education and affluence could seemingly be affixed to any item via such marketing settings; the iconography of the sporting world and the sporting body acted as an early form of fashion 'branding'. Mark Tungate quotes the contemporary fashion photographer Vincent Peters when defining the role of branding: '"What you choose to wear or not to wear has become a political statement. You don't buy clothes – you buy an identity." This identity is linked to brand values that have been communicated via marketing' (Tungate 2012, 2). Japan's transcultural cinema system, in tandem with the country's print media and commercial spaces, ensured that this political and commercial sporting 'brand identity', which entailed an overhauling of the female spectator's clothed appearance, body and familial environment, remained on constant display.

A common theme mechanism pertaining to both male- and female-targeted sports fashion imagery is a comparative dynamic existing between the star's body and the spectator's own, with the image viewed directly appealing to the spectator-as-consumer's own body image and self-perception. The goods marketed rely on this process generating anxiety, in which the spectator fails to see the star's bodily physique reflected in their own, and as a result seeks out consumer products in order to change this. The concept of body image being manipulated via media can be thought of as both a contemporary problem, exacerbated by social media's increasingly immersive role, and a 'female' problem, with female-identifying consumers existing as the chief 'victims' of this process. Suzanne Winfield and Yvonne Richardson note that in recent years 'several governments worldwide have registered concern about the negative impacts of body image', particularly highlighting the effect of fashion media imagery on women, referring to government surveys conducted in the UK in 2013 (Winfield and Richardson 2016, 53). Winfield and Richardson describe how conventional fashion media marketing has been justified by the rationale that 'consumers would be put off buying from brands that used models considered to be "too next-door" or "too real,"' with recent 'alternative campaigns' featuring a variety of different women as models, such as the Dove Real Beauty campaign initiated in 2004, existing as a fresh (and equally lucrative) counter (Winfield and Richardson 2016, 53–4). My research shows that this 'alternative' approach, which both acknowledges the potential for fashion media to cause distress to the female viewer's own self-image and employs this knowledge for profit by reassuring her, is not a 'new' phenomenon – my examples date from as early as 1935. This is not to say that contemporary coverage of the role of body image in fashion media marketing wholly ignores its historic context – Maggie Wykes and Barrie Gunther's 2005 study 'The Media and Body Image: If Looks Could Kill' acknowledges that 'since the creation of cinema, "stars" have been used to sell products and endorse ideologies and lifestyles'; however, they attribute this process wholly to 'the burgeoning of women's magazines and the recognition by commerce of the consumption power of the female audience' (Wykes and Gunther 2005, 103). I agree with their analysis of the cinematic star as a 'perfect mythic symbol' with the ability to 'leak between and blend mass media discourses', which my work fully substantiates. However, Wykes and Gunther's study focuses entirely on female reception, and this is an approach also followed by Kate Fox on behalf of the Social Issues Research Centre in 1997, justified by the findings that 'men generally have a much more positive body-image than women – if anything, they may tend to over-estimate their attractiveness', whereas 'women are continually bombarded with images of the "ideal" face and figure' (Fox 1997). The advertising techniques observed in my study are predominantly female-focused – I assert that specifically in the case of images of the fit sporting Japanese body of the 1920s and 1930s the female body is employed to provoke both women and men to part with their cash in exchange for the opportunity to 'own' such a body either in a self-focused or sexual context. However my study does depict a body-focused anxiety also directed at the male consumer – an anxiety which does not merely originate from the star's greater dexterity, strength and physical 'beauty' (described using a variety of categorised vocabulary – not dissimilarly to how 'type' was employed in marketing to female spectators) but also from his race – actual race in the case of the Hollywood star, who is frequently presented in a state of undress, and illusory race in the case of hybridised stars such as Suzuki Denmei. Suzuki embodied a state in which the Japanese male heterosexual spectator could envision himself inhabiting a body which sat comfortably between both conventionally 'Japanese' and 'Western' screen stars, equalling the Hollywood stars' physical prowess and stature, and, in his successful blending of the two archetypes presented by Fairbanks and Valentino, actually exceed their appeal. Like the hybridised female star, Suzuki existed as an adaptable star personality – he could either provide a Japanese analogue of popular Hollywood heroes or reapply their appealing physical attributes to become a new, stronger, but most definitely Japanese hero. While a hybridised fashion aesthetic marketed to men appears to be less prevalent in the cinema of this period than that worn by female characters onscreen, when it does appear, particularly in an athletic or sporting context, it is this concept of a new and improved Japanese male body which is represented.

At the end of Part I, I proposed the question, 'Can the theoretical bases for the spectator-as-consumer relationship proposed by Hansen and Doane in the female context be applied to other genders?' By applying Mulvey's concept of the female star as the recipient of a male-focused 'gaze', which transforms her own body into that of a desirable product, we can identify how the heterosexual male spectator may self-identify with the cinematic hero, his body and its adornment, and seek to purchase these items for himself in an effort to, by proxy, 'purchase' the body of the female star. This analysis specifically focuses on these aspects in relation to a 'fit' and healthy Western-style sporting archetype, with Suzuki Denmei's star persona employed as a case study. The way Suzuki's body is filmed in order to exaggerate both his dexterity and his tall, strong physique, alongside the emphasis upon his Western-style sporting history and persona in his youth sports films narratives, provided an onscreen hero with whom Japanese male audiences could self-identify, in a similar manner to the mechanism which formed the 'shop window and mirror' which 'trapped' the female spectator as described by Doane. The key difference between these processes is the spectator's object of desire: while the 'lure' identified by Doane in the female spectator's context is the replacement of her own body with that of the female star in order to access her glamorised surroundings, in the context of the male spectator's experience he must replace his own body with that of the male star in order to access the female star's body itself. This provokes the question of whether the male star could also incite the male spectator to purchase consumer goods in order to assume his surroundings, in a process directly emulating the experience of the female spectator. Could the male star exist as a method of inciting consumption of Western-style fashion goods outside of their bodily context? In other words, could the male spectator be inspired to purchase fashion goods fuelled purely by the desire to emulate a male star's 'look', without the need for a female star to act as the anchor point of this process?

Notes

1. *Shinpa,* literally meaning 'new school', is a form of theatre focusing on melodramatic stories originating in the Meiji era.
2. *Jidai-geki* refers to the genre of any historical costume drama; *chanbara* is an action-focused sub-genre of *jidai-geki* focusing on sword-fighting samurai – essentially the Japanese equivalent of the Western swashbuckler genre.
3. *Bata-kusai,* a derogatory term used to describe Western – especially Americanised – concepts and activities with negative racial undertones.

Part III

Menswear and the Modern Boy: Ozu Yasujirō and Western style for men

Chapter 7

Historically contextualising Japanese male fashion: Western-style menswear, the cinema and space

I have discussed the means of targeting the female consumer via the cinema, utilising the work of Mulvey, Doane and Hansen as theoretical bases for these processes. The key features of the spectator-as-consumer process are a sense of momentary sensory immersion, an awareness of the female star body's position as 'gazed-upon' object and the female star's presentation within a perfected, beautiful screen world which the viewer wishes to transfer from the cinematic world to her own everyday sphere via her purchases. In Part II, I discussed how this process intersected with the Japanese state-endorsed concept of a 'cultured life', which, like many of the images seen by the female spectator-as-consumer onscreen, combined imagery of Western-style home comforts, technological advancement, attractive body adornment and enjoyable leisure time, albeit without the subversive connotations of the cinema's Hollywood-inspired Modern Girl imagery. Indeed, the 'cultured life' of the middle classes could be employed as a 'gateway' onscreen to entice the middle-class female to purchase Western-style consumer goods not purely for herself, but for the rest of her family and the shared familial home, with the female-focused screen-as-shop-window dialogue becoming extended to her husband and children. As seen within the context of marketing sportswear and related health products, the ownership of the fit female star body (either directly embodying it or sexually consuming it) was presented as a goal for male- and female-identifying spectators alike. What is yet to be discussed is whether lifestyle imagery could be employed to provoke the male spectator to consume Western-style fashion products in a similar process to the female consumer. Could the male star also incite the male spectator to purchase consumer goods in order to assume his surroundings, or is a female star body a necessary object in this process? The Modern Boy consumer image is an apt test subject for my query – I have already identified the qualities which made the Modern Girl such a successful and prolific commercial image in both the cinematic setting and beyond, but could these same mechanisms be viewed in marketing to the male-identifying spectator? Could he, too, be inspired to purchase Western-style fashion goods fuelled by the desire to emulate a male star's 'look' and its related marketable consumer identity imagery?

In order to respond to these queries, the historical link in the specific Japanese context between Western-style fashions for men and the desire to visually construct one's own identity must be defined. I will then explore the position of cinematic images of Western-dressed men in new modern urban spaces, followed by an analysis of the response of print media commentators and Japanese studios to imagery of Japanese male stars in Western-style clothing. By then analysing the connotations of the Modern Boy style and terminology in reference to Ozu's own diaries, print media consumed by Ozu himself (particularly the work of Nakamura Shinjirō for *Shinseinen* magazine) and his film output as a case study, the dialectic between the Western-style male star, his related fashion commodities and the male-identifying audience member may be evaluated.

This question of how male fashion consumers respond to male screen stars has yet to be answered, or even asked, not only in the Japanese 1920s–1930s context, but also in the wider academic discourse on men's fashion, which focuses largely on the Western contemporary context. Tim Edwards cites the reason for this as being due to an academic treatment of fashion as a primarily feminine pursuit with a principally aesthetic purpose – 'fashion for men is rarely taken as seriously as fashion for women, and menswear is seen primarily in terms of utility – a perspective which cannot account for the specific forms and meanings of menswear' (Edwards 2016, 3). In the Japanese context, men have been keen consumers of fashion products (replete with Edwards' 'specific forms and meanings' as socio-economic signifiers, thrown into even more stark relief when viewed in regards to the feudal class system) since at least the Edo period, when new textile dyeing techniques (which were strictly controlled by the Shogunate's 'sumptuary laws') 'fostered in Japanese men and women a keener sensitivity to things and thus a modern transformation to a social system where social relations were mediated through commodities' (Slade 2009,154–5). Perhaps this early form of male fashion consumerism is largely disregarded due to the similarity of male and female clothing at this time, prior to the state-supported implementation of Western clothing: Slade notes that 'costume was moderately homogenous in the Edo period – gender differentiation being primarily signalled with colour and pattern' (Slade 2009, 108). Yet, in the contemporary Western context, Edwards laments that men's fashion is academically ignored despite the fact that 'men's clothes are produced and consumed in much the same way as women's' – therefore you would expect this overtly homogenous quality of the Edo fashion climate, with both genders equally consuming fashion goods, to act as a facilitator for the study of men's fashion in the Japanese context, rather than a detractor (Edwards 2016, 3). Yet despite Slade's extensive research on Japanese fashion history, he too falls into the trap of masculine 'utility' described by Edwards, focusing on the implementation of Western-style uniforms during the Meiji era and its usage of the Western-style suit in the official sphere rather than developments at the consumer level. Edwards illustrates his assertion that in the contemporary context 'men's clothes are produced and consumed in much the same way as women's' via analysis of identifiable marketable 'looks' such as the 1980s 'New Man', but to date English-language literature on the interwar Japanese context, its gaze averted by the flashy distractions of the Modern Girl, has failed to analyse the mechanisms at play in the period's own 'New Men' appearing in the 1920s and 1930s alongside her.

An intriguing factor which raises the question of why menswear has been historically ignored in the Japanese context is the fact that the wearing of Western-style clothing itself, amongst all genders, was initiated by men – this was orchestrated predominantly by the official sphere, taking the form of European-inspired uniforms (Slade 2009, 65). This move towards Western clothing did also exist in the civilian sphere, as can be seen in a return to Kon's 1925 survey of dress modes in Ginza, Tokyo, the female element of which I discussed in the previous chapter. Kon's summary image dictates that a wholly Western-style dress aesthetic was fairly widespread amongst men, with 67 per cent of men classified in this group (Kawazoe 2004, 33). I have already raised my issues with the methods of Kon's survey in Chapter 4; however, the survey image does give some idea of both the prevalence of Western clothing amongst fashionable male Tokyoites (in comparison to the wearing of predominantly 'Japanese' ensembles) and of what fashion items Kon classified as specifically 'Western'. These 'Western' items include not only the obvious overcoat, three-piece suit, tie and leather shoes, but also facial hair – the 'Japanese' section of the image is clean-shaven (Kawazoe 2004, 33). Interestingly, there are two items which when worn in a female context are specifically 'Western', but when worn by a man become interchangeable: spectacles and hats (Kawazoe 2004, 33). From Kon's perspective, in the male context these two items themselves become intrinsically 'hybridised', rather than existing as items which cause the hybrid outfit to exist as in the female context; he provides an additional breakdown of whether the hats sighted featured as part of an otherwise 'Japanese' or 'Western' ensemble (Kawazoe 2004, 36). This indicates a perception of hats or spectacles as fashion items that have become such ingrained parts of a man's dress aesthetic that they cease to have their own 'nationalised' existence; yet in the case of spectacles (and, to a lesser extent, some styles of men's hats) these have also existed as Hollywood cinema-related fashion 'trends'. Round spectacles, known as 'Lloyd' (*Roido*) glasses, were worn by fashionable young men throughout the 1920s inspired by the comedian Harold Lloyd, with the spectacles themselves becoming so widespread that they were subsumed into American cartoon caricatures of Japanese men, despite the spectacles themselves originating from Hollywood itself (Close 2014, 138). Unlike in the case of women's clothing, which is for the most part categorised solely with illustrations, the men's fashion items observed are frequently discussed via written vocabulary in *katakana*, as in the case of various classifications of coat, for example *rēnkōto*, 'raincoat', or *supuringukōto*, 'spring coat' (Kon 2011, 122). Rather than the coats purely existing as 'Western-style coats', they are instead presented as part of a seasonal and stylistic fashion system, with each version carrying its own characteristics, expected to be known and understood by the reader via this specific vocabulary. While Slade views Western men's clothing as something 'utilitarian', existing in order to profess the might of the new, modern Japanese state, it is clear that according to Kon and Iwamoto, these fashion items held more individualistic roles, with the readers of this survey being aware of the specific qualities of fashion items within a sophisticated men's fashion system. Furthermore, it is indicative that by this time Western clothing items were deeply entrenched in men's dress culture, almost to the extent that their signification as 'Western' fashion items – rather than simply just 'fashion items' – had become irrelevant. It is evident that men had a plethora of items from which to construct the aesthetic of their desire, rather than a proscribed state-endorsed uniform of utility.

This 'desire' element of the men's Western clothing pantheon is acknowledged by Kon in two additional illustrations which were printed in *Fujin kōron* in 1925, which document the experiences of people not in the affluent Ginza area, but of the impoverished Honjo and Fukagawa districts of Tokyo, which had been devastated by the 1923 earthquake. The two images (Figures 7.1 and 7.2) both depict a single figure surrounded by a variety of goods and their prices – however, the way in which they are titled suggests two very different approaches to the items on display: the female image is titled 'Things Honjo-Fukagawa Women Need', while the male image is titled 'Things Honjo-Fukagawa Men Want' (Kon 2011, 132–3). The commodities pictured, in the case of both images, were 'goods that can be seen in a Honjo-Fukagawa shop', indicating that, so long as they had the economic means, the residents of these areas did have actual physical access to these items (Kawazoe 2004, 40–1). The items 'wanted' by men are almost exclusively Western-style clothing items and fashion accessories – caps, gloves, shirts, trousers, rubber boots, waistcoats and belts. The female image is an almost complete reversal of the male imagery; the only clothing items depicted are a white apron and two different examples of *geta* clogs while wholly Western-style clothing is entirely absent (as noted

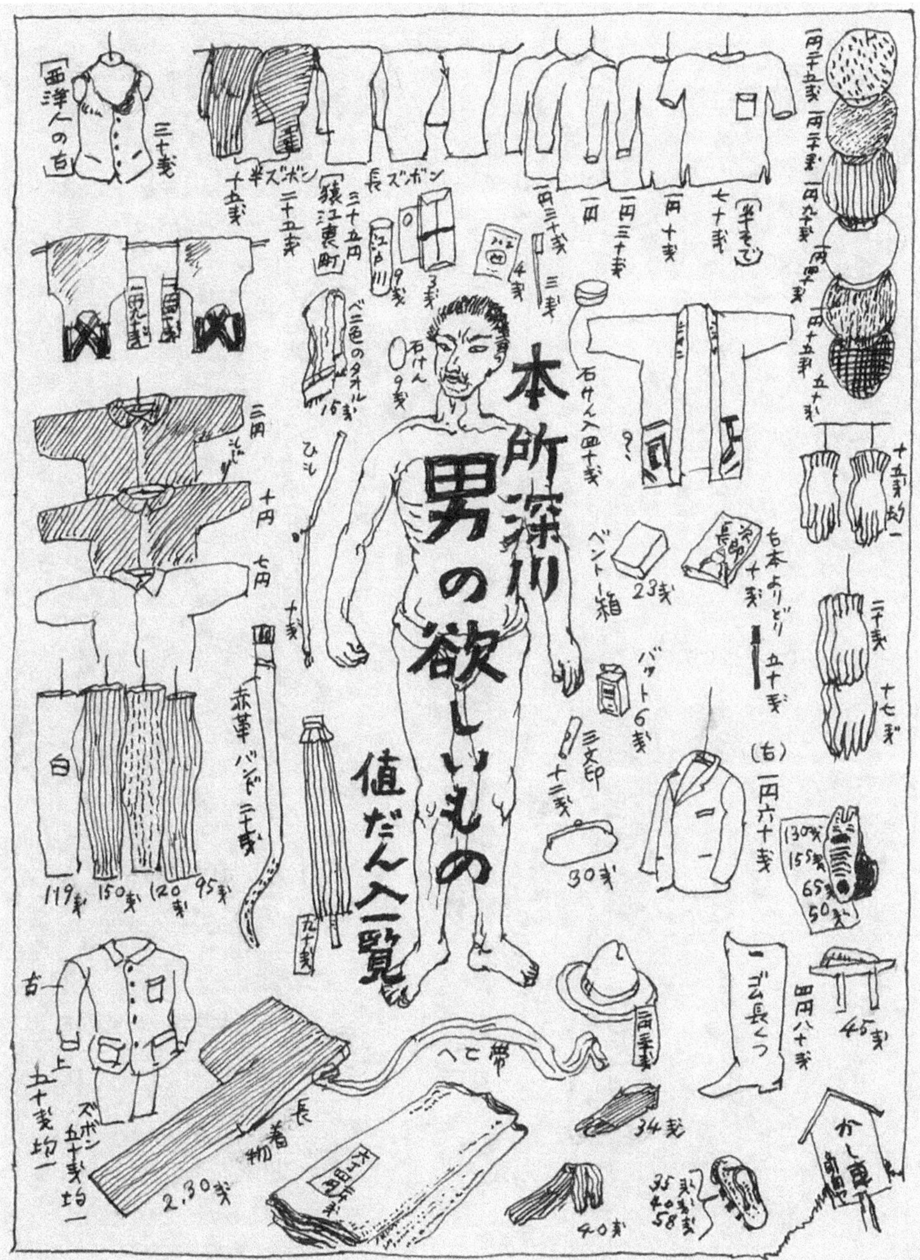

Figure 7.1 'Things Honjo-Fukagawa Men Want,' documented by Kon Wajirō in *Fujin kōron*, 1925. Courtesy of Kogakuin University Library.

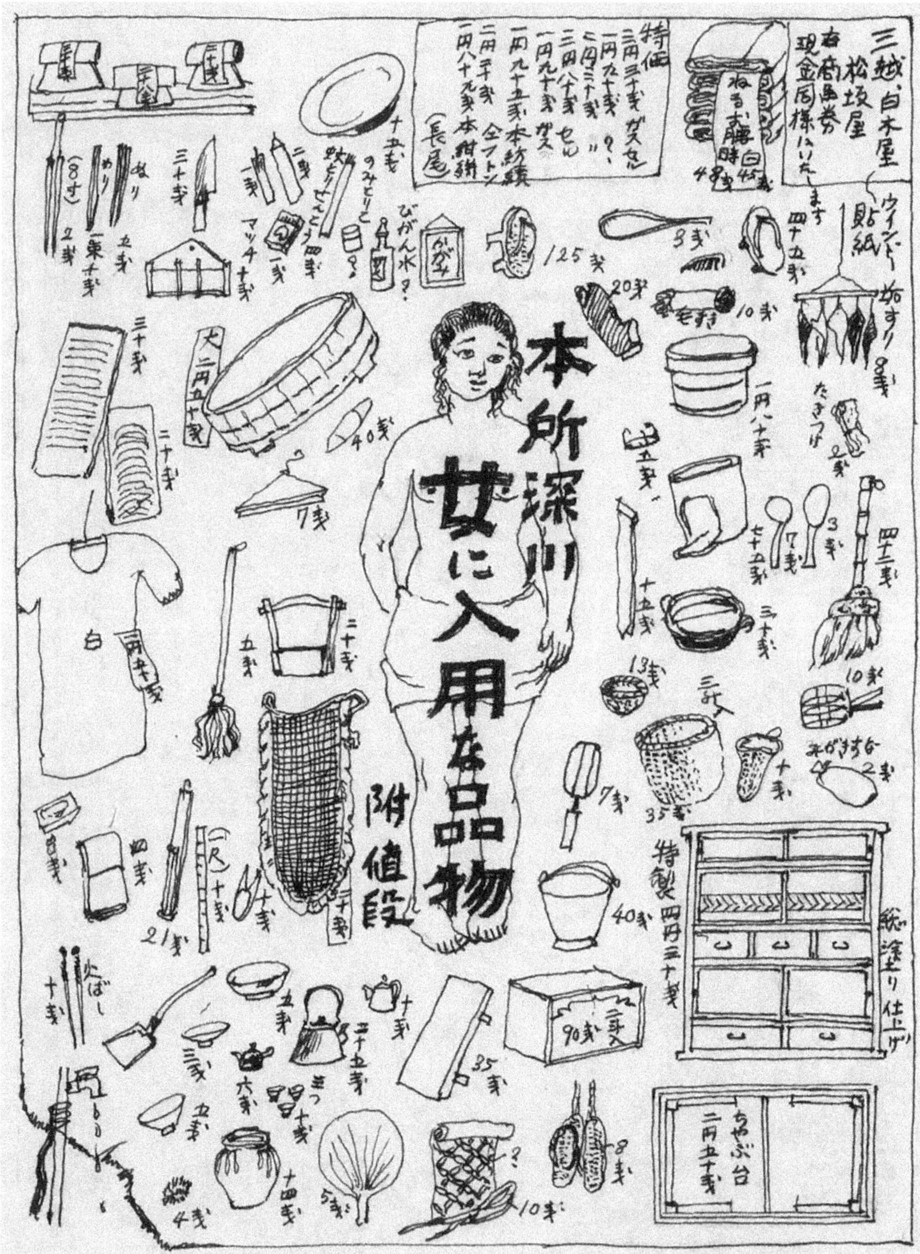

Figure 7.2 'Things Honjo-Fukagawa Women Need,' documented by Kon Wajirō in *Fujin kōron*, 1925. Courtesy of Kogakuin University Library.

in Chapter 4, Kon considered the apron to be a hybridised garment, worn by both the Modern Girl cafe waitress and the middle-class housewife). Kon's Honjo-Fukagawa woman is surrounded by household goods, many of which are typical of Western-style homes, ranging from coat hangers, kettles and kitchenware, to mops and entire shelving units. The image also provides some examples of the premises from which such goods may be purchased, including the department stores Mitsukoshi and Matsuzakaya, both of which as I have discussed were known for marketing women's ready-to-wear Western-style clothing. In one respect, this image is consistent with my discussion of how middle-class life was marketed to women via the cinema in Chapter 4 – rather than focusing on cultivating her own appearance, the focus is impressed upon a woman's need to cultivate an efficient, 'modern', Western-style home. The fact that the woman portrayed here by Kon is from a less economically privileged background than the Ginza women (Kawazoe Noboru notes that this survey existed as a comparative companion to his earlier survey for *Fujin kōron*) perhaps illustrates an emphasis on this household-focused facet of seeking to live a 'cultured life', rather than via individualistic (and expensive) self-adornment channels (Kawazoe 2004, 37). The two images, viewed in tandem, show a total reversal of Edwards' account of how men's fashion is conventionally academically discussed; women are portrayed as utilitarian consumers, while men are portrayed as aspirant fashion consumers.

An explanation for this can be found in what Slade describes in the Meiji era context as 'inner and outer conceptual barriers, wearing Western clothes in the street but kimono at home, or through a reduction of Western styles to play, insisting that they were not a serious challenge by treating them with a faddish, playful enthusiasm rather than with the reverence reserved for native styles' (Slade 2009, 137). Superficially, this rationale justifies the absence of Western clothing from the plethora of items presented as being what the Honjo-Fukagawa woman 'needs'; as her domain was to be the familial home, then she would have no need for the external 'uniform' that Western clothing provided. It similarly justifies the allure of Western clothing for the Honjo-Fukagawa man; Kon noted the area's high levels of unemployment, meaning that the association of Western clothing with the middle-class salaryman's 'outside world' held a certain lustre (Kawazoe 2004, 37). But in his analysis of Kon's survey, Kawazoe notes that even though these people were poor, 'this did not mean they were poorly dressed – in fact it appears that the opposite was true. Kon and [co-investigator] Yoshida Kenkichi noticed that the light blue overalls they called "*shokkōfuku*" ["workwear"], worn under a Western-style jacket, were everyday wear in the slums' (Kawazoe 2004, 38). Despite the lack of economic resources available to these men, according to Kon they placed significant value on Western-style fashion goods which extended beyond the 'faddish enthusiasm' of the Meiji era described by Slade. While their clothing fulfilled the utilitarian approach Edwards describes as being prioritised in the study of men's clothing, they also exhibited a desire to purchase Western clothing to be worn in public life external to the working sphere, as seen in the consumer fashion system depicted in Kon's earlier Ginza survey. So how did Western-style fashion items become both desirable, and accessible to men at various levels of urban society?

A clear distinction between the uniform-centric Meiji-era context described by Slade and the post-1923 context is how Western-style fashion, and its related marketable persona images, was presented to the urban Japanese citizen. Continuing with Slade's assertion of clothing being relevant to its wear in either 'inside' or 'outside' spaces in the Japanese context, post-1923 Tokyo presented the male spectator with not only new attitudes to the interior home space (which clothing, too, adapted to accordingly) but a plethora of new, Western style 'outside' spaces, accompanied by new social and sartorial customs. Most prominently, the young men of the 1920s and 1930s had the immersive transnational cinema and its related print media from which they could draw influence, inspiration and identity. The cinema of course existed as one such 'modern' space, but also as a means of interpreting other such spaces and their related commodities; Wada-Marciano proposes that 'examining how these interwar films[1] circulated cultural knowledge with the spectator's cultural norms – of what is modern and what has value as a commodity – allows us to formulate a historical account of the relation between space and "modernity"' (Wada-Marciano 2008, 17). Wada-Marciano's analysis focuses on the relationship between the depiction and use of space onscreen and articulations of modernity; however, it is her discussion of how screen spaces (as allegory for the spectator's own experience of the constantly evolving urban space) articulate the value of commodities within this dynamic which is of key interest when considering the male spectator's desire to consume fashion items. In its very nature the transnational cinema landscape was composed of both domestic and international (predominantly Hollywood) productions, exposing the spectator to both 'Japanese' and 'foreign' conceptions of both 'outside' urban spaces and the various identities that inhabit them. Wada-Marciano notes that despite many of the themes of 1930s (and, I argue, 1920s) *gendai-geki* contemporary dramas drawing their characterisation from Hollywood tropes, 'clearly the images cannot be interpreted simply as a reflection of Westernization or an imitation of the West; rather they were moulded for the Japanese consumers' own desires' (Wada-Marciano 2008, 33). The cinema performed a role which both reflected and generated the evolution of Japanese urban space. According to *The Annual Records of Cinema in 1930*, the average Japanese person would attend the cinema at least once every two months, with a higher rate of frequency for inhabitants of cities, which had greater access to cinemas and a range of films (Wada-Marciano 2008, 17). Outside of these hours, the city inhabitants' cinematic experience of the city as a hybridised, constantly evolving modern space continued, epitomised by the cafe: Merry White notes that 'by the time of the 1923 Tokyo earthquake, Japanese tea shops had been mostly replaced with Western-style coffeehouses, especially in the fashionable Ginza area' (White 2012, 44). Matchbooks surviving from the 1920s and 1930s, distributed to advertise Tokyo's nightlife services, feature a variety of both Japanese and Western-inspired imagery and personae, linking these recognisable character archetypes to the spaces they advertised. One example, produced for the Tenka tea-house, aptly named to mean 'the whole world' (literally 'beneath the heavens'), depicts a geisha (signified by her *okobo* platform shoes) entertaining a male customer behind a *noren*, a conventional Japanese curtain positioned outside tea-houses. But it is clear this isn't the geisha establishment of yore; the matchbook touts 'fresh beer' served alongside fish-based *sukiyaki* and *kohachimono*,[2] and most prominently the two figures depicted are only visible from the knees down – the male figure wears a pair of brown leather shoes and smart black dress trousers, enacting a contrast with the geisha's kimono. The fact that the two figures are depicted wearing shoes at all in what is purportedly a geisha tea-house screams subversion and a mixing of new Western-style spaces with conventionally 'Japanese' ones; White adds that 'for many, this was a new kind of intimate space – relaxing with one's shoes on was not conventional' (White 2012, 44). This kind of new 'intimacy', entwined with the eroticism of female entertainment (not necessarily the geisha, but more commonly her Modern Girl counterpart, the cafe waitress) becomes innate to the images used to advertise these establishments, channelled via references to the cinema's representation of romantic relationships; red-haired Modern Girls à la Clara Bow abound – however, the men in these matchbox advertisements also reference cinematic figures. An example produced for the 'Popular' (*Taishū*) Bar features a cartoon moustachioed gentleman wearing a sharp pinstripe suit cradling a cocktail glass, smiling gleefully; another, for 'Cafe Mitsuwa', depicts a gentleman with short hair and a Charlie Chaplin moustache being approached for a kiss by a red-lipped Modern Girl; the 'Western-ness' of the image is made clear by the image's accompaniment of a glass of red wine and a dish to be eaten with knife and fork. White states that during the 1920s 'cafes became Japanese and were no longer seen as offering foreign experiences'; she also coins (in a contemporary context) the term 'private-in-public space' to describe how 'the cafe offers society in place of isolation, or isolation when society is too demanding' (White 2012, 20, 44). With cafes and other recreational spaces drawing their aesthetic influences from conventionally 'Hollywood'-inspired cinematic imagery, and these spaces themselves acting as intermediaries between public and private spaces, these recreational urban areas become sites of both a continuation of the immediate momentary sensation of the screen and social disorientation. These spaces did not fit neatly into pre-cinema conventions of 'inside' and 'outside' space, which so easily divided the consumer's choice to wear 'Japanese' or 'Western' clothing, and not only the spaces themselves, but their ubiquity amongst the urban landscape, popular culture and day-to-day interaction (matchbooks, neon lighting and other advertising, print media, descriptions in literature . . .) ensured that the quasi-cinematic experience and its iconography remained constantly in view of the spectator-as-consumer, with these spaces equally adapting and evolving in line with the iconography of the cinema itself.

Discussing the European context, Elizabeth Wilson draws on the work of Georg Simmel to define the key role of fashion in allowing the individual to assert their position within the city's constantly shifting interpersonal dynamics and the experience of anonymity even in populated 'public' spaces:

> A heightened sense of individual personality and ego developed when men and women moved in wider social circles, and the constant friction of self with a barrage of sensations and with other personalities generated ... a more intense awareness of one's own subjectivity than the old uniform and unwavering rhythm of rural and provincial life. In the city the individual constantly interacts with others who are strangers and survives by the manipulation of self. Fashion is one adjunct to this self-presentation and manipulation. It is the imposition of this newly found self on a brutally indifferent and constantly fluctuating environment. (Wilson 2011, 138)

The added challenge of the interwar Japanese urban experience was the negotiation of this 'new' experience of sensation and socialisation with what were already understood to be 'Japanese' experience, customs and norms, and particularly the possibility to assert the position of one's own identity within this dynamic. The *gendai-geki* genre became an arena in which this experience of the urban spectator could be both reflected and further defined. Mulvey states that

> Man controls the film phantasy ... This is made possible by structuring the film around a main controlling figure with whom the spectator may identify ... The character in the story can make things happen and control events better than the subject/spectator ... The male protagonist is free to command the stage of spatial illusion in which he articulates the look and creates the action. (Mulvey 1975, 10)

Cinematic depictions of the city generate the sensory-immersive experience of a fantasy space of possibility in which the male spectator is hyper-able, with actual real-life spaces which reference the cinema (such as the establishments promoted by the matchbook examples) providing consumerist simulations of the protagonist's controllable narrative – particularly, in the case of cafes and cabaret bars, the simulation of relationships with women in a pastiche of the Hollywood romance. The bar in Naruse Mikio's *Every Night Dreams* (*Yorugoto no yume*, 1933), the workplace for single mother Omitsu (Kurishima Sumiko), is presented as a space devoted entirely to male entertainment and control, in which men are doted upon by openly smiling women (in both Japanese and Western-style dress, acting as stand-ins for the cinematic starlet) enjoying both female company and consumable goods such as cigarettes, the branded packaging of which is shown in close-up. Another Naruse film released the following year, *Street Without End* (*Kagirinaki hodō*, 1934), similarly portrays the cafe space (and even the Ginza itself, with the film's opening scenes portraying smartly Western-dressed men and women viewing expensive commodity goods, such as jewellery, in shop windows) as a facsimile of the cinematic romantic setting, with cafe waitress Sugiko (Shinobu Setsuko) not only resembling the cinematic female star, but directly embodying her, not only via her material quality, external to the film itself, as an actual film actress, but via the film's narrative. At the onset of the film, she is shown attentively serving two smartly dressed young men in homburg hats, and it is revealed that she is in fact being scouted for a career as an actress herself – the two men are not merely customers, but casting agents. These events are interspersed with shots of cityscapes showcasing neon advertising (for goods such as Meiji chocolate and Club cosmetics), often including crowds of Western-dressed men and women moving amongst them. The cinema itself makes a spatial appearance (in the form of the characters watching a screening of Carole Lombard and Charles Laughton in the Hollywood film *White Woman*, 1933), as does its related print media – clippings from film magazine articles are presented as narrative devices at both the onset and ending of the film. In these scenes, the city space itself is presented as an arena of possibility, with the gendered dynamics of the screen ever present and ultimately sculpted in the pursuit of male pleasure within these quasi-cinematic spaces, with the cinematic female herself being portrayed as a willing participant in this process – Sugiko leaves an unfulfilling marriage in order to return to work at the cafe.

The direct spatial referencing of the Hollywood cinema also takes place frequently in Ozu's 1930s output, particularly manifesting in the form of posters prominently displayed in onscreen spaces, acting as narrative accompaniments to the events and personalities presented onscreen. To provide just one prominent example, both *Walk Cheerfully* (*Hogaraka ni ayume*, 1930) and *Dragnet Girl* (*Hijōsen no onna*, 1933) feature gym scenes shot with a poster of Clara Bow wearing boxing gloves in *Rough House Rosie* (dir. Frank Strayer, 1927, no longer extant) in full view. Both films showcase a dichotomy between Modern Girl characters (played by Date Satoko and Tanaka Kinuyo respectively) with criminal connections and their more conventionally 'Japanese' counterparts, with the male lead's affection presented as the Modern Girl's object of desire. The poster plays a dual role: it both provides a concrete link to the spatial imagery of the Hollywood cinema and provides an analogous character type and plot reference for audience members who are aware of the film's plot. The surviving theatrical trailer for *Rough House Rosie* markets the film as 'the story of a girl who got her men by treating them rough!' and features scenes of Bow in a boxing ring and fighting back against physical maltreatment by men. The inclusion of a poster advertisement for this film reflects the theme of dangerous Hollywood-inspired femininity in its plot, alongside the intrusion of women into the gymnasium – a conventionally male space. This usage of Hollywood posters to both characterise spaces and the film's characters themselves was also extended to male characters – in *I Graduated, But . . .* (*Daigaku wa deta keredo*, 1929), the unlucky university graduate lead (Takada Minoru) lives in an apartment decorated with a poster for the Harold Lloyd film *Speedy* (1928), directly aligning Takada's character with Lloyd's simultaneously comic and fashionable persona and the high-speed nature of urban life – *Speedy* opens with the caption, 'New York, where everybody is in such a hurry that they take Saturday's bath on Friday so they can do Monday's washing on Sunday'. This cross-referencing of city spaces onscreen and the positioning of cinematic imagery itself within these onscreen spaces, echoed in the iconography exhibited in real-life social spaces such as bars and cafes, creates a synchronistic relationship in which both the cinema reflects the city space, and the city space reflects the cinema. The cinema and its iconography were therefore not only in constant position *before* the male spectator-as-consumer's eyes, but he, too, found himself regularly immersed within it. If, as argued by Wilson, fashion played a vital role in the city inhabitant's process of self-definition and self-assertion within the city environment, and the cinema too provided an arena for an idealised self-identification process particularly in the case of male spectatorship (while also augmenting the aesthetic and interpersonal spatial qualities of the city itself), then it would make sense for the cinema to exist as an effective means of marketing fashion commodities to urban male-identifying spectators.

If the cinema and fashion industries marketed Western-style clothing as part of the urban spectator's self-identification process, then purchasable masculine screen identities –which were attractive to male audiences experiencing the constantly evolving Japanese city – had to be created onscreen. Considering what I have already established to be a new sense of 'Japaneseness' emerging within the city space which combined both Hollywood and 'conventionally Japanese' pre-cinema motifs, customs and behaviours, alongside the prevalence of hybridised body aesthetics and stars as covered in Part II, these identities could be drawn from either Hollywood or other European productions (which were not designed with this specific Japanese context in mind) or, alternatively, produced by Japan's domestic film industry. These identities could be anchored to star persona archetypes, which allowed for a personified blending of these two conventions – in Chapter 6 I explained how the two masculine Hollywood archetypes of Douglas Fairbanks and Rudolph Valentino were combined with the Western-style physiognomy of Japanese star Suzuki Denmei, creating one such star archetype which could be implicated in the consumer-focused identity branding process. Of course, the concept of marketing specifically Western-style male identities to Japanese men via the cinema was not alluring to all audiences; some accusations of Western-style clothing existing as a superficial, self-defensive and indulgent outer layer as seen in the Meiji era persist during the period surveyed.

One such example of an archetype which provoked these accusations was the Modern Boy. This term was intrinsically related to the new modern spaces appearing in Japanese cities, appearing frequently in contemporary Japanese- and English-language commentary on 1920s and 1930s Japanese urban youth culture. It is rarely seen in fashion-focused publications but is plentiful in Japanese newspapers of the period. While occasionally its connotations are fairly neutral (for example in a 1928 *Asahi shimbun* article describing the manner in which Japanese clothing merchants were copying Hollywood outfits in order to satisfy the Modern Boy and Girl market, recognising both their attention to style and active purchasing power) an abundance of the commentary provided associates the Modern Boy with petty crime, scandal and negative social change. *Asahi shimbun* headlines using the term during the mid-to-late 1920s, when the term is first used in the paper, include 'The Modern Boy's Vulgar Public Trial: A Man Who Was Walking Around Harassing University Students Strolling Around The Ginza and Other Modern Boys' (*Asahi shimbun* 1927, 2); 'The Imported Modern Boy and Modern Girl: Looking to England When There Are No Words for These New Things' (*Asahi shimbun* 1927, 7); 'Modern Boy and Girl Love Suicide' (*Asahi shimbun* 1928, 1), 'A Swarm of Modern Boys and Girls Invade the Ginza in Springtime: Leaving Restaurants Without Paying the Bill, Brawling and Stealing – The Authorities Worry About Managing Them' (*Asahi shimbun* 1928, 2) and 'A Country of Modern Boy and Modern Girl Panic' (*Asahi shimbun* 1929, 2). The Modern Boy is articulated as foreign, violent, and romantically passionate.

The *Asahi shimbun*'s opinion of the Modern Boy does not improve throughout the 1930s, though the frequency with which the term is used decreases towards the end of the decade, and an examination of the *Yomiuri shimbun* reveals a similar trend. To be called a 'Modern Boy', according to the usage of the term in these national newspapers, was to be called not the relatively inoffensive 'frivolous' or 'wasteful' Dandy-esque archetype as described by Iwamoto, but a subversive and invasive influence with the potential for criminality and violence. We do not see the term 'Modern Boy' in related fashion publications or in Ozu's diary, as it was used predominantly by critics rather than young urban men wearing Western clothing themselves. The term was very different to the usage of the moniker 'Modern Girl', which was openly marketed by fashion-related industries who encouraged outspoken young women who were drawn to the Hollywood-inspired appearance of stars such Clara Bow and Louise Brooks to identify themselves with the term and express their adherence to the Modern Girl ideal via their purchasing choices. Similarly, while female film stars – both of Japanese and Hollywood origin – had the 'Modern Girl' term directly ascribed to them in fan magazines, male stars are not described as 'Modern Boys', be they from Japan or otherwise. While the Modern Girl image, despite its mixed connotations, had a clear commercial allure, the Modern Boy appeared to solely be applied to panic figures, rather than existing as a fashionable archetype.

Sartorially, the two fashion items most frequently associated with the Modern Boy are his Lloyd spectacles (frequently described as not containing functioning lenses) and baggy trousers, which lend themselves to caricature; this is taken in a literal sense in the *Yomiuri shimbun*, which published a series of cartoons drawn by Sugita Santarō entitled 'City Sights: The Modern Girl and Modern Boy Revue' in spring 1929. The Modern Boys depicted in these images are always shown in large baggy trousers, usually in a bold pinstripe or check, with either a panama hat or a pair of Lloyd spectacles. The 'foreignness' of the Modern Boy is implied further by the fact that he is always depicted in these images with a comically enlarged nose, a visual trope usually associated with Japanese caricatures of white Westerners. A notable quality of these cartoons is their depiction of the Modern Boy as a peripheral satellite of the Modern Girl, rather than an identity in his own right: the fifth instalment of the series depicts two scenes in which Modern Boys are purely spectators of the Modern Girl image. The first scene depicts two Modern Boys, sweating beneath a hot sun, gazing up at a hybridised Modern Girl (Figure 7.5), wearing a boldly patterned kimono and filing her nails, accompanied by the caption, 'Trying to compose oneself: eyes rolling around more than a Merry-Go-Round' (*Yomiuri shimbun* 1929, 3). The other image (Figure 7.4), set to a backdrop of city lights, literally depicts the Modern Boy's gaze: a Modern Boy carrying a cane and wearing a checked suit and a panama hat is illustrated as gazing directly at the legs of a Modern Girl wearing vertiginous high heels and a short skirt as a similarly dressed male companion watches on, his gaze illustrated using a dotted line from his eyes to her exposed calf. The caption reads, 'Well, look at that – the

Figures 7.3–7.5 Cartoon series 'City Sights: The Modern Girl and Modern Boy Revue' drawn by Sugita Santarō, *Yomiuri shimbun* 12–13 April 1929.

worrying thing about wanting to take the Modern Girl of your dreams as a wife is her short skirt,' the implication being that this mode of dress encourages other men to look at her – and the Modern Girl's smile implies that this attention is welcome (*Yomiuri shimbun* 1929, 3). The most blatant illustration of the Modern Boy as purely a romantic accessory to the Modern Girl is in the fifth instalment of the cartoon, in which a hybridised Modern Girl is depicted reclining within a circle, surrounded by stylised love hearts, supported by six Modern Boys who peer at her (Figure 7.3). The image is captioned, 'As youth is short, the present-day girl is somewhat of a philanthropist,' referring to her implied promiscuity (*Yomiuri shimbun* 1929, 3). It is perhaps this quality of the Modern Boy image – a male archetype defined in relation to his female relationships – which posits him as an unlikely figure of fun despite his violent and criminal associations. Unlike the Modern Girl, the Modern Boy is rarely discussed in print media in his own right.

Further commentary from *The Japan Times* from both Japanese and Anglophone commentators describes the Modern Boy in both effeminate and comical terms, depicting a young urban man who is promiscuous, but stupid; frivolous and overly concerned with his appearance, but stingy. In *The Japan Times* Frances M. Fox reproduces a list of qualities pertaining to the Modern Boy as recounted by a male Japanese university student:

> 1. He is a bad boy, he has many sweethearts, he is weak-willed and can do nothing.
> 2. He has his hair parted in the middle.
> 3. Carries a stick.
> 4. He wears glasses (lensless)
> 5. Noted for gentle speech, soft words.
> 6. He acts gently (like a gentleman?) but only for women.
> 7. He is idle and spends time walking around.
> 8. He tries to attract women.
> 9. He plays a little on some foreign instrument, preferably mandolin.
> 10. At school he attends the English or French class but is absent from the classes in his main subjects.
> 11. He reads a little of Marx or Lenin, but does not read the book through; he speaks as to Marx or Lenin, but wears beautiful clothes himself.
>
> (Fox 1928, 4)

This assessment of the Modern Boy presents him as being a similarly intellectual type to the bookish 'literary youth', the *bungaku seinen* (which will be discussed in further detail in Chapter 8), with similar layabout qualities – hardly a violent criminal archetype. It is his concern with his Western-style appearance and desire for both leisurely and romantic recreation which distinguishes him from other stylish archetypes, particularly his focus on the pursuit of women.

This depiction of the Modern Boy as peripheral to the promiscuous, uncontrollable and dominant Modern Girl is reflected in Gosho's *The Neighbour's Wife and Mine* during the film's jazz sequences; the band's conductor wears the baggy trousers, neatly groomed hair and jaunty cap suggestive of the Modern Boy and moves in the typical 'swaggering' manner often associated with the archetype in print media. He is very prominent in the shots of Modern Girl jazz singer Date Satoko singing and appears to dance around her and her Modern Girl companion. He does not have any speaking role and instead exists onscreen as little more than a backing dancer; the focus is fully on the scandalous behaviour of the Modern Girl characters onscreen rather than their Modern Boy equivalent. In Fox's article for *The Japan Times*, the young men that her Japanese student source describes as 'Modern Boys' are stated to be aware of this perception of the Modern Boy persona as purely an 'accessory' to the Modern Girl, and actually wish to not be associated with women identifying with the archetype: 'it is puzzling to see that *Mobo*s do not always admit they like *Mogas*' (Fox 1928, 4). Fox provides one theory as to why the Modern Boy is not as frequently represented in Japanese media and popular culture as the Modern Girl – 'the Mobo is somewhat standardized, he is an international character, and perhaps because he is more numerous than his feminine counterpart, he is considered more respectable' (Fox 1928, 4). However, this contradicts contemporary print media which illustrates the Modern Boy as a disruptive minority, associated in some accounts with violence and criminality, and in others with effeminate frivolousness. The common denominator in all of these accounts – which may be what was misleading Fox to believe that the Modern Boy was 'numerous' – is his affinity for Western-style fashions and leisure pursuits, which was seen in Kon's survey, and the 'Cultured Life' middle-class ideals were presented as attractive commodities and experiences throughout Japanese male society.

It is difficult to specifically define the Modern Boy, particularly as it does not appear that men publicly identified themselves with the archetype presented onscreen and in print media, and this aspect was noted in the Japanese press. A 1929 *Asahi shimbun* article simply titled 'Trumpet Trousers', referring to the emblematic Modern Boy 'Oxford bags', acknowledges that press coverage of both the Modern Boy and Girl were not necessarily reflective of reality:

> Cartoonists are not realists; a cartoon of a Modern Girl drawn by one cartoonist is created and altered according to that cartoonist's personal view of Modern Girls. If many cartoonists choose to draw Modern Girls as women with fat lumpy legs, then this is the feeling towards Modern Girls and Modern Boys that will emerge amongst the contemporary public, too. In short, trumpet trousers are not the trousers of the next age, the cloche is not the hat of the next age, and jazz is not the music of the next

> age. Everything is merely floating weeds, drifting amongst the winding flow of time. Nothing about this is real. Its existence is nothing more than an illusion. (*Asahi shimbun* 1929, 3)

This commentator portrays the Modern Boy and Modern Girl as media fabrications, with no real bearing or significance on the overall state of Japanese culture – he describes the role of media bias in shaping overall public opinion of Western-dressed young urban people, rather than actual real-life activity. This acknowledgement from within Japanese print media itself provokes a difficult proposition when considering how to evaluate the position of Western-style menswear onscreen; it appears that there was no such thing as an 'authentic' Modern Boy at all. What can be seen is a conflicted caricature which provided a carnival of attractions when viewed from a cinematic context: a slick Western-style fashionable appearance and enjoyment of related leisure pursuits, a desire for Hollywood-style romantic love, the thrill of criminality and the humorous combination of pseudo-intellectualism, superficiality and foolishness. It is for this reason that films such as Ozu's *Pumpkin*, a madcap nonsense comedy, was advertised using material referencing the inclusion of Modern Boy characters, while none of his surviving works feature characters who are explicitly referred to within the film's diegesis as such – the Modern Boy acted as a simplistic, two-dimensional distillation of these basic entertainment motifs. However, the concept of, and reasoning for, distaste for Western-style menswear amongst Japanese audiences carried far more nuance than that which could only be observed in the Modern Boy archetype – this will be explored in the following chapter.

Notes

1. Here Wada-Marciano is referring to Ozu and his contemporaries, Gosho, Naruse, Shimizu and Shimazu.
2. *Sukiyaki* is a hotpot dish cooked and served at the table; *kohachimono* is a dish consisting of chopped fish and vegetables, dressed or pickled, served in a small bowl as a bar snack.

Chapter 8

Opposition to Western-style menswear and the desire for 'Authentic' Japanese male commercial identity archetypes: Shōchiku's *shōshimin eiga* and Ozu's commercially augmented everyday male life onscreen

At the age of thirty-four, Kaneko Yōbun, co-founder of the proletarian magazine *The Sowers* (*Tane maku hito*) in 1921, contributed the article 'The Appearance of Japanese People in Western Clothing' to *Eiga jidai* (*Film Age*) in 1927. Accompanied by images of Suzuki Denmei and Okada Tokihiko in sharp Western-style suiting, with the image of Okada in particular emulating Valentino's brooding persona in his expression and pose, in this article Kaneko makes his negative feelings towards Western-attired Japanese film stars (particularly Japanese *male* stars), entirely clear:

> 'The appearance of Japanese people in Western clothing is as though they are putting on the armour of the present' – [Paul] Claudel's words convey to me an interest greater than mere quotation. When I am alone, I have a busy home life, and I rarely think of these words, but I do find myself thinking of them whenever I see Japanese films; I think bitterly about the frivolousness of the inch-by-inch imitation which is derived from American films. (Kaneko 1927, 38)

Kaneko's primary criticism of the trend for Western-clothed Japanese actors was what he considered to be its 'imitative' quality, and the representation of Japan which these actors offered to the rest of the world; he begins his piece with this quotation from Claudel, at that time the French ambassador to Japan, and adds the following commentary on the place of Japanese domestic-made cinema in international relations:

> It is essential that the films we release overseas do not contain men and women wearing entirely Western clothing, or for that matter our flimsy

> Western-style rooms [*yōshitsu*]. Illustrative examples [of unsatisfactory Western-style films] include 'Five Women Around Him' [*Kare wo meguru gonin no onna*, dir. Abe Yutaka,[1] 1927], 'The Mermaid on the Land' [*Riku no ningyo*, dir. Abe Yutaka, 1926], 'The Woman Who Touched The Legs' [Ashi ni sawatta onna, dir. Abe Yutaka, 1926], 'La Traviata' [*Tsubakihime*, dir. Murata Minoru, 1927] and 'The Sun' [*Nichirin*, dir. Kinugasa Teinosuke, 1925] – all of these films are failures. Swordplay films [*kengeki*], the works of Matsunosuke[2] and suchlike are also out of the question – foreigners cannot understand why one would brandish a sword in such a fashion. (Kaneko 1927, 39)

Kaneko's criticisms of these films appear to be critical not only of the clothing featured itself, but the Western-style surroundings in which they appear and the customs and manner of the actors onscreen – the same factors which I have identified as being part of the self-recognition process for audiences experiencing the fluid and constantly changing qualities of 'modern' Japanese life depicted onscreen. Kaneko cites Western-style clothing as a 'shorthand' for these changes and is concerned about the image of Japanese life that is marketed overseas via these films – he considers this image to resemble a cheap imitation of American life as depicted in Hollywood films. He is less concerned, however, about the actual aesthetics of Western-style menswear on Japanese actors' bodies:

> People thinking this way [in favour of Japanese people wearing Western-style clothing] are increasing in number – is it not the case that young actors such as Nakano Eiji and Okada Tokihiko actually look better than foreigners in Western clothes? Of course, other than the clumsy, unsophisticated[3] Western-clothed appearance of the foreigner, you can look around places such as Ginza and see young Japanese people with Western-clothed appearances everywhere; at first glance, they look very stylish, but even if there is some kind of beauty in a Japanese person wearing Western clothing, one does not necessarily equate the other, just as film actors cannot be suddenly thrust upon the stage. But, within the Western clothed appearance of the foreigner, *yabo* will always be *yabo*, and there is no such thing as what you would call 'taste' or 'style'. There is a beauty in the traditional which has been refined over an extended period of time. So, viewing Nakano Eiji through the eyes of the foreigner, or Okada Tokihiko for that matter, I daresay that it would appear that they were wearing some kind of armour. (Kaneko 1927, 38)

Contrary to anxieties concerning the Japanese body in Western clothing discussed in Part II, Kaneko argues that the Japanese body instead actually looks better than the Western body, even when wearing 'Western' attire itself. His point of contention is that due to what he views as the superiority of what he considers to be 'traditional' Japanese conventions, refined over the centuries,

Japanese audiences should have no need to copy Western dress formats, hence his use of the defensive terminology 'armour' used to describe Western-style attire and surroundings.

This approach to Western-style clothing, considering Kaneko's preoccupation with international opinions of Japanese life, is possibly influenced by the work of foreign 'Japanologists', such as the nineteenth-century output of Basil Hall Chamberlain, who described the uptake of Western-clothing in public areas during Meiji as 'protection via mimicry' (Slade 2009, 105). An examination of Chamberlain's 1890 work *Things Japanese*, a semi-formal work intended 'for the use of travellers and others' distributed (as of the publication of the Fifth Edition in 1905) in London, Yokohama, Hong Kong and Singapore by Kelly and Walsh Limited, unearths multiple assessments of Japanese people (generally described in masculine terms) as imitative of Western behaviours and dress norms. *Things Japanese* would have been in reach of Kaneko and remained relevant in Japan long after its initial publication – an edition of the text was published in Kobe in 1927, the same year as Kaneko's article, by J. L. Thompson & Co. (Chamberlain 1927). The text's Introductory Chapter begins by describing the typical new Japanese man as follows: '[The feudal samurai's] modern successor, fairly fluent in English, and dressed in a serviceable suit of dittos, might almost be a European, save for a certain obliqueness of the eyes and scantiness of beard' (Chamberlain 1905, 1). He adds that 'speaking generally, the educated Japanese have done with their past. They want to be somebody else and something else than what they have been and still partly are' (Chamberlain 1905, 3) and grounds this desire to transform internally and externally fully within a rhetoric of imitation of Western cultural, educational and sartorial norms as a protective measure against colonialism, 'for the mob of Western nations will tolerate eccentricity of appearance no more than will a mob of roughs' (Chamberlain 1905, 5). Chamberlain presents these observations as being wide-reaching by providing further examples from other works from across Europe and the United States in the text's section on 'Japanese People', including a *Spectator* article from 1896 describing 'the Japanese upper class … as the undergraduates of the human family … they even adopt a new costume and live in constricting uniforms before the majority have given up the habit of living in a loin-cloth' (quoted in Chamberlain 1905, 257). Chamberlain depicts the Western view of Japan as a nation desperate to assert its own position in the global hierarchy via aesthetic imitation: 'no Japanese but would be delighted to pass for a European in order to beat Europeans on their own ground' (Chamberlain 1905, 261). Considering the manner in which this aesthetic imitation is entwined in these accounts with accusations of frivolousness, a sense of superficial inferiority and intellectual shallowness, it is understandable why Kaneko would be so concerned about the domestic film industry perpetuating these connotations overseas.

Kaneko appears to be particularly disparaging towards the imitation of Hollywood norms and dress styles, particularly as he feels that this is not truly reflective of Japanese Western-style aesthetic desires – he later specifies, 'if you ask both men and women, Japanese people are mostly trying to match the Western-clothed appearance of the French – however, this could take two or three hundred years from now' – considering his admiration of Claudel's judgment, on which he bases this piece, this statement appears to view French aesthetics more favourably (Kaneko 1927, 38–9). While the piece initially appears to be wholly averse to male Japanese stars wearing Western clothing (and their fans adopting Western-style attire likewise), on further inspection his view is more nuanced – *some* Western-inspired aesthetics he deems to be acceptable both on- and off-screen. Kaneko applauds other *gendai-geki* productions, namely Mizoguchi's *A Paper Doll's Whisper of Spring* (*Kami ningyo haru no sasayaki*, 1926) and *The Passion of a Woman Teacher* (*Kyouren no onna shishō*, 1926), despite them starring the notable Modern Girl stars Okada Yoshiko and Sakai Yoneko. He states that this is due to their contemporary approach to cinematography and modern take on 'classically Japanese' themes:

> These films have classically Japanese stories, but are clearly in the style of today, and I think they must be congratulated … I saw [*A Paper Doll's Whisper of Spring*], and the skilfulness of the cinematography and the brightness of its beauty never appeared to be inferior to even the best of foreign films. Furthermore, the sets I saw in *The Passion of a Woman Teacher* I would say are absolutely excellent. Yet the former films hide behind the armour of cafes, women's Western-style rooms [*yōshitsu*] and hospitals, showing a painful ugliness. (Kaneko 1927, 39)

It appears that Kaneko is most threatened by the lack of 'authenticity' of the identity represented by the Western-clothed Japanese actor, alongside the spaces he associates with this image appearing onscreen. However, it must be noted that Kaneko's criticisms are not aimed solely at male adherents – his criticism of Western-style rooms in the home is aimed squarely at women, an association I identified in Part II as a demonstrable facet of the relationship between women, the home and consumerism advocated by the *bunka seikatsu* initiative. This question of authenticity is at the heart of Kaneko's criticisms – if the filmic convention, method or aesthetic which he deems to be 'Western' faithfully represents what Kaneko deems to be 'actual' Japanese life then he considers it to be acceptable; he considers Western-clothed actors to depict false Japanese identities interacting within false Japanese spaces.

Yet Kaneko does supply an example of a form of Japanese identity which could be authentically represented onscreen via Western clothing:

> Western clothing is mostly worn by people you would call 'labourers'. And so, from the morning to the evening, it is labourers who are living the lifestyle of modern civilisation. So, unless the film's backdrop is a factory, or depicting the lifestyle of the labourer, then this 'armour' is indeed armour, and perhaps we can make a film that celebrates Claudel's words. However, I daresay that a film such as this certainly will not be born in Japan, and so this film reminiscent of Claudel's words must also only be found in two hundred or three hundred years' time. As long as I live, today's society will not change. (Kaneko 1927, 39)

This observation is compliant with Kon's survey of the Honjo-Fukagawa residents conducted only two years earlier, in which the desires of working-class men are illustrated as being entwined with Western-style garments and accessories. Of course, Kaneko's proletarian leanings cannot be ignored, with the timing of his article coinciding with a rise in left-leaning film production at both independent and studio levels. Organisations and individuals calling for Japanese proletarian filmmaking raised similar concerns to Kaneko: two months later, in November 1927, the proletarian film journal *Film of Films* (*Eiga no eiga*) published an article titled, 'American Film Addiction?', which expressed a similar dissatisfaction with the predominance of American productions in Japan and particularly their superficial aesthetics:

> Look to the right, look to the left: American films, American films, American films … There are already so many that I want to clutch my chest and just turn away – oh, there's another American film. With its great capital strength, America is turning towards Europe, looking to force out the East. This deluge of films must be affecting multiple countries – and their cultures. We are not prepared to stop this 'Americanness' … But, but! In the encouraging film *Salvation Hunters* [dir. Josef von Sternberg, 1925] there appears a distant sadness … The American films which we seek are nothing like *Don Juan* [dir. Alan Crosland, 1926], a film manufactured using that mechanical old puppet, John Barrymore. The beauty of the costumes, the large scale of the production and so forth are nothing more than just dead old things, no longer even twitching with the last throb of life. And the 'cosmetics films'[4] of Clara Bow and Louise Brooks are not remotely what we want either. (*Film of Films* 1927, 8–9)

As seen in Kaneko's acceptance of some Western-style aesthetics and techniques appearing in Japanese *gendai-geki* productions, and his acknowledgement that Japanese people in Western clothing could be considered 'stylish', the commentator in *Film of Films* is not wholly averse to Western cinematic influences or productions. For example, he praises Sternberg's *Salvation Hunters*, a film which begins with the following caption card:

> There are important fragments of life that have been avoided by the motion picture because Thought is concerned and not the Body.

> A thought can create and destroy nations—and it is all the more powerful because it is born of suffering, lives in silence, and dies when it has done its work. Our aim has been to photograph a thought—A thought that guides humans who crawl close to the earth—whose lives are simple—who begin nowhere and end nowhere. (*Salvation Hunters*, 1925)

Sternberg's focus on 'simple' lives, and a concentration upon 'thoughts' rather than 'bodies' complies with Kaneko's desire to produce Japanese films depicting the everyday lives of working people and the disdain displayed by both him and the *Film of Films* commentator concerning superficial bodily adornment; furthermore, the film's assertion that thoughts 'create and destroy nations' supports Kaneko's anxiety surrounding the role of Western-style clothing in generating negative opinions of Japanese people (particularly Japanese men) overseas.

Contrary to his prediction, Kaneko and his peers would not have to wait two or three hundred years to see Japanese films depicting the ordinary lives of working-class Japanese people. These comments only precede the foundation of the Proletarian Film League of Japan (Nihon Puroretaria Eiga Dōmei, hereon referred to by its abbreviation Prokino) by two years – Makino Mamoru notes the organisation's founding meeting taking place in 1929 (Gerow and Makino, 1994). The organisation specialised in documentary and newsreel footage – works intended as faithful (albeit politically loaded) depictions of real-life stories, as desired by Kaneko. However, Prokino also produced fiction films featuring working-class Japanese characters, blurring the distinction between fictional and documentary works via an entirely constructed 'reality' onscreen. This interaction between fiction and documentary footage extended to commercial productions, manifested in the phenomenon of the left-leaning 'tendency film' – a genre frequently associated with Mizoguchi's works for Nikkatsu, as praised by Kaneko. This blending of commercial and independent productions, united in a desire to illustrate 'real' Japanese stories and people onscreen, is mirrored in the personae linked to Prokino. The same actors whose images appear in accompaniment to Kaneko's article, and whose Western-style appearance he criticises (Suzuki Denmei and Okada Tokihiko) were listed as early supporters of the organisation via its Prokino Tomo no Kai (Society of Friends of Prokino) initiative which it announced in its journal *Shinkō eiga* in June 1930 (Takata 1930, 31). Other names listed include Mizoguchi himself, the director Ushihara Kiyohiko (who worked frequently with Suzuki on *gendai-geki* productions) and the screenwriter Noda Kōgu, who collaborated with Ozu since the onset of his directorial career, beginning with the 1927 *jidai-geki* work *Sword of Penitence* (*Zange no yaiba*) (Nornes 2003, 35). This generates a confused image of the Japanese 'authenticity' so desired by Kaneko; the same actors and studio system he criticises for their superficial 'falseness' were also in support of telling 'ordinary' contemporary Japanese stories – and the commercial studio support of such films suggest an audience thirst for them, too.

Like Kaneko and the *Film of Films* commentator, wider audiences did not respond positively to productions considered to be purely imitative of Hollywood productions, an approach initially undertaken by Shōchiku: 'Upon its founding, Shōchiku sought to be the progressive firm, hiring Japanese who had worked for American studios and making such defiantly "Western" films as Minoru Murata's *Rojo no reikon* (*Souls on the Road*, 1921). Most of the resultant films were unpopular with the general public' (Bordwell 1988, 19). This way of thinking was not restricted to Shōchiku – three of the films criticised by Kaneko were released by Nikkatsu and directed by Abe Yutaka, who was also credited as 'Jack' Abe, a former Japanese Hollywood actor. *Kinema junpō* critic Satō Yukio, reviewing *The Mermaid on the Land* (1926, no longer extant), noted the film's popular appeal to audiences, but found the film overall superficial and lacking:

> The power of the original work [Kikuchi Kan's short story] and the abundance of content will make this film successful, but it has a huge handicap from its very beginnings. A simple love triangle is never a new plot, and this is a scenario through which only a one- dimensional view of modern life can be presented. (Satō 1926, 43)

According to Satō, this one-dimensional view of modernity permeates the film; the review describes a variety of scenes reminiscent of the same Hollywood clichés criticised by Kaneko: a flapper 'posing in a solarium' amongst other scenes shot 'inside cars and banqueting halls' (Satō 1926, 43).

Similar Hollywood-style imagery appears to be used to market *The Woman Who Touched the Legs* (which is no longer extant) a month later in September 1926; an advertisement for the film in *Kinema junpō* depicts Yōko Umemura, in full hybridised Modern-Girl mode, wearing a vibrantly patterned kimono with short permed hair and clutching an elaborately decorated box bag, framed by her male co-stars, Okada Tokihiko and Shima Kōji (Figure 8.1). Both men are wearing Western-style hats (a bowler and a homburg, respectively), fitted dark-coloured suits, white shirts and dark ties. Okada wears both Harold Lloyd's spectacles and Charlie Chaplin's moustache – a direct sartorial combination of the aesthetics of two Hollywood comedy heavyweights. The accompanying copy suggests a more nuanced narrative:

> On a train dashing through the darkness: an ambitious literary youth [*bungaku seinen*] on a trip to remote Hokkaidō and a charming woman returning to her hometown. A touch by chance from one leg to another ... An erotic depiction in which the true spirit of humanity is discussed; humorous performances hinting at the mystery of fate; a skilful adaptation by a wonderful director – a perfect blend of these three factors comes to fruition in this film! (*Kinema junpō* 1926, 40)

Figure 8.1 Advertisement for *The Woman Who Touched the Legs* (1926) in *Kinema junpō*, October 1926.

While the film is advertised using the conventional Hollywood-style erotic attractions and Western-style imagery, the plot itself contains multiple specific references to the Japanese social context. The most prominent of these is the description of Tokihiko's male lead as a '*bungaku seinen*' – a 'literary youth', a specific young Japanese male identity archetype emerging in late-Meiji print media and persisting throughout the Taishō era. Considering the film's comedic focus, and Tokihiko's costuming, it is clear that in this film the 'literary youth' is not presented as an aspirational figure, but instead as a critical caricature of modern emergent male youth archetypes. Maruyama Masao notes a trend for what he terms 'privatisation' appearing in the late-Meiji literary world, centring around the *watakushi-shōsetsu*, or 'I Novel':

> Its ideas were quite different from rising individualism in the European sense of the term. The expression (favoured by Japanese naturalists), 'the sorrow and disillusionment of exposing realities,' well describes the hero in such a novel, who is neither a masculine individualist, facing the challenges of life with grand dreams for the future, nor the Nietzschean superman, courageously trampling over conventional moral restraints ... *Bungaku seinen* [literary youths] ... escaping from *seken* [the world], indulged themselves in masochistic self-disclosure. (Maruyama 2015, 508, 509)

Like the Modern Girl, the criticisms of the *bungaku seinen* were aimed at his self-indulgence: while the Modern Girl was accused of indulging herself via her consumption of self-centred Western-style fashion and beauty goods, the *bungaku seinen* instead indulged himself in seclusion and introversion in an isolated artistic pursuit of 'exposing reality' – hardly ideals in line with the modernising state's desire to generate a strong, cohesive family system to facilitate its military aims. This was further criticised due to individuals identifying with the *bungaku seinen* grouping situating themselves as being social outcasts, despite their privileged position as university students or graduates: 'the life of the self-professed *bungaku seinen* was predicated on the young writer's unshakeable faith in these Romantic ideals and involved the acceptance of a life on the fringes of social acceptability . . . Poverty stimulated them to write about their most immediate needs and concerns' (Keaveney 2004, 56). This meant that despite their thirst for writing about an impoverished 'reality', a cause not too distant from the cinematic aims of Kaneko and his contemporaries, this impoverished, isolated 'reality' was considered self-inflicted, or even a youth 'trend' by some commentators. A 1925 *Yomiuri shimbun* article entitled 'A Warning to Novelists' associates the rise in the number of youths identifying as *bungaku seinen* with the popularity of 'nonsense' literature and mentally unstable behaviour amongst established novelists, and even asks both the reader and these established novelists to empathise with these young men, rather than chastise them:

> Recently, when novelists try to think of words to say to *bungaku seinen*, ironically, as though they are stupid, they have nothing at all to say – they have mixed feelings. For most literary masters, insulting *bungaku seinen* is one of their strong points. Indeed, amongst today's youth idiots are plentiful, but none are becoming as seemingly insufferable as the *bungaku seinen* … The increasing number of *bungaku seinen* is not incredibly welcome. (*Yomiuri shimbun* 1925, 2)

The commentator's assessment of the number of young men branded as *bungaku seinen* being on the rise during the mid-1920s appears elsewhere in print media: Arimoto Hōsui, a poet credited as an 'editor-in-chief' working on a range of publications with various target audiences published by Jitsugyō no Nihonsha (*Women's World* [*Fujin sekai*], *Nihon Shonen* [*Japan Boy*] and *Japan of Business* [*Jitsugyō no Nihon*]) is quoted as stating the following: '*Bungaku seinen*, salarymen, gentlemen [*shinshi*] and ladies [*shukujo*] – I serve them all' (*Yomiuri shimbun* 1926, 4). Rather than being an eccentric minority, the *bungaku seinen* archetype appears to have been considered as a viable member group of the Japanese consumer landscape which would be instantly recognisable onscreen to a Japanese audience. Like the Modern Girl, the *bungaku seinen* took Western-inspired factors (in his case, individualist literary perspectives and practices rather than fashion aesthetics) and adapted them to a specific Japanese context; Abe's own film, too, rather than being a wholly imitative work as asserted by Kaneko appears at least to attempt to adapt conventional Hollywood themes to include specific Japanese aspects, and this is clearly employed as an audience attraction in its advertising materials in *Kinema junpō*. The trope of 'going out of town' to a remote location (for example, the Wild West) is transposed to Hokkaido, considered to be a comparable 'frontierland' in the popular imagination from 1869 onwards (Assmann 2015, 152), and while two of the film's main characters are conventional Hollywood archetypes – the beautiful but mysterious femme fatale and a haphazard detective – the addition of the *bungaku seinen* character exists as an attempt to ground the film specifically in the Japanese viewer's own experience, with the divided attitudes towards the *bungaku seinen* archetype receiving additional comedic connotations when transferred to the star persona of popular male lead Okada Tokihiko, an actor who was particularly noted for his fashionable Western-style appearance as referenced by the images accompanying Kaneko's article. As the film is no longer extant it is impossible to truly assess whether Kaneko's description of the film as a 'failure' in terms of its ability to represent a 'realistic' approach rather than existing as an imitation of existing Hollywood works is justifiable; however these elements, accompanied by the poster's proclamation of the film's ability to depict the 'true spirit of humanity' indicates an awareness at Nikkatsu that audiences had a new thirst for 'realistic' and relatable Japanese cinema experiences. The fact that the poster first appears in the issue of *Kinema junpō* published directly after the edition which contains Satō's review of *The Mermaid on the Land* (a review which questioned the film's 'one-dimensional view of modern life') suggests that the studio wished to directly respond to this criticism within the magazine itself. This is further reinforced by the link between the production of the two films advertised in the film's *Kinema junpō* synopsis – the film is described as 'a contemporary drama produced by Jack Abe directly after *The Mermaid on The Land*' (*Kinema junpō* 1926, 42). Pure imitation of American films, altered in style only by using Japanese actors, clearly were not enough to hold a general audience's attention – and even studios producing films accused of such imitation were evidently aware of this.

If one of the effective consumption-inciting roles of the cinema was as a replication of the rapidly evolving city experience, then it would make sense that this replicated sensory-reflexive environment would be populated with 'realistic' male identities which were relatable to the film's audience, whether they be the 'labourers' described by Kaneko or otherwise. While Kaneko's concerns are primarily with the role of film in articulating 'true' representations of Japanese identity both at home and overseas, this facet of 'authenticity' is also an important facilitator in the role of cinema in marketing fashion imagery via the spectator's self-identification with the star image; Helen Warner notes that 'notions of "authenticity" are central to audience and star identification practices both historically and in the contemporary period' (Warner 2014, 143). Miriam Hansen also describes the 'changing fabric of everyday life [and] the dimension of the quotidian, of everyday usage' as being key elements of her concept of 'vernacular modernism', which I have established forms the base of the sensory-immersive process which provokes consumption (Hansen 2000, 11). However, this does not necessarily position the 'labourer' everyman star advocated by Kaneko as a potential fashion icon. In Part II, I described how the perfect, yet fallible female star image was harnessed to market fashion and beauty products to women by illuminating supposed star anxieties which mirrored the female consumer's own; I also noted the presence of body-image-focused anxiety in male-focused sporting images of Hollywood and European actors, accompanied by a dearth of images of unclothed Japanese male star bodies. Clearly clothing plays a role in the construction of an 'authentic' Japanese male identity onscreen which was, like its female-focused counterpart, relatable yet distant, Western-inspired but still 'Japanese'. The distance required between the social status of the spectator and the fashionable screen image is relative to the spectator's own position; the

Western-style fashion items desired by the Honjo-Fukagawa man depicted by Kon are not the items he would wear in a manual job, but instead items more frequently associated with the middle-classes, representatives of the idealised 'cultured life' typified by the white-collar salaryman – it is feasible that other identities could be pitched at other echelons of the urban social strata. Wilson adds that this aspect of potential social mobility via fashion, too, was innate to the modernising city experience as emulated by the cinematic sphere:

> The spatial structure of these great new cities intensified the individual's experience of mobility, both geographically and socially; great wealth and dire poverty lived cheek by jowl and the speed with which an individual might run the gamut of experience from one to the other terrified and fascinated a new generation of citizens thus condemned to perpetual over-excitement and over-stimulation. Nietzsche spoke also of the fragmentation of identity caused by the 'tropical tempo' of modernity; 'modern man "can never really look well dressed", because no social role in modern times can ever be a perfect fit'. (Wilson 2011, 27)

This raises an additional facet of instability to the constantly moving and changing spheres existing in the fashion, cinematic and urban contexts; that of an unstable social identity, subject to sentiments of both optimism, in which the spectator believes his position could rise, and anxiety, as he wishes to hold his current position or not fall behind. The distance between the spectator and the character's onscreen social position motivates these processes, which could be harnessed at both commercial and state levels.

The most obvious example of a threat to male stability was the rising mobility of women. Naruse's *The Actress and the Poet* (*Joyū to shijin*, 1935) clearly illustrates this – the film centres around a successful stage actress (Chiba Sachiko), who is always shown wearing luxurious and expensive hybrid attire (short, permed hair, a fur stole and a vibrantly patterned kimono) who is contrasted with her unsuccessful poet husband (Uruki Hiroshi), who wears a simple cap and kimono throughout. The poet is not only sartorially contrasted with his successful wife, but with male characters, particularly his male neighbour, whose hats and coats are featured in close-up – the poet's lowly status is made abundantly clear. In 1920s and 1930s urban Japan the vibrations of class tensions within the city space could be keenly felt, with the state aiming to stabilise these tensions via male youth channels – Sally Ann Hastings notes the foundation of organisations such as the Harmonisation Society (Kyōchōkai) in 1920 'to bring together labor, capital, the government and the scholarly world in order to reduce the class tensions in Japan', alongside the Japan League of Young Men's Associations (Dai Nihon Rengō Seinendan), inaugurated in 1925, member associations of which facilitated social cohesion via interpersonal activities: 'as young men studied, participated in sports, and worked together, they strengthened their bond to each other and to their neighbourhood or school district' (Hastings 1995, 107, 109, 115). As is evident in the phenomenon of the 'sports film' prevalent throughout the 1920s and 1930s, the spheres of film, fashion and sporting leisure time became entwined within a 'cultured lifestyle' archetype, with the consumption of related sporting and fashion goods existing as aspirational identity coding practices – through such interpersonal activities, Young Men's Associations anchored a sense of group identity, regardless of the individual's own class distinction, also to these aspirational image ideals; these image ideals were not promoted solely to the middle classes, but to men throughout the Japanese populace via both state and commercial channels. In this time of economic uncertainty, the 'cultured lifestyle' remained aspirational but not necessarily distant. Like the flawed female star or the Western-style Japanese sports film personality, the 'cultured lifestyle' and its aesthetic and leisure accoutrements were aspirational, but attainable, with the male spectator's own socio-economic position asserted as being subject to constant possible change.

The facet of economic instability itself was not purely the domain of the working-class labourer, either – Bordwell notes that 'in the late 1920s, over two-thirds of university graduates could not find work', signifying that the middle classes themselves, while supposedly exemplifying the 'cultured lifestyle' advocated by the state, were also subject to substantial economic pressures (Bordwell 1988, 193). This also meant that the optimistic youth comedies produced by Hollywood (such as those featuring Harold Lloyd), held a particular allure, not only as depictions of an affluent, fashionable lifestyle, but of a fantasy state present not in Japan, but abroad – Lloyd's works were so lucrative that they were the subject of a nationwide organised film piracy racket in 1925:

> Nikkatsu is premiering the imported American Pathé film 'Why Worry' [marketed as 'Overcoming the Giant', *Kyojin seifuku*], starring Harold Lloyd, this spring at the Asakusa Sanyūkan cinema, and it will next be exhibited to the public in the Kansai region. However, the Tamaki Company of Kōzu, Osaka, has produced copies of the film rebranded as 'Lloyd and the Giant' [*Roido to kyojin*] on a nationwide scale, selling it for around 12 or 13 *sen*. Around 40 or 50 reels of the copies have been sold since Nikkatsu began renting out its prints at a special low price. As this trade has been going on for some time now, Nikkatsu has been left reeling by substantial losses. Their recent premiere of 'Girl Shy' [marketed as 'Lloyd Rushes Madly Ahead', *Mōshin Roido*] has also been copied by the Tamaki Company as 'Dashing Forward, Soldiering On' [*Yūshin maishin*] and already 10 copies have been sold. All of the legitimate paperwork has been collated and was submitted to the Osaka district court on 18 April 1925. The case against the Tamaki Company is infringement of the production rights of 'Girl Shy', total seizure of the offending materials and payment of damages to Nikkatsu. (*Yomiuri shimbun* 1925, 6)

The association between Lloyd's star persona and the attire of male university students pervaded not only fashion- and cinema-related media but general news reporting, signifying this association appearing in the wider public consciousness; a 1926 *Yomiuri shimbun* report on a train robbery surmises that the bespectacled culprits may be male university students, citing 'the widespread rise of Lloyd glasses amongst male students' clothing' (*Yomiuri shimbun* 1926, 6). The distance between the spectator and the star in this case is vast, crossing not only class, but international borders, yet even here the qualification of 'authenticity' for marketing fashion products remains relevant. The key criticism of why directly adapting American stories, themes and aesthetics to Japanese-made productions could be considered less commercially successful is due to the same accusations of 'imitation' levelled by Kaneko and his proletariat contemporaries – works such as Lloyd's films presented a 'genuine' American depiction of the American way of life, rather than a Japanese imitation of an imagined lifestyle as depicted by Hollywood-trained personae such as Abe Yutaka. This aspect allowed American productions to directly stimulate Japanese production of Western clothing garments: a 1928 *Asahi shimbun* article entitled, 'Watching Films as Modern Research' describes how Japanese vendors of Western clothing created copies of designs from Hollywood films in order to target the Tokyo Modern Girl and Modern Boy market:

> Look at the smart style of those Modern Boys and Modern Girls, exuberantly dancing to the Ginza march. Could you possibly think that their Western clothes are Japanese? The leading retailers of Western-style clothing attend the premieres of foreign films, then go and request the new silhouettes with such zeal that it takes on the appearance of a truly noble cause for the Modern Girls, Modern Boys and their like who are demanding these new styles. With this technique, surely we can all have an 'up-to-date' style. (*Asahi shimbun* 1928, 5)

The language used by the commentator (the words 'smart', 'style' and 'up-to-date' are all rendered in *katakana*, signifying that these terms are used with a distinct Western-inspired focus) alongside the commentator's disbelief that the clothing worn by the Modern Girls and Boys could even be bought in Japan, signify that an 'authentic' Hollywood-inspired appearance was a lucrative aesthetic goal. Furthermore, the commentator's description of this commercial process as a method of 'modern research' frames the Hollywood film as a site in which modernity itself – and how to 'be' modern – may be quasi-scientifically observed in its 'natural habitat' – another demonstration of the cinema's role in negotiating 'modern' manners, identities, norms and interaction with space. However, while this could be interpreted as one form of 'authenticity' provided by Hollywood films, they bore little resemblance to everyday Japanese life. Superficially, for companies selling Western-style products, or those linked to the concept of a Western lifestyle in the popular imagination, this was not a problem – there were few commercial motivations for depicting a 'realistic' Japanese lifestyle. While men such Kon's Honjo-Fukagawa man could have identified with the 'labourer' characters advocated by Kaneko, it is unlikely that these characters would have incited him to consume their related fashion goods – the necessary aspirational distance between his own position and that of his screen analogue is not in place to incite the desire to obtain his appearance and/or surroundings. Of course, this would not have been of any concern to Kaneko, a harsh critic of the superficiality of Western fashion, or his contemporaries; however, the challenge for commercial entities (studios and the fashion-related industries who utilised the allure of their productions in order to market their own products) was striking a balance between the audience's thirst for 'authentic' Japanese personae and stories and an aspirational, Hollywood-inspired male dress aesthetic and identity.

The Official Shōchiku History records studio head Kido Shirō as highlighting this conflict between a desire for 'ordinary' stories and commercial interests in 1929 – he is quoted as stating the following:

> [Depicting] the lives of ordinary people are out of the question; it is not the case that the business of film production should be carelessly dragged into recession too. Economic recession imprints directly upon the film product; there is no mistaking that this weakens it. Of course, a film that cost ten thousand yen will be different to one that cost seven thousand. At least in the case of film production, even if it is the case that it is presenting the authentic result of recession, its true role is still nothing more than the entertainment of the masses. (Quoted in Nagayama 1996, 581)

Notably these comments are reported to have been made following one of Kido's trips during the summer, conducted to recruit the 'actresses with shapely legs' (*kyakusenbi joyū*) which would become synonymous with the studio's Western-style productions, an initiative incited by the more widespread wear of Western clothing which exposed the shape of the calf (Nagayama 1996, 581). According to the Official History, it was this trip – a pursuit with the Hollywood aesthetic body ideal in mind – that 'made Kido extremely motivated, to the extent that from the earliest audience responses he began to instigate new plans to gradually bring together a variety of social topics – for example, due to the economic recession, there was a trend for all things to be reduced, but on the contrary, Kido stated he had decided to produce films at an economic premium, to universal surprise' (Nagayama 1996, 581). The concept of social realism in popular cinema was not new to Kido, or to Shōchiku: upon his takeover of the studio in 1924 he wished to target an 'urban female audience' via films which 'looked at the reality of human nature through the everyday activities of society', manifesting in the genre of the 'middle-class drama' film genre (*shōshimin eiga*), with early efforts directed by Shimazu Yasujirō (Bordwell 1988, 20). He also added that these films should have an optimistic quality, with a plot which rewarded the perseverance of the human spirit: 'the films might be socially critical, but their criticism was based on the hope that human nature was basically good. People struggle to better their lot, Kido believed, and this aspiration should be treated in "a positive, warm-hearted, approving way"' (Bordwell 1988, 20). However, Kido's later approach in 1929 stresses that while the cinema may comment on current issues directly affecting its audience, this must not be at the expense of the work's luxurious, alluring star quality and entertainment value.

This quandary was addressed by Ozu's *I Graduated, But …* (*Daigaku keredo*, 1929), starring Takada Minoru (who had just left the Tōa studio to join Shōchiku, and was an already established star) and Tanaka Kinuyo, one of the studio's rising stars, 'a film which had an undercurrent of director Ozu's characteristic mingling of humour and pessimism' (Nagayama 1996, 581). Only an eight-minute fragment of the film survives, but its luxurious aesthetics are highly evident, expressed not only via its star cast but their clothing and their surroundings – particularly those of Takada. Many of the surviving shots depict Takada in a sharp, perfectly tailored dark suit, paired with a striped tie and a pale-toned pocket square; he is introduced firstly by a shot only of his smart, two-toned brogue shoes ascending the office steps, and then as a tall silhouette viewed through an office door window wearing a homburg hat. He is surrounded by other (particularly older) men in Western-style clothing working in the office, but like Suzuki Denmei, he is shot in a manner which emphasises his height and Hollywood-style physiognomy; his sharp-dressed form always dominates the frame. From the surviving fragments it appears that Western clothing is entirely male-focused in this film – Tanaka wears kimono throughout. Takada's home which he shares with his wife similarly reflects an affluent Western style; although Takada wears *yukata* when relaxing at home, his backdrop in one room is a poster for Harold Lloyd's comedy *Speedy* (1928) – in another, he appears before a display of wall-mounted American university sports pennants, a prop which would reappear in subsequent university comedies directed by Ozu, providing not only connotations of the affluent university lifestyle, but of an *American* university lifestyle. The film also contains bar scenes in which Takada is depicted wearing a hybridised outfit – a *yukata* and his homburg hat – drinking German-branded beer alongside a fully Western-dressed male companion, whose outfit is complete with Harold Lloyd spectacles. At first glance, Takada's attire and the spaces in which he appears seem to be the same superficial aspects so derided by Kaneko three years earlier; however the film's storyline is decidedly less glamorous, entailing a recent graduate who is unable to secure a satisfactory job and finds himself lying to his mother and his wife about his unemployed status. Eventually, he decides to take a lowly receptionist's job only to find himself immediately promoted – his prospective boss was only testing his character all along. In light of this storyline, the film's aesthetics lose their lustre: topical themes of disillusionment following graduation, a lack of employment opportunities and of familial disappointment (particularly of female figures, emphasising anxiety surrounding evolving gender structures) ensure that the stylish fantasy world exemplified by Western-style clothing, so criticised by Kaneko and readily featured in Lloyd's comedies, is brought fully down to earth. Bordwell adds that 'the film begins and ends with a session with the tailor' – scenes which are unfortunately now lost – but when viewing the surviving scenes with knowledge of this storyline it appears that Takada's stylish Western-style fashion aesthetic carries deeper significations (Bordwell 1988, 193). The film includes close-up shots of Takada's two-toned brogues both before and after his first interview. The first shot, in which we view only Takada's legs and feet ascending the steps of the office, anchor his character as one who is literally well-heeled and in a position of privilege. The second shot of his shoes is as he leaves the office following his successful interview; he tears up the contract and his shoes are shown stomping through the torn pieces, a clear display of arrogance – in this setting, his shoes become a shorthand for the conceited frivolousness described by Kaneko. The scenes surviving of his second, humbled interview show him with a rumpled tie and creases in his suit, speaking humbly and repentantly. Following his successful interview, he is shown running home through the rain to tell his wife – he arrives at the door soaked through, trying to shake the excess water from his homburg hat. In celebration he throws the dishevelled hat to one side, and in a shot which focuses solely upon the movement of the hat, with no actors present, it lands perfectly upon a stack of books in front of the American university pennants. Considering the framing of these scenes between two trips to a tailor's shop, and the shots in which only fashion items are present, the placement of Western clothing in the film exists as a cyclical motif, which regardless of the characterisation of Takada appearing favourably or otherwise depicts the Western-style aesthetic for men as desirable. At the onset of the film, he is noticeably stylish but arrogant and foolish; at its climax he is humbled, and appears temporarily dishevelled, but through his perseverance he once again gains access to the accoutrements of a fashionable, affluent and American-inspired lifestyle.

This angle resonates with Kido's optimistic vision for the *shōshimin eiga*; however, the film's *Kinema junpō* review 'found such playfulness jarring' as 'the happy ending divorced the film from social reality' (Bordwell 1988, 193). Ozu's works would come to strike a perfect balance between Kido's glitzy optimism and a more faithful recreation of middle-class struggles; his next film, *The Life of an Office Worker* (*Kaishain Seikatsu*, 1929), similarly combined comedy and hardship, but this time *Kinema junpō* considered its happy ending to be more believable, with a more realistic depiction of a salaryman's lifestyle, citing a scene of the family exercising to the radio – an activity in line with the 'cultured lifestyle' initiatives of the time advocating the use of technology and engagement in exercise for all the middle-class family (Bordwell 1988, 194). This aspect of greater 'authenticity' within the *shōshimin eiga* drama while still featuring optimistic themes, popular stars and illustrious Western-style settings pitched his films as a cut above other Shōchiku productions: in 1931, following the release of *I Was Born, But* (*Umarete wa mita keredo*), Matsui Sakae stated, 'although there are many films dealing with the subject of *shōshimin*, most of them do not depict our struggles in daily life; they are lies and imitations. They work as consolation for our lives . . . However, I see the real figures of ourselves in [Ozu]'s films' (quoted in Wada-Marciano 2008, 147). Yet Ozu's films – and the *shōshimin eiga* made by contemporaries at Shōchiku – did not only initiate feelings of self-identification amongst the middle classes. Woojeong Joo notes that:

> The appeal of *shōshimin eiga*'s middle-classism, however, was not confined to the urban middle-class audiences who were originally targeted. Even in rural regions, *shōshimin eiga* sold better than other genre films, proving that it served as a form of cinematic voyeurism for non-*shōshimin* audiences, who [according to *Film Review* critic Shimizu Shunji] wanted to 'forget present life' by consuming the 'most progressive and chic' image of the urban petit-bourgeois. (Joo 2012, 104)

The *shōshimin eiga* genre itself was known to inspire male audiences to self-identify with the middle-class lifestyle onscreen, regardless of their own current socio-economic situation. If Ozu's films were considered to be the most 'authentic' of the *shōshimin eiga* genre, with authenticity being considered a key facet in successfully marketing Western-style fashion products, then Ozu's works become a site where the male spectator-as-consumer's relationship with Western-style fashion items onscreen may be clearly observed and analysed. Furthermore, despite Kido's initial vision of the *shōshimin eiga* being engineered to appeal to middle-class female audiences – who I have already described as a key fashion consumer market not only in terms of purchasing items for themselves, but for use of other family members as custodians of the household income – Ozu's examples predominantly revolve around male anxieties in their narrative, with the topical threats onscreen (particularly concerning the prospect of unemployment) further facilitating the male spectator's self-identification process with the fashionable images onscreen.

While Ozu had a reputation for depicting middle-class-focused narratives and characters, he did also direct films which starred working class male characters and their struggles: *Fighting Friends: Japanese Style* (*Wasei kenka tomodachi*, 1929) features a narrative centred around a pair of truck drivers. Only a fifteen-minute fragment of the film survives, but the lifestyle of these working-class characters depicted onscreen carries similar Hollywood-inspired motifs to those of Takada's middle-class character in *I Graduated, But . . .*, which was shot immediately after *Fighting Friends* in June 1929 (Shōchiku Kabushiki Kaisha 2003, 41).

The film's central characters are quite obviously coded as low-income workers – in one scene they are shown sharing an inner tube as a pillow – yet their home is hybridised. They sleep on conventional Japanese futons, with their rooms being divided by torn *shoji* paper screens, but their dining area consists of a high diner-style table and chairs, decorated with flowers presented in a cider bottle. Their walls are adorned with images of motorcars and the torn remains of a poster for Ralph Ince's *The Uninvited Guest* (1924) – a Hollywood film with its own consumerist connotations, starring model Jean Tolley (the face of 'Happiness' brand candy and Pepsodent toothpaste) and featuring one of the earliest scenes to be shot in Technicolor, a tropical scene shot in the Bahamas (Garza 2017). The two men eat their meals with a knife and fork, supplemented by an array of cruets and condiments. Despite their relative poverty, the two men appear to take pride in a Western-style appearance, if a little ramshackle; Ryukichi (Watanabe Atsushi) wears a waistcoat, shirt and cap in most scenes, in others he appears to be wearing a rugby-style striped jersey underneath his waistcoat while Yoshizo (Yoshitani Hisao) wears the typical working men's overalls identified by Kon and Yoshida in 1925, a similar flat cap and black leather shoes – he is shown shining his shoes when they stop their vehicle to help the young woman they find injured by the roadside. At first glance, the 'cultured lifestyle' of the middle classes does not appear to be too distant from the characters' working-class lifestyle depicted onscreen; however, upon closer inspection it appears that the dining-room furniture is entirely constructed from old wooden beer crates, an example of thrifty ingenuity. It is only in comparison with other characters onscreen that their lower socio-economic status is most evident. This is most clearly illustrated when their boss is introduced, a man in an immaculately fitted three-piece suit topped off with a pair of Lloyd glasses and a most sporty accessory indeed: a sun visor, headgear more suited for the tennis court or putting green than the loading yard where he first appears onscreen. In Chapter 6 I described how sportswear was not always worn in sporting situations, and instead constituted a signifier of the affluent leisure time pertaining to the middle-class 'cultured life'; the fact that this item of sportswear is worn alongside the popular Lloyd spectacles, alongside his tyrannical behaviour (he reminds Ryukichi that he is not on a break when he spots him struggling with a heavy load, but does not in any way assist him) depicts the manager as a faddishly ridiculous figure, rather than one of aspiration. The two main stars, while not glamorised, are presented as wholly relatable, adapting the concept of the Western-informed 'cultured life' to a lifestyle made possible within their current means. Rather than this lifestyle being portrayed as wholly distanced from the working-class viewer's life, it is instead portrayed as being at least partially accessible – with a little lateral thinking. Perhaps Kaneko would have approved of this approach, despite the film's commercial and Western-inspired origins (the film itself, particularly its title, was inspired by the Hollywood film *McFadden's Flats* (1927) marketed in Japan as *Fighting Friends*). Here was a film featuring working-class men wearing Western attire who were truly living a 'modern life' through their distinctly 'modern', mechanised occupation – as in the state's implementation of 'Young Men's Association' schemes, the image of the 'cultured life' was being brought closer to the spectator's own position, rather than being dangled fully out of reach. Rather than solely depicting idealised fashion imagery, Ozu's central male characters represented a variety of marketable male identities, each with his own specific relationship to Western-style fashion commodities and particular appeal to the spectator's own self-identification process at a variety of different class levels.

Notes

1. Abe Yutaka was also credited as 'Jack' Abe – Abe began his film career as a Hollywood actor before becoming a director at Nikkatsu in 1925.
2. Kaneko is referring here to Matsunosuke Onoe, an early Japanese film actor who died in 1926, one year before this article was published.
3. Kaneko uses the term '*yabo*', a conventionally Japanese word for unstylish, implying that his dislike for Western-attire stems from particularly Japanese aesthetic conventions.
4. The terminology used here is *keshōhin eiga,* literally 'cosmetics goods films', referring to the makeup worn by the stars onscreen and their ability to be used to market cosmetics to audiences.

Chapter 9

Was Ozu a 'Modern Boy'? Negotiating related sartorial archetypes

Ozu was an enthusiastic purchaser of Western-style attire, which must be considered when discussing the role of Western-style clothing in his films. In Part I, I discussed the position of 'insider' advertising in the construction of the Modern Girl consumer image, in which women self-identifying as 'modern girls' generated their own hype surrounding Tanizaki's 'Naomi', stimulating purchases of the identity-coding commodities featured in the novel. According to Shōchiku's 2003 retrospective, 'Ozu himself loved to dress with imported clothes and bought many Western articles; he was the most Westernized director in the Kamata studio' (Shōchiku 2003, 45). This presents the prospect of Ozu himself as an 'insider' figure, applying his own desire for Western-style fashion goods to the images he featured onscreen, particularly when constructing fashionable male characters. Ozu's utilisation of Hollywood imagery and narrative motifs (particularly his usage of film posters in the background of his sets, as seen in *I Graduated, But . . .*) are well documented and acknowledged; however, his own appreciation of Hollywood-style dress aesthetics is rarely referenced. The key markets of Western-style men's fashion goods were the middle-class salaryman and urban youth. Involving young urban directors who identified with the consumer and leisure practices of these archetypes themselves in the creation of *gendai-geki* productions provided the much-desired 'authentic' approach to depictions of young middle-class Japanese male lifestyles and desires onscreen, greatly facilitating the male spectator-as-consumer process. Rather than previous efforts by studios to employ directors with direct relationships to the Hollywood filmmaking context (such as Abe Yutaka's employment at Nikkatsu, which produced flawed 'imitations' of existing Hollywood films), here instead a young director is employed whose own lifestyle practices reflected Tokyo's changing urban spaces and consumer behaviours.

Young directors were a cornerstone of the new policies Kido instated at Shōchiku in the mid-1920s. Ozu followed the standard directorial pathway at the studio: 'a promising young man would be made an assistant director and would spend his time working on scripts. If he showed talent, he would start directing short comedies. Then the youth would graduate to features' (Bordwell 1988, 9). Ozu had featured fashionable style archetypes as an attraction to his films as early as his 1928 short *Pumpkin* (*Kabocha*): the *Yomiuri shimbun* advertises the film as 'a lively ridiculous drama in which professional couples [*kaishain fūfu*], children, company bosses, modern girls and modern boys, greengrocers and the like all revolve around a pumpkin' (*Yomiuri shimbun* 1928, 10). These character archetypes were also included in works by Ozu's contemporaries, including Gosho, Shimizu and Naruse. What sets Ozu's films apart, in regard to the position of male-focused Western-style fashion goods onscreen, is the manner in which he, similarly to Abe Yutaka, was marketed as a director with a Western-style, but still 'Japanese' approach to cinema.

Ozu used the pseudonym 'James Maki' in the credits of several of his films which carried specifically 'modern' themes and aesthetics, beginning with the 1930 production *Young Miss* (*Ojōsan*), a film marketed as 'bring[ing] you the nonsense of modern life' (Bordwell 1988, 211). Surviving stills show a similar Hollywood-inspired aesthetic to that seen in *I Graduated, But ...*, with the popular stars Okada Tokihiko and Kurishima Sumiko standing before the same Harold Lloyd poster for *Speedy*. While directors such as Henry Kotani, Thomas Kurihara and 'Jack' Abe Yutaka had all undertaken English pseudonyms in the USA in order to facilitate their careers as Hollywood actors playing to American audiences – foreign pseudonyms which on their return to Japan held an exotic cachet – Ozu had elected to undertake this pseudonym in order to appeal to Japanese audiences seeking this distinct blended persona (McDonald 1994, 35–6). This was not the first time that Japanese film industry figures were marketed via Western-style pseudonyms to Japanese audiences – Suzuki Denmei, an actor with a distinctly Hollywood-influenced persona, was first introduced using the pun-like moniker '*Zeya Tōgo*' (a play on the English words 'to go there') in 1921's *Souls on the Road*. However Ozu's use of his 'James Maki' persona is notable as a personified branding exercise marketing these films at the industrial level, rather than marketing the formal transferrable star personality actually seen onscreen. Standish states that the 'James Maki' pen name signified 'the result of a collaboration between Ozu Yasujirō, Kushima Akira and Ikeda Tadao ... films produced under this pen name were intended to represent a new sophisticated 'modern' style of filmmaking' (Standish 2006, 42). However, Bordwell notes that in related print media Ozu himself claimed ownership of the name in 1930, ascribing the fictional Maki with his own hybridised persona:

> James Maki has the smartness of his American father and the delicacy of his Japanese mother ... His study has a shelf covered with intricately designed paper, on which sit toys gathered from all over Japan. We

> worked through the night drinking Japanese wine and Bordeaux from the 1800s and listening to gramophone records of *The Love Parade* [dir. Ernst Lubitsch, 1929] . . . Next day we met at my house, where, fuelled by Washington Coffee, Johnny Walker, pickled squid, and tea over rice, we worked further on the gags. (Quoted in Bordwell 1988, 7)

The fictional scene that Ozu describes is reminiscent of the hybridised leisure environments discussed in Chapter 7: a marriage of 'Japanese' and 'Western' attributes. Ozu combines conventionally Japanese foods – pickled squid and tea over rice – with recognisable American brand names: Washington Coffee and Johnny Walker whisky. He combines this with a reference to vintage wine and the soundtrack to the German-American director Ernst Lubitsch's first sound film – the Western influences he cites are not strictly 'American', but a generic blend of American and European references, manifested in a recognisable, consumable form. The 'smartness' of American consumer culture – 'smart' when rendered in *katakana* (*sumāto*) being frequently applied as a buzzword for Western-style fashion goods marketed towards both men and women – is portrayed as inherently accessible via the consumption of related consumer goods, media and practices. It is envisioned as wholly compatible with existing 'Japanese' practices and even the landscape itself, embodied by the inclusion of Maki's fictional 'toys from all over Japan'.

Ozu also invented a fictional German writer, Ernst Schwartz, to whom he credited the original story of *An Inn in Tokyo* (*Tōkyō no yado*, 1933) – an equally fictional German novel entitled *16 Hours* (*16 Stunden*). However, he returned time and time again to the hybridised Maki persona. Between 1930 and 1937 Ozu used this name on the credits of eleven films, of which seven are extant. These films constituted over half of his output during this period. In reference to the 'James Maki' films, Standish notes that 'Tokyo becomes the *mise-en-scene* of modernity in all its negative aspects' (Standish 2006, 42). Considering the thirst for 'authenticity' in productions during this time, with audiences no longer being satisfied by a Hollywood-driven fantasy of modernity alone, I agree with this perspective. However, due to Kido's desire to keep producing 'expensive-looking' entertainment productions, Ozu's films retain an aesthetic veneer of what Iwamoto Kenji describes as the '"frivolousness", "brightness" and "newness" . . . of "*modanizumu*"', which he adds was personified by 'images of Modern Boys and Modern Girls' (Iwamoto 1991, 7, 50). Via the rakish, luxuriant and transnational lifestyle purportedly enjoyed by the fictional Maki, and the male characters depicted as living in similar circumstances onscreen in Ozu's films (often even in less economically privileged circumstances, as seen in *I Graduated, But . . .* and *Fighting Friends: Japanese Style*) these films could be considered as depictions of Iwamoto's concept of the Japanese experience of modernity as a constant conflict between problematic 'thought' and superficial 'image', manifested in the image of the well-dressed but troubled young man (Iwamoto 1991, 6–7).

The Modern Girl image embodied a sense of national crisis, existing as shorthand for what Jennifer Coates describes as 'encroaching Westernization and the deterioration of a Japanese "tradition" and moral code' – yet Coates adds that the Modern Boy, too, was not exempt from this criticism. In the film *Crisis Time Japan* (*Hijōji Nihon*, 1933), the War Minister, Araki Sadao, provides a narration describing both the Modern Girl and Modern Boy as 'soft and degenerate' (Coates 2016, 149). An examination of the film itself shows much of the imagery in common with Ozu's Hollywood-inspired iconography. Both archetypes are introduced with longer shots of their fashionable attributes. The Modern Boy is introduced via a close-up shot of his loose 'Oxford bag' trousers, wool overcoat and shiny leather shoes, similarly to Ozu's introduction of Okada Tokihiko's smartly dressed male lead in *I Graduated, But ...* four years earlier. These shots of the Modern Boy character are interspersed with shots of the Modern Girl, ensuring that their negative connotations are fully entwined; this association continues with shots of fashionable Modern Boy and Modern Girl couples walking down the street. These shots are overlaid with fading close-ups of Hollywood posters, another Ozu motif; all the posters feature romantic couples embracing or kissing, aligning the public actions of the 'modern' Japanese couples with Hollywood romance and the cinematic sphere. The only poster which can be specifically identified advertises *Sinners in the Sun* (1932), featuring Carole Lombard (scantily dressed in her swimsuit) being embraced cheek-to-cheek by Chester Morris – this film also has connotations which reference the fashion commodity industry, with its narrative revolving around the romantic activities of a New York fashion model. While it appears that the Modern Boy image, whether viewed alone or in association with its female counterpart, could be interpreted as a national crisis image, I assert instead that Ozu's 'James Maki' pseudonym and its related films presented a different crisis image: an image in which the young male Japanese subject must come to terms with both the positive and negative opportunities made possible by modernity by deciding his own position within it, a process made possible via his consumer lifestyle choices. I argue that Ozu too, as a young urban male Japanese subject, had to negotiate this disorientating modern cultural landscape. I concur with Standish's assessment that it is not possible to attribute the 'James Maki' pseudonym solely to Ozu himself and am not analysing Ozu's output as an auteur. Instead, I assert that via his frequent interviews in print media, and particularly his ownership of the pseudonym via his statement in 1930, Ozu can be understood as a director with a comparable sense of marketable 'star persona' to the actors I have already examined in this book. This marketable persona image identifies his works with a hybridised, leisurely Japanese masculinity, which seamlessly melded a non-specific sense of a Western lifestyle to existing Japanese aesthetics and practices via consumer choices, while 'authentically' exploring this concept via themes of urban masculine hardship. I have proposed the idea of the Japanese male consumer-as-audience-member being sold the concept of identity construction via his sartorial purchasing choices. The challenge for Ozu, as a young, urban, Japanese man, a director and avid cinema consumer himself, was constructing not only the sartorial character archetypes seen onscreen in his productions for the perusal of audiences, but also his own public and private consumer persona.

Ozu exists as a unique case study due to the publication of his personal diaries, which detailed his own fashion purchases, leisure pursuits, day-to-day working activities and his thoughts on both Hollywood and Japanese films. In contrast to his film output, which was subject to constraints imposed by the commercial studio system and wider governmental censorship controls, Ozu *was* the sole producer and creative director of his own diary, a document kept solely for his own private thoughts from January 1933 onwards. His films, viewed alongside his diaries, allow for analysis of the same film and fashion products at both the production and consumption levels, from the same consistent individual perspective. A study of the role of fashion in Ozu's work alone is not a comprehensive means of addressing the much larger query of how general Japanese male audiences responded to fashion images onscreen. However, by analysing his work and diaries within context, in accordance with Michel Foucault's concept of critical discourse analysis, I will be able to discuss the attitudes towards his own work, Western-style fashion products and Hollywood productions Ozu expressed privately in his own diaries alongside the publicly available attitudes of others to his work expressed in related print media.

A publication providing context is the men's fashion column 'Vanity Fair' (later titled 'Vogue En Vogue') published in *Shinseinen* magazine between 1929 and 1938: the same timeframe as Ozu's use of the 'James Maki' pseudonym. This was the first Japanese fashion column aimed specifically at male-identifying readers. Ozu was known to read *Shinseinen*, from which he drew the plot for films such as *That Night's Wife* (*Sono yo no tsuma*, 1930), which was based upon the short story 'From Nine to Nine' by Oscar Shisgall, published in *Shinseinen* in March 1930. The magazine was a bricolage of 'Western' and Japanese content – translated Western works sat alongside stories by Japanese authors, interspersed with lifestyle and fashion articles. 'Western' media content or items were not solely aligned with a Modern Boy lifestyle image. As seen in the blurring of boundaries between the hybridised housewife and Modern Girl consumer images, Western-style male-targeted consumer images could also experience such fluidity. I have discussed a variety of male consumer image archetypes: the middle-class salaryman, the university student (or recent graduate) and the *bungaku seinen*. A common factor amongst all these archetypes is a desire for Western-style fashion commodities which combine to generate an overall 'well-dressed' appearance, shaped by a desire amongst audiences and fashion consumers to consume media featuring 'authentic' modern Japanese identities. By viewing the responses of creators of fashion-related imagery and media (in this case Ozu and the longest-running author of the *Shinseinen* fashion column, Nakamura Shinjirō, who ran the column from January 1930 until his suicide in November 1934) to particular fashion goods within their own private spheres (for example in journals or candid photographs) and comparing this to their commercial creative output, insights may be gained into the connotations pertaining to Western-style men's fashion garments both in the commercial and individual consumer spheres. How were consumer archetypes constructed onscreen in Ozu's 'James Maki' films, and how did this construction interact with Ozu's own responses to Western-style fashion items, lifestyle activities and other films and wider print media depictions of young urban Japanese men? Was Ozu a 'Modern Boy'?

Iwamoto describes Ozu's film output as not representing the Modern Boy lifestyle, but 'Dandyism', defining it as a 'calmer' male identity archetype reflecting the 'brightness' of Japanese modernity:

> The fun and humorous conversation, the neatness of the composition and storytelling, the laid-back stylishness of the clothing and decor – Dandyism in Ozu's films can already be identified in the 1930s. If the brightness of the Modern Boy was accompanied by raucousness and showy posturing, then Dandyism's brightness was accompanied by feelings of an elegant, calm steadiness. From silent films to talkie films, even during the war and post-war change, and from slapstick laughter to the smile of a joke, while always leaning towards a typically Japanese emotional mood, I daresay that Ozu's films show us the means of achieving a typically Japanese version of Dandyism. (Iwamoto 1991, 178)

Iwamoto's assessment of the Modern Boy as superficial and 'raucous' in contrast to Ozu's laid-back, easy-going style both on- and off-screen generates a question of comparison, not only between Ozu's own appearance and this image, but between such 'raucousness' and the Modern Boy image which Iwamoto himself previously described as 'bathed in the audience's gaze – a gaze half of aspiration, and half of jealousy' (Iwamoto 1991, 50). Iwamoto's description of Ozu's 'Dandyism' as being more relaxed is concurrent with images of Ozu's personal style. Iwamoto's statement is accompanied by a selection of candid photographs taken of Ozu during the production of his film, a photographic genre known as *sunappu*, 'snaps', which were frequently featured in film fan magazines (Figures 9.1 and 9.2). Ozu typically wears a soft-brimmed fedora hat with a suit and tie, often accessorised with a cigarette

Figure 9.1 Ozu Yasujirō (centre, wearing a fedora hat), on the set of *Where Now Are the Dreams of Youth?* (1932). Courtesy of Riburopōto.

Figure 9.2 Ozu Yasujirō (centre, wearing a fedora hat) on the set of *I Was Born, But...* (1932). Courtesy of Riburopōto.

and an overall laid-back posture and style. This contrasts with Ozu's male leads, who are smartly dressed and well-groomed. A still from *An Introduction to Marriage* (*Kekkongaku nyūmon*, 1930), which features the film's male lead, Satō Tetsuo, alongside Takada Minoru, features both actors wearing stylish outfits with individualised accessories. They wear long silk scarves, crisp white wing-collared shirts with neckties, watch chains and pinstripe trousers. Both men have neatly styled hair and are depicted in an elegant bar setting. There appears to be a significant distinction between Ozu's own dress and that of his sharp-suited male leads – is this a visual depiction of the distinction between the more relaxed 'Dandy' style archetype and the more 'raucous' Modern Boy?

There is no evidence that Ozu identified with the term 'Modern Boy' himself, nor that he was described as such by external media. The term is largely absent from both Ozu's diaries – whether he is referring to himself, others, or fictional characters – and the period's male-focused fashion media. One specific link can be made between Ozu and a figure who was described as a 'Modern Boy' in the media – the fashion columnist Nakamura Shinjirō, author of the 'Vogue en Vogue' fashion column appearing in *Shinseinen* magazine. Nakamura was explicitly described as a 'Modern Boy' by the *Asahi shimbun* on 14 December 1932, following his role in an attempted double suicide which took place two days earlier. The other participant in the suicide attempt, eighteen-year-old Takanawa Yoshiko of the Shinjuku Moulin Rouge (a young woman with a known history of suicidal tendencies), had died in Nakamura's Shinjuku apartment from gas poisoning, however Nakamura had survived (Nakano 1998, 32). Nakano Masaaki describes the media reaction to the case as a 'sensation'; the *Asahi shimbun*'s commentary supports this assessment (Nakano 1998, 32). With the headline, 'Survivor of The Double Suicide, Writer Nakamura is Taken to Prison with the Calm and Collected Appearance of a Modern Boy', the article gives the particulars of the case while also recounting the details of the outfit worn at the time of his arrest, associating it with the Modern Boy's image of nonchalance. Nakamura is described as having 'the calm appearance of a modern boy in his belted overcoat' (*Asahi shimbun* 1932, 2). This was not the first time that the *Asahi shimbun* had featured Nakamura; almost a year earlier, on 22 January 1932, he had contributed an article to the paper's 'Household' ('Katei') section, a segment of the paper specifically aimed at middle-class married women. The article itself detailed permanent wave hairstyles, which in Chapter 4 I noted were touted as a modern technological novelty, not purely the preserve of the single Modern Girl but a hygienic, stylish option for the housewife (*Asahi shimbun* 1932, 5). By the time that this article was printed, Nakamura had already been heading *Shinseinen*'s 'Vogue en Vogue' column for a year, taking the reins of the magazine's fashion column (previously titled 'Vanity Fair') in January 1930. At no time during his authorship of the column did Nakamura refer to himself or others, including film archetypes, as a 'Modern Boy'; the fact that a national newspaper – particularly one which was partially government funded – deemed Nakamura fit to instruct the nation's middle-class housewives on their choice of hairstyle depicts him as a rather innocuous figure as opposed to a criminal Modern Boy archetype. Instead, it appears that Nakamura's public image became transformed in the press as a direct response to the suicide event, which fitted neatly into the previously faceless Modern Boy panic image. Following the trial, which revealed more and more details of Nakamura's private life, and which added further social misdemeanours to the case's cocktail of scandal (namely, serial womanising and raucously indulging himself in Tokyo's vibrant nightlife), the Modern Boy image became personified and identifiable, rather than a disembodied miscreant physically signified only by canes, spectacles and suits.

This association between the Modern Boy image and Western-style menswear allowed Nakamura to be seamlessly integrated within the trope. However, this does not necessarily mean that the fashion items themselves held innate Modern Boy connotations. The initial commentary on the incident provided by the *Asahi shimbun* on 13 December 1932 is summarised by a composite image (Figure 9.3): a photograph of the tragic Takanawa, staring wistfully into the camera bearing all the fashionable hallmarks of the Modern

Figure 9.3 Composite image of Nakamura Shinjirō, Takanawa Yoshiko and their signed suicide note, *Asahi shimbun*, 13 December 1932.

Girl (bobbed haircut, a string of gaudy beads around her neck, a button-down dress and Clara Bow pencil brows and red lips); a candid photograph of the shamed Nakamura, his eyes downcast, with his sleekly styled hair, suit and tie; and their co-signed suicide note. This constructed image summarises the narrative surrounding the Modern Girl and Modern Boy moral panic image (sex, scandal and sartorial flamboyance), yet this is not referenced in the surrounding copy. Even a detail which directly associates the supposedly corrupting Hollywood cinema to the personalities involved in the incident is employed to evoke sympathy, rather than fear or derision. Takanawa is described as 'having an intense love for the silver screen star [Marlene] Dietrich', and is recounted being seen by friends longingly singing to a photograph of the star hung in the corner of her room (*Asahi shimbun* 1932, 11). In this initial report, Nakamura himself is described simply as a 'writer', with his compositions both for the *Asahi shimbun* itself and *Shinseinen* cited without any further commentary; his association with friends described as 'modern writers' and 'nonsense writers' could just as easily associate him with the innocuous *bungaku seinen* archetype as with the actively malevolent Modern Boy.

Nakamura is only described as a Modern Boy once he is cited as being potentially responsible for Takanawa's death – the other components of his public persona (his penchant for Western clothing and cultural pursuits, enjoyment of Tokyo nightlife and philandering) are mere accessories to the term, not worthy of such derision without a criminal element. The *Asahi shimbun* continues to not only brand Nakamura a Modern Boy, but even compares the scale of the scandal to that of the Okada Yoshiko incident, which had similar Western, cinematic and sexual connotations (*Asahi shimbun* 1932, 11). He is also still referred to as simply 'an author of the Modern literary group' (*modan-ha zatsubunka*), even when he is eventually given a suspended sentence for murder (*Asahi shimbun* 1933, 2). One May article utilises both terms, with the word '*mobo*' highlighted as a large sub-headline; it is implied that this refers to Nakamura, acting as a popular buzzword luring in the eye of the reader – however, on closer inspection the term is in fact referring to the numerous bystanders observing the trial rather than Nakamura himself (*Asahi shimbun* 1933, 2). This appears to be the only reference made by the paper to Nakamura's following, and notably alongside his description as a 'modern writer' he is likened to a wholly Western model of a philanderer; the case is referred to as a 'Casanova Love Story', perhaps rendering him as external to Japanese male norms altogether (*Asahi shimbun* 1933, 2). In the same way that Nakamura's criminality transforms him into a Modern Boy, it has the knock-on effect of transforming the paper's opinion of his readership also, which were previously not defined in any particular manner – Nakamura is presented not only as a Modern Boy himself, but as a corruptive Modern Boy icon.

Prior to the incident, the 'Vogue en Vogue' column neither refers to itself nor its readers as 'Modern Boys'; the only time that the column had ever explicitly referenced the term was prior to Nakamura's authorship while it was still being published as 'Vanity Fair' in June 1929. The Modern Boy and Modern Girl were hardly presented as ideals for the column's readership; the article presents the terms 'chic boy' and 'chic girl' as ideals for readers to aspire to, employed as words describing 'gentlemen' (*shinshi*) and 'ladies' (*shukujo*) derived specifically from the American publications *Vanity Fair* and *Vogue*. The uncredited commentator posits these terms as specific opposites to the Modern Boy and Girl: 'Readers of [the *Shinseinen*] Vanity Fair [column] choose to use the words "Chic Boy" and "Chic Girl" . . . young men and women are still contesting the terms "Modern Girl" and "Modern Boy"' (*Shinseinen* 1929, 110–11). Similar Western-style outfits to those featured in the column were featured simultaneously in the *Asahi shimbun:* a 4 September 1933 article, with accompanying illustrations bearing similarity to those featured in *Shinseinen*, extols the virtues of 'hats for young and old', 'a new sock trend', sporty white shirts and neckties galore for the benefit of its general male readership (*Asahi shimbun* 1933, 5). Another article advertises autumn men's fashions from the Takashimaya department store in direct opposition to the Modern Boy aesthetic, with the headline 'A tough time for Modern Boys? Young men's autumn fashions are suddenly transformed into angular, broad-shouldered shapes; a farewell to trumpet trousers!', placing young men's Western-style clothing items in direct opposition to the wide-legged trousers of the Modern Boy stereotype (*Asahi shimbun* 1933, 5). This was not an observation exclusive to the *Asahi shimbun* – the move towards trousers with a slimmer fit was noted by Nakamura himself the following year (*Shinseinen* 1934, 215). Yet when the followers of the Western style represented in *Shinseinen* become spectators of Nakamura's public trial, in the eyes of the *Asahi shimbun* these Western-dressed young men become the very Modern Boys that they sought to avoid, purely by their association with Nakamura's public misdemeanours.

It is apparent that while the column advocated living a 'modern' lifestyle, manifested via a variety of Western-style fashions, commodities and lifestyle pursuits, it did not openly encourage its readers to pursue a malevolent Modern Boy lifestyle as depicted by the national newspapers. It is also apparent that while many of the commodities advocated by the paper were 'Western' in origin, this was not presented as detrimental to the wearer's 'Japaneseness'. The column presented stateless luxury, an idealised worldview focused upon global products; the participant is an ever-youthful *flâneur*. In line with the 'Japanese Dandyism' observed by Iwamoto in Ozu's films, an array of terms which reference a youthful, laissez-faire attitude to urban life is applied by the column to its male readership, both during Nakamura's period of authorship and following his departure. These include other terms with specific Western connotations, for example the term 'boy' (with no 'chic' or 'modern' identifier) in either Roman lettering or the *katakana* rendition '*boizu*', or wholly Japanese terms: '*otoko no ko*' (again, simply 'boy') and '*danshi*' ('young man', a term also associated with male university students). Nakamura does continue to use the more mature term '*shishi*' ('gentleman') as employed by his predecessor, but it is apparent that a more youthful image predominates, with this image constructed primarily via the wearing of Western clothing, which he refers to as '*danshifuku*' ('young men's clothing'). The vocabulary used to describe the reader's own fashionable identity is demonstrably important, giving the absence of the 'Modern Boy' term greater gravity.

The position of the 'Vogue en Vogue' column was as a mediator, adapting an 'authentic' Western urban experience in a way which made it accessible to the Japanese reader, utilising Western urban city settings such as New York as starting points for the reader to construct their own stateless sartorial identity. Before, during and after Nakamura's authorship of the column, the magazine provided commentary on emerging trends in New York, London and Paris, aimed at men and women. These observations were accompanied by lists of locations in Tokyo where the reader could buy the same items and indulge in the same leisure activities. This practice presented a single immersive lifestyle package, for private and public consumption. An overt example of this is Nakamura's mix of commentary on suggested outfits to be worn by men both in public and at home (his recommendations include pyjamas and different white shirt silhouettes, disputing the idea that Japanese clothing should be worn in the home) alongside a list of cocktail recipes to be made at home or requested at the bar provided in August 1931 (*Shinseinen* 1931, 230–1). The column places branded Western products at the core of this quasi-didactic process; however no preference is made for one Western country over another – they are presented as largely homogenous sources of 'authentic' Western products. An example from 1929 discusses various men's hair pomades, describing Japanese-made concoctions as 'imperfect', while French examples are described as 'rich', with 'French, German and English' examples all on a par (*Shinseinen* 1929, 143).

Superficially, this would suggest that Western products and lifestyles were portrayed as inherently superior to those considered conventionally 'Japanese'. This was the case in the pre-Nakamura incarnations of the column, particularly when it came to menswear. The 'Vogue en Vogue' column published in November 1929 begins, 'The Western-clothed lifestyle is much easier than wearing kimono,' and specifically refers to the more convenient aspects of Western-style menswear – for example, the ease with which a buttoned collar may be fastened (*Shinseinen* 1929, 152–3). However, upon closer inspection, the relationship between cultural products of Western origin and those of

Japanese origin is more nuanced, even in these earlier columns; in the 'Vanity Fair' February 1929 roundup of 'stylish stars', the Japanese male stars Okada Tokihiko, Suzuki Denmei, Kosugi Isamu, Yamanouchi Hikaru and Yūki Ichirō are awarded equal billing with Hollywood stars, including Gary Cooper (*Shinseinen* 1929, 290–1). Hollywood stars, too, are even analysed in accordance with conventionally 'Japanese' male beauty tropes: 'It appears that the likes of the *nimaime*[1] actors Ronald Colman, Ben Lyon, Gilbert Roland, Ramon Navarro are being left behind' (*Shinseinen* 1929, 290–1). While branded Western-style goods appear to carry some cachet and are presented as more desirable than Japanese clothing commodities, they do not entirely displace existing Japanese aesthetics or negate the impact of Japanese star personalities.

In these early uncredited columns, branded fashion and lifestyle goods exist primarily as fantasy objects, rather than actual real-life purchase recommendations. The motorcar provides a case study for this – riding in an appropriately branded taxi is presented as a substitute for motorcar ownership, presented in both a romantic and cinematic setting:

> If a foreigner were to watch a scene from a Japanese film, in which a gentleman [*shishi*] wearing an overcoat rides in a Ford Model T, he would probably ask, 'Is this a comedy?' ... The 'new' style Ford was released last summer and is the ultimate fashion item. But options that are close enough are the Diana, Packard, Rolls Royce and the Lincoln – whenever one of these rushes through the Ginza the driver will always look content – his roadster will take the fare of a pair of lovers out for a drive for sure. The car's speed, or the speed of civilisation – which is faster? (*Shinseinen* 1929, 288–9)

The April 1929 column showcases this fantasy of motorcar ownership to more dramatic effect, providing guidance on how to purchase a Rolls Royce, an item hardly within the grasp of the average Japanese citizen (*Shinseinen* 1929, 157). It appears that in the early incarnations of the column, while still adapted to be relatable to a Japanese context, the goods described appear as abstracted fantasy images rather than attainable commodities for purchase.

Nakamura's authorship divulged a didactic sense of wearing attainable Western clothing items 'correctly', rather than a simplified depiction of them as fantasy lifestyle goods that are inherently 'better' than their Japanese counterparts. Nakamura's proposition is that, like the Japanese male star, the male Japanese reader of his column could sit comfortably beside his Western counterpart and live an equally stylish existence – granted that he followed the column's advice. This sense of 'correctness' concerning Western clothing is expressed on an individual and accessible level in Nakamura's responses to readers' letters. These letters exhibit anxiety surrounding the 'wrong' wear of Western clothing items or conduct in Western-style leisure pursuits, comparable to the anxieties surrounding body image, clothing and media discussed in Part II: 'What looks odd for boys [*boizu*] playing sports?' (*Shinseinen* 1931, 213); 'Will a Japanese person wearing a raincoat on a clear day be laughed at? Don't they have all-weather raincoats overseas?' (*Shinseinen* 1932, 274–5). In response to queries such as these, Nakamura responds matter-of-factly; when directly addressing his readers, he is utilitarian and approachable in his instruction. In April 1932, a reader asks, 'After spring, if it is too cold just to wear your suit, so you are wearing your spring coat, is it strange to wear a raincoat too? Must you own both of these items?', to which Nakamura responds, 'Strictly speaking, you should own both of these items, but if you don't own both of these items, in Japan, just one or the other is fine' (*Shinseinen* 1932, 242–3) Rather than presenting the ideal Western-style 'look' as something to be copied meticulously, Nakamura openly encourages the adaptation of these supposed norms to the Japanese reader's own individual context. This was not to say that the lifestyle advocated by Nakamura was in any way pedestrian, as it was often outlandish, but instead he promotes a sense of individual adaptation as being innate to the modern experience, rather than the prospect of a 'modern lifestyle' existing as an entirely Western-derived concept.

Nakamura's approach to the anxiety provoked by Western-style clothing differs to the overall narrative concerning body image anxiety examined in Part II; rather than nurturing the reader's anxiety as a means of encouraging their consumption of consumer goods, Nakamura instead provides multiple routes to the same desired look and lifestyle at various entry points. This perspective is illustrated in his response to a female reader in March 1934, who is asking what to purchase for her boyfriend as a gift, stating only, 'He is 26. He is a student. He is very modern' (*Shinseinen* 1934, 302–3). To this Nakamura replies, 'As he is a modern person, the things he will be most pleased with will be either practical, commonplace items or something totally out of the ordinary. For example, a Majolica-ware coffee mug, or a cut-glass one; a toy animal or caviar' (*Shinseinen* 1934, 302–3). While providing examples of the lavish and exotic (but still in a form which was available for purchase from local department stores, rather than being wholly unattainable), Nakamura also provides a more approachable alternative in the form of 'ordinary' goods which also carried the cultural currency of a 'modern' lifestyle. While framed within a structure which stressed the 'correct' mode of style and conduct, when addressing the reader himself, Nakamura's instructive tone is more flexible than it initially appears, referring to the activities of the Western world without glorifying them. While style aesthetics and commodity ownership are integral to the column by its very nature, in a similar vein to the women's magazines aimed at the middle-class housewife a large element of the publication focuses on intellectual awareness of goods and practices, rather than actual participation in trends. Much of the column focuses on vocabulary and explanation rather than product promotion; from May 1934 onwards, Nakamura accompanied the column with an ever-growing alphabetical list of fashion-related vocabulary (*Shinseinen* 1934, 260–1). This list was not purely explaining Western trends, but instead provided an overview of the overall fashion landscape, mixing both Japanese and Western terms. The first instalment of the column situated the terms 'eyeshadow', 'iron', 'out of date', 'out of fashion', and 'atomiser' alongside '*akashi chijimi*' (a highly textured, red Japanese fabric) and '*anakagari*' (a Japanese method of stitching holes) (*Shinseinen* 1934, 260–1). The 'correct' use and knowledge of fashion terminology seemingly extends beyond exoticised foreign wording, as did the column's overall approach to the marketing of a stateless but stylish male lifestyle. Rather than being a purely superficial publication advising audiences of the correct Western-style 'look' only, with no intellectual depth (an accusation levelled at the Modern Boy archetype), Nakamura's ideal reader was a well-versed connoisseur of both the Japanese and Western sartorial world, schooled by his notion of 'correctness'.

This concept of 'correctness', while largely grounded in the customs of Western urban centres, did not necessitate an emulation of Western aesthetics. In February 1931 Nakamura criticised what he termed 'Pedantic Americanism', the concept of curating a menswear look that is *too* close in approximation to American trends (*Shinseinen* 1931, 246–7). His criticism was not aimed solely at American-style tailoring; in November 1931 Nakamura dedicated an entire section of the column, entitled 'Horrible Trends', to lambasting the most recent men's fashion trends being lauded in France, also taking aim at German and Hollywood trends in the process (*Shinseinen* 1931, 301). The starkest declaration of Nakamura's attitude to style existing as a composite of Japanese and Western aesthetics appears in his final column, published in January 1935, two months after his death by suicide on 15 November 1934:

> 1935! Although I think this at the beginning of every year, this year especially I feel that without great progress the fashion and accessories world will die. I hope that men's clothing will become more subdued! And that women's clothing will gradually move a little closer to allowing them to actually walk! These are the developments that are needed. I want to make an invitation to the producers of this clothing, from the perspective of a person who wears it – can it not be said that the manufacturing process is responsible for 90 per cent of the instances of someone wearing a strangely cut suit or dress? … Outfitters who make trousers that are so high that they conceal your chest, are not concerned about their fabrics becoming faded by sunlight and have among their staff 'designers' who simply trace designs from foreign magazines using thin paper – these are especially depressing affairs. I do wonder if Japan should be a bit more of a cultural country. Whatever the case may be, I seek liberation from

> these borrowed things – I want to gain a clear understanding of things pertaining to my own country. (*Shinseinen* 1935, 213)

Three aspects stand out as motivations for Nakamura to turn his gaze more towards Japanese design – impracticality, poor quality and poor imitation. His criticisms of Western clothing lie less so in their aesthetics or national origins, but in poor execution.

Due to Nakamura's death at just twenty-nine, it is impossible to know if his column was to pursue this direction of becoming more focused on Japanese fashion as he intended. Following his death, the column's leadership was handed to Hasegawa Shūji, a translator, writing under the female pseudonym Hara Narako, or 'Miss Hara', a convention that was common in female-focused print media (Frederick 2006, 27). While the column made some mention of Japanese garments, the column largely constituted a return to its pre-Nakamura view of Western-branded goods as the pinnacle of style, also removing the reader's letters section. Notably, the column had a greater influence from the cinema, which was predominantly discussed in spatial terms under Nakamura's leadership (i.e., what to wear *to* the cinema and how to conduct oneself within it). However, unlike the perspective of Nakamura's predecessor, the Japanese and Hollywood cinemas are no longer presented as fashionable equals:

> Foreign films are very susceptible to trends. The height of fashion is in constant use, and every studio has designers collaborating with its stars to create the chicest costumes for the silver screen. The thing is, when it comes to this, the Japanese film industry is always a little stale. Amongst both big and small stars, whoever could possibly feel totally confident wearing the authentic Japanese kimono? Particularly when it comes to the actresses appearing in *gendai geki*! (*Shinseinen* 1935, 263)

Considering the true identity of 'Miss Hara', this Hollywood-oriented approach to style is not surprising; Hasegawa is best known for providing the Japanese subtitles for the Marlene Dietrich film *Morocco* when it was first screened in Japan in 1931, having previously worked in the script departments of the Japanese offices of Fox and Warner Brothers in the Kansai region. Marketed as, 'Taking a fresh look at Vogue – through female eyes,' rather than overtly supplying this insight as a film industry insider, in this wholly fictionalised format the column instead moved back towards the imitative perspective derided by Nakamura, perhaps even to a greater extent than the column's original perspective as 'Vanity Fair' in 1929 (*Shinseinen* 1935, 268). The fact that Hasegawa wrote under a pseudonym at all removed one of the principal attractions of Nakamura's approach, what he described himself as 'the perspective of someone actually wearing these clothes' in his final column. Rather than being the personal account of the *flâneur*-esque life of a young

Japanese man enjoying the sartorial and leisure delights of both the Japanese and Western worlds, to the reader unaware of 'Miss Hara's' true identity, the new column now positioned its author in a similar dynamic to that existing between the female star image and the heterosexual male audience member, in which adopting a particular male fashion consumer 'look' was motivated by appeasement of a woman acting as an analogue for a real-world love interest rather than a definition of his own consumer identity. This dynamic was purely one-dimensional; 'Hara' held a purely didactic role, peddling a clear 'modern equals Western' message.

During Nakamura's authorship, the column's process of adapting Western-style goods and customs was its most alluring quality, rather than Nakamura's celebrity status. With his rebranding as a 'Modern Boy' in the press following the double suicide attempt and the resultant media sensation that arose, Nakamura gained a new notoriety, penning (and performing in) a play entitled *Shinjuku Souvenir* based on the pact's events (Marx 2015). The editors of *Shinseinen* magazine clearly did not want to be associated with such sensationalism, again distancing the publication from the Modern Boy image that had been foisted upon Nakamura following his indiscretions; the column in January 1934 was accompanied by a statement released by Nakamura himself, stating, 'It is the expiration of my term of office – it has been decided that in ten months I will return this column to its original writer' (*Shinseinen* 1934, 241). In practice, Nakamura's columns were published until January 1935 – it is unclear whether the contractual arrangement Nakamura is referring to is referencing the time in which he was actively writing for the column (it is clear that he was writing the columns in advance, hence two of his columns being published posthumously) or the number of monthly columns he would be publishing from the date of this announcement onwards – which possibly could imply that he reconciled with the editorial team prior to his suicide. What is clear is that the popularity of the 'Vogue en Vogue' column itself – at least from the perspective of the *Shinseinen* editors – was not reliant on the notoriety of its Modern Boy author, and despite the less accessible, and more imitative nature of the 'Miss Hara' column which followed it, it continued to be featured in the magazine until 1938. Japanese advertisers, too, continued to support the column, although they did not appear to be too perturbed by Nakamura's legal troubles either, with multiple Western-style Japanese products continuing to be advertised directly alongside the column throughout the scandal.

The *Asahi shimbun*'s description of Nakamura's followers as 'Modern Boys', inspired by a central subversive figure, conjoined with the relatively low circulation of *Shinseinen* as a magazine (William J. Tyler states that it 'did not rival other general-interest magazines in terms of circulation figures, with a monthly readership of around forty thousand') would suggest that the column's following relied on a subcultural model, similar to the self-generated Modern Girl buzz surrounding *Naomi* appearing in the previous decade (Tyler 2008, 181). The column invited readers to adapt the Hollywood lifestyle and persona seen onscreen to their own environment, with Nakamura acting as a guide, increasing this sense of accessibility for the reader and a degree of the knowledgeable 'authenticity' that cinema audiences so craved. Considering the correlation between the fashion products and cultural pursuits that appear simultaneously in the 'Vogue en Vogue' columns, Ozu's own diaries and his 'James Maki' films, it is possible to examine Ozu as both a student of *Shinseinen* and an analogous content creator, adapting the magazine's modern concept of a Westernised Japanese world to the immersive cinematic context and providing a new avenue by which the modern consumer and behavioural landscape may be understood. Neither Nakamura nor Ozu may have truly been Modern Boys, but both were equipped with the understanding of the constituent parts which constructed such media images, allowing for both personal identity and cinematic character construction. Their representations of this worldview were clearly perceived as commercially attractive by related industries, hence the support of Western-style advertisers purchasing space flanking the 'Vogue en Vogue' column and the Shōchiku studios' support of Ozu's works.

Ozu's diary depicts a young Japanese man with much in common with Nakamura and the readers of his column, particularly regarding his own media consumption, leisure activities and interest in Western-style fashions. Like the hypothetical Modern Boy described in national newspapers, Ozu's 'natural habitat' in the 1930s was the Ginza, Tokyo. Regular haunts, where he would meet with other directors and scriptwriters to work on his productions, include the Western-style Shiseido cafe, which provided a space for aspiring Modern Girls to learn about fashion and beauty services within an art deco ice-cream parlour, and Western-style bakeries and tea-rooms, specified by the name of their national cuisine only: 'the German bakery; . . . the American bakery' (Tanaka 1993, 33, 44, 77). While Ozu enjoyed many Japanese dishes and establishments, he makes more frequent note of Western-style dishes and establishments. Coffee appears to be of particular interest, with Ozu providing candid input on which establishments served the best and worst examples. A favourite bar of Ozu's, known as 'Eskimo', which he frequented with his colleagues at Shōchiku, was actively linked to criticisms of the Modern Boy in the *Asahi shimbun*; an article entitled 'Ginza Uproar' published on 30 May 1933 dubs the pun '*Eski-moboya*' in its subtitle, '*ya*' being a suffix applied to the names of shops, restaurants and drinking establishments – it is branded as an establishment frequented by Modern Boy clientele (*Asahi shimbun* 1933, 2).

Ozu describes his own activities in the Ginza as '*burabura*' – to stroll or swagger around – a term consistently applied to the Modern Boy's urban activities by national newspapers, this time directly applied by the participant himself to his leisure activities (Tanaka 1993, 122). Ozu's enjoyment of this 'strolling and swaggering' from one Western-style leisure pursuit to another is demonstrated in a December 1934 entry: 'Today is my birthday. I'm giving up work and going out for a stroll' (Tanaka 1993, 99). Yet Ozu did not only partake in Modern Boy-esque strolling – he was also a devotee of middle-class sporting pursuits. Ozu wrote about playing golf from the mid-1930s onwards and kept abreast of events in the international boxing scene. Ozu's diary is also a record of his own film viewing habits; most of the films consumed by Ozu are Hollywood productions, recorded in a mixture of English written in Latin script (*romaji*) and English rendered in the Japanese *katakana* script, usually in the form of a brief acknowledgement or note, but sometimes with supplementary commentary. The list-like recording of the names of these films is peppered throughout Ozu's diaries, alongside other incongruous English phrases and vocabulary. In April 1933, Ozu finished a diary entry with the phrase, 'Such is life!'; a month prior he recounts remembering a phrase in English said by a friend identified only as 'Tadashi': '"sophisticated idle boy"' (a phrase which could easily describe the media image of the Modern Boy) while on a train, and being amused by this (Tanaka 1993, 40, 37). These seemingly unnecessary usages of English align Ozu's own behaviour with that of the Modern Boys described as superficially repeating English phrases they had learned from films, with Ozu's 'listing' of Hollywood films embodying little more than a collector's mentality. However, unlike the Modern Boy archetype – and more akin to Nakamura's ideal of an educated, fashionable Japanese man – Ozu did not enjoy these films purely due to their superficial depiction of Western lifestyles and often provides critique. He describes *A Farewell to Arms* (1932), starring the hugely popular Hollywood star Gary Cooper, as a 'worthless product'; the Frederic March film *The Sign of the Cross* (1932) is dismissed as 'nonsense' (Tanaka 1993, 49, 38). When Ozu provides more in-depth criticism, information about his own attitude to including the influences of Western films in his own work may be attained. In May 1935, after viewing the Clark Gable film *Manhattan Melodrama* (1934) and the French production *Le Grand Jeu* (1934) Ozu provides insightful commentary on the role of 'realism' onscreen:

> The Foreign Legion have an excellent reputation, but I wasn't impressed with some of the scenes during the film. There is a literary scent, but the film is chewed up with bitterness; the Foreign Legion are as boring as simple worms. However, in 'drama', when depicting the Foreign Legion, there is no need for simple, boring things. There is no match for the representation of things exactly as they naturally are onscreen. (Tanaka 1993, 161)

Considering that many of the scenes featured in *Le Grand Jeu* were shot on location with the Foreign Legion itself under the pretence of a documentary, here Ozu shows a different angle on a commitment to showing events onscreen 'exactly as they naturally are'; the film was critically acclaimed in European media for its 'realistic' approach, yet Ozu found it boring and unsatisfying. It is apparent that the 'realistic' approach represented onscreen via the documentary style did not match the 'realistic' image of the Foreign Legion imagined by Ozu – in this sense, his desire for 'authentic' narratives, melded with entertainment value, matches Kido's commercial vision for the Shōchiku *shōshimin eiga*, which acknowledged social hardship while retaining a glossy cinematic veneer.

Ozu's fashion consumption fits this narrative; other than food, socialising and film consumption, the most frequently documented factor in Ozu's diary is his fashion consumption. Some entries describe generic Western-style items – in March 1933 he records purchasing a pair of 'red suspenders'; he refers numerous times to 'neckties' throughout the 1930s and describes purchasing a 'Panama hat', such as he was frequently pictured wearing in candid photographs, in July 1937 (Tanaka 1993, 36, 221). Many of his accounts of purchases made throughout the 1930s denote specific brand names or locations, as documented in the 'Vogue en Vogue' column. Ozu expresses no desire for the product of a particular Western country, but rather for specific brands mentioned in the column. He describes purchasing a scarf, a hatband and an opal brooch from the Mitsukoshi department store, which was particularly reputed for its sale of Western fashion goods; his desire to purchase a British Benson watch and 'Sportex' branded menswear, an imprint owned by French brand Dormeuil; and 'Knox' brand American hats (Tanaka 1993, 107, 71, 189, 192). He recounts buying an overcoat 'from the American shop' for his younger brother Shinzo, implying that the origin of the garment is of particular interest and value. (Tanaka 1993, 150). Ozu himself clearly displays a desire to own menswear as illustrated in Kon's 1926 survey – particularly foreign-made, 'genuine' Western-style menswear and accessories, and notably these purchases predominantly take place during Nakamura's leadership of the 'Vogue en Vogue' column, with the only outlier being his contemplation of purchasing a 'Benson' watch in September 1935 (Tanaka 1993, 189). While there is no overt reference to *Shinseinen*, Ozu depicts himself as not only an avid consumer of Hollywood film, which also featured many of these items onscreen, but of Japanese popular print media – he describes reading not only the film-industry-specific magazine *Kinema junpō* but the more general popular culture magazine *Sutā*, which alongside its film commentary also included a men's and women's fashion section (Tanaka 1993, 188). Considering the description of his 'James Maki' alter-ego as a fictional Japanese-American, it is clear that Ozu himself utilised these fashion objects to assert his own position in a media-augmented version of 'reality'.

Ozu's garments perform a narrative role in his diaries: descriptions of his sartorial appearance punctuate his life. When describing working overtime in February 1935, he writes, 'Going to the office is stretching out the knees in my trousers . . . it is stretching out my beard too' (Tanaka 1992, 108). The use of fashion goods to narrate events extends to Ozu's film output; involving Western-style products in onscreen narratives depicts an entertaining version of 'reality', as described in Shōchiku's retrospective:

> The decor of *Walk Cheerfully* (1930), the automobiles, typewriters, golf players, trumpets, hotels, original posters of foreign films and of boxing, guns, phonographs, English scribblings on the wall, the humorous greetings inspired by Harold Lloyd's *The Freshman* (1925) etc. constituted an 'American-like' world, far from the Japanese reality, and probably far from any reality. (Shōchiku 2003, 45)

Ozu's onscreen world in the 'James Maki' films is certainly 'American-like'; however, it was grounded, in terms of its onscreen elements, in a 'version' of Japanese reality, akin to Nakamura's vision. Ozu discusses sourcing costume items and conducting 'location hunting' in Tokyo, searching for suitable real-life Japanese spaces to film Hollywood-style scenes. The filming for *Dragnet Girl* involved 'script research' in a 'French-style bar', and was filmed in a working Tokyo boxing club (Tanaka 1993, 37). The genuine posters of Hollywood films which appear in multiple 'James Maki' films were purchased by Ozu himself specifically for this purpose, and his diaries recount his thought processes in constructing the rooms used by the characters (Tanaka 1993, 143). The media-generated 'myth' of the violent, troubled but ultimately stylish Modern Boy allowed Ozu to transport the motifs of the Hollywood gangster film directly to the Tokyo context, and to distance these disruptive archetypes from other fashionably dressed young Japanese men. The 'reality' depicted onscreen was not the 'reality' which would be known by most audience members, who were experiencing the deprivation of recession, yet its usage of recognisable media tropes and real-life immersive leisure settings rooted the consumer goods onscreen in a world which was technically possible, accessible, and Japanese. Unlike the one-dimensional print media images and descriptions provided by the 'Vogue en Vogue' columns, even with the 'first-hand' perspective of Nakamura, the didactic process of the adaptation and representation of Western-style Japanese male archetypes and their relevant environments was now presented in an analogous immersive setting to the Hollywood cinema which inspired it.

The extant 'James Maki' films employ the process of male characters negotiating a modern, Hollywood-influenced world as a narrative device, for example in *The Lady and the Beard* (*Shukujo to hige*, 1931). Starring Tokihiko Okada as a university kendo champion who is set in his old-fashioned ways, with a large, unruly beard (a role based in irony, considering Tokihiko's fashionable star persona) the film charts his journey from an old-fashioned samurai analogue to a modern man who has swapped kendo for golf, is clean shaven and in a relationship with a discerning young woman who has guided him through this process. Yet like Nakamura's 'Vogue en Vogue' column, 'Western' is not presented as innately 'better'; while Tokihiko's character is presented as unhygienic (he is shown picking clumps of his beard out in a job interview, to the interviewer's horror), frightening (he is invited to a companion's birthday party, where he is asked to dance by a group of young women in a mixture of Western-style and Japanese-clothing – his boisterous sword dance causes them to run in horror too), uncivilised (at said birthday party he sits in the corner stuffing birthday cake into his mouth) and unkempt (at his job interview he appears wearing an incredibly ill-fitting suit, in the vein of Charlie Chaplin) he is also awarded with a number of chivalrous and positive qualities, which are presented in direct opposition to Western-style conventions. He is shown to be concerned about the reputations of women when he is left alone with them – something which does not perturb his male university friend, who is the archetypal Westernised student – and comes to the aid of the woman who becomes his love interest (who notably wears kimono throughout) when she is mugged by a Modern Girl (Date Satoko). His interactions with the Modern Girl character and her Modern Boy accomplices (who are designated as such by their characteristic swagger, with their hands in their pockets with cigarettes dangling from their lips, both wearing baggy trousers and shiny leather shoes, an image alluding both to the Hollywood gangster image and to the Japanese print media Modern Boy image) particularly depict a negative perspective of imitation of Western styles. When the Modern Boy characters try to intimidate him, he waves his scabbard at them, and they immediately flee – they appear as cowardly accessories to the Modern Girl, even being shown as passengers being driven around by her in a motorcar, a notion in agreement with the print media descriptions of the Modern Boy image.

The criticism appears to be particularly levelled at female imitation of Hollywood dress styles, and even an emulation of a Hollywood-style bodily aesthetic for women; after defeating her Modern Boy cronies, Date steps forward to berate him. Tokihiko's response is to gesticulate an hourglass figure, saying, 'I could never forget your inelegant Western-style clothes.' That eventually Tokihiko convinces Date to pursue an honest life echoes the sentiments of Nakamura's final column; perhaps the rapidly Westernising Japanese world could learn by reflecting on its 'old fashioned' customs, too. Actual Western men are also criticised – while Tokihiko is working in the

Tokyo Thomas Cook Hotel (another 'genuine' Western-style Japanese location scouted by Ozu) it is revealed that an American guest has bought a counterfeit brooch for his Japanese girlfriend, claiming that it cost him 37,000 yen – he bribes a Japanese guest at the hotel to keep his secret. Like the 'Vogue en Vogue' column, brand names abound – a Lincoln car is playfully juxtaposed with a print of Abraham Lincoln (announced as '1932's Lincoln', ensuring that the audience is fully aware of both the pun and the branding); however they appear alongside Japanese names – 'Jintan' breath fresheners (a brand well-known for Western-style advertising using the Modern Girl actress Irie Takako) and a Western-style bakery sponsored by Meiji chocolate. *The Lady and the Beard,* perhaps of all the 'James Maki' films, presents a worldview which is closest to that presented by the 'Vogue en Vogue' column: Japanese and (selected) Western attributes seamlessly co-exist, on both a personal and commodity level, with the protagonist's understanding of how to navigate the modern world sartorially and socially ultimately leading him to happiness. The film translates the publication's didactic process into an immersive modern fable for the young male Japanese audience member, with the possibility for this process motivating him to consume being acknowledged by the involvement of multiple Western-style Japanese advertisers.

The Lady and the Beard's consumer process largely relies upon the involvement of a female love interest, who provides instruction to the film's protagonist – by acquiring aptitude at understanding Western-style sartorial aesthetics, the protagonist (and, by proxy, the male viewer) gains ownership of the female star body also. This model also appears in *Passing Fancy* (*Dekigokoro,* dir. Ozu Yasujirō, 1933), in which the impoverished male factory worker lead, Kihachi (Sakamoto Kihachi) visits the barber shop for a shave and haircut to impress a young woman, Harue (Fushimi Nobuko), who is working at the local tavern. This decision is motivated by viewing his own moustachioed reflection in the shop window; following the shave the other male customers all remark, 'You're looking very modern these days!' to which he responds, 'Am I not twice as handsome now as I was before?' However, in this example, despite Kihachi's efforts his older age remains as a barrier to his love interest, echoing the emphasis on male youth which appeared in 'Vogue en Vogue' – this is also directly alluded to in the film's dialogue, where Kihachi is elated when he is addressed as 'young man' by the female owner of the tavern. Here the male-consumer-female-star dynamic is presented in an oversimplified, mocking context: the assumption that a woman will be attracted to a man based on his 'modern' appearance alone is presented as foolish.

Like the letters section of Nakamura's column, frequently Western clothing and lifestyle artefacts are implicated in wholly individual male anxieties, removing the requirement for a romantic female star image in the consumption process altogether. Ozu's first all-sound film, *The Only Son* (*Hitori musuko*, 1936), directly references the plight of university graduates during the recession, in which a mother in the provinces undergoes hardship working in a silk mill to fund her son's Tokyo education. We are first introduced to the male protagonist as an adult following a view of the Tokyo landscape, shot from behind the headlamp of a motorcar, a clearly affluent image, and his sartorial appearance matches this – he wears a homburg hat, a three-piece suit and tie, and is clean-shaven, the picture of middle-class affluence. However, when his mother comes to visit it is revealed that he lives with his wife and child in a tiny house on a meagre income from school teaching – he spends his money to impress his mother, but eventually admits that 'trying in Tokyo is useless'. His Western-style appearance functions similarly to the 'armour' described by Kaneko in Chapter 8; rather than concealing a 'Japanese' interior, it conceals the disappointment of his home life, an attempt to ward off social judgement. The social value of men's Western-style clothing and lifestyle goods is even demonstrated as being relevant to children's lives in *I Was Born, But . . .* (*Umarete wa mita keredo*, 1932). In one comic scene, the group of young boys participate in a game of one-upmanship, arguing over whose father has the most impressive lifestyle goods. A boy in a striped polo shirt and an embroidered baseball cap boasts, 'My dad has tons of Western clothes,' to which another replies, 'Isn't that because your family's business is a tailoring shop?' – his misguided boastfulness results in the boy being mocked by his companions. A similar sequence revolves around motorcars, in which it is revealed that the 'best car' is in fact a hearse, much to the boy in question's embarrassment. The group of boys is presented as an allegory for wider male society, in which one's position is defined by his commodity goods and his correct understanding of their use. Ozu's 'James Maki' films, whether the main character's consumption is motivated by a female love interest or by social anxiety, implicate a further process of adaptation in the pursuit of representing a relatable 'reality', moving the already adapted but idealised Western/Japanese leisure image towards a representation of the struggles facing middle-class Japanese men in their actual everyday lives.

In conclusion, men were active consumers of Western-style fashion goods, who, like female consumers, could be incited to consume via fashionable images onscreen. Male consumers were incited to consume via two channels within the cinematic space, with either the ownership of the female star body itself as motivator, or with fashionable male consumer lifestyle archetypes in mind. Regarding the second facet of this process – in which the consumption process is purely based around a man's own image of himself – this also concerns a didactic element, in which print and screen media act as mediators, adapting Hollywood imagery to the specific Japanese context. At the core of all debates concerning the role of Western male clothing onscreen is the concept of 'authenticity' versus 'imitation', with clothing being means by which an audience thirst for 'real' Japanese stories, executed in relatable modern spaces, could be articulated. Considering the role of the audience member's self-identification with the star image in inciting the consumption of fashion products, and the role of 'everyday', recognisable imagery in generating the 'sensory-reflexive horizon' described by Hansen, this 'authenticity' also existed as a means of furthering this process by making the screen image and its related commodities relatable to specifically Japanese audiences, rather than the more fantastical Hollywood screen environment. Another facet of this concept of 'authenticity' was the notion of 'correct' ways to perform Western-style Japanese masculinity via clothing, allowing for the generation of anxiety concerning one's appearance, ownership of commodity goods and position in society. This anxiety both presented the Western-style fashion commodity as the marker of a 'successful' man, but also allowed for the generation of negative Western-clothed male media stereotypes, most prominently the Modern Boy. In contemporary English language scholarship, the term 'Modern Boy' appears to be applied to any young Japanese man in the 1920s and 1930s with a penchant for Western-style clothing and customs; however, my examination of the term's use in context reveals that self-identifying 'Modern Boys' did not actually exist at all, existing only as a filmic trope and panic image. What existed instead were a variety of different male fashion archetypes, which were defined by devotees of Western-style clothing and lifestyle pursuits themselves, both in print and onscreen. Rather than being purely 'imitative' of distant Hollywood trends as suggested by their detractors, male consumers of Western style fashion images were incited to consume these fashions filtered through a Japanese lens, adapted using both on-screen Japanese male star bodies and off-screen creators.

Note

1. *Nimaime* is a term originating from Kabuki theatre, described by Robertson in the interwar cinematic context as 'the film media equivalent of the Kabuki dandy . . . usually a pale-faced, merchant-class playboy with street smarts in lieu of swordsmanship' (Robertson 1998, 56).

Conclusion

Due to its transnational nature, the Japanese cinema of the 1920s and 1930s was a site of complex commercial imagery, with these images inciting consumption via a variety of sensory-immersive processes. These processes are rooted in Miriam Bratu Hansen's theory of the classical cinema acting as a 'sensory-reflexive horizon for the experience of modernization and modernity' via the sensory immersion of the audience member, facilitated by factors such as 'continuity editing . . . [which] creates the effect of a closed diegesis, a seemingly autonomous fictional world which the viewer can access fantasmatically as a privileged and invisible guest' (Hansen 2000, 11). I combine this concept of the cinema as a sensory-immersive arena for the experience of modernity itself with Leo Charney and Vanessa Schwartz's assessment that 'film endeavoured to freeze fleeting distractions and evanescent sensations by identifying isolated moments of "present" experience' (Charney and Schwartz 1995, 2–3). This power of the cinema allows for the illusion of stabilising the urban spectator's psychological and bodily experience of 'the rapid crowding of changing images' which Ben Singer describes as 'the psychological conditions the metropolis creates' (quoted in Singer 1995, 74). I propose that the ability of the cinema to allow its audiences to experience the immediacy of modernity via bodily sensation perpetuates the consumption of its film products; due to the impossibility of truly depicting the moment, but allowing audiences to experience the 'sensation' of it, audiences seeking this visceral 'sensation' of the modern experience continue to participate in the cinematic experience. This fundamental process applies to modern audiences of all genders; however, Mary Ann Doane specifically notes the following in regards to female audiences, linking the female star image to consumerism:

> In her desire to bring the things of the screen closer, to approximate the bodily image of the star, and to possess the space in which she dwells,

> the female spectator experiences the intensity of the image as lure and exemplifies the perception proper to the consumer. The cinematic image for the woman is both shop window and mirror, the one simply a means of access to the other. The window/mirror takes on then the aspect of a trap whereby her subjectivity becomes synonymous with her objectification. (Quoted in Petro 2002, 43)

The cinematic space and screen become a device which allows the female spectator to envision herself bodily appropriating the star's lifestyle via her image due to the sensation of immediate sensory immersion as described by Hansen, and to imagine the achievement of this via commercial participation in other modern 'feminine' spaces as an identity coding practice, such as the department store. All of these theoretical bases are intended to explain phenomena pertaining to Euro-American audiences watching Hollywood films and consuming Hollywood star images; my work demonstrates that this process also applied to female Japanese audiences viewing Western-style fashion products onscreen and in two-dimensional star images of female star bodies of both Japanese and Hollywood origin, and also that female star images could be employed in order to incite male consumption of Western-style fashion products. Considering Japan's rapid modernisation during the period of study, much of which involved appropriation of Western cultural practices, iconography and spaces, Western academic theory becomes applicable. By applying Laura Mulvey's concept of the female star as the recipient of a male-focused 'gaze', which transforms her own body into that of a desirable product, we can identify how the heterosexual male spectator may self-identify with the cinematic hero, his body and its adornment, and seek to purchase these items for himself in an effort to, by proxy, 'purchase' the body of the female star. To date this process has only been analysed in regard to female star images, as a process within which only the female star image is presented as the object of allure. Yet my study has also illuminated an analogous process occurring around male star images, in which the male star becomes presented similarly as an object of identification for the male spectator, who also wishes to possess the male star's Western-style fashionable appearance, fit body and lifestyle, and is encouraged to compare his own body to that of the male star onscreen in the same way that female cinema attendees were encouraged to do so in related print media, with the concept of an 'authentic' Western-style Japanese masculinity at its core.

The mechanisms of these sensory immersive processes are dependent on the audience-member-as-consumer's own personal gendered and socio-economic alignments. These identity alignments were made possible via the rich print media and ephemeral climate which interacted with and supported the conjoined film and fashion industries in producing a number of marketable archetypes from which the consumer could pick and choose. These images could seamlessly transit between different forms of media and space – from the privately consumed magazine, novel or matchbook (which could also be consumed in semi-public spaces such as cafes, holding a particularly mobile status), to the publicly displayed film poster and the cinematically styled department store exhibition space. This ensured that an illusion of the sensory-reflexive horizon supplied by the cinematic space itself continued into the spectator's everyday life and existence, fuelled by the repetition of these images and the spectator's own consumption practices. I concur with Miriam Silverberg's assertion, 'The consumption of images of objects rather than the objects themselves was central to Japanese modern culture' (Silverberg 2009, 23). Regardless of the consumer's own class and economic status, the manner in which images of Western-style fashion objects and related star images transited freely from the screen to other spaces – both private and public – ensured that knowledge of their value both as commodities and as symbols was constantly accessible and present.

The 'national identity' of these images existed in a realm of flux: what initially appeared to be a fashion item coded as 'Western-' or 'Hollywood'-inspired in origin easily transited between Hollywood, European and Japanese productions, to the extent that many of these items no longer held a specific connotation of geographical origin, a connotation which was instead replaced with a universal, stateless quality of fashionable desirability. At the political level, via a process of adaptation facilitated by Japanese media imagery, this allowed for some fashion items and overall looks, including an initially Hollywood-inspired star body, to be 'rebranded' as being part of the aesthetics of the new Japanese state, and in turn the new Japanese citizen and consumer. Throughout the study there are key themes which resurface, one being the significance of an isolated fashion item or fashionable characteristic onscreen or in external media (for example bobbed hair, spectacles or cosmetics) versus the position of these items within an entire marketed look, with these two factors sometimes existing in opposition. A Modern Girl character could be easily recognised onscreen by her bobbed hair and use of cosmetics (and would be unlikely to be portrayed onscreen or as a print media archetype without them), yet neither short hair (or hair styled to give an impression of a shorter length) nor the use of cosmetics were the sole reserve of the Modern Girl – these styles and fashion items were equally marketed as hygienic novelties to the eugenic modern Japanese housewife. To use a male-targeted example, Harold Lloyd-style round spectacles were used in print media and in film posters to indicate a Modern Boy character, holding a specific Westernised and subversive connotation. However, off-screen the same spectacles were openly sported by government officials and other men of various ages and from all walks of life, with Kon Wajiro situating the spectacles as a 'Japanese' fashion article in his survey. Rather than a fashion item holding a single connotation, both onscreen and in commercially motivated print media each item worked in synthesis with the imagery provided by other fashion items adorning the body and with the behaviours of the wearer in order to generate an overall purchasable persona or narrative archetype, acting both as an element of *mise en scène* within the frame, indicating to the audience the archetypal role of the character onscreen, and an imitable persona with which the spectator could identify and emulate via their purchasing and dress choices. It is this concept of the signification of clothing items being shaped by the behaviours and characteristics of the bodies wearing it that highlights the conjoined roles of cinema and fashion-related spaces and publications as didactic tools. As 'new' clothing or cosmetic items appear onscreen, introduced by Hollywood or European film productions or fashion companies, audiences and consumers were required to understand the use of these items, with such knowledge itself becoming a commodity – this learning experience itself became a marketable activity, taking place in spaces such as the cinema and the department store. Star bodies onscreen, in print media and in shop displays become literal models for promoting the purchase of not only the fashion commodities themselves but the cultural knowledge that accompanied them, including behavioural codes, as part of an identity-coding practice. This becomes a process which allows for both the state and the film and fashion industries to influence purchasing practices alongside civilian behaviours and the maintenance of the physical body. All three parts of this book note a process of adaptation enacted in order to make these commodities or purchasable archetypes more approachable, appealing or socially acceptable to Japanese spectators or audiences, many of which involve the adaptation of the characteristics of the adorned body within, for example via the marketing of Japanese 'versions' of known international stars. This process demonstrates how the sensory-reflexive environment of the cinema, and its reproduced imagery which echoed this phenomenon in the spectator-as-consumer's everyday life, encouraged the modern Japanese citizen to buy into this hybridised, adapted image, which entwined national pride, eugenics and militarism with the conveniences, mass-production and efficiency of the modern world – a compact demonstration of Iwamoto's hypothesis that the cinema allowed the rationalism of *kindai-shugi* and the 'lightness' of *modanizumu* to work together (Iwamoto 1991, 6–7).

One of the key reasons for this research to be conducted was to implement a theoretical framework via which filmic motifs may be 'read' which considers the immersive audio-visual experience of the cinema itself. My implementation of critical discourse analysis, which required an in-depth examination of the external contexts of these filmic motifs, necessitated a detailed understanding of the commercial climates of both the Japanese and global film and fashion industries which produced these images and influenced their audiences. I maintain that the approach I have adopted here may be adapted to various geographical and chronological contexts and exists as an avenue for further research in itself, having proven its value in understanding the filmic imagery which appears in the pre-war Japanese context. However, it has also revealed the value of examining many of the other issues illuminated by this book as contextual factors, particularly the relationship between audiences, onscreen fashion images and consumption. Guy Debord's *The Society of the Spectacle* (1967) notes in a Western context that 'mere images are transformed into real beings, tangible figments which are the efficient motor of trancelike behaviour' (Debord 1995, 17). This finding is markedly similar to the processes that I have analysed occurring in Japan thirty or more years prior, which produced similar 'behaviours' facilitated by an almost entirely analogous sensory-immersive multimedia, networked sales environment to that described by Debord:

> Waves of enthusiasm for particular products, fuelled and boosted by the communications media, are propagated with lightning speed. A film sparks a fashion craze, or a magazine launches a chain of clubs that in turn spins off a line of products … in the footsteps of the old religious fetishism, with its transported convulsionaries and miraculous cures, the fetishism of the commodity also achieves its moment of acute fervor. (Debord 1995, 44)

On a superficial level, this would imply that the same processes surrounding the audience-member-as-consumer viewed in interwar Japan were both transferable to other geographical contexts (which, as my analysis is based on Hansen and Doane's discussions of the classical Hollywood cinema, is already tested by this book) but also to later time periods, with different technological advances (in the 1960s experienced by Debord, for example, television and its related advertising, which brought the sensory-immersive advertisement directly into the home space). Subsequent studies should test whether the relationship between this bombardment of mobile images and the spectator-as-consumer's consumption process has changed over the course of time, and whether it will do so in future. Debord's concept of 'commodity fetishism' being analogous to (Judeo-Christian) 'old religious fetishism, with its transported convulsionaries and miraculous cures' appears to be particularly relevant to the discussions of body image in advertising I analysed in Part II. This section analysed how commodities were marketed to both men and women with the promises of alleviating bodily anxiety and overall improving the subject's lifestyle – an anxiety that was also harnessed for the betterment of the nation's health by the state. Today's world is becoming increasingly interconnected, and social media – particularly platforms focused around the exchange of images and video, such as Instagram and TikTok – has allowed the sensory-immersive sales environment not only to be constantly accessible wherever the user pleases, but to become interactive; this relationship between the spectator-as-consumer and media images requires constant re-examination.

The issue of social media, fashion marketing and body image is being analysed (Fardouly et al. 2015; Perloff 2014); however current studies describe it as a contemporary, Western and (predominantly) female problem. My survey shows a long-running, deep-rooted history of global fashion and film industries utilising body-based anxiety in order to market products to both men and women, particularly Western-style fashion commodities – it is my intention, in future studies, to consider current media developments within this historical context. A logical extension of examining these mechanisms in the Japanese context would be the expansion of the same analytical methodology employed here to the study of these images in the post-war period and beyond, particularly considering the emergence of cosmetic surgery and new connotations arising concerning both the Hollywood cinema and Western-style fashion products. A prominent archetype in this dynamic in the immediate post-war context is the figure of the '*pan-pan* girl', a term used to describe 'the street prostitutes who served the soldiers of the Allied forces, mostly from the USA, during the occupation of Japan from 1945 to 1952, and who sometimes became the local girlfriends of GIs' (Sakamoto 2010, 1). Sakamoto Rumi notes the prominence of Western-style fashion products in the *pan-pan* girl's coding in visual and literary media: 'even during the occupation, when censorship precluded reference to US GIs in Japan, *pan-pan* girls were clearly codified with their red lipstick, nail polish, cigarettes, high heels, strong perfume, and provocative dress codes . . . [including] brightly coloured Western-style dresses' (Sakamoto 2010, 5). Like the pre-war Modern Girl image, the *pan-pan* girl image linked Hollywood-style glamour iconography, consumption and sexuality – to mixed reception. Her negative connotations are obvious – Tanaka Masakazu notes accounts of such women being criticised by other Japanese men, women and children not only for subverting the marriage system and engaging in public sexual activity with American soldiers, but also for their flagrant consumerism while other Japanese citizens endured economic hardship (Tanaka 2012). Yet Tanaka also notes *pan-pan* girl imagery being associated with 'female independence, assertion of positive body images, and a sense of liberation following the chaotic aftermath of the war' (Tanaka 2012). Like the Modern Girl, the *pan-pan* girl image carried some illicitly desirable connotations, with the *pan-pan* girl's superficially extravagant consumerist lifestyle holding some allure. Sakamoto demonstrates this with a quotation from a schoolgirl which is almost entirely analogous to comments made about the attractions of the Modern Girl image: 'I'd like to be a *pan-pan* when I grow up. They have beautiful dresses and expensive shoes, and ride in cars – it looks like fun' (Sakamoto 2010, 6). Despite this glamourised materialist image, combined with the 'positive body image' described by Tanaka, the economic value of the *pan-pan* girl's body was paramount to the image's existence – a value which, due to her relationships with American soldiers, was tied to Western beauty ideals emblematised by Hollywood star images. A 1948 photograph of a group of young women described as '*pan-pan* girls', taken by the American anthropologist John W. Bennett during the Allied Occupation, substantiates this: all three women pictured have elaborately styled, permed hair; one girl wears a Katherine Hepburn-esque trouser, blouse and tank-top combination, another wears the same quasi-masculine fitted skirt suit I describe in Chapter 3 (Low 2015, 269). Morris Low concurs that this is a Hollywood-inspired sartorial appearance (Low 2015, 269). The exact same relationship between Hollywood-style, Western-style clothing, outspoken and subversive behaviour and sexuality observed in the 1920s and 1930s becomes directly transposed onto the image of the sex worker in the post-war Japanese cinema in films such as Mizoguchi Kenji's *Street of Shame* (*Akasen chitai*, 1956), which features Kyō Machiko as the ruthless 'Mickey', a sex worker who adopts an entirely Western-style persona, both in clothing and in name, and who is perhaps the post-war counterpart of her predecessor Omocha in Mizoguchi's *Sisters of the Gion* (1936).

While the everyday Japanese woman of the pre-war era was bombarded with Hollywood-inspired images of fit female bodies wearing Western-style clothing and was encouraged to shape her own body via exercise specifically in order to fit this clothing accordingly, this message resonated even more loudly for the *pan-pan* girl, penetrating through her clothed appearance to her commoditised body itself. An immediate solution lay in surgical enhancement – Elizabeth Haiken notes that in the global history of cosmetic surgery, the practice of silicone injections as a form of breast enlargement is largely considered to be a Japanese invention, citing a *New York Times* article stating that Japanese physicians utilised it to enlarge the breasts of sex workers in the post-war period (Haiken 2002, 180). An area of interest for future research is the manner in which Western-style body modifications, which encouraged the subject to physically alter their appearance in line with film archetypes, become more widespread, accepted and perhaps even normalised, beyond the stereotypes of the Modern Girl or the *pan-pan* girl. By the 1980s, Lana Thompson notes that cosmetic surgery in Japan with the specific aim of removing ethnic characteristics becomes both widespread and mainstream: '. . . Asians in Japan . . . chose to modify their typical features and not preserve their ethnicity [through procedures such as] breast augmentation, rhinoplasty and modification of the epicanthic eye fold' (Thompson 2011, 99). In 1999, Sander L. Gilman documents an increasingly popular practice of Japanese parents purchasing facial surgery for their fifteen-year-old daughters, with Dr Kamoshita Ichiro of the Hibiya Kokusai Clinic rationalising it with the same rhetoric seen in articles promoting female physical self-improvement in the 1920s and 1930s: '[Women] are being duped by . . . advertising that appeals to a woman's inferiority complex about her looks. Many women believe that if they improve their looks, their personal relations with other people will also improve' (Gilman 1999, 104). The words of one of these women purchasing surgery for their daughters acts as a succinct summary of the worldview propagated not only by advertising in the 1990s, but, as seen in this book, since the 1920s: 'pretty women just have a better time in this world, don't they?' (Gilman 1999, 105). Future research should trace the trajectory of these developments with awareness of their historical context, discussing how Western-influenced purchasable identity-related images – such as the Modern Girl – not only evolve alongside cinematic imagery, but technological and social developments in the worlds of fashion, advertising and bodily economy.

Superficially, many of the mechanisms seen in today's media marketing also appear in the interwar Japanese context, including both overt and undisclosed product placement, both of which were discussed in Part I of this book. The advertisements and their related messages I have studied here all originate from corporate or state entities themselves. With the user-generated element of social media giving rise to the 'influencer' (individuals generating their own advertising content, with or without corporate backing), the actual mechanisms involved in marketing products using this multimedia sales environment are beginning to shift. This includes the practice of manipulating the spectator-as-consumer's attitude to body image; while examples of marketing based on bodily anxiety remain (for example, a Gold's Gym billboard campaign conducted across the UK in 2016 asked consumers if they were 'tired of being fat and ugly'), brands are also choosing to collaborate with influencers publicly identifying with the 'body positive' movement. Body positivity activist and plus-size[1] model Chenese Lewis defines the term as promoting 'self-esteem and a positive body image. The body positivity movement is about health (at any size), identity, and self-respect. The ultimate goal is to combat unrealistic ideals about beauty and health, as well as to promote self-acceptance' (Dalessandro 2016) – a polar opposite to the concept of the body as something which must be fixed via consumable fashion goods surveyed in this book. Social media is 'bring[ing] the things of the screen closer' than ever before, including its stars, creating even greater advertising potential. While brands may be applauded for their increased social consciousness, as seen in the examples of more 'approachable' marketing appearing in the interwar Japanese context seen in this book, these methods are not only nothing new but also incredibly lucrative, employed as much for commercial gain as social change. 'Influencers', a rebranding of the 'star' terminology of the interwar years and beyond, primarily operate as successful marketing tools for corporations due to their perceived 'authenticity', something which is difficult to retain when melded with corporate campaigns, leading to consumer confusion and criticism – Cassidy Crawford, for the opinion site *Medium*, stated the following concerning a campaign by lingerie brand Aerie featuring body positive activist and plus-size model Iskra Lawrence: 'simply adding a body-positive caption to an advertisement photo doesn't change the fact that the women being featured are still not "real women" – they're professional models who are paid to look pretty' (Crawford 2016). A world constantly speculating on the 'authenticity' of media depictions and claims (which again my analysis shows is not a 'new' phenomenon, considering the role of the Proletariat Film movement discussed in Part III) manifests in the discourse of 'fake news'; increased media literacy and an understanding of industrial motivations for generating screen messages is becoming essential. Sonia Livingstone notes that it is 'vital . . . that people are informed about and critically able to judge what's useful or misleading, how they are regulated, when media can be trusted, and what commercial or political interests are at stake' (Livingstone 2018).

I conclude that the changing pressures on the spectator-as-consumer must be monitored and understood, and for this an understanding of the global history of this process is necessary. The commercial relationship between the spectator-as-consumer and screen media, and its related social issues, are neither exclusive to the global 'West', nor to the twenty-first century.

Note

1. The term 'plus size' used here, in line with UK modelling agency terminology, denotes sizes UK14 and up.

Bibliography

Books

Anderson, Joseph L. (2011) *Enter a Samurai*. Tucson: Wheatmark.

Aoki, Tamotsu, Kawamoto, Saburō, Tsutsui, Kiyotada, Mikuriya, Takashi and Yamaori, Tetsuo (eds) (2000) *Kindai Nihon bunkaron, Vol. 3: Hai karuchā*. Tokyo: Iwanami Shoten.

Assmann, Stephanie (ed.) (2015) *Sustainability in Contemporary Rural Japan: Challenges and Opportunities*. London: Routledge.

Atkins, E. Taylor (2001) *Blue Nippon: Authenticating Jazz in Japan*. Durham, NC: Duke University Press.

Bachelard, Gaston (1958) *The Poetics Of Space*, trans. Maria Jolas. Boston, MA: Beacon Press.

Baroni, Helen J. (2002) *The Illustrated Encyclopedia of Zen Buddhism*. New York: The Rosen Publishing Group.

Barthes, R. (1991) *Mythologies*, trans. Annette Lavers. New York: The Noonday Press.

Baskett, Michael (2008) *The Attractive Empire: Transnational Film Culture in Imperial Japan*. Honolulu: University of Hawaii Press.

Bean, J. M., Horak, L. and Kapse, A. (eds) (2014) *Silent Cinema and the Politics of Space*. Bloomington: Indiana University Press.

Blakey, Paul (2011) *Sport Marketing*. Exeter: Learning Matters (SAGE Publishing).

Blanco, Jose (ed.) (2015) *Clothing and Fashion: American Fashion from Head to Toe* [Vol. 3]. Santa Barbara, CA: ABC-CLIO.

Bock, Hans-Michael (ed.) (2009) *The Concise Cinegraph: Encyclopedia of German Cinema*. Oxford: Berghahn Books.

Bordwell, David, Staiger, Janet and Thompson, Kristin (2003) *The Classical Hollywood Cinema: Film Style and Mode of Production to 1960*. London: Routledge.

Bordwell, David (1988) *Ozu and the Poetics of Cinema*. London and New Jersey: BFI Publishing and Princeton University Press.

Braudy, L. and Cohen, M. (1999) *Film Theory and Criticism: Introductory Readings*. New York: Oxford University Press.

Brown, Kendall H. and Minichello, S. A. (2003) *Taishō Chic: Japanese Modernity, Nostalgia and Deco*. Hawaii: Honolulu Academy of Arts.

Brumann, Christoph (2012) *Tradition, Democracy and the Townscape of Kyoto: Claiming a Right to the Past*. London: Routledge.

Bruzzi, Stella (1997) *Undressing Cinema*. London: Routledge.

Buckley, Sandra (ed.) (2009) *Encyclopaedia of Contemporary Japanese Culture*. London: Taylor & Francis.

Bullock, Alan and Trombley, Stephen (2000) *The New Fontana Dictionary of Modern Thought*. London: Harper Collins.

Butler, Judith (1990) *Gender Trouble*. London: Routledge.

Cameron, D. and Kulick, D. (eds) (2006) *The Language and Sexuality Reader*. Oxford: Routledge.

Carter, C. and Steiner, L. (eds) (2003) *Critical Readings: Media and Gender*. London: McGraw-Hill Education.

Chamberlain, Basil Hall (1905) *Things Japanese*. London, Yokohama, Hong Kong and Singapore: Kelly and Walsh Limited.

Chamberlain, Basil Hall (1927) *Things Japanese*. Kobe: J. L. Thompson & Co.

Charney, Leo and Schwartz, Vanessa R. (1995) *Cinema and the Invention of Modern Life*, Berkeley: University of California Press.

Close, Frederick P (2014) *Tokyo Rose / An American Patriot: A Dual Biography*. Lanham, MD: Rowman & Littlefield.

Coates, Jennifer (2016) *Making Icons: Repetition and the Female Image in Japanese Cinema, 1945–1964*. Hong Kong: Hong Kong University Press.

Collins, Sandra (2007) *The 1940 Tokyo Games: The Missing Olympics*. London: Routledge.

Crowley, Charles Bonaventure (1996) *Aristotelian-Thomistic Philosophy Of Measure and the International System Of Units*. Lanham, MA: University Press of America.

Dalby, Liza (1993) *KIMONO: Fashioning Culture*. New Haven, CT and London: Yale University Press.

Davis, Darrell W. (1996) *Picturing Japaneseness*. New York: Columbia University Press.

De Beauvoir, S. (2011) *The Second Sex*, trans. Constance Borde and Sheila Malovany Chevallier. New York: Vintage Books.

Debord, Guy (1995) *The Society of the Spectacle*, trans. Donald Nicholson-Smith. New York: Zone Books.

Downer, Lesley (2003) *Madame Sadayakko: The Geisha Who Seduced the West*. London: Review.

Dyer, Richard (1998) *Stars*. London: British Film Institute.

Edelman, Robert and Wilson, Wayne (2017) *The Oxford Handbook of Sports History*. Oxford: Oxford University Press.

Edwards, Tim (2016) *Men in the Mirror: Men's Fashion, Masculinity, and Consumer Society*. London: Bloomsbury Publishing.

Erens, Patricia (1990) *Issues in Feminist Film Criticism*. Bloomington: Indiana University Press.

Ericson, Joan E. (1997) *Be A Woman: Hayashi Fumiko and Modern Japanese Women's Literature*. Honolulu: University of Hawaii Press.

Fairclough, N. and Wodak, R. (1997) 'Critical Discourse Analysis', in Van Dijk, T. A. (ed.) *Discourse Studies: A Multidisciplinary Introduction, Vol. 2: Discourse as Social Interaction*. London: Sage.

Fairclough, Norman (2013) *Critical Discourse Analysis: The Critical Study of Language*. London: Routledge.

Farrell, Amy E. (2011) *Fat Shame: Stigma and the Fat Body in American Culture*. New York: New York University Press.

Faure, Bernard (1998) *The Red Thread: Buddhist Approaches to Sexuality*. New Jersey: Princeton University Press.

Ferraro, Gary P. and Andreatta, Susan (2010) *Cultural Anthropology: An Applied Perspective,* California: Wadsworth Cengage Learning.

Foucault, Michel (1969) *Archaeology of Knowledge.* London: Routledge.

Francks, Penelope (2012) 'Kimono Fashion: The Consumer and the Growth of the Textile Industry in Pre-War Japan', in Francks, Penelope and Hunter, Jane (eds) *The Historical Consumer: Consumption and Everyday Life in Japan, 1850–2000.* London: Palgrave Macmillan.

Francks, Penelope and Hunter, Jane (eds) (2012) *The Historical Consumer: Consumption and Everyday Life in Japan, 1850–2000.* London: Palgrave Macmillan.

Frederick, Sarah. (2006) *Turning Pages: Reading and Writing Women's Magazines in Interwar Japan.* Honolulu: University of Hawaii Press.

Frost, Warwick, Laing, Jennifer and Williams, Kim (eds) (2013) *Fashion, Design and Events.* London: Routledge.

Fujiki, Hideaki. (2013) *Making Personas: Transnational Film Stardom in Modern Japan.* Cambridge, MA and London: Harvard University Press.

Garber, Marjorie (2006) 'Selections from *The Chic of Araby*: Transvestitism and the Erotics of Cultural Appropriation', in Stryker, S. and Whittle, S. (eds) *The Transgender Studies Reader.* London: Taylor & Francis.

Garon, Sheldon (2009) 'Middle Class', in Buckley, Sandra (ed.) *Encyclopaedia of Contemporary Japanese Culture.* London: Taylor & Francis.

Gerow, Aaron (2008) *A Page of Madness: Cinema and Modernity in 1920s Japan.* Ann Arbor: University of Michigan Press.

Gerow, Aaron (2010) *Visions of Japanese Modernity: Articulations of Cinema, Nation, and Spectatorship, 1895–1925.* Berkeley: University of California Press.

Gever, Martha (2003) *Entertaining Lesbians: Celebrity, Sexuality, and Self-Invention.* London: Psychology Press.

Gilman, Sander L. (1999) *Making the Body Beautiful: A Cultural History of Aesthetic Surgery.* New Jersey: Princeton University Press.

Goodrum, Alison L. (2013) 'A Dashing, Positively Smashing, Spectacle . . .: Female Spectators and Dress at Equestrian Events in the United States During the 1930s', in Frost, Warwick, Laing, Jennifer and Williams, Kim (eds) *Fashion, Design and Events.* London: Routledge.

Gordon, Andrew (2012) *Fabricating Consumers: The Sewing Machine in Modern Japan.* Berkeley: University of California Press.

Grant, Susan (2013) *Physical Culture and Sport in Soviet Society: Propaganda, Acculturation and Transformation in the 1920s and 1930s.* London: Routledge.

Greig, C. J. and Martino, W. J. (eds) (2012) *Canadian Men and Masculinities: Historical and Contemporary Perspectives.* Toronto: Canadian Scholars' Press Inc.

Habermas, Jürgen (1991) *The Structural Transformation of The Public Sphere,* trans. Thomas Burger. Cambridge, MA: MIT Press.

Haggerty, G. and Zimmerman, B. (eds) (2003) *Encyclopedia of Lesbian and Gay Histories and Cultures.* London: Taylor & Francis.

Haiken, Elizabeth (2002) 'Modern Miracles: The Development of Cosmetic Prosthetics', in Ott, Katherine, Serlin, David and Mihm, Stephen (2002) *Artificial Parts, Practical Lives: Modern Histories of Prosthetics.* New York: New York University Press.

Hansen, Miriam B. (1994) *Babel and Babylon: Spectatorship in American Silent Film.* Cambridge, MA and London: Harvard University Press.

Harootunian, Harry D. (2011) *Overcome by Modernity: History, Culture, and Community in Interwar Japan.* New Jersey: Princeton University Press.

Hastings, Sally Ann (1995) *Neighborhood and Nation in Tokyo, 1905–1937*. Pittsburgh: University of Pittsburgh Press.

High, Peter B. (2003) *The Imperial Screen*. Madison: University of Wisconsin Press.

Hiratsuka, Raichō (2006) *In The Beginning, Woman Was the Sun*, trans. Teruko Craig. New York: Columbia University Press.

Holmes, Su and Redmond, Sean (2012) *Framing Celebrity: New Directions in Celebrity Culture*. London: Routledge.

Horak, Laura (2014) 'Queer Crossings: Greta Garbo, National Identity, and Gender Deviance', in Bean, J. M., Horak, L. and Kapse, A. (eds) *Silent Cinema and the Politics of Space*. Bloomington: Indiana University Press.

Horne, J., Tomlinson, A. and Whannel, Garry (1991) *Understanding Sport: An Introduction to the Sociological and Cultural Analysis of Sport*. London: Taylor & Francis.

Huffman, James L. (1997) *Creating A Public: People and Press in Meiji Japan*. Honolulu: University of Hawaii Press.

Ito, R. (2008) 'The "Modern Girl" Question in the Periphery of Empire: Colonial Modernity and Mobility Among Okinawan Women in the 1920s and 1930s', in Weinbaum, A. E., Thomas, L. M., Ramamurthy, P., Poiger, U. G., Dong, M. Y. and Barlow, T. E. (eds) *The Modern Girl Around the World: Consumption, Modernity and Globalisation*. Durham, NC and London: Duke University Press.

Iwamoto, Kenji (1991) *Nihon eiga to Modanizumu 1920–1930*. Tokyo: Riburopōto.

Iwamoto, Kenji (1992) 'Sound in the Early Japanese Talkies', in Nolletti, Arthur Jr. and Desser, David (eds) *Reframing Japanese Cinema: Authorship, Genre, History*. Bloomington and Indianapolis: Indiana University Press.

Jackson, Tim and Shaw, David (2008) *Mastering Fashion Marketing*. Basingstoke: Palgrave Macmillan.

Jansen, Marius B. (ed.) (2015) *Changing Japanese Attitudes Toward Modernization*. New Jersey: Princeton University Press.

Jenkins, Eric S. (2014) *Special Affects: Cinema, Animation, and the Translation of Consumer Culture*. Edinburgh: Edinburgh University Press.

Kawamura, Yuniya (2005) *Fashion-ology: An Introduction to Fashion Studies*. Oxford: Berg.

Kawamura, Yuniya (2013) *Fashioning Japanese Subcultures*. London: Berg.

Kawazoe, Noboru (2004) *Kon Wajirō sono kōgengaku: modernologio*. Japan: Chikuma Bunko.

Keaveney, Christopher T. (2004) *The Subversive Self in Modern Chinese Literature: The Creation Society's Reinvention of the Japanese Shishōsetsu*. New York: Palgrave Macmillan.

Kinema junpō (1980) *Nihon eiga haiyū zenshū joyū-hen*. Japan: Kinema junpō-sha.

Kirihara, Donald (1992) *Patterns of Time: Mizoguchi and the 1930s*. Madison: University of Wisconsin Press.

Kon, Wajirō (2011) *Kon Wajirō saishū kōgi*. Japan: Seigensha Art Publishing.

Koszarski, Richard (2008) *Hollywood on the Hudson: Film and Television in New York from Griffith to Sarnoff*. New Jersey: Rutgers University Press.

Kramer, Eric M. (2003) *The Emerging Monoculture: Assimilation and the 'Model Minority'*. Westport, CT: Greenwood Publishing Group.

Kyo, Cho (2012) *The Search for the Beautiful Woman: A Cultural History of Japanese and Chinese Beauty*. Lanham, MD: Rowman & Littlefield.

LaMarre, T. (2009) 'Cine-Photography as Racial Technology: Tanizaki Jun'ichirô's Close-Up on the New/Oriental Woman's Face', in Morris, R. C. (ed.) *Photography East: The Camera and Its Histories in East and Southeast Asia*. Durham, NC: Duke University Press.

LaMarre, Thomas (2005) *Shadows on the Screen: Tanizaki Jun'ichirō on Cinema and 'Oriental' Aesthetics*. Ann Arbor: University of Michigan Press.

Le Fanu, Mark (2005) *Mizoguchi and Japan*. London: BFI Publishing.

Lash, Scott M. and Urry, John (1994) *Economies of Signs and Space*. London: SAGE Publications.

Lippit, Seiji M. (2012) *Topographies of Japanese Modernism*. New York: Columbia University Press.

Lugowski, David M. (2011) 'Norma Shearer and Joan Crawford: Rivals at the Glamour Factory', in McLean, Adrienne L. (ed.) *Glamour in a Golden Age: Movie Stars of the 1930s*. New Jersey: Rutgers University Press.

Manca, Luigi Daniele, Manca, Alessandra and Pieper, Gail W. (eds) (2012) *Utopian Images and Narratives in Advertising*. Lanham, MD: Lexington Books.

Maruyama, Masao (2015) 'Patterns of Individuation and the Case of Japan: A Conceptual Scheme', in Jansen, Marius B. (ed.) *Changing Japanese Attitudes Toward Modernization*. New Jersey: Princeton University Press.

Mayne, Judith (1993) *Cinema and Spectatorship*. New York: Routledge.

McClain, James L. (2002) *Japan: a Modern History*. London: W. W. Norton & Co.

McCarty, J. A., and Lowrey, T. M. (2012) 'Product Integration: Current Practices and New Directions', in Shrum, L. J. (ed.) *The Psychology of Entertainment Media: Blurring the Lines Between Entertainment and Persuasion*. London: Routledge.

McDonald, Keiko (1984) *Mizoguchi*. Boston, MA: Twayne Publishers.

McDonald, Keiko (1994) *Japanese Classical Theater in Films*. Teaneck, NJ: Farleigh Dickinson University Press.

McDonald, Keiko (2006) *Reading a Japanese Film*. Honolulu: University of Hawaii Press.

McDonald, Myra (2003) 'From Mrs Happyman to Kissing Chaps Goodbye: Advertising Reconstructs Femininity', in Carter, C. and Steiner, L. (eds) *Critical Readings: Media and Gender*. London: McGraw-Hill Education.

McLean, Adrienne L. (ed.) (2011) *Glamour In A Golden Age: Movie Stars of the 1930s*. New Jersey: Rutgers University Press.

McLelland, Mark (2012) *Love, Sex, and Democracy in Japan During the American Occupation*. New York: Palgrave Macmillan.

Meyrowitz, Joshua (1986) *No Sense of Place: The Impact of Electronic Media on Social Behavior*. Oxford: Oxford University Press.

Miller, L. and Bardsley, J. (eds) (2005) *Bad Girls of Japan*. New York: Springer Publishing.

Miller, Laura (2006) *Beauty Up: Exploring Japanese Contemporary Japanese Body Aesthetics*. Berkeley: University of California Press.

Minichello, Sharon (1998) *Japan's Competing Modernities: Issues in Culture and Democracy 1900–1930*. Honolulu: University of Hawaii Press.

Miyao, Daisuke (2007) *Sessue Hayakawa*. Durham, NC: Duke University Press.

Miyao, Daisuke (2013) *The Aesthetics of Shadow: Lighting and Japanese Cinema*. Durham, NC: Duke University Press.

Miyao, Daisuke (2013) *The Oxford Handbook of Japanese Cinema*. Oxford: Oxford University Press.

Molony, Barbara and Uno, Kathleen (2005) *Gendering Modern Japanese History*. Cambridge, MA: Harvard University Press.

Molony, Barbara (2010) 'Gender, Citizenship and Dress in Modernizing Japan', in Roces, Mina (ed.) *The Politics of Dress in Asia and the Americas*. Eastbourne: Sussex Academic Press.

Mori, T. (2007) 'All for Money: Mizoguchi Kenji's *Osaka Elegy* (1936)', in Phillips, Alastair and Stringer, Julian (eds) *Japanese Cinema: Texts and Contexts*. London and New York: Routledge.

Murguia, Salvador (2016) *The Encyclopedia of Japanese Horror Films*. Lanham, MD: Rowman & Littlefield.

Nagayama, Takeomi (1996) *Shōchiku Hyakunenshi*. Tokyo: Shōchiku Kabushiki Kaisha.

Nakamura, Momoko (2006) 'Creating Indexicality: Schoolgirl Speech in Meiji Japan', in Cameron, D. and Kulick, D. (eds) *The Language and Sexuality Reader*. Oxford: Routledge.

Nara, Hiroshi (ed.) (2004) *The Structure of Detachment: The Aesthetic Vision of Kuki Shūzō*. Honolulu: University of Hawaii Press.

Narita, R. (1999) 'The Overflourishing of Sexuality in 1920s Japan', in Wakita, Haruko, Bouchy, Anne and Ueno, Chizuko (eds) *Gender and Japanese History* (Vol. 1). Osaka: Osaka University Press.

Nayar, Pramod K. (2009) *Seeing Stars: Spectacle, Society and Celebrity Culture*. India: SAGE Publications.

Ng, Janet (2010) *The Experience of Modernity: Chinese Autobiography of the Early Twentieth Century*. Ann Arbor: University of Michigan Press.

Nicholas, Jane (2015) *The Modern Girl: Feminine Modernities, the Body, and Commodities in the 1920s*. Toronto: University of Toronto Press.

Nolletti, Arthur Jr. and Desser, David (eds) (1992) *Reframing Japanese Cinema: Authorship, Genre, History*. Bloomington and Indianapolis: Indiana University Press.

Nornes, Abé Mark (2003) *Japanese Documentary Film: The Meiji Era Through Hiroshima*. Minneapolis: University of Minnesota Press.

Ott, Katherine, Serlin, David and Mihm, Stephen (2002) *Artificial Parts, Practical Lives: Modern Histories of Prosthetics*. New York: New York University Press.

Parrill, William B. (2006) *European Silent Films on Video: A Critical Guide*. Jefferson, NC: McFarland.

Peril, L. (2006) *College Girls: Bluestockings, Sex Kittens, and Coeds, Then and Now*. New York: W. W. Norton & Co.

Petro, Patrice (2002) *Aftershocks of the New: Feminism and Film History*, New Jersey: Rutgers University Press.

Phillips, Alastair and Stringer, Julian (2007) *Japanese Cinema: Texts and Contexts*. London and New York: Routledge.

Picken, Stuart D. B. (2004) *Sourcebook in Shintō*. Westport, CT: Praeger Press.

Piga, Maria Lucia (2012) 'Masculine and Feminine Images in Italian Magazine Advertising', trans. Dolores Sorci-Bradley, in Manca, Luigi Daniele, Manca, Alessandra and Pieper, Gail W. (eds) *Utopian Images and Narratives in Advertising*. Lanham, MD: Lexington Books.

Robertson, James C. (1993) *The Hidden Cinema: British Film Censorship in Action*. London: Routledge.

Robertson, Jennifer (1998) *Takarazuka: Sexual Politics and Popular Culture in Modern Japan*. Oakland: University of California Press.

Roces, Mina (ed.) (2010) *The Politics of Dress in Asia and the Americas*. Eastbourne: Sussex Academic Press.

Said, Edward W. (2014) *Orientalism*. New York: Knopf Doubleday Publishing Group.

Sato, Barbara (2003) *The New Japanese Woman*. Durham, NC: Duke University Press.

Saussure, Ferdinand de (1974) *Course in General Linguistics*, trans. Wade Baskin. London: Fontana/Collins.

Schatz, Thomas (2004) *Hollywood: Formal-aesthetic Dimensions: Authorship, Genre and Stardom*. London: Taylor & Francis.

Shaeffer, Claire B. (2001) *Couture Sewing Techniques*. Newtown, CT: Taunton Press.

Sharp, Jasper (2011) *Historical Dictionary of Japanese Cinema*. New Jersey: Scarecrow Press.

Shimp, Terence A. and Andrews, J. C. (2008) *Advertising, Promotion, and Other Aspects of Integrated Marketing Communications*. California: Cengage Learning.

Shōchiku Kabushiki Kaisha (2003) *Ozu Yasujirō eiga dokuhon: 'Tōkyō' soshite 'kazoku' Ozu Yasujirō seitan 100-nen kinen 'Ozu Yasujirō no geijutsu' kōshiki puroguramu*. Tokyo: Shōchiku.

Shrum, L. J. (ed.) (2012) *The Psychology of Entertainment Media: Blurring the Lines Between Entertainment and Persuasion*. London: Routledge.

Silverberg, Miriam (2008) 'After the Grand Tour: The Modern Girl, the New Woman and the Colonial Maiden', in Weinbaum, Alys E., Thomas, Lynn M., Ramamurthy, Priti, Poiger, Uta G., Dong, Madeleine Y. and Barlow, Tani E. (eds) *The Modern Girl Around the World: Consumption, Modernity and Globalisation*. Durham, NC and London: Duke University Press.

Silverberg, Miriam (2009) *Erotic Grotesque Nonsense: The Mass Culture of Japanese Modern Times*. Berkeley and Los Angeles: University of California Press.

Singer, Ben (1995) 'Modernity, Hyperstimulus, and the Rise of Popular Sensationalism', in Charney, Leo and Schwartz, Vanessa R. (eds) *Cinema and the Invention of Modern Life*, Berkeley: University of California Press.

Skabelund, Aaron (2011) *Empire of Dogs: Canines, Japan, and the Making of the Modern Imperial World*. New York: Cornell University Press.

Slade, Toby (2009) *Japanese Fashion: A Cultural History*. Oxford: Berg.

Smith, Anthony D. (1991) *National Identity*. Reno: University of Nevada Press.

Smulyan, Susan (2007) *Popular Ideologies: Mass Culture at Mid-Century*. Philadelphia: University of Pennsylvania Press.

Standish, Isolde (2006) *A New History of Japanese Cinema: A Century of Narrative Film*. London: Bloomsbury Publishing.

Standish, Isolde (2013) *Myth and Masculinity in the Japanese Cinema: Towards a Political Reading of the 'Tragic Hero'*. London: Routledge.

Stockwell, Peter (2002) *Sociolinguistics: A Resource Book for Students*. London: Routledge.

Stokes, Patricia D. (2005) *Creativity from Constraints: The Psychology of Breakthrough*. New York: Springer Publishing Company.

Stryker, S. and Whittle, S. (eds) (2006) *The Transgender Studies Reader*. London: Taylor & Francis.

Sutton, Katie (2013) *The Masculine Woman in Weimar Germany*. Oxford: Berghahn Books.

Takeda, S. (1999) 'Menswear, Womenswear: Distinctive Features of the Japanese Sartorial System', in Wakita, H., Bouchy, A. and Ueno, C. (eds) *Gender and Japanese History* (Vol. 1). Osaka: Osaka University Press.

Tanaka, Masasumi (1993) *Zen nikki Ozu Yasujirō*. Tokyo: Firumuātosha.

Tanizaki Jun'ichirō (1985) *Naomi (Chijin no ai)*, trans. Anthony H. Chambers. New York: Vintage International.

Tansman, Alan (ed.) (2010) *The Culture of Japanese Fascism*. Durham, NC: Duke University Press.

Thompson, Lana (2011) *Plastic Surgery*. Santa Barbara, CA: ABC-CLIO.

Thornham, Sue (1999) *Feminist Film Theory: A Reader*. New York: New York University Press.

Thurman, Judith (2011) 'Introduction', in De Beauvoir, S. *The Second Sex*, trans. Constance Borde and Sheila Malovany Chevallier. New York: Vintage Books.

Tipton, Elise K. (2008) *Modern Japan: A Social and Political History*. London: Routledge.
Tipton, Elise K. (2009) 'Intellectual Life, Culture, and the Challenge of Modernity', in Tsutsui, William M. (ed.) *A Companion to Japanese History*. New York: John Wiley & Sons.
Tipton, Elise K. and Clark, John (eds) (2000) *Being Modern in Japan: Culture and Society from the 1910s to the 1930s*. Honolulu: University of Hawaii Press.
Tsuneo, Hazami (1955) *Shashin Eiga Hyakunen Shi* (Vol. II). Japan: Masu Shobō.
Tsubouchi, Yūzō (2000) 'Bundan no seiritsu to hōkai', in Aoki, Tamotsu, Kawamoto, Saburō, Tsutsui, Kiyotada, Mikuriya, Takashi and Yamaori, Tetsuo (eds) *Kindai Nihon bunkaron, Vol. 3: Hai karuchā*. Tokyo: Iwanami Shoten.
Tsutsui, William M. (ed.) (2009) *A Companion to Japanese History*. New York: John Wiley & Sons.
Tungate, Mark (2012) *Fashion Brands: Branding Style from Armani to Zara*. London: Kogan Page Publishers.
Tyler, William Jefferson (2008) Modanizumu: *Modernist Fiction from Japan, 1913–1938*. Honolulu: Univlrsity of Hawaii Press.
van der Merwe, Ann O. (2009) *The Ziegfeld Follies: A History in Songs*. New Jersey: Scarecrow Press.
Van Dijk, T. A. (1997) *Discourse Studies: A Multidisciplinary Introduction, Vol. 2: Discourse as Social Interaction*. London: Sage.
Vlastos, Stephen (1998) *Mirror of Modernity: Invented Traditions of Modern Japan*. Berkeley: University of California Press.
Wada-Marciano, Mitsuyo (2008) *Nippon Modern: Japanese Cinema of the 1920s and 1930s*. Honolulu: University of Hawaii Press.
Wakita, Haruko, Bouchy, Anne and Ueno, Chizuko (eds) (1999) *Gender and Japanese History* (Vol. 1). Osaka: Osaka University Press.
Warner, Helen (2014) *Fashion on Television: Identity and Celebrity Culture*. London: A & C Black.
Washburn, Dennis and Cavanaugh, Carole (2001) *Word and Image in Japanese Cinema*. Cambridge: Cambridge University Press.
Weisenfeld, Gennifer (2012) *Imaging Disaster: Tokyo and the Visual Culture of Japan's Great Earthquake of 1923*. Berkeley: University of California Press.
Weinbaum, Alys E., Thomas, Lynn M., Ramamurthy, Priti, Poiger, Uta G., Dong, Madeleine Y. and Barlow, Tani E. (2008) *The Modern Girl Around the World: Consumption, Modernity and Globalisation*. Durham, NC and London: Duke University Press.
White, Merry. (2012) *Coffee Life in Japan*. Berkeley: University of California Press.
Whitfield, Eileen (2007) *Pickford: The Woman Who Made Hollywood*. Lexington: University Press of Kentucky.
Wilson, Elizabeth (2011) *Adorned in Dreams*. London and New York: I. B. Tauris and Co. Ltd.
Winfield, S. and Richardson, Y. (2016) 'Designing-in Consumer Identity and Experience via Social Media Representation and Engagement Effects: Contesting Female Body Image and Branding', in McIntyre, Charles, Melewar, T. C. and Dennis, Charles *Multi-Channel Marketing, Branding and Retail Design: New Challenges and Opportunities*. England: Emerald Group Publishing.
Winge, Theresa M. (2013) *Body Style*. Oxford: Berg.
Wohr, Ulrike, Sato, Barbara H. and Suzuki, Sadami (1998) *Gender and Modernity: Rereading Women's Magazines*. Belgium: International Research Centre for Japanese Studies.
Wykes, Maggie and Gunther, Barrie (2005) *The Media and Body Image: If Looks Could Kill*. London: SAGE Publications.

Yamanashi, Makiko (2012) *A History of the Takarazuka Revue Since 1914: Modernity, Girls' Culture, Japan Pop*. London: Global Oriental.
Yoshimoto, Mitsuhiro (2000) *Kurosawa: Film Studies and Japanese Cinema*. Durham, NC: Duke University Press.
Young, Louise (2013) *Beyond the Metropolis: Second Cities and Modern Life in Interwar Japan*. Berkeley: University of California Press.

PhD theses

Karlin, Jason G. (2002) *The Empire of Fashion: Taste, Gender and Nation in Modern Japan*. Urbana-Champaign: University of Illinois.
Løfsgaard, K. A. (2015) 'The History of English Education in Japan – Motivations, Attitudes and Methods', Program in Asia and Middle East Studies, University of Oslo.
Nickerson, Rebecca Ann (2011) *Imperial Designs: Fashion, Cosmetics and Cultural Identity in Japan, 1931–1943*. Urbana-Champaign: University of Illinois.
Schlater, A. (2008) *Flaming Youth: Gender in 1920s Hollywood*. Loyola University Chicago.
Schmidt, C. (2008) *Second Skin: Annette Kellerman, the Modern Swimsuit, and an Australian Contribution to Global Fashion*. Queensland University of Technology.

Journal articles

Bernardi, Joanne (1997) 'Norimasa Kaeriyama and *The Glory of Life*', *Film History*, 9.
Fardouly, J., Diedrichs, P. C., Vartanian, L. and Halliwell, E. (2015) 'Social comparisons on social media: The impact of Facebook on young women's body image concerns and mood', *Body Image*, 13.
Gerow, Aaron and Makino, Mamoru (1994) 'Documentarists of Japan #5: Prokino', *Documentary Box*, 5.
Hansen, Miriam B. (2000) 'Fallen Women, Rising Stars, New Horizons: Shanghai Silent Film as Vernacular Modernism', *Film Quarterly*, 54(1).
Hirata, Yoko (2009) 'Oscar Wilde and Honma Hisao, the First Translator of De Profundis into Japanese', *Japan Review*, 21.
Joo, Woojeong (2012) 'I Was Born Middle Class, But . . . Ozu Yasujirō's *Shōshimin Eiga* in the Early 1930s', *Journal of Japanese and Korean Cinema*, 4(2).
Karlin, Jason G. (2002) 'The Gender of Nationalism: Competing Masculinities in Meiji Japan', *Journal of Japanese Studies*, 28(1).
Kobayashi, Koji, Jackson, Steven J., Sam, Michael P. (2017) 'Globalization, creative alliance and self-Orientalism: Negotiating Japanese identity within Asics global advertising production', *International Journal of Cultural Studies*, 22(1).
Komatsu, Hiroshi (2005) 'The Foundation of Modernism: Japanese Cinema in the Year 1927', *Film History: An International Journal*, 17(2/3).
Kuroda, Toshio (1981) 'Shintō in the History of Japanese Religion', *Journal of Japanese Studies*, 7(1).
Leheny, David (2000) '"By Other Means": Tourism and Leisure as Politics in Pre-War Japan', *Social Science Japan Journal*, 3(2).

Low, Morris (2015) 'American Photography during the Allied Occupation of Japan: The Work of John W. Bennett', *History of Photography*, 39(3).

Mulvey, Laura (1975) 'Visual Pleasure and Narrative Cinema', *Screen*, 16(3).

Nakano, Masaak (1998) 'Dōyō shijin no 30-nendai – mūran rūju shōshi' ['The Nursery Rhyme Poets of the 1930s – A Short History of the "Moulin Rouge"'], *Taishō engeki kenkyū*, 7(20).

Okada, Yoshiro (2011) 'WOMEN ON THE TOWN: Mitsukoshi to Paruko, Hana Hiraku Shōhi Bunka', *Ad Studies*, 37.

Perloff, Richard M. (2014) 'Social Media Effects on Young Women's Body Image Concerns: Theoretical Perspectives and an Agenda for Research', *Sex Roles*, 71(11–12).

Robertson, Jennifer (1999) 'Sexuality and shopping: eugenics and female citizenship in urban Japan, 1920–1940', *Asiatische Studien*, 53(2).

Robertson, Jennifer (2001) 'Japan's First Cyborg? Miss Nippon, Eugenics and Wartime Technologies of Beauty, Body and Blood', *Body and Society*, 7(1).

Sakai, Hiromi (2008) '"Katei" no naka no kaikyū: Taishō ki feminisuto no "jochu" koyō', *Jenda shigaku*, 4.

Sakamoto, Rumi (2010) 'Pan-pan Girls: Humiliating Liberation in Postwar Japanese Literature', *PORTAL*, 7(2).

Sanders, Charles J. (2011) 'Alpine Nippon', *Skiing Heritage Journal*, 23(4).

Sanders, Holly (2013) '*Panpan:* Streetwalking in Occupied Japan', *Pacific Historical Review*, 81(3).

Sapin, Julia (2004) 'Merchandising Art and Identity in Meiji Japan: Kyoto Nihonga Artists' Designs for Takashimaya Department Store, 1868–1912', *Journal of Design History*, 17(4).

Sato, Barbara H. (1993) 'The *Moga* Sensation: Perceptions of the *Modan Gāru* in Japanese Intellectual Circles During the 1920s', *Gender and History*, 5(3).

Shamoon, Deborah (2012) 'The Modern Girl and the Vamp: Hollywood Film in Tanizaki Jun'ichirō's Early Novels', *Positions*, 20(4).

Shoemaker, Greg (1979) 'Daiei: A History of the Greater Japan Motion Picture Company', *The Japanese Fantasy Film Journal*, 12.

Silva, Marie (2018) 'The Rise and Fall of the Weimar Woman', *The Compass*, 5(1).

Silverberg, Miriam (1992) 'Constructing the Japanese Ethnography of Modernity', *The Journal of Asian Studies*, 51(1).

Suter, Rebecca (2012) 'Orientalism, Self-Orientalism, and Occidentalism in the Visual-Verbal Medium of Japanese Girls' Comics', *Literature and Aesthetics*, 22(2).

Suzuki, Michiko (2005) 'Progress and Love Marriage: Rereading Tanizaki Jun'ichirō's "Chijin no ai"', *The Journal of Japanese Studies*, 31(2).

Tamari, Tomoko (2006) 'Rise of the Department Store and the Aestheticization of Everyday Life in Early 20th Century Japan', *International Journal of Japanese Sociology*, 15.

Weisenfeld, Gennifer (2009) 'Publicity and Propaganda in 1930s Japan: Modernism as Method', *Design Issues*, 25(4).

Online documents and resources

Ahoh, Erika (2002) *In Search of Beauty: Seiko Takada.* 16th International Congress on Dance Research. Available at <http://writings.orchesis-portal.org/index.php/en/articlesen/171-akoh-erika-in-search-of-beauty-seiko-takada-16th-international-congress-on-dance-research-athens-iofa-greece-2002> [accessed 12 April 2017].

BBC (2012) *Portrayal of Lesbian, Gay and Bisexual People on the BBC.* BBC.co.uk. Available at <http://downloads.bbc.co.uk/diversity/pdf/lgb_portrayal_update_2012_withquotes.pdf> [accessed 18 October 2018].

Crawford, Cassidy (2016) *Aerie Real Campaign: Body Positive or Body Shaming?* Medium. Available at <https://medium.com/@cassidycrawford/aerie-real-campaign-body-positive-or-body-shaming-2fb49024d7f4> [accessed 18 October 2018].

Dalessandro, Alysse (2016) *15 Definitions of Body Positivity Straight from Influencers & Activists.* Bustle. Available at <https://www.bustle.com/articles/165804-15-definitions-of-body-positivity-straight-from-influencers-activists> [accessed 18 October 2018].

Fox, Kate (1997) *Mirror, Mirror: A Summary of Research on Body Image.* Social Issues Research Centre. Available at <http://www.sirc.org/publik/mirror.html> [accessed 18 April 2017].

Garza, Janiss (2017) *The Uninvited Guest (1924): Synopsis.* AllMovie. Available at <https://www.allmovie.com/movie/the-uninvited-guest-v238575> [accessed 11 November 2017].

Gunning, Tom (1986) *The Cinema of Attraction: Early Film, Its Spectator and the Avant-Garde.* Columbia University. Available at <http://www.columbia.edu/itc/film/gaines/historiography/Gunning.pdf> [accessed 4 March 2015].

International Institute for Children's Literature Osaka (2017) *Kakube'e Jishi [The Lion Dancer].* International Institute for Children's Literature Osaka. Available at <http://www.iiclo.or.jp/100books/1868/htm-e/frame057-e.htm> [accessed 7 May 2017].

Isetan Mitsukoshi (2015) *Mitsukoshi's History.* Isetan Mitsukoshi Holdings. Available at <https://mitsukoshi.mistore.jp/store/nihombashi/foreign_customer/history/index.html> [accessed 8 May 2016].

Ishii, Kazumi (2005) Josei*: A Magazine for the New Woman.* Australian National University. Available at <http://intersections.anu.edu.au/issue11/ishii.html> [accessed 21 March 2016].

Japan Cosmetic Industry Association (2017) *A Cultural History of Cosmetics.* Japan Cosmetic Industry Association. Available at <http://www.jcia.org/n/en/info/b/> [accessed 14 August 2017].

Katherine D. Kalagher (2014) *The Invasion of the Flapper: How the College Women of the 1920s Transformed the American College Experience.* Goodwin College. Available at <https://docplayer.net/19897712-The-invasion-of-the-flapper-how-the-college-women-of-the-1920s-transformed-the-american-college-experience.html> [accessed 21 January 2023].

Livingstone, Sonia (2018) *Media literacy – everyone's favourite solution to the problems of regulation.* London School of Economics. Available at <http://blogs.lse.ac.uk/mediapolicyproject/2018/05/08/media-literacy-everyones-favourite-solution-to-the-problems-of-regulation/> [accessed 18 October 2018].

Marx, W. David (2015) *New Youth:* Shinseinen's *Suicidal Playboy.* NeoJaponisme. Available at <http://neojaponisme.com/2015/09/08/new-youth-shinseinens-suicidal-playboy/> [accessed 20 January 2018].

Rodriguez McRobbie, Linda (2015) *World War I 100 Years Later: The Classy Rise of the Trenchcoat.* Smithsonian Magazine. Available at <http://www.smithsonianmag.com/history/trench-coat-made-its-mark-world-war-i-180955397/?no-ist> [accessed 15 May 2016].

Shiseido (2023) *History of Shiseido.* Shiseido Company Ltd. Available at <https://corp.shiseido.com/en/company/history/> [accessed 21 January 2023].

Tanaka, Masakazu (2012) *The Sexual Contact Zone in Occupied Japan: Discourses on Japanese Prostitutes or* Panpan *for U.S. Military Servicemen.* Intersections, Australian National University. Available at <http://intersections.anu.edu.au/issue31/tanaka.htm> [accessed 3 November 2018].

Tilbury, Natalie (2016) *Jean Patou's Modern Sportswoman*. The Costume Society. Available at <http://costumesociety.org.uk/blog/post/jean-patous-modern-sportswoman> [accessed 29 April 2017].

Wilson, Rusty (2006) *Douglas Fairbanks and the Birth of Hollywood's Love Affair with the Olympics*. Eighth International Symposium for Olympic Research. Available at <https://go.gale.com/ps/i.do?p=AONE&u=googlescholar&id=GALE|A176818714&v=2.1&it=r&sid=AONE&asid=34ea279e> [accessed 21 January 2023].

Magazine, newspaper and ephemera articles (primary sources)

Adachi, G. (1885) 'Dai nihon fujin sokuhatsu zukai' ['An Illustrated Explanation of Women's Hairstyles in Imperial Japan']. London: British Museum.

Asahi Graph [*Asahi gurafu*] (1924) 'Suzuki Denmei', 5 May, p. 7.

Asahi Graph [*Asahi gurafu*] (1924) 'Wagering His Youth: A Nikkatsu Film', 1 October, p. 18.

Asahi shimbun (1905) 'Yokosuka Kaigun Kōshō' ['Yokosuka Naval Munitions Factory'], 19 July, p. 1.

Asahi shimbun (1907) 'Seiyō shinobi keshō no hanashi' ['The Story of Western Disguise Cosmetics'], 9 November, p. 5.

Asahi shimbun (1911) '*Madamu*' [*Madamu* advertisement], 10 August, p. 7.

Asahi shimbun (1922) 'Madamu Ekkusu' ['Madame X'], 13 January, p. 2.

Asahi shimbun (1924) '*Fujin sekai*' [*Woman's World* advertisement], 17 May, p. 1.

Asahi shimbun (1924) 'Suzuki Denmei', 3 March, p. 4.

Asahi shimbun (1925) 'Nikkatsu ni hairu: ninki otoko no Asaoka shi' ['Entering Nikkatsu: The Popular Man Asaoka'], 18 June, p. 2.

Asahi shimbun (1927) 'Mobo moga o yunyū seyo shinrashī mono o yobu kotoba no nai Igirisu e' ['Imported Modern Boy and Modern Girl: Looking to England When There Are No Words for These New Things'], 17 December, p. 2.

Asahi shimbun (1927) 'Modanbōi arashi no kōhan Ginza o aruku mobo, gakusei o kyōhaku shi aruita otoko' ['The Modern Boy's Vulgar Public Trial: A Man Who Was Walking Around Harassing University Students Strolling Around the Ginza and Other Modern Boys'], 2 October, p. 7.

Asahi shimbun (1928) 'Haru no Ginza o arasu mobomoga no mure musen inshoku, kenka, settō to, torishimari ni nayamu shokan-sho' ['A Swarm of Modern Boys and Girls Invade the Ginza in Springtime: Leaving Restaurants Without Paying the Bill, Brawling and Stealing – The Authorities Worry About Managing Them'], 3 March, p. 2.

Asahi shimbun (1928) 'Mobomoga no shinjū' ['Modern Boy and Girl Love Suicide'] 31 January, p. 1.

Asahi shimbun (1928) 'Modan kenkyū ni eiga kenbutsu' ['Watching Films as Modern Research'], 16 October, p. 5.

Asahi shimbun (1928) 'Ōsaka-sei no moga furi' ['The Osaka-Made Modern Girl Look'], 20 May, p. 7.

Asahi shimbun (1929) 'Eiga ni natta *Fue no shiratama*' ['*Undying Pearl* Has Become a Film'], 13 October, p. 5.

Asahi shimbun (1929) 'Kaigai chabanashi' ['Overseas Chatter'], 11 December, p. 2.

Asahi shimbun (1929) 'Mobo, moga kyōfu no kuni' ['A Country of Modern Boy and Modern Girl Panic'] 21 March, p. 2.

Asahi shimbun (1929) 'Rappa zubon' ['Trumpet Trousers'], 14 May, p. 3.

Asahi shimbun (1930) 'Arigatai, shingo o oboeru: Tōkī no ken'etsukandono' ['I Am Thankful for Learning a New Language, Says the Official Censoring Talkies'], 23 January, p. 7.

Asahi shimbun (1931) 'Kunisan tōkī no hareyakana shuto' ['A Bright Start for the Domestically Produced Talkie'], 3 August, p. 10

Asahi shimbun (1931) 'Zenkoku o arashimawatta dai suri-dan kenkyo saru mobo ni bakete odoriba ni mo mashu shinshutsukibotsu no 30 yomei' ['The Three Big Gangs Terrorising the Whole Country Are Arrested: Over Thirty Demons Found in Dancehalls Associated With Modern Boys and Other Evil Influences'], 19 April, p. 11.

Asahi shimbun (1932) 'Apāto rinken shinjū no kataware, Nakamura no torishirabe' ['The Apartment Is Investigated – The Survivor of the Love Suicide, Nakamura, Is Interrogated'], 15 December, p. 11.

Asahi shimbun (1932) 'Jidōsha gōtō han'nin wa mobo' ['Car Robbery: The Criminal Is a Modern Boy'], 14 December, p. 2.

Asahi shimbun (1932) 'Pāmanento uēvu ni tsuite' ['On the Permanent Wave'], 22 January, p. 5.

Asahi shimbun (1932) 'Renmei de shi no aisatsu-jō o hassō sakka Nakamura Sirō to utahime Takanawa Yoshiko jōshi Shinjuku-en apāto no 2-kai de on'na wa zetsumei, otoko wa tasukaru' ['A Jointly-Signed Suicide Note Is Sent: The Love Suicide of Writer Nakamura Shinjirō and Diva Takanawa Yoshiko on the Second Floor of a Shinjuku Apartment. She Dies, He Survives'], 13 December, p. 11.

Asahi shimbun (1932) 'Shinjū no kataware, sakka Nakamura tomeoki-ba e heiki no hira zano mobo sugata de' ['Survivor of The Double Suicide, Writer Nakamura is Taken to Prison With the Calm and Collected Appearance of a Modern Boy'], 14 December, p. 2.

Asahi shimbun (1932) 'Umi no ryūkō nozoki' ['A Peek at Seaside Trends'], 6 July, p. 10.

Asahi shimbun (1933) 'Atama kara tsumasaki made otoko no ryūkō sōshingu' ['Fashionable Men's Accessories From Head to Toe'], 4 September, p. 5.

Asahi shimbun (1933) '"Kazanovua" jōshi tokuige ni isseki utahime no shi ni karamaru Nakamura Shinjirō no shokutaku satsujin jiken kōhan' ['Casanova Love Story: A Proud Statement. The Public Murder Trial of Nakamura Shinjirō'], 16 June, p. 2.

Asahi shimbun (1933) 'Ginza no sawagi: Esukimoboya' ['Ginza Uproar: Eski-*mobo*-ya'], 30 May, p. 2.

Asahi shimbun (1933) 'Modanbōi wa mata hitokurō ka' ['A Tough Time for Modern Boys?'], 2 September, p. 5.

Asahi shimbun (1933) 'Utahime shinjū no Nakamura wa kekkyoku "shokutaku satsujin" kesa yūzai to kettei' ['Nakamura, of the Diva Double Suicide Case, Is Sentenced to Murder This Morning'], 23 April, p. 2.

Asahi shimbun (1934) 'Sekai chūshi no naka ni . . . erabareta misu Furansu!' ['Miss France – Chosen Under the Gaze of the World!'], 6 August, p. 5.

Asahi shimbun (1935) 'Dansō no reijin mata mukidō he' ['Male-Dressed Beauty Goes off the Rails Again'], 28 March, p. 11.

Asahi shimbun (1935) 'Mata mo ichi man en motte dansō no reijin iede' ['Male-Dressed Beauty Runs Away From Home Again, Takes Ten-Thousand Yen'], 28 January, p. 11.

Asahi shimbun (1937) 'Mobo no fukudoku' ['Modern Boy Takes Poison'], 24 December, p. 11.

Asahi shimbun (1938) 'Meidai shutsu no tōmoku "futari wa wakai" o kuchizusamu mobo dohi 2,000 to tomoni tōkō' ['The Leader Has Left Meiji University: A Modern Boy Humming

"We Are Young" To Himself Surrenders Alongside 2,000 Other Local Rebels'], 11 February, p. 11.

Clement, Ernest W. (1930) 'Educational Trends in Japan', *The Japan Times*, 16 March, p. 3.

Eiga jidai [*Film Age*] (1926) 'Rudolph Valentino in *Son of the Sheik*', October, p. 35.

Eiga jōhō [*The Movie Pictorial*] (1926) 'Kakusha no shin eiga' ['New Films From Each Company'], March, p. 32.

Eiga jōhō [*The Movie Pictorial*] (1926) 'Supōtsu seikatsu' ['Sporting Life'], March, p. 28.

Eiga jōhō [*The Movie Pictorial*] (1929) 'Kamata eiga shū' ['A collection of Kamata Films'], May, p. 13.

Eiga jōhō [*The Movie Pictorial*] (1929) '*Kangeki no haru*' ['*Moving Spring*'], April, p. 26.

Eiga jōhō [*The Movie Pictorial*] (1929) '*Lovers:* MGM', April, p. 24.

Eiga jōhō [*The Movie Pictorial*] (1929) 'Sutekki gāru' ['Stick Girl'], May, p. 28.

Eiga jōhō [*The Movie Pictorial*] (1930) 'Dugurasu Feabankusu shi futatabi raichō su' ['Douglas Fairbanks Visits Japan Again'] April, p. 8–9.

Eiga jōhō [*The Movie Pictorial*] (1930) 'Nikkatsu eiga' ['Nikkatsu Films'], August, p. 21.

Eiga jōhō [*The Movie Pictorial*] (1931) 'Kamata no kenkōbi joyū saiyō shiken' ['Kamata's Healthy Body Beauty Actress Employment Examination'], March, p. 13.

Eiga jōhō [*The Movie Pictorial*] (1932) 'Horehoresuru danseibi: Jōji Oburaien shi' ['Fall in Love with Male Beauty – George O'Brien'], February, p. 39.

Eiga jōhō [*The Movie Pictorial*] (1933) 'Suzuki Denmei', October, p. 8.

Eiga jōhō [*The Movie Pictorial*] (1934) 'Hansu aruberusu shi' ['Hans Albers'], May, p. 18.

Eiga jōhō [*The Movie Pictorial*] (1938) 'Eroru Furin' ['Errol Flynn'], October, p. 35.

Eiga jōhō [*The Movie Pictorial*] (1938) 'Ōiso no ginsa de' ['On Ōiso's Silver Sands'], October, p. 32.

Eiga jōhō [*The Movie Pictorial*] (1938) 'Takumashiki kenkōbi' ['A Robust Healthy Body Beauty'], August, p. 12.

Eiga no eiga [*Film of Films*] (1927) 'Beikoku eiga chūdoku?' ['Addiction to American Films?'], November, pp. 8–9.

Fasshon [*Fashion*] (1935) 'Deitorihhi no biyōhō kōkai' ['Dietrich's Beauty Regime Revealed'], May, p. 10.

Fasshon [*Fashion*] (1935) 'Edomondo Rō no oshare seppou' ['Edmund Lowe's Style Lecture'], April, p. 20.

Fasshon [*Fashion*] (1935) 'Fasshon ansāzu' ['Fashion Answers'], May, p. 7.

Fasshon [*Fashion*] (1935) 'Horiūdo yo, o, ware ga Horiūdo yo' ['Ah Hollywood . . . We Are Hollywood'], May, pp. 20–1.

Fasshon [*Fashion*] (1935) 'Inishiaru no tsukaikata' ['Ways of Using Initials'], March, p. 13.

Fasshon [*Fashion*] (1935) 'Kentō fuan to sukīyā no okeshō hihō' ['The Boxing Fan and the Skier's Makeup Secrets'], February, pp. 30–1.

Fasshon [*Fashion*] (1935) 'Ryūsenkata no shintai ni narimaseu' ['Let's Streamline Our Bodies'], September, pp. 16–17.

Fasshon [*Fashion*] (1935) 'Sōshinhō biyō sokusei' ['Quick Beauty and Weight-loss Methods'], August, p. 20.

Fox, Frances M. (1928) 'Mogas and Mobos', *The Japan Times*, 27 January, p. 4.

Fujin kurabu [*Women's Club*] (1924) 'Ohanamigoro ni fusawashii omusume-san muki no nihongami' ['Japanese hairstyles suitable for young ladies during *Hanami*'], April, p. 12.

Fujin kurabu [*Women's Club*] (1924) 'Ryūkō kamigata ni dai' ['Two Fashionable Hairstyles'], April, p. 11.

Futaba, Hikari (1935) 'Yōsō tenbou: sukāto ni tsuite (ichi)' ['Views on Western Clothing: About the Skirt, Part 1'], *Fashion* [*Fasshon*], March, pp. 6–7.

Futaba, Hikari (1935) 'Yōsō tenbou: ueisuto ni tsuite' ['Views on Western Clothing: About the Waist'], *Fashion* [*Fasshon*], May, pp. 6–7.
Hasegawa Shūji (1939) 'Nō nekutai: are wa hisho' ['No Necktie: "It" Is Cooling off for Summer'], *Style* [*Sutairu*], August, pp. 70–1.
Hashizume Ken (1925) 'Teue hōsōshitsu: Naomizumu' ['Straight From the Newsroom: Naomi-ism'], *Yomiuri shimbun*, 3 October, p. 4.
Hatoyama, Suruga (1936) 'Tōkī to haiyū no kōbō-shi' ['The History of the Rise and Fall of the Talkie Actor'], *Nihon eiga*, April, pp. 26–9.
Honma, Hisao (1922) 'Atarashiki jidai no tame no atarashiki fujin' ['New Women for a New Age'], *Shukujo gahō* [*Ladies' Pictorial*], May, p. 2–4.
Hooper, Ruth (1922) 'Flapping Not Repented Of', *The New York Times*, 16 July.
Hosokawa, Haruhiko (1928) 'Bō no yoso' ['The Goodness of Clara Bow'], *The Play and Movie*, November, p. 10.
Ishii, Bunsaku (1928) '"Are" no ohanashi' ['The Story of "It"'] *The Play and Movie*, September, p. 9.
Kamata (1931) 'Macchi Ire' ['Match Holders'], January, p. 1.
Kaneko, Yōbun (1927) 'Nihonjin no yōfuku sugata ['The Appearance of Japanese People in Western Clothing'], *Film Age* [*Eiga jidai*], September, pp. 38–9.
Kari, Yado (1928) 'A Dictionary for Everyday Use', *Japan Times*, 15 July, p. 5.
Kawakami, Kōsuke (2014) 'Let's Celebrate the Launch of Lapo's Wardrobe', *GQ Japan*, August, pp. 34–7.
Kawakita, Renshichirō (1934) 'Nihon josei no taikei to yōsō no dezain' ['The Body Shapes of Japanese Women and Western-style Designs'], *Women's Pictorial* 'Style Book' [*Fujin gahō sutairu bukku*] Spring/Summer, pp. 30–1.
Kinema junpō (1924) 'Kinsaku eiga shōkai: *Umi ni naru otoko*' ['Introducing Recent Films: *The Man Who Becomes the Sea*'], 21 September, p. 21.
Kinema junpō (1926) '*Ashi ni sawatta onna*' [Advertisement for *The Woman Who Touched the Legs*], 21 October, p. 40.
Kinema junpō (1926) 'Kakusha meisaku Nihon eiga shōkai: *Ashi ni sawatta onna*' ['Introducing Recent Japanese Films From Each Company: *The Woman Who Touched the Legs*'], 21 September, p. 42.
Kinema junpō (1926) 'Shuyō Nihon eiga hihyō: *Undōka*' ['Criticism of Major Japanese Films: *The Athlete*'], 21 March, p. 52.
Kinema junpō (1930) 'Clara Bow, Paramount Star', 1 May, p. 7.
Kinema junpō (1931) '*Madamu to nyōbo*' ['*The Neighbour's Wife and Mine*'], 11 August, p. 79.
Kinema junpō (1932) 'Junpo Guraffiku' ['Graphic, Released Every Ten Days'] May, p. 53.
Kinema junpō (1932), [Summer photo spread of various actresses – no title], 1 May, pp. 28–9.
Kinema junpō (1935) 'Kenshō boshū: zen Nihon eigakan bijin jō' ['Competition Announcement: Miss All-Japan Cinema Beauty'], 1 May, p. 22.
Kinema junpō (1936) 'Eba kurēmu' [Advertisement for Eva brand hair removal cream], 1 March, p. 186.
Madsen, Charles P. (1912) *Electric Curling-iron* [patent reference]. US1018673A.
Michaels, Hans (1933) 'In Japan Western Ways are a Veneer', *Japan Times*, 26 January, p. 1.
Misono, Teruko (1927) 'Wansa gaaru no koe' ['The Voice of a Female Extra'], *The Play and Movie*, April, p 12.
Mitamura, Genryo (1928) 'What is *Shibumi*?', *Japan Times*, 3 June, p. 5.
Mizumachi, Seiji (1936) 'Nihon eiga hihyō' ['Japanese Film Criticism'], 1 November, p. 128.

Nakano, Eitaro (1935) 'Dansō no reijin to Saijō Eriko: dōseiaishi misui no ikikatsu' ['The Male-Dressed Beautiful Woman and Saijō Eriko: The Circumstances of their Same-Sex Suicide Attempt'], *Woman's Review* [*Fujin kōron*], March, p. 161–7.

Natsumura, Senkichi (1939) 'Nikkatsu no Kazami Akiko hōmonki: "Renai ga ichiban komaru wa"' ['An Account of a Visit to Nikkatsu's Kazami Akiko: "Romantic Love is the Greatest Problem"'], *Sutairu* [*Style*], July, pp. 8–9.

Nihon eiga [*Japanese Film*] (1936) 'Hanai Ranko', August, p. 8.

Nihon eiga [*Japanese Film*] (1936) 'Kawaishi', July, p. 34.

Nihon eiga [*Japanese Film*] (1936) 'Saijō Eriko', June, p. 14.

Nihon eiga [*Japanese Film*] (1936) 'Supōtsu eiga haiyū monogatari' ['The Story of Sports Film Stars'], December, p. 75.

Nihon eiga [*Japanese Film*] (1936) 'Takehisa Chieko', August, p. 10.

Nihon eiga [*Japanese Film*] (1936) 'Yamada Isuzu', August, p. 9.

Okumura, Hanako (1924) 'Utsukushii muki no tesage' ['A Beautiful Handbag for Springtime'], *Women's Club* [*Fujin kurabu*], March, p. 7.

Osachi, Higashi (1926) 'Nihon eiga goshippu' ['Japanese Film Gossip'], *Eiga jidai* [*Film Age*], October, p. 100.

Osaka Mitsukoshi (1932) 'Meirō no san ni nendo no mōdo o hiraku' ['Presenting 1932's Bright Fashions'], January, p. 5.

Pollak, Robert (1933) 'Japan and Western Music', *Japan Times*, 10 September, p. 1.

Satō, Yukio (1926) 'Shuyō Nihon eiga hihyō: *Riku no ningyō*' ['Criticism of Major Japanese Films: *The Mermaid on the Land*'], 21 September, p. 43.

Seriba, Teruo (1939) 'Date to wa kokoroiki nari' ['Stylishness Is Spirit'], August, pp. 44–5.

Shiseido (1927) 'Katei denki kigu' ['Household Electric Appliances'], *Go-fujin techō* [*The Pocket Book for Women*], pp. 33–4.

Shiseido (1927) 'Pari' [Paris], *Go-fujin techō* [*The Pocket Book for Women*], pp. 105–6.

Shinseinen [*New Youth*] (1929) 'Uteba hibiku' ['An Immediate Result'], June, pp. 110–11.

Shinseinen [*New Youth*] (1929) 'Vanity Fair', April, pp. 156–61.

Shinseinen [*New Youth*] (1929) 'Vanity Fair', February, pp. 288–91.

Shinseinen [*New Youth*] (1929) 'Vogue en Vogue', November, pp. 152–3.

Shinseinen [*New Youth*] (1929) 'Vogue en Vogue', September, pp. 142–3.

Shinseinen [*New Youth*] (1930) 'Vogue en Vogue', September, pp. 312–13.

Shinseinen [*New Youth*] (1931) 'Vogue en Vogue', August, pp. 230–1.

Shinseinen [*New Youth*] (1931) 'Vogue en Vogue', December, pp. 209–13.

Shinseinen [*New Youth*] (1931) 'Vogue en Vogue', February, pp. 246–7.

Shinseinen [*New Youth*] (1931) 'Vogue en Vogue', November, pp. 301–3.

Shinseinen [*New Youth*] (1932) 'Nyū Yōku Dandī' ['The New York Dandy'], May, pp. 277–81.

Shinseinen [*New Youth*] (1932) 'Vogue en Vogue', April, pp. 242–3.

Shinseinen [*New Youth*] (1932) 'Vogue en Vogue', May, pp. 273–6.

Shinseinen [*New Youth*] (1934) 'Vogue en Vogue', August, pp. 214–15.

Shinseinen [*New Youth*] (1934) 'Vogue en Vogue', January, pp. 239–43.

Shinseinen [*New Youth*] (1934) 'Vogue en Vogue', March, pp. 302–3.

Shinseinen [*New Youth*] (1934) 'Vogue en Vogue', May, pp. 258–63.

Shinseinen [*New Youth*] (1935) 'Vogue en Vogue', December, pp. 263.

Shinseinen [*New Youth*] (1935) 'Vogue en Vogue', January, pp. 213–17.

Shinseinen [*New Youth*] (1935) 'Vogue en Vogue', March, pp. 268–73.

Shiseido (1922) 'Biyōka ni tsuite' ['About Our Beauty Department'], pamphlet, Shiseido, Ginza, Tokyo.

Shiseido geppō [*Shiseido Monthly*] (1926) 'Modern Girl', June, pp. 5–6.
Shufu no tomo [*Women's Friend*] (1927) 'Happyō tenrankai' ['Announcing an Exhibition'], October, pp. 15–16.
Shufu no tomo [*The Housewife's Friend*] (1932) 'Modan shanpū' ['Modern Shampoo'], postcard.
Shufu no tomo [*The Housewife's Friend*] (1932) 'Natsu no kodomo fuku issai no tsukurikata' ['The Complete Guide to Making Children's Summer Clothing', supplement.
Shukujo gahō [*Ladies' Pictorial*] (1922) 'Wafuku no ichiri' ['An Advantage of Japanese Clothing'], March, p. 2.
Shukujo gahō (1922) 'Wafuku no ichiri' ['The Advantages of Japanese Clothing'], May, p. 2.
Singer, Caroline (1932) 'Theatre Reveals Modern Japanese Life', *Japan Times*, 29 February, p. 5.
Stage and Screen (1936) '*Desire*', May, p. 1.
Sugita, Santarō (1929) 'Tokaifūkei moga mobo rebyū – 5' ['City Sights: The Modern Girl and Modern Boy Revue – 5'], *Yomiuri shimbun*, 12 April, p. 3.
Sugita, Santarō (1929) 'Tokaifūkei moga mobo rebyū – 6' ['City Sights: The Modern Girl and Modern Boy Revue – 6'], *Yomiuri shimbun*, 13 April, p. 3.
Sutā [*Star*] (1933) 'Sumairu' [Advertisement for Smile brand eye drops], August, p. 17.
Sutā [*Star*] (1933) 'Sumairu' [Advertisement for Smile brand eye drops], October, back cover.
Sutairu [*Style*] (1939) 'Bikutā no Yuri Akemi-san' ['Victor Records' Yuri Akemi'], May, p. 42.
Sutairu [*Style*] (1939) 'Jockey Club Brilliantine Cosmetique' [Advertisement], March, p. 66.
Sutairu [*Style*] (1939) 'Natsu no sugao' [Summer's Makeup-free Faces], July, p. 5.
Sutairu [*Style*] (1939) 'Nikkatsu', June, p. 30.
Sutairu [*Style*] (1939) 'Shoka' ['Early Summer'], June, pp. 13–14.
Sutairu [*Style*] (1939) 'Sukī no keshō' ['Makeup for Skiing'], February, p. 66–7.
Sutairu [*Style*] (1939) 'Sutairu saron' ['*Style* Salon'], May, p. 37.
Suzuki, Jūzaburō (1924) 'Nihon eiga ran – ō yō eiga hihyō: *Umi ni naru otoko*' ['Japanese Film Section – Summary and Film Criticism: entry for "The Man Who Becomes The Sea"'], 1 October, p. 21.
Takata, Tamotsu (1930) 'Purokino tomo no kai ni tsuite' ['About the Society of Friends of Prokino'], *Shinkō eiga*, June, p. 31.
Tamura, Yukihiko (1931) 'Nihon eiga hihyō: *Madamu to nyōbo*' ['Japanese Film Criticism: *The Neighbour's Wife and Mine*'], *Kinema junpō*, 21 August, p. 77.
Tanaka, Kinuyo (1936) 'Kamata jūnen: watashi no omoide' ['Ten Years of Kamata: My Memories'], *Nihon eiga*, April, pp. 20–1.
The Japan Times (1926) 'An Attempt to Explain Japan', 24 November, p. 1.
The Japan Times (1927) 'Office Boy's Musings, by "Kodomo" of the Japan Times Staff', 12 October, p. 2.
The Japan Times (1927) 'Office Boy's Musings, by "Kodomo" of the Japan Times Staff', 16 November, p. 2.
The Japan Times (1928) 'Office Boy's Musings, by "Kodomo" of the Japan Times Staff', 26 February, p. 3.
The Japan Times (1930) 'The Talking Films in Japan', 6 January, p. 4.
The Japan Times (1931) 'Exotic Beauties Passé in Japanese Films This Year; Healthy Types Preferred', 18 February, p. 1.
The Japan Times (1931) 'News of Notables of the Screen During the Present Week', 23 April, p. 3.
The Japan Times (1932) 'Doug Spends Day Sightseeing Here, Acts as Guide', 23 January, p. 1.
The Japan Times (1932) 'Korean Taxi Driver Has Long Vain Ride', 29 June, p. 1.

The Japan Times (1932) '"Tempura", Delight of Japanese Epicures, Much Relished by Chaplin During Stay Here', 15 June, p. 3.
The Japan Times (1932) 'Thousands Greet "Doug" As Belgenland Arrives With Globe Girdlers', 22 January, p. 1.
The Japan Times (1933) 'Japanese Press Opinions', 10 September, p. 1.
The Japan Times (1938) 'Comments on Passing Topics: Summer Sports and Police', 14 June, p. 1.
The Play and Movie (1924) 'Sakai Yoneko', May, p. 14.
The Play and Movie (1927) '*Ra Torabiata*' ['*La Traviata*'], March, p. 15.
The Play and Movie (1928) 'Futari joyū: shotaimen no omoide' ['Two Actresses: Memories of Their First Interviews'], June, p. 10.
The Play and Movie (1928) 'Futatsu no sukecchi: Faasuto Nashonaru Eiga kara Bonnō' ['Two Sketches: *Bonnō* From First National Pictures'], November, p. 4.
The Play and Movie (1928) 'it . . . It . . . IT: Clara Bow', February, p. 13.
The Straits Times (1985) 'Now for the Courtship Strut – Spike Heels Teeter Back', 22 September, p. 3.
The Travel Bulletin (1935) 'Dietrich Speaks', p. 49.
Tomoda Jun'ichirō (1936) 'Nihon eiga hihyō: *Naniwa erejī*' ['Japanese Film Criticism: *Osaka Elegy*'], *Kinema junpō*, 1 June, p. 106.
Yomiuri shimbun (1923) 'Kyokutōsenshukenkyōgitaikai: dai ni nichi' ['Far Eastern Championship Games: Day Two'], 23 May, p. 5.
Yomiuri shimbun (1923) 'Kyokutōsenshukenkyōgitaikai: dai san nichi' ['Far Eastern Championship Games: Day Three'], 24 May, p. 5.
Yomiuri shimbun (1923) 'Kyokutōsenshukenkyōgitaikai: dai yon nichi' ['Far Eastern Championship Games: Day Four'], 25 May, p. 5.
Yomiuri shimbun (1925) 'Kandan' ['Idle Talk'], 24 October, p. 4.
Yomiuri shimbun (1925) 'Roido eiga ga nageta hamon: Nikkatsu ga soshō o' ['Lloyd Films Making Waves: Nikkatsu Files Lawsuit'], 24 April, p. 6.
Yomiuri shimbun (1925) 'Shōsetsuka no chūkoku' ['A Warning to Novelists'], 16 March, p. 2.
Yomiuri shimbun (1926) 'Ma no ichi ni ressha kesa mo mata tōnan jiken shutsubotsu suru gakusei-fuku no Roido megane' ['Evil Robbery Incident on the 1-2 Train, Widespread Wearing of Lloyd Glasses as Student Clothing'], 23 August, p. 6.
Yomiuri shimbun (1926) 'Zasshi no hitobito' ['Magazine People'], 23 August, p. 4.
Yomiuri shimbun (1928) 'Eiga dayori' ['Film News'], 14 August, p. 10.
Yomiuri shimbun (1928) 'Ressha-nai no fūki o midasu mobomoga wa komari mono' ['Disruption of Public Morality in Richshaws: Modern Girls and Modern Boys Are Troublesome Things'], 16 August, p. 3.
Yomiuri shimbun (1928) 'Shisōzendō-jō gaikoku eiga no jōei o kinshi saretai' ['Based on Thought and Virtue, I Want to Ban the Screening of Foreign Films'], 17 August, p. 2.
Yomiuri shimbun (1929) 'Fūki binran no kindai-ka mobo ni mo hanbun no tsumi kondo wa furyō kyaku dai seibatsu Keishichō asa' ['The Modernisation Corrupting Public Morality: Modern Boys Are to Blame for Half of All Crime. "Now Is the Time to Tackle These Hooligans," Say Police Department'], 15 May, p. 7.
Yomiuri shimbun (1929) 'Tōkyō kōshinkyoku' ['Tokyo March'], 5 June, p. 10.
Yomiuri shimbun (1931) '1931 nen no keshō a ra mōdo' ['Cosmetics à la mode for 1931'], 24 August, p. 3.
Yomiuri shimbun (1931) '*Madamu to nyōbo*' ['*The Neighbour's Wife and Mine*'], 12 May, p. 10.
Yomiuri shimbun (1931) '*Madamu to nyōbo*' [*The Neighbour's Wife and Mine*, Advertisement], 29 July, p. 2.

Yomiuri shimbun (1933) 'Mobo no runpen? Hōridasa reta dansu kyōshi 100-mei wa dō naru' ['Unemployed Modern Boys? What Will Become of the 100 Sacked Dance Teachers?'], p. 7.
Yomiuri shimbun (1934) 'Tokei de tsumazuita mobo no "kyūzō" henzō kogawase de totonoeta minari' ['Modern Boy with a Broken Watch Makes a Hasty Construction: Falsifies Postal Order in Order to Keep Up Appearances'], 26 March, p. 7.
Yomiuri shimbun (1936) 'Okyaku katagi' ['Respectable Customers'], 8 February, p. 9.
Yomiuri shimbun (1937) 'Yokohama: Ninotani ni ningyo afuru' ['Yokohama: Ninotani Is Overflowing With Mermaids'], 9 July, p. 7.
Yōsō silhouette [*Western Clothing Silhouette*] (1939) 'SILHOUETTE', p. 1.

Filmography

A Daughter of the Gods (1916) Directed by Herbert Brenon. Hollywood: Fox Film Corporation.

A Farewell to Arms (1932) Directed by Frank Borzage. Hollywood: Paramount Pictures.

A Page of Madness [*Kurutta ippēji*] (1926) Directed by Kinugasa Teinosuke. Japan: Kinugasa Eiga Renmei.

A Paper Doll's Whisper of Spring [*Kami ningyo haru no sasayaki*] (1926) Directed by Mizoguchi Kenji. Japan: Nikkatsu.

Amateur Club [*Amachua Kurabu*] (1920) Directed by Kurihara Kusaburo. Japan: Shōchiku.

An Inn in Tokyo [*Tokyo no yado*] (1936) Directed by Ozu Yasujirō. Japan: Shōchiku.

An Introduction to Marriage [*Kekkongaku nyūmon*] (1930) Directed by Ozu Yasujirō. Japan: Shōchiku.

Crisis Time Japan [*Hijōji Nihon*] (1933) Directed by Kondō Iyokichi. Japan: Osaka Mainichi Shinbunsha.

Crossroads [*Jūjiro*] (1928) Directed by Kinugasa Teinosuke. Japan: Kinugasa Eiga Renmei.

Days of Our Youth [*Warera no wakaki hi*] (1924) Directed by Suzuki Kensaku. Japan: Nikkatsu.

Desire (1936) Directed by Frank Borzage. USA: Paramount Pictures.

Dishonored (1931) Directed by Josef von Sternberg. USA: Paramount Pictures.

Don Juan (1926) Directed by Alan Crosland. USA: Warner Brothers.

Dragnet Girl [*Hijōsen no onna*] (1933) Directed by Ozu Yasujirō. Japan: Shōchiku.

Every Night Dreams [*Yorugoto no yume*] (1933) Directed by Naruse Mikio. Japan: Shōchiku.

Fighting Friends: Japanese Style [*Wasei kenka tomodachi*] (1929) Directed by Ozu Yasujirō. Japan: Shōchiku.

Five Women Around Him [*Kare wo meguru gonin no onna*] (1927) Directed by Abe Yutaka. Japan: Nikkatsu.

Fujiwara Yoshie's Hometown [*Fujiwara Yoshie no furusato*] (1930) Directed by Mizoguchi Kenji. Japan: Nikkatsu and Mina Talkie.

Girl Shy (1924) Directed by Fred C. Newmeyer and Sam Taylor. USA: Pathé.

I Graduated, But ... [*Daigaku wa deta keredo*] (1929) Directed by Ozu Yasujirō. Japan: Shōchiku.

I Was Born, But... [*Umarete wa mita keredo*] (1931) Directed by Ozu Yasujirō. Japan: Shōchiku.

Izu Dancer [*Izu no odoriko*] (1933) Directed by Gosho Heinosuke. Japan: Shōchiku.

Japanese Girls at the Harbour [*Minato no nihon musume*] (1933) Directed by Shimizu Hiroshi. Japan: Shōchiku.

Kageboshi: The Noble Thief of Edo [*Edo kaizoku-den: Kagebōshi*] (1925) Directed by Futagara Buntarō. Japan: Toa Makino.
La Traviata [*Tsubakihime*] (1927) Directed by Murata Minoru. Japan: Nikkatsu.
Le Grand Jeu (1934) Directed by Jacques Feyder. France: Pathé-Natan.
Little Caesar (1931) Directed by Mervyn LeRoy. USA: First National Pictures.
Love Troops [*Aijō Butai*] (1939) Directed by Sasaki Yasushi. Japan: Shōchiku.
Madame X (1920) Directed by Frank Lloyd. USA: Goldwyn Pictures.
Manhattan Melodrama (1934) Directed by W. S. Van Dyke. USA: Metro-Goldwyn-Mayer.
Marching On [*Shingun*] (1930) Directed by Ushihara Kiyohiko. Japan: Shōchiku.
McFadden's Flats (1927) Directed by Richard Wallace. USA: First National Pictures.
Miss Europe [*Prix de Beauté*] (1930) Directed by Augusto Genina. France: Sofar-Film.
Miss Nippon [*Misu Nippon*] (1931) Directed by Murata Minoru. Japan: Nikkatsu.
Morocco (1930) Directed by Josef von Sternberg. USA: Paramount Pictures.
Night Tales of Honmoku [*Honmoku yawa*] (1924) Directed by Suzuki Kensaku. Japan: Nikkatsu.
No Blood Relation [*Nasanu naka*] (1932) Directed by Naruse Mikio. Japan: Shōchiku.
Osaka Elegy [*Naniwa erejī*] (1936) Directed by Mizoguchi Kenji. Japan: Dai-Ichi Eiga.
Our Neighbour, Miss Yae [*Tonari no Yae-chan*] (1934) Directed by Shimazu Yasujirō. Japan: Shōchiku.
Pandora's Box [*Die Büchse der Pandora*] (1929) Directed by G. W. Pabst. Germany: Süd-Film.
Passing Fancy [*Dekigokoro*] (1933) Directed by Ozu Yasujirō. Japan: Shōchiku.
Pumpkin [*Kabocha*] (1928) Directed by Ozu Yasujirō. Japan: Shōchiku.
Queen of Modern Times [*Gendai no joō*] (1924) Directed by Mizoguchi Kenji. Japan: Nikkatsu.
Roses of Remembrance [*Tsuioku no bara*] (1936) Directed by Tasaka Tomotaka. Japan: Nikkatsu.
Rough House Rosie (1927) Directed by Frank Strayer. USA: Paramount Pictures.
Salvation Hunters (1925) Directed by Josef von Sternberg. USA: United Artists.
Seven Seas Part One: Virginity Chapter [*Nanatsu no umi zenpen: shōjo hen*] (1931) Directed by Shimizu Hiroshi. Japan: Shōchiku.
Seven Seas Part Two: Frigidity Chapter [*Nanatsu no umi kōhen: teisō hen*] (1932) Directed by Shimizu Hiroshi. Japan: Shōchiku.
Sinners in the Sun (1932) Directed by Alexander Hall. USA: Paramount Pictures.
Sisters of the Gion [*Gion no kyōdai*] (1936) Directed by Mizoguchi Kenji. Japan: Dai-Ichi Eiga.
Song of Youth [*Seishun no uta*] (1924) Directed by Murata Minoru. Japan: Nikkatsu.
Souls on the Road [*Rojō no reikon*] (1921) Directed by Murata Minoru. Japan: Shōchiku.
Speedy (1928) Directed by Ted Wilde. USA: Paramount Pictures.
Stick Girl [*Sutekki gāru*] (1929) Directed by Shimizu Hiroshi. Japan: Shōchiku.
Street of Shame [*Akasen Chitai*] (1956) Directed by Mizoguchi Kenji. Japan: Daiei.
Street Without End [*Kagirinaki hodō*] (1934) Directed by Naruse Mikio. Japan: Shōchiku.
Symphony of the Backstreets [*Uramachi no kōkyōgaku*] (1935) Directed by Watanabe Kunio. Japan: Nikkatsu.
The Actress and the Poet [*Joyū to shijin*] (1935) Directed by Naruse Mikio. Japan: Shōchiku.
The Athlete [*Undōka*] (1926) Directed by Suzuki Shigeyoshi. Japan: Nikkatsu.
The Four Horsemen of the Apocalypse (1921) Directed by Rex Ingram. USA: Metro Pictures.
The Good Fairy (1935) Directed by William Wyler. USA: Universal Pictures.
The Groom Talks in His Sleep [*Hanamuko no negoto*] (1935) Directed by Gosho Heinosuke. Japan: Shōchiku.
The Lady and the Beard [*Shukujo to hige*] (1931) Directed by Ozu Yasujirō. Japan: Shōchiku.

The Life of an Office Worker [*Kaishain seikatsu*] (1929) Directed by Ozu Yasujirō. Japan: Shōchiku.
The Man Who Becomes the Sea [*Umi ni naru otoko*] (1924) Directed by Kondō Iyokichi. Japan: Nikkatsu.
The Mermaid on the Land [*Riku no ningyo*] (1926) Directed by Abe Yutaka. Japan: Nikkatsu.
The Neighbour's Wife and Mine [*Madamu to nyōbo*] (1931) Directed by Gosho Heinosuke. Japan: Shōchiku.
The Only Son [*Hitori Musuko*] (1936) Directed by Ozu Yasujirō. Japan: Shōchiku.
The Passion of a Woman Teacher [*Kyōren no onna shishō*] (1926) Directed by Mizoguchi Kenji. Japan: Nikkatsu.
The Sheik (1921) Directed by George Melford. USA: Paramount Pictures.
The Sign of the Cross (1932) Directed by Cecil B. DeMille. USA: Paramount Pictures.
The Stylish Retainer [*Oshare hatamoto*] (1935) Directed by Tsuji Yoshiro. Japan: Nikkatsu.
The Sun [*Nichirin*] (1925) Directed by Kinugasa Teinosuke. Japan: Rengo Eiga Geijutsuka.
The Uninvited Guest (1924) Directed by Ralph Ince. USA: Submarine Film Corporation.
The Woman Who Touched the Legs [*Ashi ni sawatta onna*] (1926) Directed by Abe Yutaka. Japan: Nikkatsu.
This Mother Is Sinful [*Kono haha ni tsumi ariya*] (1931) Directed by Shimizu Hiroshi. Japan: Shōchiku.
Tokyo March [*Tōkyō kōshinkyoku*] (1929) Directed by Mizoguchi Kenji. Japan: Nikkatsu.
Tokyo Rhapsody [*Tokyo rapusodei*] (1936) Directed by Fushimizu Osamu. Japan: Tōhō.
Undying Pearl [*Fue no shiratama*] (1929) Directed by Shimizu Hiroshi. Japan: Shōchiku.
Wagering His Youth [*Seishun wo toshite*] (1924) Directed by Ōboro Genga. Japan: Nikkatsu.
Walk Cheerfully [*Hogaraka ni ayume*] (1930) Directed by Ozu Yasujirō. Japan: Shōchiku.
Why Worry (1923) Directed by Fred Newmeyer and Sam Taylor. USA: Pathé.
Woman of Tokyo [*Tokyo no onna*] (1933) Directed by Ozu Yasujirō. Japan: Shōchiku.
Youth Olympics [*Seishun Orinpikku*] (1938) Directed by Hisamatsu Seiji. Japan: Shinkō Kinema.

Index

Note: page references with 'n' indicate chapter notes; *italic* references refer to images.

EU representative:
Easy Access System Europe
Mustamäe tee 50, 10621 Tallinn, Estonia
Gpsr.requests@easproject.com

www.ingramcontent.com/pod-product-compliance
Lightning Source LLC
LaVergne TN
LVHW061220100826
845148LV00004B/809

* 9 7 8 1 4 7 4 4 9 7 7 1 8 *